WARRANTING ASSENT

SUNY Series in Speech Communication
Dudley D. Cahn, Jr., Editor

WARRANTING ASSENT

Case Studies in Argument Evaluation

edited by

Edward Schiappa

STATE UNIVERSITY OF NEW YORK PRESS

Published by
State University of New York Press, Albany

© 1995   State University of New York

Production by Susan Geraghty
Marketing by Fran Keneston

Printed in the United States of America

For information, address State University of New York Press,
State University Plaza, Albany, N.Y., 12246

Library of Congress Cataloging-in-Publication Data

Warranting assent : case studies in argument evaluation / edited by
    Edward Schiappa.
        p.   cm. — (SUNY series in speech communication)
    Includes bibliographical references (p.) and index.
    ISBN 0-7914-2363-8 — ISBN 0-7914-2364-6 (pbk.)
    1. Persuasion (Rhetoric)—Case studies.   I. Schiappa, Edward,
    1954- . II. Series.
    P301.5.P47W37   1995
    808—dc20   94-13642
                                                                CIP

10 9 8 7 6 5 4 3 2 1

CONTENTS

ACKNOWLEDGMENTS

Chapter 1 of this book is an elaboration of an essay originally written by Marilyn J. Young, Michael K. Launer, and Curtis C. Austin as "The Need for Evaluative Criteria: Conspiracy Argument Revisited," *Argumentation and Advocacy* 26 (1990): 89–107. An earlier version of chapter 5 by Ralph E. Dowling and Gabrielle Marraro appeared as "Grenada and the Great Communicator: A Study in Democratic Ethics," *Western Journal of Speech Communication* 50 (1986): 350–67.

Earlier versions of chapters 3, 10, and 12 were presented as papers at the fifth conference on Argumentation sponsored by the Speech Communication Association, the American Forensic Association, and the University of Utah, and appeared in *Argument and Critical Practices: Proceedings of the Fifth SCA/AFA Conference on Argumentation*. Earlier versions of chapters 2 and 8 were presented at the seventh conference and appeared in *Argument in Controversy: Proceedings of the Seventh SCA/AFA Conference on Argumentation*. Both proceedings were published by the Speech Communication Association.

Previously published portions of these essays are used with permission of the publishers.

INTRODUCTION

Edward Schiappa

"Argument evaluation" refers to rendering an explicit judgment that an argument is valid or invalid, sound or unsound, good or bad, strong or weak, ethical or unethical. One can make judgments about aesthetic considerations or the effectiveness of an argument with a particular audience, but that is not what is generally meant by the term "argument evaluation" in this book. Even so narrowly described, most argumentation scholars would agree that one appropriate and important function of criticism is to render judgments of the worth of individual arguments and that argument evaluation is an important part of argumentation studies. Argument evaluation has many uses, including improving argumentative competence, teaching critical thinking, and improving decision making. The benefits of argument evaluation are coterminous with the benefits of the study and practice of argumentation itself, for one cannot be successful at either without the ability to recognize the difference between good and bad arguments.

If it is agreed that argument evaluation is an important task for argumentation scholars, it follows that argument evaluation should be published. Argument evaluation is not something fit only for the privacy of the classroom; rather, evaluation is a function of criticism that deserves recognition *as* scholarship. Publication of argument evaluation can be defended as a means of testing argument theory, for furthering pedagogical goals by providing exemplary work, or it can be defended as a valid end in itself; that is, as scholarship, argument evaluation is at least as valuable as other sorts of criticism.

Despite the common view that argument evaluation is a very important function of argument analysis and criticism, there are remarkably few examples in the scholarly literature of argumentation studies that represent argument evaluation qua argument evaluation (Schiappa 1991). Argumentation studies recently has been dominated by theoretical and descriptive work that generally sidesteps the sort of explicit normative judgments that are unavoidable in argument evaluation. If one is reasonably strict about differentiating argument evaluation from other activities sharing the "argument criticism" umbrella, then argument evaluation will be found to be, by far, the least popular modus operandi of the publishing argument scholar. This book is intended, in part, to further the process of correcting this imbalance.

FINDING A PLACE FOR ARGUMENT EVALUATION

The factors rendering argument evaluation a relatively unpopular scholarly endeavor are, no doubt, numerous and complicated. Some causes may be clearly personal, such as the fact that some scholars may find argument evaluation insufficiently challenging or interesting. Some factors combine the personal and the material, such as the fact that more professional journals in the field of communication studies focus on rhetoric than on argument. Even in conferences and publications self-identified as committed to argumentation studies, argument is often "translated" as rhetoric. All too often, unfortunately, once a text is designated for the purposes of study as a rhetorical artifact as opposed to an instance of argument, our critical expectations are altered. The questions we ask of an instance of rhetoric are usually different than those we ask of argument. Typically, from the standpoint of argument evaluation, our standards are lowered once a text is dubbed rhetoric. For example, Robert Rowland advocates a three-part test for the evaluation of an argument, including a test of internal consistency, a test of evidence, and a "dialectical" test for the cogency of warrants and consideration of "reasonable alternatives" (1985, p. 130). Certainly these are very reasonable minimal standards for an argument to meet. Yet such questions are rarely relevant when a text is approached as a rhetorical artifact. For example, Thomas Kane's essay "Rhetorical Histories and Arms Negotiations" argues that "the use of historical events as rhetorical artifacts has served to sustain cold war assumptions and attitudes" (1988, p. 143). Arguing that "the cold war is a rhetorical enterprise," Kane undermines the persuasiveness of cold war "rhetorical histories" in part by calling attention to their rhetorical nature. At the same time, by characterizing rhetorical histories as part of an ongoing process of symbolic inducement, Kane conceptualizes rhetorical events as objects whose meaning is independent of "reality" and of truth considerations: "whether American or Soviet, these events acquired their meaning less from what really happened than the collective set of assumptions and perceptions about them that have been handed down from previous discourse, arguments, experiences and interpretations" (p. 144).

Kane's essay thoroughly documents the symbolic power of interpreted historical events. However, from the standpoint of argument evaluation, a distinctly rhetorical analysis relieves the discourse under consideration of certain burdens. When historical events become "rhetorical histories" used in the process of symbolic inducement the issue becomes primarily one of *effectiveness*: rhetorical histories are persuasive even if they are unreasonable. By contrast, if one were to examine, say, Jack Kemp's use of historical "examples" as "evidence" for specific argumentative "claims" he has set forth, a very different evaluative picture would emerge. Put a different way, rhetorical criticism and argument evaluation represent different sets of "terministic screens"; hence what the critic looks for and finds may differ depending on which screen is employed.

As another example, Rebecca S. Bjork's "Reagan and the Nuclear Freeze: 'Star Wars' as a Rhetorical Strategy" is a provocative portrayal of how Reagan's campaign for the Strategic Defense Initiative undercut the persuasiveness of the nuclear freeze movement (1988). Once again, the results of the study are somewhat different from what the perspective of argument evaluation would have provided. Examining Star Wars as a rhetorical strategy leads Bjork to focus primarily on the effectiveness of Reagan's manipulation of symbols rather than the soundness or validity of specific arguments. The arguments of the nuclear freeze movement are characterized as "vocal demands." Star Wars is a "vision" that renders the arguments of the freeze movement "not appealing" or "not believable" to the general public. Bjork makes at least a dozen references to Reagan's rhetoric as "effective," "successful," "accomplished," "masterful," and as possessing "advantages." Bjork's analysis is solid as rhetorical criticism, but by focusing primarily on "effectiveness," the strength or weakness of Reagan's arguments escapes close scrutiny. Even though Bjork makes her negative feelings toward the arms race fairly clear, no sustained case is made that there is anything unsound or invalid about Reagan's position.

Argumentation scholars also have been discouraged from publishing explicit evaluations of arguments by disciplinary norms that can be described as "methodological injunctions." These norms are sometimes made explicit in argumentation studies' "social knowledge" (Farrell 1976), but mostly function implicitly as a "tacit component" of the "personal knowledge" gained during socialization as graduate students and young scholars (Polanyi 1958).

There are at least three identifiable methodological injunctions that function to discourage argument evaluation. The first can be described as the "enduring versus ephemeral" injunction. Karlyn Kohrs Campbell's argument is that scholarly rhetorical criticism ought to focus on "enduring" analysis in which "what we learn about the specific rhetorical acts is secondary; they become illustrations or means through which the reader apprehends the nature of symbolic processes themselves" (1974, p. 12). Such studies are enduring "because rhetorical theory deals with symbolic processes that are inherent in the human condition and recur in different times, in different places, and in response to different issues" (p. 12). As important as evaluation of contemporary communicative acts may be, Campbell suggests that their study is usually inappropriate as a scholarly exercise: "the social criticism of ephemeral, contemporary events belongs in the mass media, where much of it now appears, and the audience it needs to reach is the general public" (p. 10).

Campbell's position is widely shared in our field (whether specifically acknowledged in individual essays or not), and functions as a sort of methodological injunction. A specific example can illustrate how the "enduring versus ephemeral" injunction discourages argument evaluation. If during the Reagan Administration a critic were to evaluate Ronald Reagan's time-bound arguments in support of Star Wars, that critic would be engaging in ephemeral criticism. Within such a perspective one could make the case that some of Reagan's arguments were weak or misleading. For example, as Bjork points out, one of Reagan's key arguments in favor of Star Wars was that it can "save lives" by rendering nuclear weapons "impotent and obsolete" (1988, pp. 187–88). In fact, Reagan consistently argued for Star Wars on the grounds that it could offer successful population defense. As an argument such a claim is open to serious challenge. William Broad's research has documented that from the start advisors and SDI researchers have acknowledged the impossibility of successful population defense and have advocated SDI as missile defense (1984, pp. 206–20). Since 1983 the SDI program has been redirected to focus on missile defense, though this reorientation is rarely acknowledged by the White House (Waller and Bruce 1987). Nonetheless, Reagan's arguments on behalf of SDI continued to stress the virtues of total population defense (Schiappa, 1989). As an argument, Reagan's position can be judged as weak and misleading. Such a judgment, however, is clearly "ephemeral" criticism since the only "enduring" principles involved (arguers should not mislead) are obvious and "trivial" when viewed as contributions to theory. By contrast, the ability to describe Reagan's strategy as "transcendence," the "stealing of symbols," and "casuistic stretching" (Bjork 1988) allows a critic to move from a time-bound evaluation of arguments to the description of timeless "processes that characterize human communication" (Campbell 1974, p. 12).

The second methodological injunction that functions to discourage argument evaluation can be described as the "truth-avoidance" criterion. The foremost spokesperson for this criterion is Forbes Hill, though his articles have been cited with approval by others. Hill argues that assessments of the truth-content of speakers' arguments are inappropriate in scholarly criticism in part because such assessments assume that the critic knows "the truth, the whole truth, and nothing but the truth" (1983, p. 122; 1972). Hill charges that, at the very least, assessments of truth privilege the critic's claims over the rhetor and therefore require detailed arguments that fall outside the scope of scholarly criticism.

It should be noted that Hill's arguments are directed toward rhetorical criticism and not argument evaluation. Also, Hill's case has been answered, at least to some critics' satisfaction, by Karlyn Kohrs Campbell (1972, 1983) and Philip Wander (1983, 1984). Nonetheless, there is some indication that his truth-avoidance injunction is at least an implicit part of our field's social knowledge and that it has discouraged argument evaluation. Often various topics investigated by rhetorical or argument critics are portrayed as highly contested, with strong advocates on both sides. The implication is that "the truth" is in doubt; therefore, the analysis that follows can "bracket" truth as an issue and avoid ethical judgment or an evaluation of argumentative soundness.

For example, consider two articles published in a special issue on nuclear criticism in the journal now called *Argumentation and Advocacy*. The essays, by Thomas J. Hynes and Cori E. Dauber, are predominantly descriptive, though both make certain critical judgments. After describing the "stratified and highly differentiated group of audiences" for arguments concerning arms negotiations and the presupposition-bound nature of the evidence in such disputes, Hynes draws the conclusion that rational evaluation and resolution are highly unlikely (1988). Similarly, Dauber's study suggests that the interdisciplinary nature of arguments over Soviet nuclear policy intentions makes the development of "validity standards" difficult and that absent such standards "resolution is in fact impossible" (1988, p. 176). Dauber also analyzes a debate over Soviet naval strategy and suggests that one author's position is more probable than another's based on the thoroughness of his methodology. Based on the two examined debates Dauber concludes that work by argument scholars "cannot be of real help" since the determination of appropriate validity standards must be established by "the peculiarities of the dispute at hand" (180). In short, both Hynes and Dauber conclude that, in some cases, argument evaluation is pointless if not impossible because the critic cannot claim to know the truth of the matter.

Obviously the force of my claim that argument evaluation would provide a unique and valuable perspective is undercut if it is concluded that argument evaluation is not a live option with respect to certain public issues, such as those regarding nuclear policy. It can be argued, however, that useful argument evaluation is possible with respect to any issue that is actually argued in the public sphere. Even if a specific clash of arguments cannot be resolved, it does not follow that the debate cannot be usefully evaluated. Speaking of nuclear policy debates Goodnight has suggested that dead-end arguments must be transcended by the critic in order to "open up new possibilities for understanding" such that we "reconstitute the confidence necessary for sober public appraisal and decision" (1983, p. 320).

Hynes and Dauber are quite right to point out that what constitutes evidence for nuclear policy arguers is often bound up with the arguers' presuppositions concerning the Soviet Union and the general desirability of arms control. However, such evidentiary problems are not unique to foreign policy disputes, nor is it evident that they are a barrier to argument evaluation. In the philosophy and history of science, for example, the theory-dependency of observation, data, and empirical evidence is well known. Yet this does not stop scientists from making reasoned choices of theories (Kuhn 1977). Similarly, the influence of presuppositions on the interpretation of evidence in some nuclear policy disputes has not stopped nuclear policy "experts," politicians, and concerned citizens from engaging in argument and making better or worse reasoned choices. Hynes is able to describe some uses of evidence and argument as "Wonderland like," "easily refuted," and dependent on suspect sign reasoning (1988, pp. 165–66). Furthermore, Dauber's suggestion that one writer's arguments concerning Soviet naval policy are more probable than another's is based on the field-independent values of thoroughness and rigor, even if the instantiation of those values is field-specific (1988, pp. 179–80). Argument evaluation is not the explicit purpose of either scholar's essay. Nevertheless, even as the authors describe the difficulty of providing "easy" resolution to the issues, they provide indications of how they have, apparently, already evaluated the probable truth of some of the conflicting arguments. What an argument evaluation can seek is not necessarily a definitive, final, or "clear" resolution of a controversy, but a comparative assessment of which advocate has made the best case. Accordingly "validity" and "truth" become relative constructs that the argument critic judges at a given point in time. From the perspective of argument evaluation, to do any less is to admit that a preference for a position is arbitrary and nonrational.

Obviously, if one strictly applies Hill's truth-avoidance injunction to the study of argument, then argument evaluation is virtually impossible. One cannot weigh the soundness of competing claims and evidence without some notion of probable truth. Fortunately, scholars like Kane have not completely refrained from comparative assessments such as between rhetorical histories and "what really happened" (1988, p. 144). Also, evaluations such as those gathered in this book either assert truth-claims or at least cite the deficiencies of selected arguers' truth-claims. Nonetheless, on balance, it is likely that another factor in the relative scarcity of argument evaluation is the sentiment reflected in Hill's truth-avoidance injunction.

The third methodological injunction that functions to discourage argument evaluation can be described as the nonadvocate stance or the principle of nonpartisanship. The clearest exposition of this position is by Rowland, who warns that "the danger in criticism is that the critic will become so involved in the evaluation that he or she will become an advocate for a position. Thus a liberal might not merely critique the arguments of the Reagan administration, but implicitly advocate a Democratic alternative" (1985, p. 129). The solution, according to Rowland, is to avoid "partisan advocacy" and to adopt Scriven's "Principle of Charity" when interpreting and evaluating an argument. The "problem" of advocacy "can be controlled if the critic remembers that his or her role is not to label a claim as wrong, but to expose weaknesses in the argument both to aid the audience in judging the argument and so that the argument can be improved" (p. 129).

Sentiments similar to Rowland's can be found also in recent works by V. William Balthrop and David Zarefsky. Balthrop describes partisan evaluation as reducing the scholar from "sage" to "hack." The hack "is clearly and irresolutely grounded in the political, at least at first appearances. The ideal partisan is concerned with advocacy, with promoting a particularly ideological stance; but the discourse allegedly 'criticized' functions only as pretext and not as exigence" (1987, p. 27). Zarefsky has helped sound the alarm against the "dangers" of partisan ideological criticism by warning that locating critical authority "in the person of the interpreter" can lead to an "extreme nihilism" and a "vicious relativism" (1987, p. 54).

The combined weight of such diatribes is a strong presumption against evaluative judgments by critics that could be called "partisan" or "advocacy." The problem with such a presumption is that—taken at face value—it rules out argument evaluation as such. How can one evaluate an argument as ethical or unethical, good or bad, sound or unsound, without at least implying a preference for certain values, views of reality, or courses of action? A cautious reader might object at this point that the distinctions among advocacy, partisanship, ideology, and value-preference are being blurred here. But in the act of argument evaluation these seemingly separate categories become difficult to distinguish: all evaluation expresses values; all language use is sermonic and advocates a partial point of view; and, if the argument under assessment is of public interest, the values and point of view cannot help but have a political dimension. Challenging the belief that there is an amoral, nonideological language for scholars to use, Michael Shapiro has suggested that "standard disciplinary practices have made us obtuse to the political content sequestered in the subjects, objects, and relationships we have inherited within both our ordinary and our disciplinary ways of speaking and writing" (1987, p. 366).

Significantly, Balthrop and Zarefsky provide important qualifications to the warnings quoted earlier. Both acknowledge that *all* criticism functions ideologically on one level or another and thus involves partisanship. For example, as Philip Wander has argued, even the act of selecting a text for study has an ideological dimension (1983, 1984). If one selects a text that is not relevant to contemporary issues, one is "choosing" to use criticism in a way that serves to preserve existing social order and power relations. If one selects a politically relevant text, then *any* stance the critic selects will function in a partisan manner. Zarefsky acknowledges this and advocates a stance that is presumptively sympathetic to the speaker; he calls for a "melioristic bias" that "privileges the rhetor's point of view" (1987, p. 56). In short, the notion of value-free, nonideological, nonadvocate, nonpartisan criticism is admitted to be illusory even by those who fear the excesses of the hack.

To say that all criticism and all evaluation are necessarily partisan does not imply that "anything goes." Argument evaluation, like any good scholarship, demands careful attention to the text, defensible methodology, and well-reasoned arguments. At the same time, the methodological injunction identified here as the nonadvocate stance or the principle of nonpartisanship is clearly in need of amendment lest it function as a prohibitive presumption against the value of argument evaluation. Otherwise we risk reducing the role of the argument critic to that of the argument "consultant." It is arguably the case that a self-conscious partisan evaluation of a politically significant argument by a "hack" is preferable to scholarship that *pretends* to be value-free or nonpartisan, but is not.

The norms I have described here may be appropriately labeled *modernist* in orientation. Interestingly enough, despite the deep suspicion of rationality one finds in most postmodernist writings,

most argumentation scholars have relatively little difficulty recon-
ciling argument evaluation with postmodern theories. As pointed
out in a number of essays in *Argument and the Postmodern Challenge* (McKerrow 1993), argumentation studies has long
embraced most of the antifoundationalist, antiessentialist tenets
embraced by postmodern theorists. Furthermore, it is not uncom-
mon to find prominent postmodern theorists that champion the
preservation of "practical reason" to continue what they feel is the
best of the Enlightenment project. In "What Is Enlightenment?"
Michel Foucault calls for a radical continuation of the "critical
task" of the Enlightenment project (1984). Jacques Derrida
(1988, pp. 111–54) defends the ability to evaluate arguments—
including the strength and truth of claims—and denies that he is
an irrationalist: "To the contrary, I am for a certain type of reason, *Aufklärung* [Enlightenment] rationality" (in Gonzáles-Marin
1987, p. 181, translated by Ramsey Eric Ramsey). And Ernesto
Laclau claims that, in the absence of any "ultimate ground" for
argument, we need to return to the "Aristotelian notion of *phro-
nesis*" to evaluate claims since it is through argument that we construct "social reality" (1988, p. 79). To be sure, the "rationality"
sought here is more modest than that envisioned in the past; postmodern theorists are more conscious of historical and cultural
contingency, more cautious of power and privilege, and more sus-
picious of claims of what is "normal" and "natural," than their
Enlightenment foreparents. But it is clear from a brief reading of
any postmodern author that one can admit that one's arguments
are only *probably* true, time-bound, and thoroughly ideological
and *still* want to make claims—including claims about the usefulness, validity, or strength of other arguers' claims.

I will resist the temptation to provide further theoretical justification for the project of argument evaluation. The point of this
book is to feature case studies of argument evaluation, not add yet
another volume to the "theory wars" of argumentation studies.
Argument theory is important, but the ability to utilize and apply
a theory to explicate and evaluate an argument is even more
important. Unless scholars and students of argument can *use* a
theory, such a theory is—by definition—use*less*. It is at that point
that argument scholars end up quite literally just talking to themselves.

THE CASE STUDIES

This book brings together a set of exemplary essays that demonstrate the art of argument evaluation. Collectively the essays serve as a bridge between more abstract, theoretical works, such as those found in Cox and Willard's *Advances in Argumentation Theory and Research* and Williams and Hazen's *Argumentation Theory and the Rhetoric of Assent*, and the many argumentation and debate textbooks on the market. Too often, provocative theories of argument are generated that never engage historically situated examples of argument. Or, in the case of most textbooks, the examples of fallacies provided are so patently problematic that they can be critiqued with little to no familiarity with advanced argumentation theory or other sorts of scholarly literature. The virtue of the essays assembled in this collection is that they apply a variety of theoretical approaches to specific, historically situated arguments in order to render a specific normative judgment. Furthermore, by bringing to bear knowledge of argumentation theory along with expertise pertaining to the specific arguments under investigation, the essays illustrate the utility of argument evaluation as a discrete mode of scholarly engagement.

The essays are divided into four parts. The first three gather together works that share common presuppositions concerning the purpose of argument evaluation. The fourth pulls together three different approaches to a single, extended argument. Part 1, Epistemological Approaches to Argument Evaluation, brings together three essays that are fueled by the premise that argument is epistemic (cf. Thomas). Believing that argumentation is a useful process through which to produce knowledge about the world, each essay purports to assess the epistemic usefulness of a particular set of arguments. Marilyn J. Young and Michael K. Launer bring to bear a traditional set of evaluative criteria on conspiracy arguments in general, and conspiracy arguments regarding the shooting down of Korean Air Lines Flight 007 in particular. Following David Zarefsky, the authors believe that conspiracy argument has become a "staple of American political discourse" and hence demand the attention of argumentation scholars. Focusing on David Pearson's influential article, "K.A.L. 007: What the U.S. Knew and When We Knew It," the authors identify argumentative moves that made the article persuasive as well as critique what they believe to be crucial flaws in Pearson's argument. By analyzing Pearson's sign reasoning, methods of amplification, and quasilogical arguments, the authors provide a convincing critique of Pearson's case. Equally important is their move to situate their "formalist" critique as an alternative to Walter Fisher's narrative paradigm as a means of understanding conspiracy discourse.

Carol K. Winkler shares the uneasiness of the authors of the previous essay with respect to the persuasive influence of narrative. Though Winkler does not deny the idea that narratives are epistemic, her study argues that some stories provide better ways of knowing than others. Specifically, Winkler critiques George Bush's use of a "terrorist" narrative to define, explain, and defend his military actions during the Persian Gulf War. Her argument is that by reframing the conflict between the United States and Iraq within a terrorist narrative, Bush was able to recast the arguments regarding military action in terms much more favorable for him that mark "an important shift in the conventional public debate about decisions to go to war." Winkler expresses concern that such a narrative positions the American citizenry as "onlookers to a terrorist event" rather than as active collaborators forging a national decision whether to go to war. Not only did Bush's argumentation shift the burden of proof to opponents of the war, but it sets the stage for similar "storytelling" in the future. Winkler sounds an important warning that "the redefinition of what constitutes an acceptable rationale for military engagement obfuscates a more conventional, cautious approach to entry into war."

Dennis S. Gouran's essay also focuses on argument in a decision-making process; in this case the decision to launch the ill-fated space shuttle *Challenger*. Gouran argues that the decision to launch the *Challenger* in the face of what now appear to be obvious risks was based on a combination of a gradual shift of presumption (that one had to prove a launch was *unsafe* rather than *safe*), faulty risk analysis, and fallacious reasoning on the occasion of this particular launch. In addition to failures that "even a beginning student in logic" should catch, Gouran suggests there was also a failure of persuasive argument. Different arguers' definition of their "place" and claims cast in pseudoneutral language, for example, encouraged a less than robust decision-making environment. Gouran's essay nicely illustrates the utility of social psychological research for the understanding and evaluation of situated argumentation, while simultaneously noting the importance of traditional models for evaluating specific chains of inference.

Part 2, Axiological Approaches to Argument Evaluation, is comprised of three essays that make ethical appraisals of arguments. Kathryn M. Olson's essay is an ethical appraisal of arguments among members of the Commission for a New Lutheran Church (CNLC) regarding whether the new church should have mandatory "inclusiveness percentages" for church governing bodies. Weaving together elements of Henry W. Johnstone's "Basic Imperative" for ethical argument and Wayne Booth's criteria for an effective "rhetorical stance," Olson praises certain advocates for aligning "ethicality and effectiveness" in persuading the group to adopt inclusiveness standards. Through a judicious combination of Johnstone and Booth, Olson suggests that critics can avoid the apparent extremes of amoral descriptions of argument effects and normative yet pragmatically vacuous assessments. Two other aspects of Olson's essay are noteworthy. First, her essay examines "situated" argument in the most obvious sense of the word. That is, her study involved field work in which she tape-recorded and transcribed many hours of argument among the members of the CNLC. Such original research, especially in argumentation studies, is all too rare. Furthermore, her essay concentrates on the positive characteristics of the arguments she observed. Setting aside purely effects-oriented studies in argumentation, how many studies are there that result in positive assessments? Not many. Thus, Olson's essay is exemplary in terms of its theoretical contribution, data collection, and ethical purpose.

Ralph E. Dowling and Gabrielle A. Ginder offer a critical assessment of Ronald Reagan's arguments in defense of his decision to invade Grenada in 1983 based on a "democratic orientation" to argumentation. While Olson derives her ethical precepts from Johnstone's ontological approach to argument, Dowling and Ginder's are based on Dennis G. Day's and Thomas R. Nilsen's explication of ethical norms that are necessary for free and open political decisions. In a democracy, Dowling and Ginder maintain, one not only needs to produce defensible decisions (ends), but they must be arrived at through an ethical process (means). Dowling and Ginder contend that democratic decision making depends on an ethic requiring that important evidence is made available, that arguments are made clearly and understandably, and that arguments are directed toward audiences with respect for their well-being. Through a careful study of the arguments advanced by the Reagan administration on behalf of the military action in Grenada, Dowling and Ginder suggest that they were the antithesis of ethical argument. The authors do not pull their punches: "the President lied" to the American people and concealed or withheld the information necessary for an informed public opinion. Their conclusion, which may seem obvious but is far from trivial, is that democracies cannot survive unless the ethical norms required for political argument are respected.

Jeffrey L. Courtright turns to a set of specialized texts that are too often neglected by scholars of argument: dissenting opinions in Supreme Court decisions. In addition to making the case that this much-maligned genre of argument deserves our careful study, Courtright provides a case study of an ethical assessment of one dissenting opinion in particular. Like Olson, Courtright turns to Johnstone's work for a set of ethical precepts with which to analyze his text; in this case, Justice Sandra Day O'Connor's dissent in *Metro Broadcasting, Inc. v. FCC*. After carefully describing O'Connor's "rhetorical situation," Courtright analyzes her dissenting opinion in light of four ethical duties identified by Johnstone: resoluteness, openness, gentleness, and compassion. Courtright contends that O'Connor's dissenting opinion does, in fact, instantiate Johnstone's ethical duties—a conclusion made all the more compelling by a provocative conclusion in which Courtright contrasts O'Connor's dissenting style with that of Justice Anthony Kennedy. Courtright's and Olson's essays are useful complements as collectively they illustrate the utility of Johnstone's ethical framework for "lay" and "expert" arguers alike.

The essays that make up Part 3, Ideological Approaches to Argument Evaluation, are united by an interest in the political dimensions of argumentation studies. All three essays share the beliefs that public discourse is typically (or always) infused with ideological interests, that an appropriate task of the critic is to identify such interests and commend or condemn them, and that the critic's discourse is also infused with ideological interests. In the essay by Kathryn M. Olson and Clark D. Olson, the competing positions articulated by the prosecuting attorneys and the defendants in the so-called sanctuary trial are examined for their respective ideological commitments. Olson and Olson illustrate that the arguments proffered by each side represent incompatible constellations of ontological, epistemological, and axiological beliefs. They argue that the prosecution benefited by the judge's ideology which, after all, is the one most able to direct the course and outcome of the trial. As a result, Olson and Olson suggest that "jurors may have been drawn to the prosecution's ideology because it was the only complete, internally consistent position" allowed to be presented in court by the judge. In contrast, Olson and Olson provide their own, self-admittedly partisan, set of reasons for preferring the ideological commitments represented by the defendants' position.

Mary Keehner's essay is a feminist critique of current arguments that are framed as fetal "versus" women's rights. Keehner examines the arguments concerning companies' legal right to exclude women from jobs that may represent a hazard to future (potential) fetuses and suggests that they are infused with assumptions that are patriarchal, class-biased, and rooted in a gendered liberal legal theory. Such assumptions are harmful to women in three ways. First, important economic interests are obfuscated that impact women and men unevenly. Second, current arguments take the male as "normal" and define women as "other," thereby reinforcing sexism in general. Third, current arguments pit women against their own potential unborn children, thereby framing other issues related to women's rights as a zero-sum gain—what the woman gains, unborn children lose. Keehner's critique is distinctive because she offers an alternative framework for understanding fetal protection; one that replaces the male body as "normal" with that of the pregnant female. Such a framework, Keehner suggests, would enhance workplace safety for men and women, cease to pit women against fetuses, and serve as a counterweight to seeing women as "other."

Rebecca S. Bjork's study identifies and critiques the ideological functions served by arguments concerning the desirability of the "Global Protection Against Limited Strikes" (GPALS) missile-defense program. Bjork contends that in post–cold war foreign policy, anticommunist ideology has been replaced by a political understanding that sees the most significant antiAmerican threats coming from the so-called third world. Drawing from Edward W. Said's analysis of Orientalism, Bjork suggests that the argumentative discourse used to justify U.S. hegemony in foreign policy in general, and particularly to support the Persian Gulf War and the GPALS program, defines Americans and "others" with a set of overly simplistic dualisms (modern/backward, civilized/savage, rational/irrational, good/evil). Bjork suggests that arguments on behalf of the program perpetuate the ideology of colonialism, "along with its racist and sexist implications." Like the previous two essays, Bjork's essay is explicitly self-reflexive. She notes her own ideological commitments and calls upon all scholars to be "vigilant and aware of the power and implications of their work."

The fourth and final part of this book consists of three approaches to arguments in and about the 1986 *Final Report of the Attorney General's Commission on Pornography* (hereafter *Report*). These three essays illustrate very different approaches to the practice of argument evaluation. Not surprisingly, the authors end up with distinct results. Ian Fielding focuses very specifically on the causal argument presented in the *Report* between exposure to pornography and subsequent acts of sexual violence. Fielding contends that the causal argument plays a crucial role in the over-all *Report* and is decisive for determining its usefulness for public policy decisions. Fielding charges the *Report* with various weaknesses, including a lack of clarity in its definition of "pornography" and "harms," and the lack of specific standards for assessing evidence, especially that provided by witnesses. Drawing on Stephen Toulmin's model of argument, Fielding suggests that the crucial warrant and backing connecting the *Report*'s evidence of harms with the claim that pornography is the cause is simply inadequate for the purposes of public policy-making.

While Fielding's concerns are epistemological, Catherine Helen Palczewski's interests are ideological. Her essay is an in-depth feminist analysis of how "survivor testimony" regarding the effects of pornography is framed and assessed by different audiences. Criticisms such as Fielding's, Palczewski suggests, are fueled in part by ideological commitments that devalue the concrete lived-experiences of women. For Palczewski, feminism "is defined by the politicization of the personal," thus the assessment of testimony of witnesses who have suffered the effects of pornography is an inescapably political act. Palczewski's response to critiques such as Fielding's is straightforward: "personal testimony should not be dismissed so easily." Palczewski traces the history of the *Report*'s survivor testimony back to similar hearings on an antipornography ordinance in Minneapolis (proposed by Catharine MacKinnon and Andrea Dworkin). Palczewski sees important differences between the two hearings, however, which result in very different argumentative uses of the witnesses' testimony. While leaving space for other forms of argument and evidence on the effects of pornography, Palczewski defends survivor testimony as a useful form of argument from example that empowers survivors and speaks important truths.

Gerard A. Hauser's essay approaches the *Report* axiologically as an "argumentative instrument of legitimation" that functions to reconfigure public discourse. "The expressed hope of the commission," Hauser notes, "was to encourage public discussion on the issue of pornography's effects on its consumers and on the community." However, such discussion did not materialize. Hauser suggests there were, in effect, two reports by the commission. One was a digest of the commission's findings by Frederick Schauer. Hauser finds this report "scholarly," "evenhanded," and "reasonable," yet its substance received scant attention. The "second" report was that which was seized upon by the press. Hauser suggests that the media focused on such factors as the commission's composition, its scanty budget, the *Report*'s methodological flaws, the *Report*'s extensive sections that claimed to document the harms of pornography, and the perception that the *Report*'s antipornography stance was a done deal even before they had begun work—all of which Hauser regards as fair game for criticism. Hauser suggests that if what he calls the first version of the report—the Schauer summary—had been the focus, a productive "national debate on pornography might have ensued." But because the *Report* was perceived by the press as a strident, all-out assault on freedom of expression, debate in the media focused on the propriety of the commission's activities and methods. Ultimately, Hauser concludes, the Meese Commission bears the responsibility for this misdirected debate: The *Report* "did not promote discussion on pornography because it did not provide insight into pornography."

As the preceding summary demonstrates, the essays collectively engage an important and interesting range of issues. Obviously, a number of senses of "argument" are at work, reflecting the variety of methods and theories now popular in argumentation studies in general. Yet all of the essays imply a commonly shared belief that argumentation is a type of discourse that we expect more of than other sorts of communication. Or, put another way, the argumentation *perspective* enacted in these essays encourages readers to ask more of the discourse they encounter.

Furthermore, all of these essays demonstrate the authors' fluency in the expert literature most relevant to the topic of their essays. They encourage readers not only to learn more about argumentation theory, but to learn something more about the Supreme Court, foreign policy, feminisms, pornography, and a host of other topics. Most important, they encourage us to see the crucial link between what are often viewed as timeless, abstract theoretical principles and the timely, concrete practical questions that face us every day. By providing models for deciding how and when to grant our assent to argument, I can think of no better illustration of the usefulness of argument evaluation.

REFERENCES

Balthrop, V. William. 1987. The criticism of argument, the argument of criticism. In *Argument and critical practices: Proceedings of the Fifth SCA/AFA Conference on Argumentation*, ed. Joseph W. Wenzel. Annandale, Va.: Speech Communication Association.

Bjork, Rebecca S. 1988. Reagan and the nuclear freeze: "Star Wars" as a rhetorical strategy. *Journal of the American Forensic Association, 24,* 181-92.

Broad, William. 1985. *Star warriors.* New York: Simon and Schuster.

Campbell, Karlyn Kohrs. 1972. "Conventional wisdom—Traditional form": A rejoinder. *Quarterly Journal of Speech, 58,* 451–54.

———. 1974. Criticism: Ephemeral and enduring. *Speech Teacher, 23,* 9–14.

———. 1983. Response to Forbes Hill. *Central States Speech Journal, 34,* 126–27.

Cox, J. Robert, and Charles Arthur Willard, eds. 1982. *Advances in argumentation theory and research.* Carbondale: Southern Illinois University Press.

Dauber, Cori E. 1988. Through a glass darkly: Validity standards and the debate over nuclear strategic doctrine. *Journal of the American Forensic Association, 24,* 168–80.

Derrida, Jacques. 1988. *Limited inc.* Evanston: Northwestern University Press.

Farrell, Thomas B. 1976. Knowledge, consensus, and rhetorical theory. *Quarterly Journal of Speech, 62,* 1–14.

Foucault, Michel. 1984. What is enlightenment? In *The Foucault reader,* ed. Paul Rabinow. New York: Pantheon.

Gonzáles-Marin, Carmen. 1987. Entrevista, Jacques Derrida: Leer lo ilegible. *Revista de occidente, 62/63,* 160–82.

Goodnight, G. Thomas. 1983. On questions of evacuation and survival in nuclear conflict: A case study in public argument and rhetorical criticism. In *Argument in transition: Proceedings of the Third Summer Conference on Argumentation*, ed. David Zarefsky. Annandale, Va.: Speech Communication Association.

Hill, Forbes. 1972. Reply to Professor Campbell. *Quarterly Journal of Speech*, 58, 454–60.

———. 1983. A turn against ideology: Reply to Professor Wander. *Central States Speech Journal*, 34, 121–26.

Hynes, Thomas J. 1988. You can't prove it here: Nuclear arms negotiations and the testing of evidence. *Journal of the American Forensic Association*, 24, 155–67.

Kane, Thomas. 1988. Rhetorical histories and arms negotiations. *Journal of the American Forensic Association*, 24, 143–54.

Kuhn, Thomas S. 1977. Objectivity, value judgment, and theory choice. *The essential tension*. Chicago: University of Chicago Press.

Laclau, Ernesto. 1988. Politics and the limits of modernity. *Universal Abandon? The politics of postmodernism*, ed. Andrew Ross. Minneapolis: University of Minnesota Press.

McKerrow, Raymie E., ed. 1993. *Argument and the postmodern challenge*. Annandale, Va.: Speech Communication Association.

Polanyi, Michael. 1958. *Personal Knowledge*. Chicago: University of Chicago Press.

Rowland, Robert C. 1985. On argument evaluation. *Journal of the American Forensic Association*, 21, 123–32.

Schiappa, Edward . 1989. The rhetoric of nukespeak. *Communication Monographs*, 56, 254–72.

———. 1991. Toward more argument evaluation: Identifying the constraints. In *Argument in controversy*, ed. Donn W. Parson. Annandale, Va.: Speech Communication Association.

Shapiro, Michael J. 1987. The rhetoric of social science: The political responsibilities of the scholar. In *The rhetoric of the human sciences*, ed. John S. Nelson, Allan Megill, and Donald N. McCloskey. Madison: University of Wisconsin Press.

Thomas, David A. 1980. *Argumentation as a way of knowing*. Falls Church, Va.: Speech Communication Association.

Waller, Douglas C., and James T. Bruce. 1987. SDI's covert reorientation. *Arms Control Today*, 17, 2–8.

Wander, Philip. 1983. The ideological turn in modern criticism. *Central States Speech Journal*, 34, 1–18.

———. 1984. The third persona: An ideological turn in rhetorical theory. *Central States Speech Journal*, 35, 197–216.

Williams, David Cratis, and Michael David Hazen. 1990. *Argumentation theory and the rhetoric of assent*. Tuscaloosa: University of Alabama Press.

Zarefsky, David. 1987. Argumentation and the politics of criticism. In *Argument and critical practices: Proceedings of the Fifth SCA/AFA Conference on Argumentation*, ed. Joseph W. Wenzel. Annandale, Va.: Speech Communication Association.

PART 1

Epistemological Approaches to Argument Evaluation

CHAPTER 1

Evaluative Criteria for Conspiracy Arguments: The Case of KAL 007

Marilyn J. Young and Michael K. Launer

Many contemporary theorists would have the critic abandon traditional forms of argument analysis and evaluation; they endorse instead an audience-centered perspective that focuses on explanations of how argumentative discourse operates in a given context. For example, Fisher (1984, 1985) advocates using the tenets of narrativity, focusing on an argument's coherence and fidelity as measures of its worth. Indeed, it is particularly tempting to apply the principles of narrativity to the subject of the present essay—the analysis of conspiratist discourse—because much of the task of the conspiratist rhetor lies in stringing together the anomalies of a troubling situation into a coherent, compelling narrative. Nevertheless, in this essay we seek to recreate the responsibility of the critic to fuse evaluation with explanation. In so doing, we address two significant questions: How should the critic approach examples of the conspiratist genre—with traditional criteria for evaluating argument or with audience-centered analysis? What evaluative tools will facilitate the critical process?

We contend that the most revealing evaluation is provided by close textual analysis that blends the ability of audience-centered

We would like to express our gratitude to Ray McKerrow for his support and guidance. We would also like to thank Curtis Austin for his contribution to the original version of this essay.

approaches to explain the persuasive appeal of conspiratist argument with the ability of formal approaches to assess logical structure and evidentiary strength. In order to demonstrate this process, we have chosen to analyze a specific instance of conspiratist rhetoric—David Pearson's "K.A.L. 007: What the U.S. Knew and When We Knew It," an article that appeared just prior to the first anniversary of the 1983 destruction of Korean Air Lines Flight 007 over Sakhalin Island (USSR) by jet fighters of the Soviet Air Defense Forces (Pearson 1984).[1]

Belief in conspiracy as the force behind social phenomena is "older than historicism" (Popper 1959, p. 281). Simply put, conspiratism is "the view that an explanation of a social phenomenon consists in the discovery of the man or groups who are interested in the occurrence of this phenomenon . . . and who have planned and conspired to bring it about" (Popper 1950, pp. 287–88). In recent years, the locus of such rhetoric has moved away from the extremist fringe and closer to the mainstream, becoming a staple of American political discourse (Zarefsky 1984).

Observations on the argumentative power of conspiratist interpretations are common. Zarefsky (1984) has considered the techniques of argumentation that help make conspiracy arguments credible and the social circumstances that make such charges believable to moderates as well as zealots. He notes that "conspiracy arguments become widely accepted when they explain a pattern of anomalies"; moreover, it is precisely "when a large number of (anomalous) events occurs, and the anomalies seem to have a pattern, [that] the search for an explanation intensifies" (p. 72). Warnick (1987) suggests that Fisher's notion of the narrative paradigm may provide insight into the description of some conspiracies (such as the "Prince of Evil," the Nazi explanation of Germany's problems). Goodnight and Poulakos (1981) have furnished a useful explanation of how conspiracy theories that have become accepted by society are integrated into social history.

While such literature has been useful in describing conspiratist rhetoric, it has failed to evaluate the arguments propounded. For instance, Goodnight and Poulakos (1981) discuss only those conspiracies that are proven to exist; they argue from the a posteriori vantage point of knowing that the Watergate conspiracy actually occurred and was exposed. (Nixon and his forces lost the battle for belief in their version of the truth.) Far more common and, therefore, more interesting and compelling to the student of argument are those claims of conspiracy that are never resolved to the satisfaction of significant segments of society. It is in these instances that the essential nature of conspiratist argument resides, for it is here the rhetor manipulates anxieties described by Neumann (1957, p. 259), exploiting—even creating—the very ambiguity that attends anomalous situations. One means for achieving conspiratorial persuasiveness is to join the characteristic causal, deductive claims of conspiratist rhetoric (Creps 1981, pp. 205–7) with dramatistic form—what Farrell (1979) has called a "Burkean syllogistic progression" (see also Young and Launer 1988b, chap. 8). This melding of logos and pathos gives urgency to the need for critical tools to evaluate conspiratist argument, since "the threshold level of plausibility for conspiracy theories is quite low" (Creps 1981, p. 4). We would contend that *the argumentative characteristics of the conspiratist text demand the application of formalist criteria to explicate the content or substance of the rhetoric.* Campbell and Jamieson (1976, p. 27) explicitly call for close reading of a text as a requirement for establishing the generic character of that text.

Indeed, as Warnick (1987) points out, it is precisely in the cases of stories that make "too much sense" that the critic is not well served by abandoning the conventions of formal and informal logic (p. 176). Moreover, Rowland (1987) has argued that narrative fidelity and probability "must test not merely the story, but the story in relation to the world." When such tests are applied in this manner "they become essentially equivalent to the tests of evidence and reasoning that are traditionally applied to public argument" (p. 270). Warnick (1987) continues: "A narrative such as Hitler's is invidiously persuasive precisely because of its narrative fidelity. . . . The narrative in *Mein Kampf* provides a convenient mode for responding to any questions or issues that those who are not 'true believers' might want to raise" (pp. 176–77). The example Warnick has chosen is fortuitous. It illustrates the difficulty of disproving the conspiratist claim—what Zarefsky terms the "self-sealing nature" of conspiratist argument—and in so doing, it underscores the necessity for rhetorical critics to address appropriate ways to praise or blame a particular argument (Zarefsky 1984; Warnick 1987, pp. 176–77). This is especially true if Zarefsky is correct in observing that conspiracy argument has become a staple of American politics. In analyzing

Pearson's essay as a case study of mainstream conspiratist rhetoric, we shall examine the evidence adduced on behalf of this specific conspiracy claim and shall demonstrate that, while factually and logically inadequate as proof, the text nonetheless artfully creates its own internal consistency—one that is seductive to the noncritical reader.

Thus, in the analysis that follows, we attempt to assess the communicative factors operating in "K.A.L. 007: What the U.S. Knew and When We Knew It." The present authors do not presume to know whether or not the airliner was actually engaged in a spy mission when it was shot down over Soviet territory; nor is it our intent to decide a winner in this contest. Our interest is focused on answering the following questions: How did this conspiratist marshal his arguments? Inasmuch as Pearson's article makes the type of "deductive, causal claim" described by Creps (1981), how might one evaluate the components of that claim? How accurate are the technical and linguistic assertions underlying the claim? How do stylistic choices within the text support the rhetor's conspiratist arguments? How are all of these structural elements drawn together to create a convincing story? Of necessity we examine the extent to which there exists independent confirmation or refutation of specific charges contained in our exemplar, the use to which this rhetor puts any independent confirmation, and the manner in which he deals with seemingly discrepant evidence. To do this requires that a judgment be rendered concerning the extent to which claimed anomalies are indeed anomalous.

CONSPIRATIST RHETORIC: A CASE STUDY

On the night of August 31/September 1, 1983, Korean Air Lines Flight 007 was intercepted by Soviet air defense fighter planes and ultimately shot down. All 269 persons aboard perished in the Sea of Japan. Much speculation and controversy surrounded the entire incident: President Reagan, who termed the tragedy a "horrifying act of violence," stated simply that KAL 007 flew off course accidentally; the Soviet Union, on the other hand, claimed the airliner was on a spy mission purposely planned and executed by U.S. intelligence services. The world press devoted considerable attention to the story through mid-November.

Subsequently, a number of books and articles appearing in the West purported to substantiate the spy plane scenario.[2] One of these was "K.A.L. 007: What the U.S. Knew and When We Knew It." Published on the eve of the first anniversary of the tragedy, the essay is an attempt to demonstrate the culpability of the American government in the destruction of KAL 007. Not only did the *Nation* highlight this article in an advertising campaign, but the unanswered questions raised by David Pearson caught the attention of such syndicated columnists as Tom Wicker of the *New York Times* (1984a, 1984b, 1985a, 1985b, 1986).

Pearson's essay is an excellent example of how one artful construction of a story can be transformed into "evidence" of a conspiracy. It is important because of all the studies that advance the hypothesis of an American role in the KAL tragedy, none has gained greater notoriety and none has influenced other investigators more. As Murray Sayle (1985) observes, "Pearson . . . has faced the choice between accident and conspiracy, and he gives us the heaviest possible nudge in the direction of conspiracy" (p. 49). In the opinion of Sayle, a veteran journalist whose reportage on KAL won praise in England, that article in the *Nation* was the "serious authority" relied on by Oliver Clubb (1985) and "many another conspiracy enthusiast" (p. 49). The most recent addition to the list of adherents is R. W. Johnson (1986), who used much of Pearson's material to support his own version of the conspiracy theory in *Shootdown: KAL 007 and the American Connection* (1986), which itself became the basis for an NBC television movie. HBO also broadcast a made-for-television movie, *Tailspin*, in 1989. Pearson's article is also important in that it demonstrates the potential power of the conspiracy argument to focus and direct public debate: his interpretation heavily influenced subsequent public understanding of the tragedy.[3] A 1986 survey, for example, revealed that 25 percent of the public believed "The airliner was equipped with devices for spying and intentionally went off course to spy."[4]

In his *Nation* article, Pearson contended that the U.S. government knew (or should have known) the situation into which KAL 007 had placed itself; the U.S. government, on the other hand, has consistently maintained that KAL was an "unarmed civilian aircraft" that had innocently strayed over Soviet territory unbeknownst to anyone, including its crew (U.S. Department of State 1983, p. 1).[5] Because of Pearson's persuasive account of the incident, the U.S. position was perceived by at least part of the public as a fabrication. To be sure, the American government unwittingly did much to erode the believability of its own position (Young and Launer 1988a, 1988b), but this merely created an opportunity for conspiratists by establishing a field of battle. As is usually the case, the initial odds of winning such a battle still were stacked in favor of the challenged authority (Goodnight and Poulakos 1981, p. 306; Smith 1985).

Sign Reasoning: The Associative Power of Narrative

Textual analysis of David Pearson's article reveals four underlying themes, or leitmotifs, which he uses to establish a frame of reference for the reader. Intertwined in the introductory section entitled "A Predictable Event," and continuing throughout the text, these themes provide a skeletal structure on which the author's arguments are assembled. Simultaneously, they supply the reader with "relevant" history to make sense of the story the author is telling (see Jervis 1985, pp. 513–14), thus providing the basis for a kind of sign reasoning (see Toulmin, et al. 1984, pp. 222–25). The first of these themes concerns the timing of recurrent intrusions by U.S. planes into Soviet airspace. The second is embodied in Pearson's observation that the United States "has usually cited radio or navigational difficulties as the cause of such intrusions into Soviet airspace, even when the aircraft took evasive action" (p. 107). Pearson introduces his third leitmotif when, in discussing the interceptions of previous intruders, he emphasizes the care with which Soviet pilots are said to follow accepted procedures— opening fire only when all other methods fail. The author's fourth and final theme is prophetic of his argument regarding the fate of KAL 007: "[T]he United States . . . places a very high priority on penetrating Soviet airspace, sometimes at the expense of human life" (p. 107). This quotation is the last statement before, "That is the context in which the tragedy of Flight 007 must be understood" (p. 107). Accordingly, there can be no doubt about the writer's intent in this extended introduction, starting with the section title: he has created a scenario in which the tragedy of KAL 007 would indeed be "a predictable event."

In constructing this worldview, the author offers no direct proof—in the legal sense of that term—to support the version of history in which he grounds his argument; he builds his case almost entirely on suggestion and the structural device of narrative position. It is significant that narrative structure *alone* provides the driving force behind whatever plausibility may reside in these assertions. Indeed, the association of disparate ideas in the course of storytelling is the foremost device available to the conspiratist to create the self-sealing argument that is required to proselytize for his beliefs.

In other words, Pearson uses the tactic of association to establish the narrative fidelity of his story. As Fisher (1984, p. 8; 1985, p. 364) observes, it is the power of association that makes stories function—as the individual tests the story against that which he or she already "knows." Lacking documentation, the entire fabric of this narrative depends on association. The difficulty, of course, lies in knowing how to determine if the claimed association is legitimate.

One may well ask: Wherein lies the capacity of association to produce plausibility in narrative discourse? The answer, it would seem, resides in reasoning from sign—a basic intellectual process that enables humans to order and organize experience. Toulmin et al. (1984) state: "Whenever a sign and its referent can reliably be expected to occur together, the fact that the sign is observed can be used to support a claim about the presence of the object or situation the sign refers to" (p. 223). While sign reasoning does not necessarily suggest causation, or even a time-ordered relationship, it does allow us to assume that certain phenomena are symbols or codes for the occurrence of other phenomena, creating an association. This suggests that the critic might profitably evaluate the reliability of the sign-to-inference framework established by the conspiratist rhetor.

With specific reference to this case study, one discerns the following instances of reasoning from sign in each of Pearson's leitmotifs:

1. He claims that border intrusions have often been timed to "sensitive moments" when important Soviet-American meetings were scheduled, and such meetings were imminent at the time of 007.

2. He associates radio or navigational difficulties with "evasive action" from which he imputes intent, and KAL 007 had reported radio problems throughout its flight.

3. He claims that Soviet PVO forces fire on intruders only as a last resort, and Soviet forces fired upon KAL 007.[6]

4. He recalls that loss of life has been heavy in the aftermath of several intentional border violations by U.S. military aircraft, and 269 people died when KAL 007 was destroyed.

In this frame of reference the imminence of bilateral Soviet-American talks, the claim of radio difficulties, the very fact of the shoot-down, and the ensuing loss of life are all meant to suggest that the Korean airliner was deliberately sent into Soviet airspace and that the consequences of this deliberate action were indeed predictable.

An allied tactic is a variant of the halo effect, one that might be defined for our purposes as "credibility by association." For example, in the *Nation* article (p. 111) Pearson argues:

(A) The Soviets were correct about the location of the mission orbit of the U.S. reconnaissance plane, an RC-135, which was in the area.

(B) They were correct about the point at which KAL 007 entered Soviet airspace. Therefore,

(C) the Soviets must also be correct about the RC-135 making a second loop outside its mission orbit in order to rendezvous with KAL 007.[7]

Pearson cites confirming evidence to support his analysis on the first two points (p. 107). Unfortunately, no evidence whatsoever is presented in support of the existence of the second loop. Indeed, Pearson's presentation makes it seem as though the U.S. government admitted the presence of the RC-135 in response to Soviet charges, which is not the case. Nevertheless, the effect in the 1984 *Nation* article is to create an aura of legitimacy for the entire Soviet version of events, including the unsubstantiated "double loop" theory.

The process of assent embodied here is similar to what Burke (1968) terms a "qualitative progression," in which "the presence of one quality prepares us for the introduction of another" (pp. 124–25). The technique of qualitative progression involves not so much logical entailment—as is the case with syllogistic progression—but the creation of an after-the-fact feeling of "rightness."

Thus, the citation of items A and B (known to be correct) prepares, or perhaps induces, the audience to accept item C as well.

Lesser Facts, Greater Facts: In the Absence of Proof

In public argument, the lack of direct proof often leads a proponent of a pet hypothesis to adopt an associative tactic one might call "lesser facts, greater facts." In using this technique, the rhetor accumulates a multitude of tangentially relevant details in order to give the impression that he knows more than is actually proved, enabling him to overclaim his evidence. As Creps (1981) points out, "[T]he persuasive force of the conspiracy case is produced not by a single portion of testimony, but by the simultaneous consideration of hundreds of pieces of evidence" (p. 45; see also Hofstadter 1965, pp. 36–37).

Pearson's article contains a great many assertions of evidence that in reality are only tangentially related to the points at issue: Did the RC-135 rendezvous with Flight 007? Did U.S. radar pick up the errant jetliner? Was the airliner on a spy mission for the U.S. government? A clear example of the effect this tactic can have on narrative structure is found in the following reference to an earlier incursion into Soviet airspace: "[A] U.S. RB-47 reconnaissance aircraft packed with long-range cameras, mapping cameras and electronic equipment for checking sites and frequencies of aircraft detection systems was attacked by two Soviet MiG-17 fighters over the Barents Sea" (Pearson 1984, p. 106).

The wealth of trivial detail in the participial construction "packed . . . systems" serves no true informational function—after all, what other kind of equipment would one expect a reconnaissance plane to carry? But Pearson, by providing this detailed description and using the verb "packed" (rather than "equipped" or "carrying"), gives the reader the subconscious impression that this RB-47 was somehow different, "extraordinary," rather than a routine, scheduled mission over international waters. The detail carries the burden of demonstrating the author's point. In this way, the onus on the Soviets for shooting down the plane is somewhat lessened. Perelman and Olbrechts-Tyteca (1958/1969) analyzed this stylistic device in their discussion of the "relation between art and argumentation": "In order to discern the argumentative use to which a term is being put, it is important to know the words or expressions the speaker might have used and to which he preferred the word he selected. . . . The terms comprising a [word-] family form an aggregate by relation to which any given term is specifically determined: they are . . . the background against which the selected term stands out" (pp. 150–53).

In the next section of his essay, entitled "The Role of the RC-135," Pearson asks what might explain the proximity of the American reconnaissance plane to KAL 007 prior to the airliner's intrusion over Kamchatka. This segment contains the notion of monitoring a Soviet missile test (a function explicitly allowed by the SALT agreements), as well as a more sinister possibility—that the RC-135 was watching as Soviet radar reacted to KAL, an intelligence opportunity the author terms "extraordinary" and a "bonanza." The passage is dominated by a wealth of technical detail and logistical information, but the question posed at the outset (What was a reconnaissance aircraft doing in such close proximity to an intruder in Soviet airspace?) is never actually answered.[8] Rather, the author reaches this conclusion: "Whether the RC-135 was in the area because of the SS-X-25 test or because it was coordinated with K.A.L. 007's intrusion into Soviet airspace, it must have observed the Korean airliner and had ample time to take steps to correct its course, but it did not do so" (p. 115). The unanswered question that initiated this segment of the article has been obscured by a proliferation of tangential facts. More important, both the initial question and the subsequent conclusion assume the accuracy of the claim that the reconnaissance aircraft rendezvoused with the airliner. As Burke (1931/1952) noted, "[a]trophy of form follows hypertrophy of information" (p. 144).

Quasi-Logical Argument: The Facade of Logic as a Rhetorical Tool

Perelman and Olbrechts-Tyteca (1958/1969) have defined as "quasi-logical" those arguments that "claim to be similar to the formal reasoning of logic or mathematics. . . . [S]ince there are formal proofs of recognized validity, quasi-logical arguments derive their persuasive strength from their similarity with these well-established modes of reasoning" (p. 193). Perelman and Olbrechts-Tyteca are not referring exclusively to fallacious arguments; they include all arguments that offer the appearance of logic. Their point is simply this: quasi-logical arguments are persuasive despite failing formal tests of validity. Included in this characterization, however, must be the fallacies most often used by conspiratist rhetors; for, to the extent those arguments are persuasive, they clearly derive their strength from an apparent similarity to rational forms. Thus, a component of the proposed methodology for evaluating the intellectual rigor of mainstream conspiratists must be the analysis of reasoning.

Close analysis of the *Nation* article confirms the impression: in addition to more traditional rhetorical strategies, Pearson often substitutes logical fallacy for evidence and reasoned argument. However, the technical detail combined with the anomalies obscures the fallacious reasoning. The overarching flaw is that the entire article amounts to a false dilemma: it is claimed that the failure of American forces to monitor the airliner means one of two things—either this was a major intelligence breakdown on the part of the U.S. military or the American government actually did know what was going on and is covering it up. The author argues, in effect, that U.S. monitoring capabilities are so extensive that the first scenario is impossible. Thus, it must be the case that the U.S. government is hiding something. And if the government is hiding something, it must be true either that officials decided to take advantage of an accidental situation or that they planned the entire operation:

> The most charitable interpretation is that U.S. military and intelligence agencies suffered an extraordinary series of human and technical failures which allowed the airliner to proceed on its deviant course. . . . However, a much more likely and frightening possibility is that a conscious policy decision was made by the U.S. government . . . to risk the lives of 269 innocent people on the assumptions that an extraordinary opportunity for gleaning intelligence information should not be missed and that the Soviets would not dare shoot down a civilian airliner. (1984, p. 106)

Despite the existence of evidence to the contrary to which Pearson had access (for example, reports of the International Civil Aviation Organization [ICAO] and its Air Navigation Commission), the article assumes that the U.S. military had the technical capability to track KAL 007 throughout the course of its flight; that any such equipment should have been used in this fashion; that if it was not, this, in and of itself, constitutes a failure. This construction constitutes a form of argument from ignorance, based on a combination of lack of information on the part of the audience and the difficulties inherent in proving a negative—that the United States did not engage in a spy operation. Thus, one is presented here a conundrum on the order of "Have you stopped beating your wife?" Ultimately, the position depends on points that the author never establishes: that the capability exists; that the equipment, if technically capable of such monitoring, was set up to do so; that the monitoring, if done, was done in "real time" (which is necessary if the tragedy were to be averted); and that those watching were aware of what was happening. Obviously, many steps are omitted from the overall proof.

Hiding those gaps in the enthymematic structure of this argument are masses of irrelevant technical detail and many logical fallacies. For example, an instance of false cause occurs in the analysis of the route of the RC-135, the U.S. reconnaissance aircraft that was on station near Kamchatka as KAL 007 headed toward Soviet territory. The Soviets allege that the RC-135 performed a control function in an espionage operation, that both it and the Korean airliner changed course in order to rendezvous. In Pearson's words, "That loop [in the route of the RC-135] . . . may have been an anomaly undertaken to bring the aircraft into close proximity to K.A.L. 007" (p. 110). But the only extant evidence for this "double loop" theory is the reconstructed map (not actual recorded radar data) displayed by the Soviets at their press conference.[9] Of course, the existence of this extra loop is essential to proving the allegation that the RC-135 was involved in this event, and a role for the RC-135 is crucial to the conspiracy theory. Despite the absence of any hard evidence (such as radar recordings or independent corroboration),[10] the author assumes this Soviet assertion to be true throughout the remainder of the article, justifying this position in part because the U.S. government has steadfastly refused to release any information concerning the reconnaissance plane's mission orbit: "Why would the United States consider that information sensitive? Because the time during which the two aircraft were in closest proximity was about a half hour before K.A.L. 007 first entered Soviet airspace—plenty of time to warn the jetliner, call ground stations or notify higher authorities" (p. 111). In this instance of the post hoc fallacy, it is useful to test the negative syllogism (if not B, then not A), yielding the following:

> If (and only if) KAL 007 had not penetrated Soviet airspace thirty minutes after the airliner and the RC-135 were in closest proximity to one another, then the U.S. government would not consider information concerning the mission orbit of the RC-135 sensitive.

For that statement to be true, reconnaissance routes would have to be public knowledge at other times. This is obviously not the case, since it is highly unlikely that the U.S. government is willing to make such information public under any but the most extreme circumstances.

This passage also represents another use of the false dilemma, for the reader is again presented with a binary choice: either the RC-135 was involved in the "spy mission" or the United States would release the pertinent information about its route.

Circular Reasoning: Assuming the Conclusion

The strategy of false cause tends to impute conscious behavior when, in fact, none may exist. Such *post hoc* fallacies may be persuasive when the alleged relationship can be made to *appear* reasonable. In this section, we examine specific uses of logical deficiencies as a structural device designed to induce the reader's participation in the rhetorical process, the linguistic means applied to reinforce this effort, and the extent to which discrepant information is ignored by the author. Reasoning from sign—the driving force behind associative thinking—is particularly useful in this process. But it is the associative power of narrative that allows circular reasoning to succeed. For example, if there were a conspiracy involving the CIA, the National Security Agency, and Korean Air Lines, the U.S. government certainly would want to hide the fact of a rendezvous between KAL 007 and any reconnaissance plane that was supervising its actions. But the failure to release information regarding the route of the RC-135 is not, in and of itself, an evidentiary fact leading to the inference that such a conspiracy existed. However, narrativity, which is grounded in reasoning from sign, allows the auditor to create such a relationship. In this instance, the false cause depends on an unproven assumption and the argument becomes circular: that is, the explanation makes sense only if one assumes a priori the existence of a conspiracy and the need to cover it up; yet the refusal to reveal classified information is used as proof of the conspiracy, illustrating the self-sealing nature of the conspiratist argument. Similarly, the refusal to reveal previously classified information cannot be taken as a sign of conspiracy or cover-up. A requirement of sign reasoning is that the sign and its referent can reliably be expected to occur together (Toulmin et al. 1984, p. 223), and only the totally cynical would assert that each instance of such reluctance signals a conspiracy or cover-up.

The fabric of much of the argumentation in Pearson's article follows this formula of assuming conclusions that need to be proven. For instance, in a passage explaining why the Soviet Air Defense Forces "had trouble figuring out what the intruder was," Pearson accepts the disputed rendezvous as fact: "Because of the complex flight path of the reconnaissance aircraft, its convergence with the flight path of K.A.L. 007, the airliner's reported change of altitude at the moment of convergence and its changed course shortly thereafter, it is not difficult to imagine at least some confusion" (p. 118). Although stated as fact by Pearson and by the Soviets, these allegations are specifically left open by the ICAO.[11] Of course, the general reader, not having access to this report, is left at the mercy of the author's interpretation of the two conflicting versions.

The conspiracy theory for which Pearson so eloquently argues depends absolutely on two of his allegations: that the airliner was under surveillance by the United States, and that the Korean pilot took evasive action. Unless the flight of KAL 007 was monitored, the alleged "intelligence bonanza" could not materialize.[12] Likewise, if the pilot did not take evasive action, there is no evidence to demonstrate he was aware his aircraft was in Soviet airspace.

As noted earlier in this essay, Pearson bases his analysis of the technical capabilities of U.S. military intelligence radar installations in the Western Pacific on assumptions supported by seemingly relevant, but insufficient, evidence. The issue centers on the question of whether the United States had over-the-horizon radar, an assumption which Pearson never establishes as fact. Instead, once again, he depends on the strategy of "lesser facts, greater facts," and the reader is in no position to evaluate the accuracy or significance of this information.

Pearson uses two disputed events to demonstrate his thesis that the Korean plane engaged in evasive maneuvers: the question of whether the airliner was flying with navigation lights extinguished and the issue of a voice inquiry by the intercepting Soviet pilot. The source of the problem can be found in the author's analysis of the recorded comments of Soviet interceptor pilots; the English language translation of this air-to-ground transmission is Pearson's sole support for these allegations. With respect to the issue of navigation lights, in reporting the confusion as the Soviets first scrambled fighters over Kamchatka, Pearson states: "If K.A.L. 007 was flying with its air navigation lights (ANOs) on at that time, the Soviet fighters should have seen it in the clear sky at 33,000 feet from as little as twenty miles away. That they did not suggests the airliner's ANOs were not on" (p. 118). But the linguistic evidence provided by the Russian transcript indisputably contradicts Pearson's allegations.[13] Based on this misapprehension, Pearson incorrectly interprets the Soviet pilot to be saying later, over Sakhalin, that he has turned on his own lights as the first step in the intercept procedures (pp. 119–20). Because he is wrong here, Pearson has no evidence that the pilot of KAL 007 knew he was being intercepted and, therefore, no independent reason to believe that he took evasive action, except the authority of the Soviet government. Indeed, according to the ANC *Report,* "available information suggests that the flight crew of KE007 was not aware of any of the interceptions reported by the USSR. . . . [There was] no reference to any visual or radio contact by KE007 with intercepting aircraft" (UNO 1984, p. 8). Pearson, however, ignores this information, concluding that the argument he has developed "leaves us with the most persuasive theory: that the airliner made a deliberate, carefully planned intrusion into Soviet territory with the knowledge of U.S. military and intelligence agencies" (p. 122). Unfortunately, a majority of the allegations in this article, and particularly this last one, are actually unproven. The writer nevertheless assumes their validity and employs them as premises in later arguments, substituting repetition for proof.

Only a close textual analysis will reveal the conspiratist's method of operationalizing this strategy. In the *Nation* article, clues to the linguistic underpinning of the process can be found in the author's discussion of variant U.S. and ICAO translations of a crucial line in the transcript. The author writes:

> At 1813:16, the pilot of the SU-15 replied to another instruction from ground control. "Roger," he said. Ten seconds later, according to the U.S. translation of the transmissions, the pilot reported back to ground control, "The target isn't responding to

I.F.F. [Identification/Friend or Foe]." If I.F.F., a military proce-
dure, was used, it is clear the Russians believed they were dealing
with a hostile military aircraft. But in its final report, the
I.C.A.O. team investigating the incident translated that message
as, "The target isn't responding to the call." "The call" might
refer to an attempt to contact K.A.L. 007 on the international
hailing frequencies of 121.5 or 243.0 megaHertz. . . . If the
I.C.A.O. translation is correct, the Soviet pilot may well have
used the international hailing frequency in accordance with
accepted interception procedures. *Yet* the transcripts show no
response from K.A.L. 007. (p. 120, emphasis added)

Fleshing out Pearson's reasoning, we arrive at the following: (1) If
the ICAO translation is correct, the Soviet pilot may have used the
International Hailing Frequency. (2) If the Soviet pilot used the
International Hailing Frequency, KAL 007 should have
responded. (3) KAL did not respond. Conclusion desired: KAL
007 was being evasive.

It is the word "yet" that colors the entire passage, because
there would be no false reasoning without it: if one were to substitute "in any event"—an equally pedestrian connector—the
statement would become one of co-occurrence, coincidence,
rather than causality. But claims of causality are essential to vindicate the conspiratist's stance: for it is precisely coincidences that
have no credibility within this worldview. As we have noted, a
hallmark of the conspiracy argument is its "deductive, causal
claim." Further, it is "the deductive logic of this appeal . . . that
can transform all data into indisputable 'evidence'" (Creps 1981,
pp. 96, 100).

The importance of this argumentative structure rests on the
simple fact that Pearson does not prove the International Hailing
Frequency was actually used. Indeed, all hard evidence is to the
contrary and the "evidence" on which Pearson relies is hypothetical. The conclusion that KAL 007 engaged in evasive maneuvers
does not follow from the evidence presented. Nor does it make
any sense: it would clearly have been in the Korean pilot's interest
to respond, identifying his craft as a civilian plane with passengers
aboard, particularly if, as the Soviets—and Pearson—allege, a
civilian aircraft was specifically chosen as a cover for the spy operation to ensure safety. The obvious conclusion must be that the
"call" was not a verbal inquiry made on the 121.5 MHz Interna-

tional Hailing Frequency. Nevertheless, this last possibility is not made available to the naive reader.

In the context of the building narrative, the hypothetical nature of Pearson's claim is lost in his attempt to demonstrate that the Soviet pilot was following established intercept procedures. He makes no mention of the ICAO *Report,* which states that there was no evidence of the interceptor pilot having made any significant effort to follow international procedures for intercepting aircraft (UNO 1983, p. 43). Failure to establish this claim would undermine one of his four leitmotifs. In addition, since a voice call on 121.5 MHz is a *requirement* of those procedures, Pearson's entire argument would be vitiated if it could be demonstrated that no such call was made. Significantly, the Air Navigation Commission concluded: "There is no record or other information of any calls on 121.5 MHz having been heard by any civil or military ground unit or by other aircraft within VHF range of the intercepting aircraft, or any record of such transmissions having been received via the search and rescue satellite (SARSAT) system" (UNO 1984, p. 9).[14] It should be noted, as Kang has demonstrated (see Launer et al. 1986, p. 70), that when the U.S. government supplied evidence to refute the Soviet Union's claim it inadvertently proved the falsity of its own position as well. If the Soviet pilot made an IFF inquiry minutes prior to shooting down the aircraft, then it must not be true that Soviet military officials knew all along what sort of aircraft they were dealing with, because the only thing an IFF interrogation could prove was that KAL 007 was not a Soviet military aircraft. Had that been clear for over two hours, there would have been no necessity to complete such an electronic inquiry so late in the interception sequence.

EXAMINING THE FOUNDATIONS OF CONSPIRATIST RHETORIC: THE PROBLEM WITH NARRATIVE APPROACHES

We began this essay by posing the following question: How does one evaluate examples of the conspiratist genre? A good starting point for analysis is the conspiratist's worldview or frame of reference. As Jamieson (1976) states, "A rhetor's *Weltanschauung* manifests itself not only in the premises he assumes but also in his structuring of arguments, his rhetorical tone, his use of language and in the types of evidence he educes" (pp. 4–5). Importantly, the very nature of the data can contribute to the plausibility of an alleged conspiracy. In cases such as the Korean airliner disaster, complex scientific, technical, and linguistic evidence is central to any discussion, including claims of conspiracy. The inherent plausibility of conspiracy is undoubtedly enhanced by the highly technical nature of some incidents. Consequently, one reason Pearson's article succeeds is the author's reliance on the ignorance of his audience. Fisher (1987) tells us that the role of experts in public moral argument is to act as counselors. "Only experts can argue with experts, and their arguments . . . cannot be rationally questioned by nonexperts" (p. 72). It is not clear what should be the role or the subject of the "counsel" that Fisher espouses. If experts refute technical error, they are engaging in the discourse-stifling practices that Fisher condemns. On the other hand, failure to so refute leaves the public as ignorant and error-prone as before (see Rowland 1987; Benoit 1988). Unfortunately, Fisher sheds no light on what the critic should do with a case such as the present one.

Although Pearson is not an expert in the sense that Hans Bethe and Edward Teller are experts on nuclear weapons (cf. Fisher 1987, p. 72), he nevertheless provides an overwhelming amount of technical detail that helps in the development of the rhetorical worldview he is creating. The reader, of course, is in no position to judge the accuracy, significance, or relevance of this information. For example, Pearson makes a point about additional fuel taken on by the airliner prior to leaving Anchorage: "According to data contained in the [ICAO's] final report on the incident, K.A.L. 007's pilot added 9800 pounds of fuel at Anchorage which were neither needed for his scheduled flight nor accounted for in his subsequent position reports to air traffic controllers" (p. 107). This sounds like a lot of fuel, but in fact it was only 3.8 percent of the minimum required for the flight, and constituted, in the view of many experienced pilots, a prudent reserve, referred to as "grandmother fuel."[15] As Perelman and Olbrechts-Tyteca (1958/ 1969) observe, "Generally speaking, absolute figures have a greater impact on the imagination [than relative figures] . . ." (p. 148). The effect of accumulating technical detail is to enhance the believability of Pearson's story; the naive reader will assume Pearson is an expert, hence credible as a witness. Details such as Pearson provides are crucial for strengthening narrative probability and narrative fidelity, yet their accuracy and relevance can be tested only if experts argue in the traditional mode.

When faced with arguments that depend on sophisticated technical knowledge, the American public—which usually is favored by freedom of information—is no better off than the Soviet public, which historically has had no access to such information. In the case of KAL, the American public could not even determine who the real experts were, since television and the press, which mediated all information concerning the KAL disaster, made no more critical judgments than did the public. Indeed, the press tends to seek a complete story, even if inaccurate—favoring those who profess to know what happened, while passing over those who insist the data are inconclusive or incomplete (see Boot 1990).

Although the public may be swayed by the ethos or verbal skills of a rhetor to accept such evidence at face value, it must be pertinent to any critical judgment to assess the factual accuracy and evidentiary relevance of all specialized data (see Baskerville 1961). Indeed, conspiratist argument invites such critique. By its very nature, conspiratist rhetoric purports to be an evidentiary process, though in fact what makes the rhetoric work is its narrativity. Thus, one can assess the worldview of the conspiratist—the ground on which the charge of conspiracy rests—by examining the rhetorical use of quasi-logical argument (Perelman and Olbrechts-Tyteca 1958/1969, pp. 193–260), the perceived stylistic use of language, and the factual accuracy of technical details adduced as evidence.

More specifically, Creps (1981) defines the substance of conspiratist rhetoric as its "propositional, thematic, logical, and evidential content." The evidentiary methodology is particularly significant as a critical tool, because it evaluates the conspiratist claim on its own terms, and cuts through the maze of association obfuscating enthymematic gaps in the proof structure. For example, conspiratist rhetoric characteristically employs the false dilemma (a dissociative construct that imposes upon the auditor a seemingly binary choice). Associative strategies frequently employed by the conspiratist rhetor include a kind of "credibility by association," reliance on circular and post hoc reasoning, and a variant of the halo effect that we have called "lesser facts, greater facts" (the use of trivial detail to imply knowledge of more important issues). Each of these associative/dissociative techniques functions effectively within the narrative structure of the conspiratist argument to produce narrative probability. Perelman and Olbrechts-Tyteca (1958/1969) explain association as a quasi-logical structural device: "[T]wo terms are presented as if their insertion into the same class went without saying, and there is a formation of a class *ad hoc* through the union of the two terms on a plane of equality. . . . [E]lements placed side by side in this way to form a class should react on each other in the [auditor's] mind, and it is because of this that the technique assumes its argumentative value" (p. 129).

As Warnick (1987) has noted, "[I]t is precisely because of the ambiguity and implicitness of its claims that narrative can be used to account for seemingly discrepant facts" (p. 176). We understand "implicitness" to mean the implicative character of storytelling structure. Ambiguity becomes manifest as the absence of a precise connection between parts of the argument. "The [auditor] is left free *to imagine . . . a relationship* that by its very lack of precision, assumes a mysterious, magical character . . ."—an argument form that Perelman and Olbrechts-Tyteca (1958/1969) term "parataxis" (see pp. 157ff., emphasis added). Once associations are adduced in order to impute causality, they operate in the subsequent narrative as if causality were already proven. It would seem, then, that the process of creating narrative probability has the capacity to overshadow the need to demonstrate narrative fidelity.

In our exemplar, Pearson effectively associates his hypothetical premises and conclusions with what is known about the incident. Association/dissociation is probably the most powerful tool of persuasiveness and the most basic human thought process. It is the means by which we classify experience. As a rhetorical tool it is not only the standard by which stories are judged; it is the very substance of the narrative act. Thus, the lack of definitive evidence bearing on this case allows association to prevail; and the associative power of stories allows circular reasoning to succeed. Hypothetical premises, as well as the conclusions drawn from them, take on the status of proven fact and can be repeated as such in subsequent arguments. Each argument becomes an artistic element in the narrative development, achieving, finally, a symbiosis of argument and poetic in which traditional rhetorical fallacies are utilized as artistic devices. Consciously crafted language carries the intellectual burden of argument, and the dramatistic elements of the story overshadow the lack of evidence. But such ambiguity, of course, can be misleading, and it is from this absence of formal argumentation that conspiratist narration derives its persuasiveness. The use of association, then, is one characteristic that allows for—indeed, creates—the self-sealing attribute observed by Zarefsky (1984) and others. Warnick (1987) recalls Burke's characterization of Hitler's power: "If those skeptical of Hitler's account pointed out the existence of Jewish workers not conforming to his stereotype, his response would be '[t]hat is one more indication of the cunning with which the Jewish plot is being engineered'" (p. 176). Accordingly, discrepant evidence can be dismissed by the conspiratist as some sort of red herring consciously designed by the conspirators to confuse the unwary and the gullible.

Because an auditor is constrained to choose between two carefully selected alternatives, employing the false dilemma as a rhetorical tactic serves to delimit choices artificially, hence polarizing the alternatives purportedly available to decision makers. False dilemmas are simplistic—which is both their virtue and their vice. Hence, it follows that the conscious use of false dilemma (or other logical fallacies) as a rhetorical tactic distorts the communicative nature of the rhetorical act. Furthermore, such devices thrive in the medium of narration precisely because of the absence of formal argumentation.

The human desire for explanations of all natural phenomena—a drive that spurs inquiry on many levels—aids the conspiratist in the quest for public acceptance. Moreover, the primary characteristic of conspiratist rhetoric that allows it to be adopted by other audiences is its ability to conceal ambiguities and points of contention by means of rhetorical coercion. In contrast, the tests of evidence that we have outlined are specifically designed to reveal those places where a story isn't sound and, especially, those places where it is not possible to discern the truth on the basis of the available information.

Accordingly, we contend that the central task of argumentative analysis lies in determining whether or not the conspiratist's weltanschauung interacts with coercive elements in the rhetoric to delimit the rhetorical choices available to the audience. The objects of analysis are (1) those textual elements that project the ideology of the rhetor, and (2) the techniques employed to convey that ideology. If the critic can utilize the immanent structural characteristics of a rhetorical text to demonstrate the presence of a weltanschauung that is consistent with the ideology described above, one of the cornerstones of conspiratist rhetoric shall have been discovered. In addition, the "deductive, causal claim" described by Creps (1981) can be evaluated on its own terms: Are the purported facts accurate and relevant? That is, what is the quality of the conspiratist's evidence? If it can be demonstrated that the conspiratist employs false dilemmas, inaccurate technical data, or other flawed tactics to establish consistency, to claim causality where only anomaly logically resides—and if it is claimed that conspiracy is the causal factor—then it is proper for the critic to focus attention on the nature of these tactics. For when such devices adumbrate within a well-constructed text, a spurious sort of narrative plausibility—narrative fidelity—may be created. A reader cannot test narrative fidelity—the test against real-world knowledge—unless that reader actually has the requisite knowledge.

Perelman and Olbrechts-Tyteca (1958/1969) state that the primary requirement of argumentation is that it provide "the means of obtaining the adherence of the audience through variations in the way of expressing thought" (p. 163). Accordingly, the form of a discourse must not be separated from its substance, nor should stylistic structures be studied "independently of the purpose they must achieve in the argumentation" (p. 142). Such analysis makes it "possible to track down [i.e., to discern the motive for] the choice of a particular form" (p. 143). It is, of course, this notion that lies at the root of the generic mode of criticism.

We contend that the task for the critic of conspiratist narrative may rightly include the application of universal criteria in assessing that rhetor's "ulterior motives" (Fisher 1985, p. 364), particularly if those criteria are applied to evidence that resides within the conspiratist narrative itself. Warnick (1987) correctly argues that the internal coherence of a text, its narrative probability, "is inadequate for the judgment of narratives used rhetorically" (p. 177; see Shlapentokh 1986, pp. 22, 36) and, further, that it "cannot function as the sole means for . . . assessing [a] text's adequacy as the response to a rhetorical situation" (p. 178; see Bitzer 1968), because, simply stated, rhetoric attempts to persuade. Hence, the rhetor who utilizes narrative in order to achieve the goal of promulgating a particular weltanschauung may be held accountable by the critic for the value criteria that underlie that vision.

One may view a conspiratist (Pearson) as the "critic" of "narrative used rhetorically" (the U.S. government's explanation of the KAL incident). From this point of view, one can see in Pearson a critic with no external criteria other than his own moral values. However, to the extent that Pearson (functioning as the rhetor who propounds his own "narrative used rhetorically") advocates a particular weltanschauung, one may also judge that his narrative constitutes "a mask for ulterior motives" (Fisher 1985, p. 364). This statement might also apply, ipso facto, to the position maintained by the U.S. government.

CONCLUSIONS

At one level, Pearson's article is persuasive simply because he tells a better story, successfully exploiting a confluence of public knowledge about past espionage activities, traditional American distrust of government, a concomitant faith in technology, and the administration's unwillingness to reveal sources and methods of intelligence. And, in an age of skeptics, government complicity does not seem unreasonable. Indeed, conspiracy theories are almost never unreasonable; they are merely too monistic.

Nevertheless, we have suggested that it is fruitful to evaluate conspiratist rhetoric from the standpoint of rhetorical behavior intended to expand possibilities for meaningful dialogue and compromise versus strategies that limit real communication. One major aspect of much conspiratist rhetoric that has not been discussed by previous authors is the potential use of the false dilemma as a rhetorical strategy. In our opinion, the use of logical fallacy, particularly the false dilemma, exemplifies coercive communication.

Forcing audiences into a simple binary choice between alleged good and alleged evil is a standard ploy that has ancient roots: "He who is not with us is against us." One can also pose an issue in such a manner that the audience is offered a choice between willful evil and inadvertent evil, but evil nonetheless. Thus, Robert Welch, founder of the John Birch Society, characterized President Eisenhower as either a conscious Soviet agent or an unwitting dupe of the communist conspiracy. Similarly, David Pearson argues that U.S. claims of failure to monitor KAL indicate a concerted effort to cover up either a failed intelligence operation or, at the very least, a major U.S. intelligence breakdown. After setting up this dichotomy, Pearson then argues for his perception of a malevolent reality, with inadvertent evil reserved as the only refuge for nonbelievers.

One arrives at a symbiosis of poetics and argumentation: various logical fallacies are used as artistic devices in the structure of a conspiratist tract qua rhetorical text, while consciously crafted language carries the intellectual burden of argument further by use of emotion than the rhetor could otherwise achieve through induction.

In this way, Pearson can be seen to utilize structural devices— fallacies and argument from ignorance—to create the anomalies that are then explained by claims of conspiracy: technical material and dramatistic style are fused to create internal consistency while the deductive causal form overrides it all to create an image of inexorability. In this way, the rhetor transforms the rhetorical act, distorting its communicative nature, engaging in rhetorical coercion.

Of course, this is the traditional, rational view of argument; nevertheless, we would contend that it is the best, perhaps the only, means of coming to grips with conspiratist claims because it is often the case that this type of argumentation consciously violates the standards of rationality. The appeal of the conspiracy story is its self-sealing nature: it provides a worldview that is complete, capable of answering—by subsuming—all uncomfortable questions. Its apparent internal cohesiveness provides the narrative fidelity and probability that make it persuasive. Thus, conspiracy argument proves Fisher's (1987) theory correct: auditors test a story by their own lights. Yet, because the narrative paradigm is not normative (p. 66), analysis of conspiracy argument also provides the rationale for resisting the seduction of Fisher's position.

REFERENCES

ABC News. 1983, September 22–26. *ABC News/Washington Post Poll* (Survey #0084). New York: Author.

Abcarian, G. 1971. Political deviance and social stress: The ideology of the American radical right. In *Social control and social change,* ed. J. P. Scott and S. F. Scott. Chicago: University of Chicago Press.

Andrews, J. R. 1969. Confrontation at Columbia: A case study in coercive rhetoric. *Quarterly Journal of Speech*, 55, 9–16.

Andrjushkov, Col. A. 1986, April 6. Ia idu na taran [I'm going to ram it]. *Krasnaja zvezda*.

Anonymous (P. Q. Mann). 1984, June. Reassessing the Sakhalin incident. *Defence Attaché*, 41–56.

Archer, J. 1969. *The extremists: Gadflies of American society*. New York: Hawthorn.

Auerbach, E. 1946. *Mimesis. Dargestellte Wirklichkeit in der abendländischen Literatur*. Bern, Switzerland: A. Francke.

Bailyn, B. 1967. *The ideological origins of the American revolution*. Cambridge: Harvard University Press.

Baskerville, B. 1961. The illusion of proof. *Western Speech*, 25, 236–42.

Bell, D., ed. 1964. *The radical right*. New York: Anchor Books.

Benoit, W. L. 1988. Review of Fisher, 1987. *Argumentation*, 2, 535–38.

Bitzer, L. 1968. The rhetorical situation. *Philosophy and Rhetoric*, 1, 1–14.

Boot, W. 1990, January–February. The accidental journalist. *Columbia Journalism Review*, 17–21.

Bormann, E. G. 1972. Fantasy and rhetorical vision: The rhetorical criticism of social reality. *Quarterly Journal of Speech*, 396–407.

———. 1985. *The force of fantasy. Restoring the American dream*. Carbondale: Southern Illinois University Press.

Bosmajian, H. A. 1974. *The language of oppression*. Washington: Public Affairs Press.

Brockriede, W., and R. Scott. 1970. *Moments in the rhetoric of the cold war*. New York: Random House.

Bunzel, J. 1967. *Anti-politics in America*. New York: Alfred A. Knopf.

Burke, K. 1968. *Counter-statement*. Berkeley: University of California Press.

Campbell, K. K., and K. H. Jamieson. 1976. *Form and genre: Shaping rhetorical action*. Falls Church, Va.: Speech Communication Association.

Chalmers, D. M. 1965. *Hooded Americanism: The first century of the Ku Klux Klan: 1865 to the present*. Garden City: Doubleday.

Clubb, O. 1985. *KAL FLIGHT 007: The hidden story*. Sag Harbor, N.Y.: The Permanent Press.

Cohen, J. 1978. *Conspiracy fever*. New York: Macmillan.

Creps, E. G., III. 1981. The conspiracy argument as rhetorical genre (Ph.D. diss., Northwestern University, 1980). *Dissertation Abstracts International*, 42, 3320A. (University Microfilms No. 8104701)

Curry, R. O., and T. M. Brown, eds. 1972. *Conspiracy: The fear of subversion in American history*. New York: Holt, Rinehart and Winston.

Cutler, R. B. 1986. *EXPLO 007: Evidence of conspiracy.* Beverly Farms, Mass.: Author.

Dallin, A. 1984. *Black box: KAL 007 and the superpowers.* Berkeley: University of California Press.

Davis, D. B. (comp.) 1971. *The fear of conspiracy: Images of un-American subversion from the Revolution to the present.* Ithaca: Cornell University Press.

Dobbs, M. 1983, September 20. Soviets: 747 was part of spy network. *Washington Post,* A1, A11.

Donahue. 1986, September 16. Nationally syndicated telecast.

Dudman, R. 1962. *Men of the far right.* New York: Pyramid.

Epperson, A. R. 1985. *The unseen hand: An introduction to the conspiratorial view of history.* Tucson: Publius Press.

Farrell, T. B. 1979. Rhetoric in two voices: The continuing epistemic conversation of Kenneth Burke. Northwestern University. Cited in Creps (1981), p. 56.

Fisher, W. R. 1970. A motive view of communication. *Quarterly Journal of Speech,* 56, 131–39.

———. 1984. Narration as a human communication paradigm: The case of public moral argument. *Communication Monographs,* 51, 1–22.

———. 1985. The narrative paradigm: An elaboration. *Communication Monographs,* 52, 347–67. [Reprinted as "An elaboration" in *Human communication as narration,* pp. 85–101].

———. 1987. *Human communication as narration: Toward a philosophy of reason, value, and action.* Columbia: University of South Carolina Press.

Foreign Broadcast Information Service. 1983, September 12. KAL Incident. *Daily Report, Soviet Union,* DD1–43.

Goldberg, A. 1968. *Conspiracy interpretations of the assassination of President Kennedy: International and domestic.* University of California Security Studies Project Paper No. 16. Los Angeles: University of California Press.

Golden, F. 1984, December. Seeing a conspiracy in the sky. *Discover,* 8.

Goodnight, G. T., and J. Poulakos. 1981. Conspiracy rhetoric: From pragmatism to fantasy in public discourse. *Western Journal of Speech Communication,* 45, 299–316.

Griffin, L. M. 1964. The rhetorical structure of the "New Left" movement: Part I. *Quarterly Journal of Speech,* 50, 113–35. Reprinted in *The rhetoric of our times,* ed. J. Jeffery Auer. New York: Appleton-Century-Crofts.

Hersh, S. M. 1986. *"The target is destroyed."* New York: Random House.

Hoffer, E. 1951. *The true believer.* New York: Harper and Brothers.

Hofstadter, R. 1965. The paranoid style in American politics. In *The paranoid style in American politics and other essays*. New York: Alfred A. Knopf.

Hook, S. 1953. *Heresy, yes—Conspiracy, no*. New York: Day.

Illesh, A., and A. Shal'nev. 1989, November 13. Kak èto bylo. Kommentarii k knige "Raskapyvaja sovetskie katastrofy" [The way it was. Commentary on the book *Uncovering Soviet disasters*]. *Izvestija*, 6.

Jakobson, R. O. 1956. Two aspects of language and two types of aphasic disturbances. *Fundamentals of language*, part 2. The Hague: Mouton. Reprinted in: Roman O. Jakobson. 1971. *Studies on child language and aphasia*. The Hague: Mouton. Also reprinted in v. 2 of *Selected writings*.

Jamieson, K. H. 1976. The rhetorical manifestations of *weltanschauung*. *Central States Speech Journal*, 27, 4–14.

Jervis, R. 1985. Hypotheses on misperception. In *International politics. Anarchy, force, political economy and decision making*, ed. R. J. Art and R. Jervis. 2d ed. Boston: Little, Brown. Reprinted from April 1968 issue of *World Politics*, 20, 454–79.

Johnson, R. W. 1983, December 17. 007: License to kill? *The Guardian*, 15.

———. 1986. *Shootdown: Flight 007 and the American connection*. New York: Viking.

Jones, V. 1988, November 29. Was jumbo jet crash a hoax? *Globe*, 11.

Larry King Live. 1986, September 2. Cable News Network telecast.

Launer, M. K., M. J. Young, and S. Kang. 1986. Correspondence. *Bulletin of Concerned Asian Scholars*, 18, 67–71.

Ligon, D. 1978. *Thesis of conspiracy, 1778–1945. Philosophs, Freemasons, Jews, liberals, and Socialists as conspirators against social order*. Dijon, France: University of Dijon.

Lipset, S. M., and E. Raab. 1978. *The politics of unreason: Right-wing extremism in America, 1790–1977*. 2d ed. Chicago: University of Chicago Press.

Lucaites, J. L., and C. M. Condit. 1985. Reconstructing narrative theory: A functional perspective. *Journal of Communication*, 35, 90–108.

McEvoy, J. 1966. *Letters from the right: Content-analysis of a letter writing campaign*. Ann Arbor: University of Michigan. Center for Research on the Utilization of Scientific Knowledge.

Maertens, T. 1985, September. Tragedy of errors. *Foreign Service Journal*, 25–31.

National Strategy Information Center. 1986. *National Survey 6320, June 7–11, 1986*. Santa Ana, Calif.: G. Lawrence Company.

Neumann, F. 1957. *The democratic and the authoritarian state*. Glencoe: Free Press.

Newman, R. P. 1970. Under the veneer: Nixon's Vietnam speech of November 3, 1969. *Quarterly Journal of Speech*, 56, 168–78.

Oberg, J. E. 1985, October. Sense and nonsense: A reader's guide to the KE007 massacre. *American Spectator*, 36–39.

———. 1988. *Uncovering Soviet disasters. Exploring the limits of glasnost.* New York: Random House.

Ogden, C. K., and I. A. Richards. 1923. *The meaning of meaning.* Cambridge, England: Cambridge University Press.

Overstreet, H., and B. Overstreet. 1964. *The strange tactics of extremism.* New York: W. W. Norton.

Parenti, M. 1969. *The anti–Communist impulse.* New York: Random House.

———. 1986. *Inventing reality. The politics of the mass media.* New York: St. Martin's Press.

Payne, P. S. R. 1975. *The corrupt society: From ancient Greece to present-day America.* New York: Praeger.

Pearson, D. 1984, August 18–25. K.A.L. 007: What the U.S. knew and when we knew it. *The Nation*, 104–24.

———. 1987. *KAL 007: The cover-up.* New York: Summit.

Pearson, D., and J. Keppel. 1985, August 17–24. Journey into doubt: New pieces in the puzzle of flight 007. *The Nation*, 104–10.

Perelman, Ch., and L. Olbrechts-Tyteca. 1969. *The new rhetoric. A treatise on argumentation.* Trans. John Wilkinson and Purcell Weaver. Notre Dame: University of Notre Dame Press. (Original work published 1958).

Popper, K. 1950. *The open society and its enemies.* Princeton: Princeton University Press.

———. 1959. Prediction and prophecy in the social sciences. In *Theories of history*, ed. Patrick Gardiner. New York: The Free Press.

Rohmer, R. 1984. *Massacre 747.* Markham, Ontario: PaperJacks Ltd.

Rowland, R.C. 1987. Narrative: Mode of discourse or paradigm? *Communication Monographs*, 54, 264–75.

Sampson A., and W. Bittorf. 1984, September 24 and October 1, 8, and 15, [four parts]. 'Sinken auf eins-null-tausend . . .' Der Todesflug des Korea-Jumbo. *Der Spiegel.*

Sayle, M. 1985, April 25. KE007: A conspiracy of circumstance. *New York Review of Books*, 44–54.

Shlapentokh, V. 1986. *Soviet public opinion and ideology. Mythology and pragmatism in interaction.* New York: Praeger.

Shootdown 1988, November 28. National Broadcasting Company telecast.

Smith, D. 1985, November. *KAL 007: Making sense of the senseless.* Paper presented at the annual convention of the Speech Communication Association, Denver, Colo.

Thayer, G. 1967. *The farther shores of politics.* New York: Simon and Schuster.

Toulmin, S. E. 1958. *The uses of argument.* Cambridge, England: Cambridge University Press.

Toulmin, S., R. Reike, and A. Janik. 1984. *An introduction to reasoning.* New York: Macmillan.

UNO [United Nations Organization], International Civil Aviation Organization. 1983, December. *Destruction of Korean Air Lines Boeing 747 over Sea of Japan, 31 August 1983. Report of the ICAO fact-finding investigation.* Montreal, Quebec: Author.

UNO [United Nations Organization], ICAO, Air Navigation Commission. 1984, February 16. *1818th report to council by the president of the Air Navigation Commission* (Document C-WP/7809). Montreal, Quebec: Author.

U.S. Department of Defense, Joint Chiefs of Staff, Special Operations Division. 1983. *Soviet news and propaganda analysis based on Red Star [the official newspaper of the Soviet defense establishment], 3 (9).* Alexandria, Va.: Defense Technical Information Center.

U.S. Department of State, Bureau of Public Affairs. 1983. *KAL flight #007: Compilation of statements and documents. September 1–16, 1983* (1983-421-412: 672). Washington, D.C.: U. S. Government Printing Office.

U.S. House of Representatives, Committee on Science and Technology, Subcommittee on Transportation, Aviation and Materials. 1983, September 19. *Aircraft navigation technology and errors* [Hearing]. Washington, D.C.: U.S. Government Printing Office.

Warnick, B. 1987. The narrative paradigm: Another story. *Quarterly Journal of Speech, 73,* 172–82.

Wicker, T. 1984a, September 7. A damning silence. *New York Times,* A27.

———. 1984b, October 21. Silence on flight 007. *New York Times,* E23.

———. 1985a, September 3. A disintegrating story. *New York Times,* A21.

———. 1985b, September 6. The final word? *New York Times,* A23.

———. 1986, September 21. Before the shootdown. *New York Times,* E25.

Windt, T. O., Jr. 1982. Administrative rhetoric: An undemocratic response to protest. *Communication Quarterly, 30,* 245–50.

Young, M. J. 1975. The conspiracy theory of history as radical argument: Students for a Democratic Society and The John Birch Society (Ph.D. diss., The University of Pittsburgh, 1974), *Dissertation Abstracts International, 35,* 6276A. (University Microfilms No. 75-6384)

Young, M. J., and M. K. Launer. 1988a. KAL 007 and the superpowers: An international argument. *Quarterly Journal of Speech*, 74, 271–95.
———. 1988b. *Flights of fancy, flight of doom: KAL 007 and Soviet-American rhetoric.* Lanham: University Press of America.
Zarefsky, D. 1984. Conspiracy argument in the Lincoln–Douglas debates. *Journal of the American Forensic Association*, 21, 63–75.

CHAPTER 2

Narrative Reframing of Public Argument: George Bush's Handling of the Persian Gulf Conflict

Carol K. Winkler

"And the bottom line is this: Kuwait's night of terror has ended" (Bush 1991f, p. 245). With this statement to the members of the Armed Forces stationed in the Persian Gulf, George Bush concludes the final chapter of the military response to the Iraqi invasion of Kuwait. The statement provides an ending to a story that substantially infuses the administration's public stance regarding the conflict from January to March 1991.

The use of storytelling, or narratives, in political discourse is pervasive. Lance Bennett and Murray Edelman (1985) argue that "Stories are among the most universal means of representing human events" (p. 156). Karlyn Campbell and Kathleen Jamieson (1990) surmise that for war discourse in particular, the reliance on narratives represents one of the defining elements of the genre. They reason that the widespread use of narratives occurs because of the need for the chief executive to garner public support for "the presidential assumption of the office of commander in chief" (p. 112).

In war rhetoric, as in the broader realm of human communication, narratives function to help individuals interpret and react to the situations they face. Since a narrative reduces the perceivable elements in a situation to a story complete with characters, scenes, and plots, it provides a structuring of events readily interpretable to public audiences (Fisher 1984). If well-crafted, a narrative "can motivate the belief and action of outsiders toward the actors and events caught up in its plot" (Bennett and Edelman 1985, p. 156).

The meaning derived from narratives comes, in part, from the interrelationships that a given story has with other narrative accounts (Katriel and Shenhar 1990). Bennett and Edelman argue that "every acceptance of a narrative involves a rejection of others" (1985, p. 160). While not all scholars view narratives as exclusive accounts, the process of comparing two narratives can yield important critical insights. As Robert Entman (1991) observes, "Unless narratives are compared, frames are difficult to detect fully and reliably, because many of the framing devices can appear as 'natural,' unremarkable choices of words or images. Comparison reveals that such choices are not inevitable or unproblematic but rather are central to the way the . . . frame helps establish the literally 'common sense' (i.e., 'widespread') interpretation of events" (p. 6).

While a comparison of narratives could concentrate on a number of different aspects, this analysis will focus on an assessment of the arguments recurrent in war discourse. Specifically, it will compare the arguments common to stories of conventional military foes with those used by Bush beginning in January 1991 in what will be termed "the terrorist narrative." A terrorist narrative frames the characters, scenes, and events of hostilities in accordance with the means and motivations of political terrorists; it provides a sharp contrast to alternative characterizations of foes that plan direct military assaults on the nation's soil or its citizenry.

An attempt to compare all the arguments used in military and terrorist narratives would be a daunting, if not impossible, task. Instead, this analysis will focus on those lines of argument that recur in the genre of war rhetoric. Comparing only the generic claims of a particular type of discourse allows the critic to examine how narratives address the central expectations of the public. While each narrative will bring its own interpretative frame to a rhetorical situation, it must also accommodate generic constraints of the discourse or risk failing to meet the audience's expectations.

The generic expectations of war rhetoric used in this analysis rely on the findings of Campbell and Jamieson's *Deeds Done in Words: Presidential Rhetoric and the Genres of Governance* and of Robert Ivie's essays entitled "Images of Savagery in American Justifications for War" and "Presidential Motives for War." Campbell and Jamieson explain the rationales for recurrent arguments of narratives found in the war genre, while Ivie discusses the motivations that prompt the recurrent stock arguments of such discourse.

Absent a generic discussion of presidential rhetoric specific to terrorism, this study relies on previous scholarship that addresses the characteristic means and motivations of terrorists in general, as well as the policies and conventional expectations of the U.S. response to such individuals. Recurrent public portrayals of terrorists and the government's response to them become the backdrop for judging the implications of invoking the terrorist narrative.

The need to demarcate January 1991 as the starting point for the Bush administration's use of the terrorist narrative stems from the former president's rhetorical choices. From August to December 1990 the Bush administration publicly floats numerous rationales for U.S. involvement in the Persian Gulf conflict that are consistent with conventional military narratives. Bush (1990a, 1990b) maintains that the nation's military presence is necessary to: (1) stem the aggressive tendencies of Iraq; (2) come to the defense of Saudi Arabia; (3) defend national security interests; (4) protect the lives of American citizens abroad; (5) set the stage for the new world order; (6) curb the proliferation of chemical, biological, ballistic missile, and nuclear technologies; and (7) protect the security and stability of the Persian Gulf. Unsuccessful in his bid to garner substantial popular support for U.S. military involvement, he reframes the more conventional narratives for military engagement to a consistent terrorist narrative in January 1991. This essay will argue that pursuant to the transformation in Bush's rhetoric, the public appears to accept a fundamentally altered view of the threat posed by Iraq and the subsequently appropriate response of the United States.

When presidents replace one familiar narrative framework with another, they ask the populace to interpret their public arguments and actions according to an altered set of standards. This analysis will assume that regardless of the particular narrative a president uses, certain argumentative standards of evaluation should be operable in judgments about war rhetoric. Working from the assumption that war should be avoided if possible, the study evaluates the terrorist narrative according to whether it promotes uninformed judgments by the public in the consideration of a military response. Specifically, the analysis examines whether the arguments used in the terrorist narrative encourage a balanced assessment of the enemy's motivations and means, whether they encourage discussion of any American culpability for hostilities, and whether they promote a cautious, thoughtful scrutiny of the alternatives to war.

To begin, the essay will outline the terrorist narrative as presented in the Bush administration's rhetoric from January to March 1991. Afterwards, the analysis will show how the terrorist narrative allowed Bush to resolve tensions with the generic expectations of war discourse concerning the cause of the hostilities, the nature of the enemy, and the appropriate response. Conclusions will be drawn concerning the evaluative standards established for narratives used in war rhetoric.

THE TERRORIST NARRATIVE
OF THE BUSH ADMINISTRATION

Bush's depiction of the Iraqi leadership during its occupation of Kuwait mirrors the characteristic motivations of a terrorist. At no point does Bush argue that Iraq is a nation at war with another nation due to some irreconcilable difference. In the administration's rhetoric, Iraq's intentions are much more sinister. Iraq represents "a worldwide threat to democracy" (1991e, p. 15) and "an assault on the very notion of international order" (p. 16). In this description, Hussein's ultimate motivations exceed the conquest of Kuwait; they threaten all established and emerging democracies around the globe.

The means by which the Iraqi leadership will carry out its ultimate goals become the focus of Bush's public arguments. Describing each Iraqi move as another act of terrorism, Bush reinforces the transformation of the Persian Gulf conflict from a conventional military confrontation to a fight against terrorism. He describes the occupation of Kuwait as "a systematic campaign of terror on the people of Kuwait—unspeakable atrocities against men and women and among the maimed and murdered, even innocent children" (p. 16). He portrays Iraq's moves to expand their oil reserves as a means to "finance further aggression, terror and blackmail" (p. 15). When Iraq sets the oil wells in Kuwait on fire, Bush labels the act "tragic and despicable environmental terrorism" (1991a, p. 95). He frames Iraq's pursuit of chemical and biological weapons in terrorist terms by reminding the public that Iraq previously used chemical weapons against "innocent villagers, his own people" (1991e, p. 15). Regardless of the act, Bush interprets all Iraqi moves and motivations in terrorist terms.

The use of timing in the construction of the narrative reinforces the notion of Saddam Hussein as a terrorist. Bush's description of the relevant events in the Persian Gulf conflict begins on August 2, the day that Iraq began occupying Kuwait. By avoiding a discussion of events prior to the invasion, Bush focuses attention on the means by which Iraq attempts to accomplish its objectives. If the narrative begins earlier, either one week before when the United States and Iraq are engaging in diplomatic discussions or when the OPEC nations refuse to raise the price of oil to Iraq's satisfaction, the frame would invite discussion about Iraqi motives for the attack. By excluding the foreign country's motivations from the public version of the story, Bush places emphasis on the unacceptable means that Iraq employs, rendering these actions an unreasoned episode of terrorism.

In addition to the chronological starting point for the narrative working to reinforce Saddam Hussein's terrorist tendencies, Bush uses the timing embodied in the structure of the narrative to underscore his message. In his depictions of the Iraqi leadership, Bush employs what Mieke Bal ([1980] 1985) refers to as "external retroversions" of previous events that inform the audience's interpretations of the narrative. Bush reminds the audience repeatedly that Iraq has used chemical weapons against its own people in the recent past. Coupled with the actions against Kuwait, Bush establishes a pattern of behavior by the Iraqi leadership. By indicating that Saddam Hussein has engaged in terrorist activities in the past, and continues to do so in the present, Bush invites the audience to fill in the conclusion that failure to stop the Iraqi leader now will lead to more terrorist acts in the future. Bush's use of the narrative, then, establishes the terrorist acts of the Iraqi regime to be character traits rather than isolated acts in response to particularized circumstances.

As the most obvious victim of the terrorist assault, Kuwait becomes a hostage in Bush's scenario. Bush describes Kuwait like the conventional hostage, as an innocent civilian, randomly selected to suffer the brutality of the terrorist. Imprisoned against its will and suffering unspeakable atrocities, Kuwait shifts from a nation engaged in its own defense to an individual waiting to be freed from the hands of the terrorist. Bush personifies Kuwait as "a peaceful neighbor" (1991a, p. 90) and "a small and helpless neighbor" (1991b, p. 50) to highlight its civilian status in the conflict. Reinforcing both the personification and the helplessness of Kuwait, Bush metaphorically relies on crimes against primarily women to characterize Iraqi misdeeds. He labels the initial Iraqi invasion to be "a ruthless, systematic rape of a peaceful neighbor" (1991a, p. 90). The use of the metaphor of rape and the personification of the nation function to reinforce the powerlessness of the Kuwaitis to affect their own fate. The rhetorical move is critical to the characterization of Kuwait in the narrative. Without the status as an innocent individual, the public might readily expect Kuwait to take up its own defense.

The relatively small emphasis Bush places on the characterization of Kuwait is consistent with the expectations of the terrorist narrative. By devoting comparable time to other events in the conflict, Bush equates the atrocities that Kuwait suffers to the other acts of Iraqi terrorism past and present. The shifting of the scene from the seas and sands of the Gulf to the locations of the emerging democracies worldwide reinforces the notion that the attack on Kuwait is only one of many settings suffering at the hands of the Iraqi terrorists. Kuwait has suffered only one in a series of random attacks; the country's motives and prior actions become secondary concerns. The characteristic traits of Iraq as a terrorist become the paramount issue, taking precedence over all others in the crisis.

In response to the Iraqi acts of terrorism, the United States must assume a leadership role in Bush's scenario. The president argues that the United States is uniquely qualified and responsible for coming to the defense of the civilized world. He states, "Among the nations of the world, only the United States of America has both the moral standing and the means to back it up. We're the only nation on this Earth that could assemble the forces of peace. This is the burden of leadership and the strength that has made America the beacon of freedom in a searching world" (p. 95).

As the leadership opposed to terrorist acts, Bush disassociates the United States from Iraq. Morally, he insists that the United

States opposes threats to the international order. America respects the rule of law and "will lead the world in facing down a threat to decency and humanity" (p. 90). Bush claims the United States wants a new world order, "a world where the rule of law, not the law of the jungle, governs the conduct of nations" (1991b, p. 51). Toward that end, he indicates that the objective of the coalition has never been the conquest of the Iraqi people (1991f). Aligning America with peaceful intentions, Bush maintains that the United States wants to be the defender of the international principles of justice and law.

Bush also attempts to distinguish the means of the United States from those of terrorists. He insists that the United States will not target innocent civilians. He credits military technology as the distinguishing feature that allows the United States to fight a war without inflicting multiple civilian casualties. In his 1991 State of the Union Address, Bush argues that "The quality of American technology, thanks to the American worker, has enabled us to successfully deal with difficult military conditions and help minimize precious loss of life" (p. 94). Not only does the high-tech weaponry place America's offensive capabilities within the frame of nonterrorist activities, but it contributes to a morally superior defensive force as well. Bush notes later in the same speech that "with remarkable technological advances like the Patriot missile, we can defend against ballistic missile attacks aimed at innocent civilians" (p. 95). Opposed to both the philosophy and tactics of terrorism, the United States emerges as the natural leader of the coalition against Iraq.

The timing of the narrative reinforces the choice of the United States to be the leader of the international response to Iraq. Using another external retroversion, Bush places the narrative in the context of the end of the cold war. Justifying the need to establish a new world order, Bush (1991b) refers to the timing of the response to the Iraqi invasion as "an historic moment." He notes that "We have in the past year made great progress in ending the long era of conflict and cold war. We have before us the opportunity to forge for ourselves and for future generations a new world order" (1991b, p. 51). Placed in this perspective, the United States naturally surfaces as the optimal choice to lead the coalition. Its victory over the Soviet Union, arguably a much greater threat, infers that it can achieve victory over the Iraqi forces.

Bush's placement of the narrative in the context of the victory in the cold war offers a sharp contrast to alternative settings, whose appropriateness he explicitly denies. Repeatedly, he reminds the public that the conflict in the Persian Gulf will not be another Vietnam. He insists that "Our troops will have the best possible support in the entire world, and they will not be asked to fight with one hand tied behind their backs" (p. 51) as they were in Vietnam. Bush attempts to disassociate the efforts on behalf of Kuwait from the military failure in Vietnam by indicating that he will not limit the level of military engagement.

The final players in Bush's scenario are the United States' allies in the conflict. Referred to as "coalition partners," these nations take on the role of friendly, supportive advisors. Bush consults with them before reaching conclusions about specific actions required to enforce the twelve UN resolutions passed in response to the Iraqi invasion of Kuwait. Between these consultations, they remain "resolute" in their opposition to Iraqi aggression. Perhaps their largest role in the conflict is to contribute monetarily to the war effort.

Taken together, Bush depicts Iraq as a terrorist committing continual atrocities against defenseless neighbors. Only a united world effort, led by the morally and technologically superior United States, can rid Iraq of its terrorist capabilities. Only through decisive action, supported by each of the coalition partners, can the world send a message to future would-be aggressors. In his 1991 State of the Union address, Bush insists that "The world can, therefore, seize this opportunity to fulfill the long-held promise of a new world order, where brutality will go unrewarded and aggression will meet collective resistance" (p. 95).

The Iraqi invasion of Kuwait offers an opportunity for the terrorism narrative to resonate with the American public. Stereotypes of Middle Eastern dictators, Iraq's previous use of chemical weapons on the Kurds, and the Iraqi decision to hold hundreds of foreign nationals as "guests" all contribute to the persuasiveness of the characterization of Saddam Hussein as a terrorist. Kuwait offers a palatable victim, as the small size of the country and the relative weakness of its military render it an unworthy opponent for the Iraqi military. Foreign countries unable to resolve the conflict on their own fall naturally into the role of partner in the worldwide effort. Finally, the United States, armed with technologically superior weaponry capable of primarily targeting military installations, sets the stage for the confrontation of good versus evil in the terrorist arena.

IMPLICATIONS FOR WAR RHETORIC

Since the use of any narrative inevitably reduces the potential range of situational elements to an interpretable set of events, implications exist for how the narrative, if accepted, transforms the evaluation of public arguments. Rather than envision the Gulf conflict to be a war scenario, Bush encourages the public to adopt the posture of onlookers to a terrorist event. In the process he quells conventional evaluations of public argument during times of war. Instead, he invites the acceptance of a hardline response generally supported by the public in response to terrorist threats since the Iranian hostage crisis. Specifically, the narrative helps explain the public's interpretations of arguments concerning the cause of the conflict, the nature of the Iraqi threat, and the response deemed appropriate by the nation and its leadership. In each instance, abrupt shifts in public opinion polls are consistent with the President's recasting of the conflict.

Cause of the Crisis

Robert Ivie (1980) argues that presidents leading the United States into a military confrontation have the obligation to place the blame for the hostilities on the enemy. As he explains, "a people strongly committed to the ideal of peace, but simultaneously faced with the reality of war, must believe that the fault for any such disruption of their ideal lies with others. Hierarchic guilt would otherwise threaten to drive the nation toward some form of self mortification" (p. 280). Campbell and Jamieson (1990) articulate the result when they state that the narrative tends "to recast the conflict as aggression by the enemy, which legitimizes presidential initiatives as actions to defend the nation" (p. 107).

With the Iraqi invasion of Kuwait, however, the responsibility for the conflict is not clear. From the early days following the attack, concern arises regarding the United States' potential culpability for the affair. The Iraqis insist that the United States had the opportunity to preempt the attack and opted not to do so. The Iraqis release a transcript that allegedly records a meeting between

April Glaspie, U.S. ambassador to Baghdad, and Saddam Hussein less than one week prior to the invasion. In the transcript, Glaspie tells Hussein that "we have no opinion on the Arab-Arab conflicts, like your border dispute with Kuwait" (Sciolino and Gordon, 1990, p. A12). The statement, embedded in a series of mixed messages from the Departments of Defense and State arguably implicates the United States for failing to preempt the Iraqi attack. The incident blurs the issue of who is responsible for hostilities. With Glaspie unavailable to the press and State Department officials confirming that the Iraqi transcript is "essentially correct" (Friedman, 1991, p. A6), the blame for the conflict is left unclear.

The terrorist narrative resolves the argument concerning who is responsible for the invasion of Kuwait. The labeling of an individual as a "terrorist" or a "hostage-taker" places the emphasis on the means used by that individual to achieve political goals. The reasons an individual chooses to undertake such methods are of secondary importance. The American representative to the United Nations indicates the irrelevance of the motives in arguments about terrorism at a Draft Convention Against the Taking of Hostages: "Just as certain forms of violence, such as acts committed against protected persons, including diplomatic agents, were inadmissible regardless of circumstance, so the act of taking hostages which endangered human life was inadmissible in all cases" (Aston 1981, p. 146).

As the terrorist in Bush's narrative, the Iraqi leadership becomes the responsible agent for the hostilities. The narrative, which begins on the day of the invasion, excludes consideration of the motivations the Iraqis might have for attacking their neighbor. With the dominant focus on the means used to accomplish its political objectives, Iraq's actions render it solely responsible for the military conflict.

When the Bush administration permits April Glaspie to speak to the press about her diplomatic exchanges with Saddam Hussein, she reinforces the terrorist narrative. Shifting from the State Department's original assessment of the Iraqi transcript as "essentially correct," Glaspie insists that Iraq omits a portion of the meeting where she sternly warns that the United States would not tolerate certain *means* to resolve the border dispute. She claims to have emphasized to Hussein several times that "we would insist on settlements being made in a nonviolent manner, not by threats, not by intimidation, and certainly not by aggression" (Friedman,

1991, p. A15). With Iraqi motivations subordinated, Glaspie's account arguably resolves the tension between the perception of events immediately following the Iraqi invasion and the expectation that Iraq would be totally responsible for the conflict.

Prior to the consistent use of the terrorist narrative by the Bush administration, the public concerns itself with the motives of both the United States and Iraq to enter into the conflict. When asked "Why do you think we are involved in the Iraqi situation and why are the troops in Saudi Arabia" in polls taken August 16–19, November 15–18, and November 20–December 2, the largest percentage of the public (39%–49%) think that the United States is attempting to defend its oil interests, while only 11 to 23 percent state that the United States is attempting to stop Iraqi aggression (*Gallup*, December 1990).

Once the Bush administration consistently adheres to the terrorist narrative, the polls shift to indicate that Iraq is primarily responsible for the United States' involvement in the conflict. Fifty-five percent think that the United States is preparing to go to war to stop Iraqi aggression and protect other countries in the Middle East. Only 32 percent think the United States is there to protect its supply of oil and its economic interests (*Gallup*, January 1991).

Nature of the Enemy

The enemy in generic U.S. war rhetoric is one that represents a substantial threat to American notions or ideals. Specifically, Ivie (1980) argues that the general antagonist will be "a coercive brute driven to subvert international law in an active effort to subjugate the civilized world . . . upon whose shoulders can be placed the full weight of responsibility for the breach of the peace" (p. 292). Campbell and Jamieson (1990) emphasize that the threat generally "imperils the continued existence of the nation . . . and the future of civilization itself" (p. 107).

In the early days following the invasion, the Bush administration faces some difficulty making a credible argument that Iraq poses a threat to the civilized world. The administration's recent foreign policy, reflected in Glaspie's rhetoric in her meeting with Saddam Hussein, has been to improve relations between the two countries to help moderate Iraq's behavior (Sciolino and Gordon, 1990). As recently as the summer of 1990, administration officials have attempted to block efforts by the U.S. Congress to impose sanctions against Iraq. Assessing the Iraqi buildup on the Kuwaiti border up until August 2, the consensus opinion of the State Department has been that Iraq would not attack. With a policy of appeasement toward Iraq, Bush faces rhetorical obstacles to immediately transforming Saddam Hussein into a world menace.

The terrorist narrative provides an explanation for why the Bush administration would initially misjudge Iraqi intentions. Terrorists tend to target their victims randomly in an effort to instill fear in the broadest possible group of potential victims (Schrieber 1978). Frequently, the goal of the terrorist is to do precisely the unexpected to reduce the likelihood that an effective response will be forthcoming. The stereotype of the psychologically unbalanced terrorist (Hacker 1976) implies that such individuals are not subject to rational modes of behavior. The Bush administration could be logical in assuming that the Iraqi plan to attack Kuwait would be ill-conceived. Nevertheless, an emotionally unstable leader such as Saddam Hussein would be unlikely to consider the reality that his forces had been substantially weakened in their lengthy confrontation with Iran. The desire for publicity alone can motivate some terrorists to undergo extraordinary personal risks (Dowling 1986).

Besides providing an explanation for the initial inaction by the United States, the terrorist narrative also elevates Iraq to a level sufficient to render it a threat to the civilized world. Terrorists' goals are not limited to an isolated set of circumstances; they oppose the values and ordering of civilized society. Stephen Sloan (1986) maintains that "Terrorism always poses an unacceptable challenge to the principles on which organized society rests, for those acting in this way seek to arrogate to themselves, and use in perverse ways, powers exclusively reserved to the state" (p. 9). By labeling Iraq a terrorist, Bush transforms the attack on one small country into a potential threat to all the civilized nations of the world.

Terrorism not only elevates previous actions of the Iraqi government to a dangerous level, but also invites fear of escalating future threats. As terrorists become frustrated by an inability to achieve political objectives, chances increase that they will resort to more desperate means to achieve their ends. Neil Livingstone (1981) calls terrorism a "war without limits" (p. 83), a phrase that implies that future deeds will exceed the present level of hostilities.

Saddam Hussein's possession of chemical and nuclear capabilities means that his ultimate act of desperation could have devastating consequences. Even if the United States and its allies have the capability to overwhelm his forces, Saddam Hussein's potential to employ weapons of mass destruction heighten the risks of his arsenal.

In a cyclical, escalating process, terrorism heightens the threat that the enemy poses. Initially, many terrorist groups act in order to prompt a target government to respond by instituting repressive measures (Celmar 1987). If the government does take action to preempt terrorist assaults, it frequently interferes with the normal daily operations of the public. The decision, for example, to inspect luggage at major airports on domestic flights during the Gulf conflict meant that the public experienced the impact of terrorism firsthand. With the intensified, personal sense of risk, the public may clamor for tighter and tighter controls that impact on their individual freedoms.

Prior to the Bush administration's consistent use of the terrorist narrative, the public appears unconvinced of the terrorist nature of the Iraqi threat. While 70 percent of public indicate that they would favor going to war if they knew that Iraq and Saddam Hussein would have nuclear weapons in two years in December 1990, only 48 percent favored going to war for any reason (*Gallup*, December 1990). By February 1991, one month after the onset of the president's use of the narrative, the vast majority of Americans appear convinced of Iraq's terrorist nature. Eighty-four percent think that a likely outcome of the war will be Iraq's unleashing of new major threats to the region's environment; 82 percent think Iraq will eventually end up using chemical, biological, or nuclear weapons against the allies; and 77 percent say that U.S. citizens will become the victims of Iraqi terrorism (*Gallup*, February 1991).

Nature of the Response

In any conflict, governments have three options for responding to outside threats: diplomatic negotiations, economic sanctions, and military engagement. The conventions of war rhetoric specify when each of these strategies is appropriate. As Ivie (1974) notes, "War is recommended only after demonstrating that peaceful methods—such as remonstrances, expostulations, negotiations, and embargo—have failed to restore the ideal or to prevent the disharmony" (p. 344). Campbell and Jamieson (1990) offer that the reason for such an ordering of response options is to make the decision to intervene militarily appear a product of thoughtful consideration, not anger. By exhausting the peaceful avenues, the nation's leadership also keeps itself disassociated from the evil motives and tactics of the antagonist.

In the diplomatic realm of the Iraqi conflict, Bush faces the argumentative burden of convincing the public that he has exhausted options for diplomatic negotiation. In a January 9 news conference, Bush (1991d) pronounces the meeting between Secretary of State Jim Baker and Iraqi Foreign Minister Tariq Aziz a failure, indicating that the United States has exhausted all bilateral discussions with Iraq. Despite this proclamation, however, both Germany and France publicly maintain that the bilateral meeting does not constitute the last effort for a peaceful solution. Subsequently, the Secretary General of the United Nations travels to Iraq to attempt to resolve the conflict. The Soviet Union reopens the questions as to whether diplomatic options remain when they engage the Iraqi leadership in talks immediately prior to the onset of the ground war. Repeatedly, then, several of the coalition partners raise doubts regarding whether the proper time has come to engage the use of military force.

The terrorist narrative provides a public argument for why Bush has exhausted all potentially fruitful diplomatic options. Claiming in the same news conference that he "sent Jim Baker to Geneva not to negotiate, but to communicate" (Bush 1991d, p. 23), Bush evokes the no-negotiation, no-concessions rhetoric of a hostage crisis. The no-negotiation, no-concession stance redefines the conventional interpretation of diplomacy, recasting it as a refusal to negotiate. As Nehemia Friedland (1983) explains, "The core of the conflict between politically oriented terrorists and a government committed to 'no ransom' consists of largely indivisible political entities. Consequently, the process characteristic of hostage negotiations is rarely one of distributive bargaining, accommodation, and reconciliation, but of brinkmanship" (p. 211). Within the terrorist narrative, the United States fails if it makes any concession to a terrorist. Based on prior rehearsals of the narrative, the audience expects that any concession would embolden not only Iraq to claim a victory over the United States in this instance, but would send a message to all future terrorists that the United States is willing to negotiate.

While recasting conventional interpretations of diplomacy, the terrorist narrative allows Bush to remain consistent with the generic expectation that he has exhausted all opportunities for a peaceful settlement of the crisis. When the Soviet Union attempts to negotiate a peaceful solution prior to the start of the ground war, Bush proclaims immediately that the proposal "falls well short of what would be required" (Rosenthal, 1991, p. A1). In a framework that allows no concessions, the presidential response seems fitting. Only when the Soviet Union publicly rebukes Bush for commenting on the Kremlin's peace initiative does Bush slightly soften his rhetoric opposing the proposal. But even while admitting that the initiative is "useful" (Dowd, 1991, p. A6), Bush retains his leadership role in the narrative by refusing to make any concessions to Iraq.

A shift in the public's willingness to support negotiations and concessions is consistent with the administration's reliance on the terrorism narrative. Prior to the rhetorical stance in December 1990, 81 percent of the public agree that the United States should instigate a face-to-face meeting with Iraqi envoys to negotiate a possible solution. Seven out of ten favor a concession that would involve the United States hosting an international summit to discuss the problems of the Mideast (*Gallup*, December 1990). By February 79 percent indicate that Bush has been correct in his decision to dismiss the peace proposal negotiated between the Soviet Union and Iraq (which includes the very concession approved of by 70 percent of the American public two months earlier). Seventy-two percent agree with Bush's insistence on an unconditional withdrawal from Kuwait. Only 36 percent of the public remain willing to discuss some concessions with Iraq (*Gallup*, February 1991).

As noted earlier, presidents must not only exhaust diplomatic alternatives for averting a military confrontation, but must explore the potential effectiveness of economic sanctions as well. In January 1991 Bush faces a Congress and nation split regarding whether economic sanctions have had sufficient time to work. In an extremely close congressional vote, U.S. lawmakers narrowly agree to a resolution authorizing Bush to use all means necessary to drive Iraq out of Kuwait. Throughout November and December the general public remains equally divided as to whether the leadership has exhausted sanctions as an alternative to war (*Gallup*, January 1991).

The terrorist narrative reevaluates the wisdom of the policy of exhausting diplomatic and economic remedies prior to the use of force. The convention takes time; time plays into the hands of the terrorist. Enabled by months of negotiations and economic sanctions, terrorists have the opportunity to maximize their strengths. They can refortify their weaknesses and gradually escalate their atrocities against vulnerable citizens. Bush relies precisely on this depiction of the Iraqi regime in his address to the nation announcing the use of military action in the Persian Gulf. Repeating the phrase "while the world waited," Bush (1991b) argues that Iraq has raped, pillaged, and plundered Kuwait, added to its chemical weapons arsenal, fortified its military forces, and undermined the economies of nations throughout the world. As a terrorist, Iraq can only be expected to take maximum advantage of any delay.

Exhausting diplomatic and economic alternatives not only allows terrorists an opportunity to strengthen their positions, but also inhibits the ability of the United States to respond effectively. As with generic war rhetoric, presidents responding to terrorism in the past have insisted publicly on exhausting diplomatic and economic avenues prior to the use of force. The results of this strategy of gradual escalation in the terrorist arena have not been positive. The case of Jimmy Carter is illustrative. From the beginning of the Iranian hostage crisis, Carter (1980) vows publicly to exhaust diplomatic and economic options prior to any use of force. When he resorts to an ineffective use of force following a supposed exhaustion of diplomatic and economic avenues, Carter loses credibility regarding further strategies to obtain the hostages' release. Offering an alternative to the Carter approach, Ronald Reagan implies that a president must have the full arsenal of responses available against terrorists at all times; to do otherwise would alert the terrorist as to what response to expect (Reagan 1985, p. 802).

Relying on the logic of the Reagan administration's response to terrorism, Bush explains that he will use diplomatic, economic, and military responses simultaneously. When asked at a news conference the week prior to military engagement if he is ruling out further diplomatic contacts with Iraq, Bush (1991d) flatly denies that the reporter's assumption is correct, claiming "I want to use everything in my power to encourage people to try" (p. 27). By bringing the full range of responses against Iraq in no predetermined order, Bush maintains that he maximizes the coalition's advantage over the terrorist.

The public appears to accept Bush's assessment of the role of economic sanctions within the totality of the United States' response. Prior to the use of the terrorist narrative in December 1990, 47 percent feel that the president should give sanctions more time to work, while 46 percent feel that the time has come to use force. One month later, after the narrative frames the president's rhetoric, only 36 percent feel that sanctions should be given more time to work. Fifty-seven percent consider it time to begin using force (*Gallup*, January 1991).

When the Bush administration, in consultation with the coalition partners, determines to remedy the Kuwaiti situation with military measures, reasonable objections persist. Despite the possession of the world's largest and most powerful military, questions linger about how long the United States will remain committed to military action. Memories of Vietnam leave in doubt whether the American public will continue to support a military engagement that results in numerous American causalities. Given that Bush's approval ratings for his handling of the crisis mirror those of Lyndon Johnson at the initiation of the Vietnam conflict (*Gallup*, December 1990), the staying power of the public support remains in question.

The terrorist narrative bolsters the rationale for a long-term military engagement. It insinuates that the United States and its coalition partners are risking little in the confrontation with Iraq. Lacking the means to militarily engage authoritative structures, terrorists represent minimal opposition when engaged in conventional military assaults. As Ralph Dowling (1986) observes, "Too small or weak to obtain a military victory, terrorists are forced to use violence rhetorically" (p. 13). Facing such a diminished threat, the public can be reasonably confident that the United States will achieve a military success.

The setting of the terrorist narrative reinforces the minimization of the threat. Assuring the public that the conflict in the Persian Gulf will not be another Vietnam (Bush 1991a), Bush sheds the image of the American military as a force without the will to see a conflict through to its completion. He replaces it with repeated references to the end of the cold war. Recalling the lengthy history of the United States' struggle against the Soviet

Union, Bush encourages the audience to think of the constancy of American determination used to defeat the aggressive tendencies of their historical foe. By contrast to the military strength of the Soviet Union, the Iraqi forces become a reduced threat.

Finally, the terrorist narrative provides a means by which the public can counterbalance the potential loss of life to American soldiers. Successful acts of terrorism beget future attempts at terrorism. Dowling (1986) argues that the standard for success by the terrorist can be quite small. Terrorists may be satisfied with a simple moral victory or just the notion that they still have the strength to act on world events. In this climate, other terrorists may become emboldened, with the result that the threat to the world order extends far beyond that originally posed by the perpetrator. Bush (1991a) offers the remedy of a continued commitment to the troops: "we will succeed in the Gulf and when we do, the world community will have sent an enduring warning to any dictator or despot, present or future, who contemplates outlaw aggression" (p. 95). The public can expect minimal American casualties, but only if they remain committed to wiping out the terrorist threat before it spreads throughout the civilized world.

As before, the public responses to opinion polls remain consistent with the implications of the terrorist narrative. When compared to polls taken at the beginning of January, polls taken in the last half of that same month show the public has decreased their expectations of the number of casualties they would expect from the conflict (*Gallup*, January 1991). By February 81 percent approve of the president's decision to begin the ground war against Iraq, despite the fact that almost half expect at least several thousand Americans will be killed or injured in the conflict (*Gallup*, February 1991).

SUMMARY AND CONCLUSIONS

Facing public uncertainty about the Persian Gulf conflict, George Bush uses the terrorist narrative to reconcile situational tensions with the generic expectations of wartime discourse. By altering the standards by which the public evaluates his arguments, Bush provides a frame for a more favorable evaluation of his handling of the crisis. He places the blame for the hostilities on Iraq by exploiting the narrative's focus on unacceptable means for achieving political objectives. He characterizes the enemy as a threat to the civilized world by evoking the narrative's assumptions of irrationality and desperation as inherent traits of the terrorists. He exhausts peaceful avenues of conflict resolution by redefining both when certain options have been exhausted and the appropriate order of their use. Finally, he assumes a military victory by relying on the narrative's depiction of the terrorist as a weak military threat and by reminding the nation of even larger future consequences should they fail to support the strongest possible response.

Public opinion polls beginning in January 1991 indicate that the public accepts the logic of the terrorist narrative as applied to arguments about Iraq. Polls related to the cause of the conflict, the nature of the enemy, and the response of the coalition are all consistent with the interpretation of Iraq as a terrorist nation. If such support does indicate an acceptance of the narrative, Bush's public success may be larger than generally assumed. Not only would Bush have provided a victory to avenge the loss of the Vietnam War as numerous commentators have suggested, but he may also have achieved success against terrorists, a war the United States is arguably losing even before the Iran-contra scandal.

The public victory, however, is not without consequence. Using the three standards for evaluating arguments used in war discourse outlined earlier, Bush encourages an uninformed acceptance of his assumption of the powers of commander-in-chief. To begin with, he prompts an unbalanced assessment of Iraq's motivations for engaging in the conflict. By invoking terrorism as the frame, he subordinates discussion of the motivations of the Iraqi leadership to an exclusive focus on the means used to accomplish objectives. Whether Iraq has a historical claim to Kuwait or whether it had been gauged economically by the oil policies of its neighbor received little public discussion. While not arguing that either reason would necessarily justify the August 2 assault on Kuwait, the public should have been given the opportunity to decide with a full consideration of Iraqi motives.

The Bush administration's arguments also discourage discussion of potential U.S. culpability for the hostilities. By subordinating Iraq's motives for the attack, Glaspie's comments regarding the United States' unwillingness to become involved in border disputes are relegated to the level of an insignificant consideration, rather than a diplomatic blunder arguably important in Iraq's decision to go to war. By relying on stereotypical assumptions about terrorist behavior, the Bush administration is not held accountable for failed intelligence and foreign policy judgments that continued from the summer of 1990 up to the day of the attack. Given the consequences that were inevitable in such a conflict, careful public consideration of the role of our diplomatic blunders and failed intelligence should have occurred.

Finally, the arguments used by the Bush administration undermine the cautious, thoughtful scrutiny generally required before military engagement. By reducing diplomacy to a pledge of no-negotiation/ no-concessions, the narrative undermines potentially successful diplomatic avenues for preventing the conflict. By redefining the exhaustion of economic sanctions from a necessary precursor to military engagement to one of three simultaneous avenues for addressing terrorism, the narrative undermines an avenue for avoiding war. Finally, by insinuating the unworthiness of the military opponent and by raising the level of acceptable casualties in the conflict, the arguments make the choice to go to war an easier one.

Certainly, critics could disagree with the standard that war should be avoided if possible or that the public should be informed about the decisions of their government. But if public acceptance of the terrorist narrative permits the government to avoid responsibility for its role in hostilities and undermines the thoughtful considerations of alternatives to war, critical attention to the strategy should continue.

REFERENCES

Aston, Clive C. 1981. The UN convention against the taking of hostages: Realistic or rhetoric. *Terrorism*, 139–60.

Bal, Mieke. 1985. *Narratology: Introduction to the theory of narrative.* Trans. Christine van Boheemen. Toronto: University of Toronto Press. (Originally published as *De theorie van vertellen en verhalen* [Muiderberg: Coutinho, 1980].)

Bennett, W. Lance, and Murray Edelman. 1985. Toward a new political narrative. *Journal of Communication, 35,* 156–71.

Bremer, Paul. 1988. Countering Terrorism: Successes and failures. *Department of State Bulletin, 88,* 59.

Brodsky, Claudia J. 1987. *The imposition of form: Studies in narrative representation and knowledge.* Princeton: Princeton University Press.

Bush, George. 1990a. Address before a joint session of the Congress on the Persian Gulf crisis and the federal budget deficit. *Weekly Compilation of Presidential Documents, 26,* 1358–63.

———. 1990b. Address to the nation announcing the deployment of United States Armed Forces to Saudi Arabia. *Weekly Compilation of Presidential Documents, 26,* 1216–18.

———. 1991a. Address before a joint session of the Congress on the state of the Union. *Weekly Compilation of Presidential Documents, 27,* 90–95.

———. 1991b. Address to the nation announcing allied military action in the Persian Gulf conflict. *Weekly Compilation of Presidential Documents, 27,* 50–52.

———. 1991c. Message to allied nations on the Persian Gulf crisis. *Weekly Compilation of Presidential Documents, 27,* 16–17.

———. 1991d. President's news conference on the Persian Gulf crisis. *Weekly Compilation of Presidential Documents, 27,* 23–28.

———. 1991e. Radio Address to the Nation on the Persian Gulf Crisis. *Weekly Compilation of Presidential Documents, 27,* 15–17.

———. 1991f. Radio address to United States Armed Forces stationed in the Persian Gulf region. *Weekly Compilation of Presidential Documents, 27,* 245–46.

Campbell, Karlyn Kohrs, and Kathleen Hall Jamieson. 1990. War rhetoric. In *Deeds done in words: Presidential rhetoric and genres of governance.* Chicago: University of Chicago Press.

Carter, Jimmy. 1980. Interview with the president, question and answer session with foreign correspondents. *Public Papers of the President,* 670.

Celmar, Marc A. 1987. *Terrorism, U.S. Strategy, and Reagan policies.* New York: Greenwood Press.

Cohen, Steven, and Linda M. Shires. 1988. *Telling stories: A theoretical analysis of narrative fiction.* New York: Routledge.

Coste, Didier. 1989. *Narrative as communication.* Minneapolis: University of Minnesota Press.

Deming, Caren J. 1985. *Hill Street Blues* as narrative. *Critical Studies in Mass Communication, 2,* 1–22.

Derrida, Jacques. 1981. The law of genre. Trans. Avital Ronell. In *On narrative,* ed. W. J. T. Mitchell. Chicago: University of Chicago Press. (Originally published in *Glyph* 7. Baltimore: Johns Hopkins University Press, 1980.)

Dowd, Maureen. 1991, February 22. Soviets say Iraq accepts Kuwait pullout linked to truce and an end to sanctions. *New York Times,* A1, A6.

Dowling, Ralph E. 1986. Terrorism and the media: A rhetorical genre. *Journal of Communication, 36,* 12–24.

Entman, Robert. 1991. Framing U.S. coverage of international news: Contrasts in narratives of KAL and Iran air incidents. *Journal of Communication, 41,* 6–27.

Fisher, Walter R. 1989. *Human communication as narration: Toward a philosophy of reason, value, and action.* 2d ed. Columbia: University of South Carolina Press. (Originally Published Columbia: University of South Carolina Press, 1987.)

———. 1984. Narration as a human communication paradigm: The case of public moral argument. *Communication Monographs, 51,* 1–22.

———. 1985a. The narrative paradigm: An elaboration. *Communication Monographs, 52,* 347–67.

———. 1985b. The narrative paradigm: In the beginning. *Journal of Communication, 35,* 74–89.

Friedland, Nehemia. 1983. Hostage negotiations: Dilemmas about policy. In *Perspectives on terrorism,* ed. Lawrence Zelic Freedman and Yonah Alexander. Wilmington: Scholarly Resources.

Friedman, Thomas L. 1991, March 21. Envoy to Iraq, faulted in Crisis, says she warned Hussein sternly. *New York Times,* A1, A6, A15.

Gallup Poll Monthly. 1990. Nos. 299–303.

———. 1991. Nos. 304–305.

Genette, Gerard. 1988 *Narrative discourse revisited.* Trans. Jane E. Austin. Ithaca: Cornell University Press. (Originally published as *Nouveau discours du recit* [Editions du Seuil, 1983].)

Hacker, F. J. 1976. *Crusaders, criminals, crazies: Terror and terrorism in our time.* New York: Norton.

Ivie, Robert L. 1980. Images of savagery in American justifications for war. *Communication Monographs, 47,* 280–94.

———. 1974. Presidential motives for war. *Quarterly Journal of Speech, 60,* 337–45.

Katriel, Tamar, and Aliza Shenhar. 1990. Tower and stockade: Dialogic narration in Israeli settlement ethos. *Quarterly Journal of Speech, 76,* 359–80.

Kirkwood, William G. 1983. Storytelling and self-confrontation: Parables as communication strategies. *Quarterly Journal of Speech, 69,* 56–74.

Leitch, Thomas M. 1986. *What stories are: Narrative theory and interpretation.* University Park: Pennsylvania State University Press.

Livingstone, Neil. 1981. States in opposition: The war against terrorism. *Conflict, 3,* 83–141.

Lucaites, John Louis, and Celeste Michelle Condit. 1985. Reconstructing narrative theory: A functional perspective. *Journal of Communication, 35,* 90–108.

McGee, Michael Calvin, and John S. Nelson. 1985. Narrative reason in public argument. *Journal of Communication, 35,* 139–55.

Mellard, James M. 1987. *Doing tropology: Analysis of narrative discourse.* Urbana: University of Illinois Press.

Reagan, Ronald. 1985. Informal exchange with reporters. *Weekly Compilation of Presidential Documents, 21,* 802.

Rosenthal, Andrew. 1991, February 20. Bush criticizes Soviet plan as inadequate to end war: Iraqi may revisit Moscow. *New York Times,* A1.

Schrieber, Jan. 1978. *The ultimate weapon: Terrorists and world order.* New York: William Morrow.

Sciolino, Elaine, and Michael R. Gordon. 1990, September 23. U.S. gave Iraq little reason not to mount Kuwait assault. *New York Times,* A1, A12, A18.

Sloan, Stephen. 1986. *Beating international terrorism: An action strategy for preemption and punishment.* Maxwell Air Force Base: Air University Press.

White, Hayden. 1981. The value of narrativity in the representation of reality. In *On narrative,* ed. W. J. T. Mitchell. Chicago: University of Chicago Press.

CHAPTER 3

The Failure of Argument in Decisions Leading to the "Challenger Disaster": A Two-Level Analysis

Dennis S. Gouran

In the months following the ill-fated and widely publicized flight of *Challenger*, the Rogers Commission identified "flaws in the decision making process" as the "contributing cause" (Report of the Presidential Commission on the Space Shuttle Challenger Accident 1986, p. 82 [hereafter Report]). Most notable among the factors involved was the "propensity at Marshall [the Marshall Space Flight Center in Huntsville, Alabama] to contain potentially serious problems and to resolve them internally rather than communicate them forward" (Report 1986, p. 104). At least one of these "potentially serious problems"—O-ring failure in the solid rocket booster field joints—had been an object of continuing concern, however, since at least 1977 (Cook 1986) and subsequently proved to be the actual physical cause of the explosion that destroyed the shuttle and sent the crew members to their unfortunate deaths. For nine flights prior to 51-L, moreover, evidence of the problem was consistently available to NASA officials and part of virtually every engineering assessment from 1984 forward (Cooper 1986). These facts prompted the Rogers Commission also to conclude that the destruction of *Challenger* was "an accident rooted in history" (Report 1986, p. 120).

Substantial portions of the source material consulted in the preparation of this essay were located by Amy E. Martz and Janet Reynolds Bodenman. The author gratefully acknowledges his appreciation for their assistance.

As one sifts through the volume of facts and testimony that have surfaced in investigations of the Rogers Commission, the House Committee on Science and Technology, and scores of independent journalists, the conclusion that the decision-making process was flawed seems hardly subject to dispute. Why the process in arriving at launch decisions failed, however, is a matter worthy of further inquiry. The Rogers Commission locates the problem in the procedures NASA established, but I would contend that the system failed not so much as a result of the procedures involved, but because of weaknesses in argument. The failure in the particular case of *Challenger*, further, was the culmination of a set of historical circumstances in which argument, conceived both as reasoned judgment and persuasive influence, played an important role.

The purpose of this essay is to examine the ways in which argument misfunctioned in the decision to launch *Challenger* and to explore some of the reasons for its failure. More specifically, the essay deals with logical deficiencies and inadequacies in attempts at influence displayed by various parties involved in the decision-making process. It further identifies psychological, social, and ethical factors that may have contributed to the weaknesses noted.

THE FAILURE OF ARGUMENT AS REASONED JUDGMENT

In an occasionally scathing review of events leading to the *Challenger* disaster, Henry Cooper (1986) notes that, in questioning various parties involved in the decision to launch, members of the Rogers Commission frequently appeared "to have been dumb-founded at the convoluted logic they employed," as officials "argued on many occasions that black was white" (p. 86). To be sure, one finds many instances of highly questionable reasoning in the transcripts of the commission hearings that are supportive of Cooper's claim. Possibly the most important of these, insofar as the launch decision is concerned, occurred during a teleconference that included administrators at the Marshall Space Flight Center and managers as well as engineers at Morton Thiokol, the manufacturer of the controversial solid rocket booster. Thiokol's engineers were concerned that low temperatures expected for January 28 fell outside the available database. This condition left them unconfident that the O-rings in the solid rocket booster field joints would seal properly. In fact, the engineers had good reason to believe that they would not because the rings were made of a type of rubber that lost flexibility at low temperatures. Reduced flexibility along with the loss of pliability in sealing putty, the engineers believed, would increase the risk of blow-by of the escaping gas from the booster motor, which could, in turn, ignite fuel in the tank of the main rocket.

Lawrence Mulloy, the Solid Rocket Booster Project Manager at Marshall, was reportedly disturbed by Thiokol's engineering analysis and took the position that blow-by had occurred at temperatures much higher than the 53 degrees Fahrenheit being recommended as the minimally acceptable launch temperature. Since, in his judgment, there was no correlation between temperature and the likelihood of blow-by, Mulloy could see no grounds for delaying the scheduled liftoff (Official Transcript Proceedings before Presidential Commission on Space Shuttle Challenger Accident 1986, pp. 1520–30). The implicit line of reasoning here is that if one could not predict the effects of temperature within a known range, he or she would have no basis for predicting them outside that range. Consequently, Mulloy argued, Thiokol had no reason for believing that the O-rings would malfunction.

When one carefully examines Mulloy's thinking, he seems to be arguing that uncertainty justifies risk, when the appropriate conclusion, if anything, would be that it warrants caution. Commissioner William Rogers pointed this out in his response to Mulloy's analysis: "But they [documents assessing the O-ring problem] don't say the worst conditions would be acceptable" (Official Transcript 1986, p. 2668). George Hardy, Deputy Director of Science and Engineering at Marshall, reasoned in a similar fashion in his observation to the commission that the inconclusiveness of the data presented by Thiokol provided greater justification for moving toward launch than for postponement or cancellation (Official Transcript 1986, p. 1590). In response to a question concerning his awareness of the possible catastrophic consequences from blow-by of the O-rings in the field joints, Hardy's response was that this was "true of every other flight we have had" (Official Transcript 1986, p. 1590).

The callousness evident in the preceding statement is perhaps rivaled only by the fallaciousness of its argument. Hardy seems to be asserting that unwise actions in the past warrant their continuation. The underlying assumption of such an argument is analogous to that of the criminal who continues to commit crimes because he or she has not been apprehended. But simply because an event that could occur has not occurred, it does not follow that it will not. The appeal to ignorance (Capaldi 1971, p. 120) in Hardy's thinking is clear. Since opponents could not prove him wrong, he was therefore right, at least in his own judgment.

As another illustration of questionable logic, those responsible for the launch proceeded under conditions far less favorable than ones that only five days earlier had resulted in a decision to scrub. According to Richard Cook (1986), former budget analyst in the controller's office of NASA, the launch originally scheduled for January 24 was cancelled by the acting administrator of NASA, William Graham, on January 23 on the grounds that the weather conditions were expected to be poor (p. 21). In fact, the weather turned out to be reasonably good, but even if the expectations had proved correct, the weather predicted was not nearly as unfavorable as the known conditions under which the rescheduled launch of January 28 occurred. There is a certain irony, if not clear logical inconsistency, in thinking that would lead to postponement of a launch under weather conditions only expected to be unfavorable, but a decision to launch under conditions actually known to be much worse.

Although some critics have disputed their claims (see Sanger 1986), NASA officials at Levels I and II—especially Jesse Moore— who were responsible for the decision to launch testified to being generally unaware of the concern about possible failure of the O-rings that had been expressed by the engineers at Thiokol headquarters in Utah.[1] They did not deny, however, being aware of concerns separately voiced by the head of the ice inspection team and representatives from Rockwell International, designer of the orbiter, who feared that heavy ice might break loose during the launch and damage the shuttle craft. Charles Stevenson, who was in charge of ice inspection, testified to the House Committee on Science and Technology that he had advised the shuttle launch director against liftoff (Broad 1986c). In addition, Martin Cioffoletti, Rocco Petrone, and Robert Glaysher, all employees of Rockwell, reported to the Rogers Commission having told Arnold Aldrich, head of the Mission Management Team, that they were worried about ice damage and could not guarantee the shuttle's safety (Official Transcript 1986, pp. 1804–07). Hence, even in the absence of knowledge about the difference in opinion over the O-rings in the solid rocket booster between Thiokol's engineers and Level III officials at Marshall, sufficient doubt about the wisdom of proceeding with the launch based on other factors was being expressed that the reasonable and logical course of action would have been to delay or reschedule the flight. For whatever reasons, those with the final responsibility failed to arrive at this conclusion.

The failure to heed concerns was symptomatic of a developing mentality that several individuals characterized as being expected to prove that it was unsafe to launch (see, for example, testimony by Russell, Lund, Boisjoly, and McDonald in the Official Transcript 1986, pp. 1487, 1456–57, 1421–22, and 1303–4, respectively). The reasoning among those anxious to proceed with the flight appeared to be that if one could not prove it unsafe to fly, then, by implication, it was safe. One suspects that not even a beginning student in logic would be forgiven this obvious fallacy of using one's inability to prove a negative to establish its opposite.

The sorts of ill-formed judgments the preceding examples represent are hardly isolated cases. In fact, there appears to have been a history of questionable judgment that spanned at least a decade and a half. For instance, some critics have charged that the original decision to award the contract for building the solid rocket booster to Thiokol in 1973 was an invitation to eventual disaster (Broad 1986d). It is noteworthy that the contract was awarded to Thiokol over three competitors whose designs had all been rated superior to Thiokol's by the federal government's independent Source Evaluation Board (Cooper 1986, p. 109). Cost considerations, of course, were involved. Still, there is something disquieting about the choice under circumstances in which safety should have been a paramount concern and a logic that permits one to conclude that the least highly regarded design would satisfy such a concern.

Perhaps more indicative of a lack of reasoned judgment were the developments occurring in early tests of the solid rocket booster. Cooper (1986) describes the situation:

> In 1977, in test firings of the solid-rocket booster, Thiokol engineers found that the rocket's casing—specifically, the four major segments of the midsection, which can be disassembled for refuelling—expanded at ignition to such a degree that the so-called field joints . . . were opening slightly, instead of tightening as they had been designed to do. Thiokol managed to convince NASA that the situation was not "desirable, but is acceptable." This was

the first in a series of reversals of logic: something that did the exact opposite of what it was supposed to was approved. (p. 26)

Although the solid rocket booster design functioned in a way that increased the risk of explosion, the O-ring seal carried a classification of Criticality lR for five years. Such a classification indicates that a component is part of a redundant system and that its failure, while serious, would be offset by another component serving the same function that would not fail. Repeated testing and flight experience indicated the system was not redundant, as mounting evidence revealed that explosive gas was escaping past the primary O-ring and eroding (scorching) the secondary seal. As a result, the component was reclassified in 1982 to C1. A rating of C1 is assigned to any element in a system whose failure alone is sufficient to cause destruction. A C1 classification also automatically poses a launch constraint, which means that a mission may not proceed until the problem has been solved. Launch constraints may be waived, however, and in the case of the O-ring, the constraint was waived routinely from 1982 on (Cooper 1986, p. 89).

The process of reasoning that permitted this type of inconsistency is questionable at best. If the potential problems caused by the O-ring component were serious enough to warrant a C1 classification and resulting launch constraint, one can only wonder by what means responsible parties arrived at the conclusion that the constraint could be safely ignored. Particular NASA officials and administrators at Thiokol seemed to be maintaining that even though the system was not redundant, it was close enough to being redundant that they need not observe the constraint or take the requisite corrective action (see, for example, the testimony of Jerald Mason, Official Transcript 1986, p. 1348). As Commissioner Sally Ride so aptly pointed out, however, a system is either redundant, or it is not, and the absence of failure of the system does not constitute evidence that the potential problem a C1 designation signals is any less serious (see Official Transcript 1986, p. 1349). The implications of this type of thinking are all the more frightening when one considers that over nine hundred items in the shuttle system carried a classification of C1 (Broad 1986b, p. C9).

The inconsistency of establishing and routinely waiving a launch constraint is further accentuated by Lawrence Mulloy's having accused Thiokol of trying to make temperature a constraint when it did not appear on the official list (Official Transcript 1986, pp. 1537–41). He had no compunction about waiving constraints imposed to reduce risk, but was singularly unreceptive to a suggestion ostensibly aimed at increasing safety. Moreover, there was no policy that prevented decision makers from considering factors not included in the list of launch constraints if the safety of the craft and crew was in doubt. Mulloy's behavior was consistent, but his pattern of thought was not. The feeling that one must observe the rules when deviation would increase safety is somehow logically incompatible with the feeling that it is acceptable to ignore constraints intended to assure safety.

Of all the examples of questionable logic displayed in the history leading to the *Challenger* disaster, none seems so conspicuous as the recurrent tendency of some individuals to assume that success warranted the continuation of shuttle flights, even in the face of clear and apparently increasing evidence of risk. According to Charles Perrow (1986), who has written extensively about inherently risky technological systems, the air force had calculated the odds of failure for the solid rocket booster at one in thirty-five. NASA officials, on the other hand, testified to the Rogers Commission that they believed the odds to be one in one hundred thousand (p. 349). Although these officials gave no indication of the source of their estimates, in either case, the probability of failure for any given flight would be low. Such odds change rather substantially for a series of flights, however. For example, for the twenty-four missions, including *Challenger*, the probability of at least one failure can be calculated by one minus the probability that the solid rocket booster would function properly twenty-four times in succession, or $1 - P^{24}$, where P is the probability of success for a single flight. For the air force's figures, one fatal accident was almost a virtual certainty in as many as twenty-four missions.

The preceding estimate is borne out by the fact the *Challenger* mission failed and makes sense in light of the fact that more than nine hundred components individually could cause such an accident. NASA's own assessment might be more convincing if the calculations were for any single component, but with such a large number that could malfunction in nonredundant systems, and with evidence establishing that at least one of these (the O-ring) was not functioning as designed, there was little to warrant the judgment that it was safe to fly, especially on the extremely ambitious schedule that had been set for 1986 through 1990. The sheer number of flights effectively precluded the possibility—at least, in the short run—that sufficient attention would be paid to the sorts of engineering problems and related hazards the O-ring posed.

The fact that NASA had in July 1985 ordered seventy-two new casings designed to trap escaping gas from the solid rocket engines in the vicinity of the field joint (see Broad 1986a) suggests that at least some officials were aware of the seriousness of the O-ring problem and that estimates of failure presented to the Rogers Commission were grossly understated. Unfortunately, not everyone saw the implications of the action taken. In explaining the order, Deputy Associate Manager Thomas Moser contended, "I don't think you can say NASA was flying with a system it regarded as inadequate. The design was seen as marginal but adequate. It's just that there was an opportunity to increase the margin of safety" (cited by Broad 1986a, p. B8). That a system characterized as only marginal in respect to the functions it was expected to serve and requiring redesign could still be viewed as safe is an exercise in logic that is difficult to comprehend. One presumes that if the new design was adopted in the interest of preventing escaping gas from reaching and igniting fuel in the main rocket, then the existing design was structurally deficient and inherently unsafe. At least, it seems reasonable to assume that flights would be discontinued until the recently ordered casings could be installed.

The new design was first proposed in 1981, but continued flight success again appears to have contributed to the perception that the likelihood of the booster's failing was diminishing. In fact, there was no less reason in 1986 for believing that the solid rocket booster system was safe than there was five years earlier, at which time responsible officials agreed that a better, potentially less hazardous design was necessary. If anything, the experience with blow-by and erosion of the secondary O-ring seal in a succession of flights preceding 51-L constituted evidence that continued risk taking was indefensible. As of January 28, however, only three of the new casings were even under production, and NASA's schedule would not permit the length of delay replacement of the old casings required. Hence, luck was pushed once more, but this time to the great misfortune of the agency, the nation, and the crew of the *Challenger* and their families.

THE FAILURE OF ARGUMENT AS PERSUASIVE INFLUENCE

Although particular individuals involved in the decision to launch *Challenger* were clearly guilty of less than well reasoned judgment on important issues, others were not and made a genuine effort to prevent the flight from proceeding as scheduled. On the night preceding the launch, Thiokol engineers led by Roger Boisjoly and Arnold Thompson had all but convinced their superiors Joseph Kilminster, Jerald Mason, and Robert Lund to recommend to NASA officials at the Marshall Space Flight Center that the launch of *Challenger* be scrubbed or, at least, postponed until the temperature at the Kennedy Space Center reached a minimum of 53 degrees Fahrenheit. This led to the well-publicized teleconference in which Thiokol managers eventually reversed their position and transmitted a recommendation to proceed with the flight.

Since Thiokol had designed the solid rocket booster, the fact that its engineers were not confident it would function properly under the expected weather conditions should have been sufficient to warrant rescheduling or, at least, delay. In fact, to prevent the flight, the managers need only to have withheld approval. Launch regulations are such that all Level IV units (the contractors for various aspects of the shuttle project) can halt a flight simply by refusing to certify that it is safe to fly, insofar as the components for which they have responsibility are concerned (Report 1986). Overruling a recommendation not to launch would have serious consequences for the parties involved. Instead of exercising this authority, the managers at Thiokol engaged in a discussion with officials representing the Marshall Space Flight Center, in which Lawrence Mulloy, George Hardy, and Stanley Reinartz questioned the logic of Thiokol's engineering staff and intimated that the company was contributing to inordinate delay in the overall launch schedule. Hardy, who was reportedly "appalled" (Official Transcript 1986, p. 1599) by Thiokol's original recommendation, testified that his response to it was, "My God, Thiokol, when do you expect me to launch, next April?" (Official Transcript 1986, p. 1540).

The disagreement ultimately reduced to whether Thiokol's engineering data, in regard to the functioning of the O-rings, were conclusive or inconclusive. Marshall officials took the position that they were inconclusive. As a result, Thiokol's managers asked for time to caucus. During this period, the managers decided to give the go ahead, despite continued opposition voiced by Roger Boisjoly and Arnold Thompson. Following the caucus, the teleconference resumed, with Thiokol now reporting that its recommendation was to proceed. Kilminster was asked to put the recommendation in writing and to fax a copy to Marshall.

The preceding account reveals two points at which argument as persuasive influence failed. First, Thiokol managers were unsuccessful in convincing officials at Marshall that inconclusive data constituted grounds for caution, not risk. Had the argument been stated that way, it may have had more persuasive force.[2] Instead, managers assumed a defensive posture and tried unsuccessfully to demonstrate that the solid rocket booster had a strong likelihood of malfunction. In the words of Robert Lund, "[W]e got ourselves into the thought process that we were trying to find some way to prove to them that it wouldn't work, and we were unable to do that" (Official Transcript 1986, pp. 1456–57). In the second instance, Thiokol's engineers were unsuccessful in their attempts to convince their own managers to stick with the original recommendation. Having reversed themselves once, the managers stiffened in their resistance to further persuasive influence.

In the hours following the teleconference, three other expressions of opposition to proceeding with the launch occurred. Of these, the effort of Allen McDonald was surely the most intense—albeit as ineffective as all others' attempts. McDonald, Thiokol's manager for the Space Booster Project, was present at Cape Kennedy along with Lawrence Mulloy and Stanley Reinartz of the Marshall Space Flight Center. Dissatisfied with the disposition of the controversy surrounding the O-ring question, McDonald persisted in his opposition. He reportedly was informed that the issue was resolved to the satisfaction of Level III managers, to which he claims responding, "I sure wouldn't want to be the person who had to stand in front of a board of inquiry to explain why we launched this outside of the qualification of the solid rocket motor on any shuttle system" (Official Transcript 1986, p. 1295). The fear appeal was without impact.

McDonald's credibility may have been suspect, inasmuch as only six weeks previously he had written a memorandum urging that the O-ring problem be closed out. "Close-out" in this context refers to a problem's having been solved. McDonald was apparently eager to jump the gun because three of the previously mentioned casings were in production and would be used in flights at some future point (see Cooper 1986, p. 91). His reversal, therefore, may not have been taken very seriously by the representatives from Marshall and could have been construed simply as a show of support for his colleagues at Thiokol. On the other hand, the tone of his remarks would seem to make it clear that he was very serious.

Undeterred by the lack of responsiveness to his concern about the possibility of the failure of the solid rocket booster, McDonald offered two other reasons for either cancelling or delaying the mission: inclement weather that could hamper the positioning of recovery vehicles and the possibility of ice damage to the orbiter. Again, his efforts proved fruitless; however, on this occasion, he was assured that his concern about possible malfunction of the joints would be communicated to appropriate parties at Level II (Official Transcript 1986, pp. 1296–97). The concern, he later learned, was not sent forward as promised.

In addition to McDonald's input, NASA officials had a recommendation from Charles Stevenson, head of the ice inspection crew, not to proceed with the launch. On a tape uncovered by the House Committee on Science and Technology, Stevenson is heard commenting to Horace Lambert, Director of Shuttle Engineering, "I'd say the only choice you've got is not to go" (cited by Broad 1986c, p. A14). Stevenson later had the opportunity to repeat his recommendation against proceeding to higher officials but failed to do so.

Stevenson's reluctance to restate his recommendation proved unfortunate because representatives of Rockwell were independently recommending against launching the *Challenger* at approximately the same time as the ice-crew report was being communicated. At least from their perspective, these individuals were recommending against launch. To everyone's regret, Rockwell's representatives never exercised their prerogative to abort the mission. Rather, they appeared to feel that such statements as, "[W]e do not have the database from which to draw any conclusions for this particular situation," and, "Rockwell cannot assure that it is safe to fly" (Official Transcript 1986, pp. 1803–06) were sufficient expressions of concern to lead to the appropriate course of action. In dealing with individuals who interpreted the inconclusiveness of data as grounds for taking risks, however, this type of obliqueness could only serve to reinforce the presumption that it was safe to fly unless one could prove that it was not. It could, moreover, represent an instance of assimilation, that is, the tendency to see another's position as closer to one's own than it actually is (see Sherif, Sherif, and Nebergall 1965).

As in the case of the failure of argument as reasoned judgment, NASA, it has been revealed, had a history of the failure of argument as persuasive influence in several key areas related to the shuttle program. As Cooper (1986) notes, "[E]ngineers at Marshall and elsewhere . . . were not pleased with the design of the joints," but feeling there was little they could do about the existing booster, they invested their energy in trying to "influence the design of future ones" (p. 86). From the outset of the shuttle program, Thiokol's design was controversial. Yet those advocating other choices, or even questioning the wisdom of this particular choice, showed little in return for their efforts. Senator Frank Moss, for instance, questioned James Fletcher as far back as 1973 about the cost effectiveness of a program in which rocket boosters manufactured across the country would have to be produced and shipped in pieces for assembly at the launch site (see Broad 1986d, p. 50). Fletcher was not influenced, or apparently even impressed, by the line of questioning. Those who were more vigorous in their criticism of the choice met with a similar indifference (NYT 1986, p. A34).

Among the other instances of external critics', concerned scientists', and lower echelon personnel's inability to influence important decisions are ones involving the commitment to make the shuttle program the centerpiece of space exploration and development, agreements to pursue an overly ambitious and probably unrealistic flight schedule, and the shift in emphasis from research and development to the delivery of commercial payloads. These and other failures in argument concerning the directions in which NASA was beginning to move are detailed in recently published histories by Joseph Trento (1987) and Malcolm McConnell (1987). Their mention here merely serves as a reminder that there is a historical context in which significant actions were taken in the face of sometimes strenuous opposition, and when the justifications of the opposition were often stronger than those of officials responsible for deciding policy. In addition, there was a reluctance among many of those within the agency to push very hard on matters of importance. As William Broad (1986b) has observed, "Few knowledgeable individuals wanted to press questions that could halt the program" (p. C9). This, of course, would make the comments of more vocal opponents appear to be unrepresentative and, therefore, more easily dismissible. When one considers such a history, the failure of argument as persuasive influence in the particular context of the *Challenger* episode is less difficult to understand.

The public image of NASA prior to this incident was that of highly efficient and effective agency—one serving as a striking counterexample to the typical bureaucratic institution in this society, especially the typical governmental bureaucracy. This image was fostered by numerous successes, an effective public relations program, and a highly sympathetic press corps (Lindee and Nelkin 1986). *Challenger* shattered that image—one that in light of the agency's more recent history was probably ill-deserved. Until that time, however, image was a matter of considerable importance, and the preoccupation with it undoubtedly had much to do with the resistance to concerns about safety some of NASA's officials displayed.

REASONS FOR THE FAILURE OF ARGUMENT

Although discussion of the full set of reasons for the failures in argument is beyond the scope of this essay and the knowledge of its author, several contributing factors in addition to those already identified are evident, or can be inferred from the public record. In the cases portrayed as the failure of argument as reasoned judgment, possibly the most critical influence was the shift in presumption so frequently mentioned by parties opposed to the launch. Apparently, the succession of twenty-three consecutive successful shuttle flights induced the feeling that the burden of proof was now on those opposed to launching the *Challenger*. At the base of this shift was the fact that at a public level, at least, there existed what Irving Janis (1982) has referred to as the "illusion of invulnerability." Richard Feynman, one of the members of the Rogers Commission and Nobel laureate in physics, reinforces this notion in his observation that "space agency officials would 'agonize' over whether to launch a shuttle because booster seals had eroded on the previous flight. But then, if they decided to launch and the flight succeeded, they lowered their standards on the next flight because they 'got away with it the last time'" (cited by Broad 1986b, p. C9).

Despite the apparently low odds that a genuinely defective system could function without incident in so many previous flights as a basis for assuming the success of ensuing ones, overconfidence was not an appropriate response. As Perrow (1986) points out, with inherently risky technological systems, a number of conditions must typically exist before malfunction occurs. Accidents in such systems, he contends, necessarily have a low probability in the individual case, but when they do come about, the consequences can be very serious, if not catastrophic. Three Mile Island and Chernobyl are cases in point. This suggests the need for an even greater preoccupation with safety and an attitude favoring caution, that is, continuing to presume in the case of shuttle launches that they should not occur unless relevant evidence is very strongly supportive of a decision to proceed. The successes were apparently too convincing for NASA officials to retain the presumption to which a technically complex and dangerous system would logically obligate one. Were they less ego-involved and not subject to other pressures, they may not have so easily shifted the presumption. One senses that these very same individuals would neither be impressed by data showing, for instance, that twenty-three subjects taking an experimental drug improved nor presume from such figures that the drug is safe for general use, unless proved otherwise. Yet with an infinitely more complex situation, they did precisely that.

Another factor contributing to the failure of responsible parties to arrive at appropriate conclusions about the wisdom of proceeding with the flight of *Challenger* is the sheer number of components that, by virtue of their C1 classification, posed threats to the safety of the spaceship and its crew. With more than nine hundred items bearing this classification, one wonders why any mission was ever permitted, let alone that of the *Challenger*. In retrospect, it seems clear that the shuttle program, according to relevant criteria, had never been operational. Since risks were taken without incident and since most of the items seemed to function according to design expectations, the number of components carrying the C1 classification seems to have lost its significance.

Statistical data in this volume easily obscure the individual item, even if there is good reason to be concerned about it (see Nisbett and Ross 1980). Perceptually speaking, the fact that one among more than nine hundred items was especially problematic would seem less a cause for concern than would be the case if one of, say, only two items was problematic. In addition, large numbers can influence perceptions of likelihood and estimates of probability. The chances that one item in a compilation of nine hundred plus could malfunction are considerably greater than the chances that one of two items that could malfunction will. Nevertheless, it is the greater probability that many would take to be the lesser. Even highly trained individuals with a background in probability theory display these sorts of mental lapses and miscalculations from time to time.

Yet another explanation for the failure of central figures in the decision-making process to make appropriate judgments is offered by Arie Kruglanski (1986), who argues that "People are more likely to stick with a decision . . . if they don't have access to evidence that the judgment could be incorrect" (p. 48). When a judgment has been reached, moreover, decision makers often exhibit a corresponding tendency to bolster the judgment and to discount conflicting information (Janis and Mann 1977). Mulloy, Reinartz, and Hardy, in particular, evidenced such a propensity. The tendency, which Kruglanski refers to as "freeze-think," has even been noted in cases involving such judgmental tasks as Norman Maier's famous horse-trading problem. L. Richard Hoffman (1965) reports that in cases involving problems for which the correct solution can be mathematically or otherwise logically demonstrated, some individuals will stubbornly cling to an erroneous judgment. How much easier it must be to display this type of perseverance under circumstances in which one is unable to offer "proof" that a judgment is in error or can demonstrate that fact only after some action traceable to the judgment has occurred.

If there is a common element in the judgments of those favoring the launch of *Challenger*, it would have to be the consistent miscalculation of risk. The preceding explanations all point to this conclusion. What may have led to such miscalculations, however, requires further exploration. Utility theory suggests that a preferred choice is one that has the greatest "expected utility" (see Arkes and Hammond 1986), a value one derives from a consideration of both benefits and costs as well as their likelihood of occurrence. Calculations of benefits, costs, and their associated probabilities, however, are often subjectively determined and, therefore, can be influenced by a variety of psychological and perceptual factors that result in distorted estimates.

Additionally, under conditions in which one is not likely to be directly affected by the course of action a particular judgment implies, it may be more easily possible to underestimate the risks involved. In fact, Richard Cook, one of the sharpest of NASA's internal critics for its failure to attend to risks associated with the O-ring problem, and who wrote a memorandum in July 1985 warning of possible catastrophe resulting from defective booster field joints, testified to having lost sensitivity to the problem: "NASA gets overloaded," he observed. "How many booster joints can you worry about? I had just written an 80-page report on Centaur. How many of these can you handle?" (cited by Broad 1986b, p. C9).

The insensitivity to risk and, hence, the tendency to misperceive it resulting from the large volumes of data to which Cook alludes might be less pronounced if those involved in the calculation of risk were the ones subjecting themselves to it. In line with this possibility, Eugene Krantz, current Director of Missions Operations at NASA, reported a tendency to underestimate risk as the distance between those subjected to it and those making decisions increased (see Cooper 1986, p. 93). In the early days of the space program, there was a closeness between astronauts and administrators that, for all intents and purposes, had ceased to exist by 1986. At one time, however, administrators thought like astronauts and could project themselves into the astronaut role. This is probably a major reason why the Rogers Commission strongly recommended that astronauts become more directly involved in NASA's decision-making machinery, and especially in the realm of launch decisions (Report 1986, p. 199). Even if astronauts are no more accurate in assessing risk than NASA's principal decision makers, their errors would more likely be in the direction of overestimation and, thereby, lead to the exercise of greater caution.

Undoubtedly, some of the same factors that help us understand the failure of argument as reasoned judgment had an important bearing on the failure of argument as persuasive influence. Particularly likely is the possibility that the previously mentioned tendencies to bolster preferred choices and to engage in selective perception were at work and led to heightened resistance to persuasive influence. Commitment can be a very powerful deterrent to persuasion and counterargument (see Brehm 1966; Janis and Mann 1977). As one examines the available information, however, other factors unrelated to judgmental and perceptual processes, but which nonetheless provide reasonable explanations for the failure of argument as persuasive influence, are evident.

There can be no question that the failure of argument as persuasive influence is largely attributable to the resistance displayed by the targets of influence. But why were they so unreceptive? Surely, they did not wish to see any harm come either to the crew of *Challenger* or to their program. One explanation is that they perceived themselves to be under considerable external pressure. Although there is no convincing evidence that the officials involved were under externally generated pressure to proceed with the launching of *Challenger*, the agency was at a point in its evolution where the expectations of others outside the organization influenced decisions. NASA had been progressively shifting to the model of a commercial business. By 1986 it was "serving clients," "delivering payloads," and committed to a schedule from which little deviation could be tolerated for fear of "losing business" to competitor nations (Cooper 1986). The agency, according to one observer, even found itself "adopting the business principle that the client is always right" (p. 100). Under these conditions, one must wonder whether the appropriate strategy for opponents to take might not have been to argue that proceeding with the launch could be "bad for business."

The influences contributing to this change in conception of the type of agency NASA expected to become and, in fact, had gone a long way toward becoming, are chronicled by McConnell (1987) and Trento (1987). Neither account offers a very charitable view of the transformation or the parties most directly involved in bringing it about. The subtitle of McConnell's book, for example, suggests the forces he sees as primarily responsible: "politics, greed, and the wrong stuff." The worst in business and the worst in politics, according to these critics, had found their way into the day-to-day life of the agency and were at the base of a tragedy that need not have occurred. Whether McConnell and Trento have overstated the case is difficult to say. But one thing that emerged in both of their inquiries seems hardly controversial. From the perspective of top officials, the viability of the agency was directly related to its ability to demonstrate immediate and tangible returns on the taxpayer's investment. This required high visibility and the dependable delivery of services. Proposals that would interfere with the achievement of these objectives were threatening. The *Challenger* mission had been postponed several times, and the latest proposal to delay constituted a threat to the agency's credibility, at least from the perspective of some top officials. Under other conditions, they may have been more receptive to arguments about safety, but under the existing circumstances, the preoccupation with image may simply have overpowered other concerns.

A comparatively charitable, and perhaps more convincing, basis for interpreting resistance to persuasive influence than that offered by either McConnell or Trento is developed by Alex Roland, who served as a NASA historian from 1973 to 1981. Roland acknowledges the roles that pride and loyalty unquestionably played in creating the sort of climate in which a very reasonable request could engender so much resistance as the recommendation to postpone the flight of *Challenger* did. Most critical in Roland's judgment, however, was the fact that "They [NASA officials] had put the whole future of the space program on the shuttle," and therefore, "There was no way out. Overwhelming problems were just denied. They were kidding themselves as much as anybody" (cited by Broad 1986b, p. C9). This type of self-deception, prompted by a need for the shuttle program to succeed at all costs, makes it more understandable how the communication of problems and concerns about the readiness of the shuttle for flight would be greeted somewhat less than enthusiastically and why the burden of proof was placed on those who were opposed.

It is tempting to attribute the failure of argument as persuasive influence exclusively to the sources of resistance. A more complete understanding, however, requires an examination of the behavior of those attempting to exert influence. In a separate analysis, two colleagues and I (see Gouran, Hirokawa, and Martz 1986) found evidence of a rigid observance of role boundaries and a corresponding reluctance on the part of those opposed to persist in arguing their case as factors affecting the decision to launch *Challenger*. Despite his spirited effort to halt the launch, for example, Roger Boisjoly accepted Thiokol's reversal as final. As he testified to the Rogers Commission, "I had my say, and I never take any management right to take the input of an engineer and then make a decision based upon that input, and I truly believe that" (Official Transcript 1986, p. 1421). McDonald similarly testified to being unwilling to exceed his authority even though NASA policy required that critical concerns be brought to the attention of Level II and Level I managers (Official Transcript 1986, p. 1310). As another illustration, when Stanley Reinartz, following the caucus, asked whether there was any disagreement with Thiokol's final recommendation, none of the engineers spoke out (Official Transcript 1986, p. 1666). Finally, Rockwell's representatives seemed quite unwilling to go beyond their vague and indirect assertions that they could not be "100 per cent sure" that it was safe to fly. Sadly, in the case of these individuals, they possessed the authority to cancel the mission, as did the managers at Thiokol who, rather than take the risk of losing business, permitted others to take far greater risks with the lives of the *Challenger* crew.

Whether a greater degree of assertiveness or a willingness to go over the heads of superiors would have altered the outcome in the *Challenger* case, of course, is a matter of conjecture. From Charles Perrow's (1986) perspective, however, the answer to the question is, "Probably not." As he has observed:

> [I]t was not the procedure but the goal at NASA that was at fault. NASA's goal was not primarily the safe economical exploration of space. Instead, it appears that the agency had other priorities; its desire to beat out foreign and private competition; its effort to regain public enthusiasm by putting people into daring adventures; its willingness to satisfy the pressure for high profits from its contractors, who were, in turn, willing to falsify tests and fake their invoices; its extraordinary sensitivity to the military's demand for increased payloads that would validate President Reagan's Strategic Defense Initiative, or "Star Wars." (p. 354)

The pressures against "whistle-blowing" that going outside channels would have represented, moreover, were such that higher-level officials may not have been very receptive to the arguments about safety that were being voiced at Level IV. Boisjoly and McDonald were later to discover, as a result of their testimony to the Rogers Commission, that the cost for challenging the judgment of one's immediate superiors can be high. Despite the fact that NASA presently encourages whistle-blowing (see Wilford 1987), at the time of the *Challenger* launch concerned parties probably had good reason to believe that pressing their case or ignoring channels would do very little good, and might prove to be personally costly. They may also have perceived that, at best, their concerns would be dismissed as the urgings of bothersome Cassandras.

In spite of the possibilities that greater effort to halt the mission would have had a limited chance of succeeding, it remains less than clear that argument as persuasive influence was given the best possible chance to work by those who engaged in it. And that alone, in the atmosphere of defensiveness being displayed by those in positions of authority, would virtually assure its failure.

CONCLUSION

Tragic as the accident was, the timing of the *Challenger* disaster may have proved fortunate. According to Perrow (1986), the ensuing flight was to carry forty-seven pounds of plutonium, which for the kind of malfunction in *Challenger*'s solid rocket booster and the explosion of the oxygen and hydrogen fuel mixture to which it contributed very likely would destroy the casing in which the plutonium was to be housed and result in substantial nuclear destruction. The "what might have been" aspect of this case suggests all the more reason for one's being concerned about the failure of argument in both of the senses in which it has been explored. We have the knowledge with which to minimize the likelihood of bad decisions, and the events surrounding the fateful launch of *Challenger* should serve as a constant reminder of the need for that knowledge to be widely shared.

REFERENCES

Arkes, H. R., and K. R. Hammond, eds. 1986. *Judgment and decision making*. Cambridge, Mass.: Cambridge University Press.

Brehm, J. W. 1966. *A theory of psychological reactance*. New York: Academic Press.

Broad, W. J. 1986a, September 22. NASA had solution to key flaw in rocket when shuttle exploded. *New York Times*, A1, B8.

———. 1986b, September 30. Silence about shuttle flaw attributed to pitfalls of pride. *New York Times*, C1, C9.

———. 1986c, November 5. NASA official advised against liftoff. *New York Times*, A14.

———. 1986d, December 7. NASA chief might not take part in decisions on booster contracts. *New York Times*, I50.

Capaldi, N. 1971. *The art of deception*. Buffalo, N.Y.: Prometheus Books.

Cook, R. 1986, November. The Rogers Commission that failed. *The Washington Monthly*, 13–21.

Cooper, H. S. F. 1986, November 10. Letter from the space center. *The New Yorker*, 83–114.

Gouran, D. S. 1984. Principles of counteractive influence in decision-making and problem-solving groups. In *Small group communication: A reader*, ed. R. S. Cathcart and L. A. Samovar, 4th ed. Dubuque, Iowa: William C. Brown.

Gouran, D. S., R. Y. Hirokawa, and A. E. Martz. 1986. A critical analysis of factors related to decisional processes involved in the Challenger disaster. *Central States Speech Journal, 37,* 119–35.

Hoffman, L. R. 1965. Group problem solving. In *Advances in experimental social psychology,* ed. L. Berkowitz. Vol. 2. New York: Academic Press.

Janis, I. L. 1982. *Groupthink.* 2d ed. Boston: Houghton Mifflin.

Janis, I. L., and L. Mann. 1977. *Decision making.* New York: Free Press.

Kruglanski, A. W. 1986, August. Freeze-think and the Challenger. *Psychology Today*, 48ff.

Lindee, S., and D. Nelkin. 1986, November. Challenger: The high cost of hype. *Bulletin of Atomic Scientists*, 16–18.

McConnell, M. 1987. *Challenger: A major malfunction.* Garden City, N.Y.: Doubleday.

Nisbett, R., and L. Ross. 1980. *Human inference: Strategies and shortcomings of social judgment.* Englewood Cliffs, N.J.: Prentice-Hall.

Official transcript proceedings before presidential commission on space shuttle Challenger accident. 1986. Washington, D.C.: Alderson Reporting.

The past in the shuttle's future. 1986, December 9. *New York Times*, A34.

Perrow, C. 1986, October 11. The habit of courting disaster. *The Nation, 329,* 347–56.

Report of the presidential commission on the space shuttle Challenger. 1986. Washington, D.C.: U.S. Government Printing Office.

Sanger, D. E. 1986, December 21. Top NASA aides knew of shuttle flaw in '84. *New York Times*, 124.

Sherif, M., C. W. Sherif, and R. E. Nebergall. 1965. *Attitude and attitude change: The social judgment approach.* Philadelphia, Pa.: W. B. Saunders.

Trento, J. J. 1987. *Prescription for disaster.* New York: Crown.

Wilford, J. N. 1987, June 5. New NASA system aims to encourage blowing the whistle. *New York Times*, A1, B5.

PART 2

Axiological Approaches to Argument Evaluation

CHAPTER 4

Aligning Ethicality and Effectiveness in Arguments: Advocating Inclusiveness Percentages for the New Lutheran Church

Kathryn M. Olson

Evaluating whether an argument is ethical is a perennial problem for those interested in rhetoric. At the core of the problem is the issue of what type of standard is acceptable as an evaluative criterion. Many proposed ethical standards for argument are problematic because they either make rhetoric subordinate to ethics generated by other disciplines or evaluate ends instead of means. Initially, standards that require one to look outside the realm of argumentation itself to make an evaluation of either an argument's ends (i.e., goals or purposes) or means (i.e., processes or strategies for attaining ends) are unsatisfactory because they make rhetoric dependent on other disciplines, such as philosophy or religion. Such dependency subordinates rhetoric to an ethical standard completely external to it, which is undesirable because rhetoric becomes

> no more than the means used to achieve an end nonrhetorically certified as good. But once this position is taken, and the autonomy of rhetoric surrendered, it becomes impossible to say why rhetoric rather than some other means—perhaps a more effective means—should be used. If the hedonistic calculus tells us that x should be brought about, and x can be brought about by sticks or drugs as well as by rhetoric, then why not use the sticks or drugs? In the end, there is no longer any way to identify rhetoric except as a relatively weak kind of *force*. (Johnstone 1971, p. 82)

The justification for convincing others through reasoned, evidenced arguments instead of securing their assent by coercion or other means that might be more directly effective than argument is surrendered by standards that treat rhetoric strictly as one means to ends that are certified as desirable by other disciplines. The issue of whether an argument's ethicality can be evaluated on the argument's own merits is eclipsed in the process.

A second related complication for choosing an ethical criterion by which to evaluate arguments concerns the problem of standards that evaluate an argument by referring to its goal or telos instead of scrutinizing the means or rhetorical processes by which it pursues those goals. Teleological standards that evaluate an argument based on whether it aims at an end deemed "good" or "ethical," even were it possible to so certify the end by an exclusively rhetorical method and so avoid the preceding criticism,[1] are unacceptable for several reasons. First, teleological standards promote an "ends justify the means" approach to argument. Even a passing familiarity with the arguments examined in the Iran-contra hearings should convince one of the grave consequences that such an "ends justify the means" approach can produce. Furthermore, in pursuit of an end deemed to be "good," consistency forces teleological evaluative standards to allow argumentative practices that even a lay person would exclude from the realm of ethical argument: lying, plagiarism, taking evidence out of context. Resistance to Plato's notion that it is permissible for leaders to lie in what they believe to be the best interest of the community (*The Republic* III.389b–c) illustrates recognition of this problem with employing teleological standards and underscores the difference between an ethic focused on arguments' ends and one focused on argumentative means or processes. One final difficulty with teleological standards is the practical lack of agreement on which ends are "good" or "ethical." In contemporary America, the abortion issue provides a prime illustration of a fundamental division over the evaluation of arguments' ends.

Numerous theorists have proposed argument evaluation standards that avoid the shortcomings of dependent and/or teleological criteria. Many of these standards focus on the importance of bilaterality and respect for other participants in the process of arguing. For example, Franklyn S. Haiman (1952) endorses the "democratic ethic"; Wayne Brockriede (1972) suggests that an ethical arguer will approach the opponent or audience as a lover rather than as a seducer or rapist. Henry W. Johnstone Jr. offers a relatively comprehensive standard for ethical argument among those criteria that are neither dependent on other disciplines nor teleological in nature. While acknowledging the need in certain contexts to end discussion, at least temporarily, in order to make a decision, Johnstone contends that an ethical arguer will use arguments preserving the possibility of future argument ([1973] 1978, p. 85).

Although in much of his writing Johnstone is concerned primarily with philosophical argumentation, in 1981 he elaborated a more general standard for ethical argument, the "basic imperative." Modeled after Kant's categorical imperative, the basic imperative states, "So act in each instance as to encourage, rather than suppress, the capacity to persuade and to be persuaded, whether the capacity in question is yours or another's" (p. 310). Johnstone bases this standard on two assumptions: (1) that humans are characterized distinctively by being persuading and persuadable beings, and (2) that what is distinctively human ought to be perpetuated. To argue against the basic imperative would involve using a distinctively human capacity to promote its own termination (pp. 306–7).

Johnstone's "ethic of rhetoric" is both independent of other disciplines and not teleological. Though modeled after an earlier philosophical ethic, Johnstone's basic imperative rests squarely in the realm of rhetoric. It does not depend on philosophy or other disciplines to determine what makes an argument ethical nor to certify ends as "good" for the sake of evaluating the arguments advocating these ends. The basic imperative makes rhetoric self-sufficient and process-centered in that it establishes a rhetorical duty to protect the possibility of future arguments that may challenge, modify, dissolve, or reassert the claim of the initial argument. Instead of depending on other disciplines and/or focusing on teleological concerns for evaluative judgments, Johnstone's ethic is deontological, or based on the concept of duty. It assumes that rightness or wrongness inheres in an act itself, rather than in the act's consequences. One's duty to perform or refrain from a particular act thus is determined by evaluating the act itself (1981, p. 309). With respect to argumentation, the basic imperative suggests that an argument is ethical if it protects a space for future arguments on the issue; it is unethical if it seeks to foreclose all argumentative responses. Of course, actual arguments meet this standard to varying degrees. Since there is a continuum of variations between arguments that completely preclude any further arguments and those that preserve extensive opportunity for ongoing discussion and future reconsideration of decisions, such process evaluations find arguments to be more or less ethical instead of sweeping all arguments and their nuances into a dualistic, totalizing scheme that simply labels them either completely ethical or completely unethical.[2]

While the basic imperative seems to be an appealing choice for argument evaluation because it avoids either making rhetoric dependent on other disciplines for evaluative criteria or relying on teleological criteria, it does not speak to the issue of an argument's effectiveness. An effective argument is one with a high probability of being persuasive to its intended audience. Since people generally make arguments to forge agreement on issues currently characterized by disagreement, arguers ideally should strive to make arguments that are both ethical and effective. While effectiveness and ethicality do not accompany each other necessarily in arguments, too often people favor the other extreme and view these two qualities as operating competitively rather than synergistically. For instance, rhetors such as Adolf Hitler and Jim Jones were skilled at offering highly effective arguments that fail to meet deontological, or even most teleological, standards for ethical arguments. However, since arguers usually offer arguments specifically for the purpose of convincing people, those interested in ethics of arguing cannot ignore the relationship between arguments' effectiveness and ethicality. Conversely, a deontological standard that encourages an argumentative process so open that effective arguments automatically are judged unethical is no more acceptable than are teleological standards.

There is a need, then, for an argument evaluation standard that appreciates both ethicality and effectiveness. I suggest a concept based on the *alignment* of deontological ethicality and effectiveness. While it may be possible for an argument to be ethical according to the basic imperative and yet be ineffective and vice versa, alignment prescribes that superior arguments unite ethicality and effectiveness; in fact, as the following example demonstrates, ethicality and effectiveness mutually support each other in the most well-aligned instances. The touchstone of effectiveness employed here is Wayne C. Booth's "rhetorical stance." Booth ([1963] 1972) argues that three elements must be in balance in order for an act of discourse to be effective: the available arguments, the interests of the audience, and the voice or character of the speaker, a triad similar to the concepts of logical, pathetic, and ethical artistic proof that Aristotle develops in his *Rhetoric.* While Booth raises some ethical concerns, mostly in the sense of evident ethical violations to avoid, his essay concentrates primarily on rhetorical effectiveness without actively developing an affirmative ethical standard. My argument is that developing an evaluative position that considers both effectiveness and deontological ethicality requires more than balancing internally the three elements of Booth's rhetorical stance and striving for the self-perpetuating argumentative process implied by Johnstone's basic imperative; it also requires aligning the constellation of the rhetorical stance's three elements with the constellation created by the four duties that must be fulfilled to realize the basic imperative in practice. When an argument reflects internal consonance among the elements making it effective and among the duties making it ethical *and* there is harmony between that trio of effectiveness elements and the quartet of duties undergirding a deontologically ethical argumentation process, then the argumentative position in question should be both effective and ethical and so a superior example of argument. In fact, the qualities that make it effective and those that make it ethical will be related integrally, rather than being discrete.

Developing and illustrating how the synergistic alignment of effectiveness and deontological ethicality can function in argument evaluation requires a paradigm case. The discourse of advocates for inclusiveness percentages who participated in the 1982–86 deliberations of the Commission for a New Lutheran Church (CNLC) provides such an exemplar. A brief background section on the CNLC's inclusiveness deliberations precedes an analysis of how the very aspects of the inclusiveness percentages proponents' argumentative position that made it ethical by Johnstone's deontological standard also made it effective on Booth's terms.

ALIGNING ETHICALITY AND EFFECTIVENESS IN ARGUMENTS

Background of the Controversy

On September 8, 1982, after years of discussing possibilities for greater Lutheran unity, the American Lutheran Church, the Lutheran Church in America, and the Association of Evangelical Lutheran Churches voted to pursue unification. Their merger would create the fourth largest Protestant church in the United States (Thunderous Majorities 1982). The CNLC was the body charged with designing the new unified church. The Committee on Lutheran Unity, the body responsible for crafting the composition of its successor, recommended that the seventy-member CNLC be at least 50 percent lay people, at least 40 percent men, at least 40 percent women, and at least 16.6 percent people of color (Trexler 1991, pp. 40–41). To keep decision making as close to all church members as possible, principles of grassroots' input, a theological basis for action, and decisions by consensus when possible guided the work of both the Committee on Lutheran Unity and the CNLC (p. 23). Consistent with these principles, the key values characterizing the CNLC's deliberations in particular were newness, unity, and inclusiveness. Although the commissioners agreed on the importance of these three values, they often differed on how the new church should achieve them in practice (Olson 1987, pp. 56–94).

While many issues that the CNLC addressed were relatively uncontroversial, the challenge of assuring significant participation in decision making at all levels of the new church by lay people, women, and people of color or with a primary language other than English (hereafter shortened to "people of color") proved contentious throughout the commission's operation. Much of the debate over a proposed inclusiveness percentages system focused specifically on the percentages for people of color; this provision was the most vulnerable aspect of the plan because only a tiny proportion of the existing churches' memberships were people of color. The commissioners ostensibly agreed that it was important to include all these groups in the new church's decision making, but they differed on how to achieve such inclusiveness in practice. Some argued that, given the old churches' tendencies to grant disproportionately great decision-making power to whites, males, and clergy, the only effective way to insure adequate inclusiveness in the new church was to institutionalize inclusiveness percentages for decision-making bodies. Other commissioners rejected the need for a structured system of percentages, claiming that a strong affirmation of the inclusiveness principle coupled with the new church's "good faith" commitment would suffice. For the sake of convenience, members advocating percentages hereafter are termed "proponents," and those opposing percentages are called "opponents." The two conflicting groups offered recurring sets of arguments over the course of the commission's work.

Opponents called the proposed percentages "quotas" and advanced three main lines of argument. First, they argued that it would be impossible or impractical to implement percentages for people of color. With less than 2 percent of the current churches' memberships being people of color, there would be a shortage of members to fill the "quotas" for the new church's many decision-making bodies (Staples 1983, p. 5; Commission Proposes 1984; Trexler 1991, p. 82). Consequently, these commissioners concluded that the commitment to inclusiveness would not be taken seriously and/or the percentages system would be abused and circumvented.

Second, opponents argued that "quotas" are unnecessary because a strongly stated commitment to inclusiveness and the "good faith" of those in the new church would effect inclusiveness in practice. Its advocates grounded this argument in the powerful opposition Lutherans perceive between law and gospel. According to Lutheran theology, the Old Testament recounts how God gave people laws to guide their actions. Because, by their very nature, people could not keep the laws perfectly, God sent His Son to pay the penalty for humans' failure to keep the laws themselves and to offer a model of the godly life. The New Testament "gospel," which means "good news," tells how reconciliation between imperfect humans and a perfect God finally became possible. Consequently, what could never be accomplished by laws (i.e., the possibility of imperfect humans "earning" reconciliation with God by their own actions) was achieved and superseded by gospel (i.e., the good news that Christ had died in people's place so they could be reconciled to God simply by accepting His sacrifice and gift of grace). At the risk of being simplistic for the sake of brevity, a primary reason that Luther led the Reformation was the Catholic Church's retreat from gospel to law. The Catholic Church at Luther's time led people—most of whom could not read the Bible for themselves either because of illiteracy or lack of access to a copy—to believe that they could be saved by their own actions (or the purchase of "indulgences" from the Church to compensate for their failure to keep the law) rather than being justified by faith in God's saving grace alone. Consequently, linking a position to law as opposed to gospel tinges it with a certain unsavoriness for many

Lutherans. In this case, opponents suggested that "quotas" were legalistic in a way unbefitting a church based on gospel; a "good faith" assurance that the new church would strive to include people from diverse groups in its decision-making bodies should be an adequate guarantee for those who accept that their church is centered on gospel principles, opponents argued.[3]

Finally, some opponents claimed that, while inclusiveness is an important value, in practice it competes with other equally or more important values. The competing values advanced include the ideas that representation should reflect accurately the existing demographics of current churches' memberships and that congregations have a right to elect whomever they want to represent them at decision-making assemblies.

While it included some powerful white men, both clergy and lay, the group of proponents was comprised largely of women and people of color. Proponents termed inclusiveness percentages "goals" instead of "quotas" and relied primarily on three lines of argument. One argument claimed that the nature of the Lutheran Church and of the surrounding culture's democratic system demands that more equitable access to decision making be realized in the new church's practices. According to proponents, a more fair distribution of power cannot be delayed for poor reasons like the existing churches' continuing failure to achieve memberships more closely reflecting the demographics of the U.S. population. Since the merging churches had not accomplished inclusive decision making during their tenures, proponents concluded that assuring inclusiveness now must take priority over opponents' proposed competing values, such as congregations' freedom to choose whichever representatives they wanted. A second argument drew on historical evidence to prove that the merging churches' "good faith" and general commitments to inclusiveness had not succeeded sufficiently in the past. Proponents insisted that intentional action, such as a mandatory percentages system, was necessary if inclusiveness in church decision making ever was to be achieved in practice. Third, some proponents argued that a percentages system is desirable because it could bring a broader range of useful perspectives to decision making and so would actualize the abstract values of newness, unity, and inclusiveness in the new church.

Analysis of the Proponents' Argumentative Position

The discourse of CNLC percentages proponents illustrates how deontological ethicality and effectiveness may be aligned in an argumentative position. In advancing their position, proponents used an argumentative process conforming to the four duties of Johnstone's basic imperative. Furthermore, many of the features making the proponents' discourse ethical also made it effective according to Booth's rhetorical stance. While these aspects operated simultaneously and dynamically, for the purpose of analysis I will examine and exemplify them in turn.

In elaborating his ethic, Johnstone discusses two duties to self and two duties to others that an arguer performs in enacting the basic imperative. One's duties to self are resoluteness and openness. One's duties to those before or with whom one argues are compassion and gentleness. All four duties must be observed for one to argue in a manner maximally consistent with the basic imperative's call for a process perpetuating the human capacity to argue.

Proponents' arguments for inclusiveness percentages manifest observance of all four duties. First, the duty of resoluteness declares that one ought not capitulate helplessly to another's rhetorical demands; one has a duty to self to "take a stand and bring [one's] own persuasive powers into play with respect to propositions of which others are trying to persuade [one]" (Johnstone 1981, p. 310). Proponents were determined to demonstrate the need for an institutionalized plan to effect inclusive decision making. One woman of color used figures showing the current gender composition of recent church conventions to prove the need for a governance system based on more than "good faith" promises; she argued, "If it is an issue of trust, again I go to the polls, opinion polls, that were received where 11,000 were male and 4,000 were female at our conventions. This is trust!" At another CNLC meeting, an Hispanic clergyman expressed a similar conviction: "I believe in promise, but I also believe in things . . . I can see. We are leading by faith, but I'd like to see the figures, too." Proponents took a stand in demonstrating the practical lack of inclusiveness in current church decision-making bodies.

In the face of such an obvious lack of inclusiveness in the existing churches' decision making, other commissioners resolutely argued that the CNLC's role was to lead, even if this tack met some resistance. For example, one proponent argued,

> [T]here are times when the commission has to say to the entire church, "We were appointed to do a certain kind of job. We want you to get a certain signal. The signal that we want you to get from us is a leadership view. We intend for you to take it very, very seriously. . . . We've heard your signal; now we want to send this signal back to you." And that signal is that we intend that we should include persons of color in meaningful terms in the same way that we talk about lay persons and women.

Rejecting the law and gospel opposition as framed by the opponents, proponents determinedly showed that the need for inclusive decision making was so compelling that intentional action must be prescribed.

In refuting concerns about the practicality of inclusiveness percentages for people of color, proponents raised the problems with a less intentional system. One white male proponent used evidence of current practices to illustrate the problems of relying on a less deliberate system for achieving inclusive decision making:

> It seems to me, in every community in American life, there are people of color. They're there. And the only problem is they're completely invisible, because often we simply don't regard them as persons such as ourselves, and therefore we don't see them. And if you leave a loophole, what really happens is that you sit on your church council and suddenly you start looking at something like this, what you are required to do. And if there's a loophole, then you simply manage to get out of it. . . . I notice it in my own congregation, and we're in the inner city. We've never worried about minorities.

Another white male proponent, who held a decision-making position in an existing church hierarchy, stressed the need for resoluteness on this matter, even at the cost of creating some discomfort among those who traditionally exercised the churches' power positions. He demonstrated that he had listened to opponents' arguments and empathized, yet he also gently indicated that the percentages system must be instituted for inclusive decision making actually to occur: "And I think [the amendment to add 'where possible' to the directives for inclusiveness percentages] waters down the concept we are putting out, makes it too easy for any of us who are still struggling, even myself, are struggling . . . with the fact that maybe I have to give up my chair in order that either a woman or a person of color or other language might sit, because we cannot continue to put more chairs around the table." Commissioners of color agreed that, in their experience, "when needed, whatever possible would be used" to avoid including them in a meaningful way.

Although relying on "good faith" would be the more comfortable, less confrontational option, history clearly demonstrated that this alternative was inadequate to effect truly inclusive decision making at all levels of the church. As their arguments illustrate, proponents were determined to defend the position that they believed best insured that the theologically inclusive nature of the Lutheran Church would be reflected in its governance. They thus demonstrated resoluteness.

In ethical argument, resoluteness in using one's persuasive abilities to defend a position must be complemented by arguing with compassion for the others involved. According to Johnstone, compassion is the duty to listen to others' arguments more for their sakes than for one's own (1981, p. 310). One must not only be willing to persuade others, but also must remain open to being persuaded by them. CNLC proponents of percentages balanced their resoluteness with compassion. While resisting efforts to eliminate percentages altogether, proponents heard and responded compassionately to constituents' and opponents' contentions that it would be difficult to fulfill the proposed 20 percent goal for people of color, given the current membership composition. Although they had the votes to insist on their original plan, proponents consented to reduce this goal from 20 to 10 percent. Furthermore, their decisions suggest that proponents listened with compassion to arguments such as this one, which centers on protecting the present churches' staff members from feeling that their often lifelong contributions are being devalued on the basis of gender, race, language, or clergy status:

> I am a white male over fifty. I'm a colleague with a number of people serving three church bodies. I do not believe that each and every one of those persons is going to be chosen to be a staff member in the new church, but I do believe that the adoption of a statement such as this [one applying inclusiveness percentages

to the new church's staffing choices] will be a . . . signal that could be very detrimental and very injurious to the existing staff. . . . Therefore I have to speak against [the motion to apply the inclusiveness percentages to church staff positions] and then reiterate what I said at the beginning, making a strong commitment to being an inclusive church by adding strong personnel policies that will provide such inclusiveness, but asking you, my colleagues, not to vote for [percentages for staff positions] in respect to that which has been given as service by the Christian staff members of the three church bodies.

The arguer urges that inclusive staffing be achieved by means other than the strict inclusiveness percentages used for elected decision-making assemblies for the sake of those on whose behalf he speaks. And proponents agreed to compromise, exempting certain groups, such as the church staff, from specific inclusiveness percentages and allowing a grace period for the system to become operational. Thus, compassion as well as resoluteness characterized the proponents' comportment.

Johnstone's remaining duties to self and others are similarly complementary. The second duty to self is openness. Openness denotes one's duty to listen to and consider others' arguments for one's own edification; one ought not be impassive and self-centered (1981, p. 310). The proponent who admitted to struggling with the personal implications of inclusiveness percentages and the one who accepted responsibility on behalf of his own inner-city congregation for overlooking people of color in the past exemplify the practice of openness in arguing. Both apparently had listened to opponents' arguments and recognized their own complicity in the existing distribution of decision-making power.

Demonstrating openness from the viewpoint of one often excluded, one woman of color accepted opponents' statements that the church members were people of integrity and good faith. She interpreted the practical lack of inclusiveness in existing church decision-making structures in a gracious way, even as she urged the acceptance of the percentages system:

> I feel that, while there are many who do not intentionally include people of color and the others on their delegations, in their delegations, I feel that it's not always an intentional matter. But I think that there are still those who are, because of their comfortableness in that, they forget. And I think this would be a way of bringing to the forefront of their minds that they should be ever

mindful of those people around them who should be involved, who should be included.

At a different meeting, another proponent took a similar stand, balancing resoluteness with openness: "I do understand what X was saying and also, recognizing what X was saying, I would pray that there are some people, just like you said, who would not be aware of the need to include or involve people of color or other than English-speaking. And so, because of that, I would go back to the principle that's involved here. And I will also go back to the very, very specific and very prominent need our consciousness raises." Though they were not persuaded to reject their commitment to establishing a percentages system, these commissioners showed significant sensitivity to the opposition's arguments. Some appeared to rethink their interpretations of the current inequitable situation, rejecting outright attributions of evil intent to those currently in power in favor of allowing that forgetfulness, a lack of awareness, or simple inertia could perpetuate the existing state of affairs. While remaining open to new interpretations of motivation and to different assignments of responsibility for the current lack of inclusiveness, however, proponents still defended the necessity of inclusiveness percentages; in fact, benign footings for noninclusive behavior should be overcome even more easily than any malicious ones through a percentages system assuring the continuous practical recognition of the importance of effective inclusiveness.

Johnstone describes gentleness as the duty to influence others using persuasion instead of violence (1981, p. 310). Gentleness is the obverse side of openness as it concerns one's duties in persuading others more than those involved when being persuaded by them (Johnstone 1981, p. 310). As a rhetorical body with only the power to recommend, not mandate, its proposed design, the CNLC as a whole necessarily observed gentleness. In striving to include percentages in the design, however, proponents exceeded this minimum threshold of gentleness. Most important, proponents refused to simply force the percentages system into the new church design by majority vote. Throughout the CNLC's existence, the tenor of the debate suggested that a majority consistently favored some type of percentages system. The demographics of the CNLC provide additional evidence that the votes were available to force the percentages issue, had proponents so desired: the seventy-member commission included twenty-eight women and fifteen people of color, some of whom were also women, of course (Trexler 1991, pp. 45–46). Most of this group approved of an intentional percentages system for insuring inclusiveness in the new church's decision making. With the addition of those white male commissioners advocating inclusiveness percentages, proponents need not have taken such pains to explain, evidence, advocate, and compromise on the specifics of their proposal. However, a gentle approach was more consistent with their commitments to decisions by consensus, responsiveness to grassroots' input, and unity. Instead of using an actually or symbolically violent approach, proponents of percentages chose to argue in accordance with gentleness. Thus, proponents' argumentative position exhibits an internal harmony among Johnstone's basic imperative's four duties; compassion offset resoluteness, and gentleness balanced openness. This consonance speaks only to the argumentative position's deontological ethicality, however.

Having examined the proponents' arguments in terms of their internal balance on the issue of deontological ethicality, the next step is to evaluate the balance among the arguments' effectiveness elements. As argued earlier, effective rhetoric should manifest what Booth calls the rhetorical stance. The rhetorical stance depends on the discovery and maintenance of "a proper balance among the three elements that are at work in any communicative effort: the available arguments about the subject itself, the interests and peculiarities of the audience, and the voice, the implied character, of the speaker" ([1963] 1972, p. 220). If an arguer overemphasizes any one of these three elements, the equilateral triangle formed by an appropriate balance among the three points is distorted, blunting the discourse's effectiveness. For example, an arguer may rely so heavily on statements or information about the subject matter that he or she ignores the intended audience or underplays the relationship between the speaker and the audience (p. 221).[4] Consequently, the sense that arguments are made for a particular audience within a certain context and relationship is lost. Second, an advocate may overvalue the outcome of an argument and so undervalue its subject matter and implications for his or her implied character (p. 223). In this case, one distorts the triangle by excessively privileging the peculiarities and interests of a particular audience, willingly sacrificing some integrity and veracity in presenting arguments to get the desired results from the targeted auditors. Finally, an arguer's inordinate concern to draw attention to the self by concentrating disproportionately on exhibiting personality and charm detracts from a discourse's effectiveness (pp. 223–24). This third perversion of the rhetorical stance sacrifices the subject matter and the interests of the audience to the speaker's need for attention.

Conversely, when an advocate balances the available arguments, interests of the audience, and his or her own voice or implied character, his or her argumentative position has the best chance of being effective. The discourse of CNLC percentages proponents reflects a balance among the rhetorical stance's three elements, often through the same argumentative practices that display its deontological ethicality. While it is at least as awkward to treat Booth's three elements separately as it was to isolate the four individual duties implied by Johnstone's basic imperative, it is important for ultimately illustrating the evaluative process of alignment.

First, while remaining true to the evidence and the logical consistency of their position, proponents tempered their arguments with an eye toward the audience's concerns, their own implied characters, and the ongoing relationships among the people involved. From the set of available arguments, proponents chose those that not only resolutely expressed their position on percentages, but also showed respect for their auditors and concern for protecting a continuing relationship between proponents and opponents. For instance, as noted earlier there was overwhelming evidence that inclusive decision making was not the norm in the existing churches, more than enough to drive home harshly the point that "if we're not intentional about [a system of inclusiveness], we're just simply not going to do it! . . . [A]nd this basically then would, for all intents and purposes, shut the door on intentional representation of minorities within the church," if proponents so chose. However, recognizing that they all must work together in the new church, proponents avoided simply overpowering the opposition, either with a strong-arm vote or by bludgeoning them relentlessly with evidence of the power inequities within the existing churches. In the process, proponents avoided overt accusations of racism, sexism, and malicious intent, choosing instead the gentler approach of petitioning for a more equitable power distribution. For instance, one commissioner of color appealed, "[W]e [the people of color or primary language other than English] will have to find [a] sense that we belong to this church. And that's only what other people will grant." Another proponent's comment makes the balance of Booth's three elements especially clear: "There are men of good faith [in the church]. . . . We know the church has good faith now, but maybe down the line we need to remember to be reminded, and [a system of percentages] certainly will help make it secure." This argumentative approach allowed the opposition to save face and nurtured a positive relationship among arguers on different sides of the issue, even if the percentages system appeared in the final organizational design.

Because both factions agreed that inclusiveness was an important abstract value, the main point of contention was the means for its enactment in the new church. Although they could show historically that "good faith" alone was an ineffective means for achieving inclusive decision making, proponents did not rely solely on past evidence. In 1986 one commissioner pointed to the lack of inclusiveness evident in those portions of the ongoing merger process not governed by inclusiveness percentages. He stated,

> There is a saying in Puerto Rico that goes like this, "The way to heaven is paved with good intentions done." We all received the summary from X about the composition of the transition teams so far. It shows that, although . . . we have expressed our intentions, we are not really trying. It's not so easy . . . to change something that has been done for generations by other people. So we need something strong enough to mold people, something to break the inertia. A road can be made only if we are pushed.

This argument exemplifies how advocates offered persuasive arguments that did not violate their relationships with opponents or degrade those on the other side of the dispute. In fact, the advocate's use of "we" instead of "you" or "they" downplays the placement of blame in favor of promoting a collectively supported, affirmative response to the persistent lack of practical inclusiveness. With respect to the effectiveness balance internal to the rhetorical stance, then, percentages proponents did not overemphasize the subject matter at the expense of either the audience or their own voices.

Second, proponents also argued in ways that took into account the interests and peculiarities of their audience, without overvaluing pure effect. One illustration is their repeated grounding of arguments in sacred texts and principles that both sides valued. For example, one proponent referred to the belief that the nature of the church is inherently inclusive; he appealed to opponents' concerns that instituting inclusiveness percentages would conflict with other values, saying, "It seems to me if the inclusive principle is based on the nature of the church that the representative principle takes a second place to that principle." Another acknowledged opponents' contention that operating on "good faith" would be preferable, but indicated that, in the current imperfect world, gospel principles sometimes need the assistance of law to be fulfilled in practice:

> This is like building the kingdom of God. It is building a just ecclesiastical structure. And on that basis, I think we should be as intentional as possible with regards to the effecting of justice within the institution. Every single one of us deplores a quota of ten percent tithing in the Old Testament. And every single one of us preaches every Sunday for a goal of ten percent stewardship. In the kingdom of God, I want tithing among personnel comparable to our wallets.

This and similar arguments acknowledge the opponents' concern about the perceived tension between law and gospel, but indicate either that, in this case, law is necessary and/or that the law-gospel tension is germane only to matters of salvation, not church organization.

In addition to demonstrating the percentages system's congruence with the existing churches' understanding of sacred texts and principles, proponents' arguments stressed how instituting a percentages system also would enact other important values of concern to the whole commission (i.e., newness, unity). A woman of color commented, "[F]or me, [adoption or rejection of inclusiveness percentages] will have a great deal to do with whether this church is new or not." Another proponent commented similarly on the interaction between the CNLC's commitments to inclusiveness and newness:

> People turn to me and say, "What is this newness that we talk about in the church?" . . . One of the things that's going to make this church new in the next ten to twenty years is that there is going to be introduced into the decision-making process of this new church the views of women, the views of lay persons, the

views of minorities, of persons of color, in a way which I think
has not been done before. . . . [I]t offers the possibility for more
new ideas, more new perspectives; and that often means that,
after the discussion with a new perspective and new ideas, that
what you come out with may be just a little bit righter, a little
bit more fair, and it may be just a little bit closer to what we are
called to do in the mission of the church.

While acknowledging that percentages may produce some discord
initially, proponents implied that such an effective commitment to
inclusiveness ultimately would yield greater church unity because
those who currently feel excluded would gain a new sense of
belonging and participation.

Thus, without compromising the integrity of their subject
matter or their own implied characters, proponents adapted their
arguments to the interests and peculiarities of their audience and
the assumptions they shared with that audience. Furthermore,
proponents respected their opponents' contributions; this respect
is exhibited in the proponents' willingness to compromise on certain details, to try to understand the opponents' point of view, and
to eschew forcing percentages into the design rather than convincing opponents to accept the proposal. The way that the proponents argued also guarded the dignity of auditors who opposed a
percentages system. Proponents usually avoided an accusatory
tone, offered face-saving explanations for currently inequitable
power distributions, and sought to frame the inclusiveness issue in
a way that allowed opponents to embrace a percentages system
without admitting that their original position might have been
flawed.

The third element to be balanced with the rhetorical stance's
two other elements is the speaker's voice or implied character.
Again, proponents maximized the effectiveness of their position
by balancing their voices and personalities with the available arguments and the interests of the audience. In the case of the CNLC
inclusiveness debates, many proponents were from groups consistently under-represented in the existing church power structures.
Consequently, these advocates had firsthand experience in being
excluded from or under-represented in decision making, especially
at the upper echelons of the existing church hierarchies. While
such experience bestowed credibility on many of the proponents'
claims, it potentially could have made the percentages issue an
opportunity for revenge or personal celebrity. Though they easily

could have done so, proponents chose not to glorify the previous exclusion of groups they represented demographically at the expense of the broader subject matter or concern for the audience. Rather than accusing, they used their experiences to sensitize others to existing inclusiveness problems and the need for a more effective solution than "good faith" commitments. Proponents' characters also showed in the fact that these commissioners argued consistent with a deontological ethic; they rejected a "win at any cost" attitude, although they felt that they argued for a just cause. Finally, the willingness to be somewhat flexible on the specific percentages and their range of applicability illustrates how the proponents refused to be absolutists who would not consider counterarguments or the sensibilities of their audience. In these ways, proponents balanced the voice or character implied by their discourse with the available arguments and the needs of the audience. They refused to exploit their history of exclusion or extol their personal roles in the struggle for more inclusive decision making, preferring instead to work with integrity toward an effective future solution that their opponents could accept.

CONCLUSION

The discourse of CNLC inclusiveness percentages proponents exhibits two constellations of argument elements, each with its own internal balance. On the dimension of ethicality, proponents balanced their duties of resoluteness with compassion and of openness with gentleness. On the dimension of effectiveness, they balanced the available arguments, the interests and peculiarities of the audience, and the voice or implied characters of arguers; no single effectiveness element was stressed at the expense of the other two. Furthermore, the elements of the proponents' rhetorical stance were not only balanced but were also consistent with each other. When these three elements are not internally consistent, it blunts the effectiveness of even an argumentative position balancing its arguments, audience, and voice. To illustrate, in the sanctuary trial *U.S. v. Aguilar* the defense team used arguments characterizing their clients as law-abiding. However, the defense team undercut that message by resisting the judge at every turn, thus projecting a voice or character that appeared disrespectful of laws and authority. Although no one element was overemphasized, the defense attorneys' arguments and voice conflicted and so decreased their argumentative position's effectiveness (see Olson and Olson 1991).

More important for the purpose of this essay is consideration of the alignment between ethicality and effectiveness in the example analyzed. In this particular case, the very argumentative aspects that made the case for inclusiveness percentages ethical were the ones that simultaneously made it effective. While ethicality and effectiveness do not in practice join forces so well in every case, their integration makes arguments exemplary because that which makes them effective and that which makes them ethical are mutually supportive and often selfsame; neither internally balanced constellation of effectiveness elements or of ethical duties is simply tacked on in the service of the other. Interestingly, in this example, even the teleological goal of proponents' discourse is aligned with its deontological argumentative process. The proponents' telos was to insure a space in the new church for the future arguments of women, laity, and people of color. Inclusiveness percentages would perpetuate the opportunity for a diversity of voices to continue to be heard in the decision making of the new church. So, while it is the harmony between an argument's deontological ethicality and its effectiveness that makes it especially commendable according to my alignment standard, an argument synthesizing these two qualities sometimes also pursues a teleological end consistent with its deontological argumentative process.

Finally, it is important to note that the means people use to restrict the flow of argument can be ordered hierarchically. For example, the opponents of inclusiveness percentages implied that protecting congregations' freedom to choose whichever representatives they wanted also preserved open argument. While this position has merit, proponents' evidence indicated that such freedom had led in practice to significant exclusions of certain groups from the existing churches' argumentative and decision-making processes. Such de facto exclusion more seriously restricts participation in the argumentative process because it virtually eliminates, rather than only somewhat limiting, the participation of particular individuals or groups; thus, practical noninclusiveness is more confining than the restriction on freely choosing one's congregational representatives (i.e., the insistence that a certain proportion of delegates be women, lay people, and people of color) and so is a greater threat to a deontological argumentative process. Consequently, on this point, the proponents' argumentative position is more ethical than the opponents' because it better preserves access to the ongoing argumentative process for a broader range of arguers.

Although evaluating arguments will continue to be a challenge, the concept of alignment proposed here is one approach to the task worthy of further consideration and development. By examining the fit between deontological ethicality and effectiveness, as well as evaluating the internal balance among the elements constituting each constellation, alignment provides a relatively complete approach to argument evaluation. This approach avoids the main pitfalls associated with adopting teleological ethical standards or criteria that make rhetoric dependent on other disciplines and demands that one accept the responsibility of considering ethical concerns in conjunction with arguments' effectiveness rather than simply evaluating an argument by measuring its success with an audience.

REFERENCES

Aristotle. 1926. *"Art" of rhetoric.* Cambridge, Mass.: Loeb Classical Library.

Black, Edwin. 1970. The second persona. *Quarterly Journal of Speech,* 56, 109–19.

Booth, Wayne C. [1963] 1972. The rhetorical stance. In *Contemporary Rhetoric: A Reader's Coursebook,* ed. Douglas Ehninger. Glenview, Ill.: Scott, Foresman.

Brockriede, Wayne. 1972. Arguers as lovers. *Philosophy and Rhetoric,* 5, 1–11.

Charland, Maurice. 1987. Constitutive rhetoric: The case of the *peuple Québécois. Quarterly Journal of Speech,* 73, 133–50.

Commission Proposes Statement of Faith. 1984. 16 March. *The Lutheran Standard,* 23.

Haiman, Franklyn S. 1952. A re–examination of the ethics of persuasion." *Central States Speech Journal,* 3, 4–9.

Herrick, James A. 1992. Rhetoric, ethics, and virtue. *Communication Studies,* 43, 133–49.

Johnstone, Henry W., Jr. 1971. Some trends in rhetorical theory. In *The prospect of rhetoric,* ed. Lloyd Bitzer and Edwin Black. Englewood Cliffs, N.J.: Prentice-Hall.

———. [1973] 1978. Rationality and rhetoric in philosophy. In *Validity and rhetoric in philosophical argument: An outlook in transition,* ed.

Henry W. Johnstone, Jr. University Park, Pa.: The Dialogue Press of Man and World.

———. 1981. Toward an ethics of rhetoric. *Communication*, 6, 305–14.

Olson, Kathryn Marie. 1987. Toward uniting a fellowship divided: A dramatistic analysis of the constitution-writing process of the Evangelical Lutheran Church in America. Ph.D. diss., Northwestern University.

Olson, Kathryn M., and Clark D. Olson. 1991. Creating identification through the alignment of rhetorical enactment, purpose, and textually implied audience. In *Proceedings of the Second International Conference on Argumentation*, ed. Frans H. van Eemeren, Rob Grootendorst, J. Anthony Blair, and Charles A. Willard. Amsterdam: International Centre for the Study of Argumentation.

Plato. 1974. *The Republic*. New York: Penguin Books.

Staples, Mark A. 1983, 16 November. Our unfinished minority goals. *The Lutheran*, 4–6.

Thunderous Majorities for Union. 1982, 20 September. *Time*, 79.

Trexler, Edgar R. 1991. *Anatomy of a merger: People, dynamics, and decisions that shaped the ELCA*. Minneapolis: Augsburg Fortress.

White, James Boyd. 1984. *When words lose their meaning: Constitutions and reconstitutions of language, character, and community*. Chicago: University of Chicago Press.

CHAPTER 5

An Ethical Appraisal of Ronald Reagan's Justification for the Invasion of Grenada

Ralph E. Dowling and Gabrielle A. Ginder

On Tuesday, October 25, 1983, the U.S. military invaded the island of Grenada. A debate ensued concerning the justification for the attack. The Reagan administration, in attempting to justify the incident and win the support of the American people, gave three main reasons for the attack. First, it claimed that its primary goal was to protect Americans on Grenada who faced imminent danger. Second, it told the American public there was a strong communist threat on the island and that the attack was an attempt to preserve Grenada's democracy. Finally, the administration claimed that the United States had responded to a request from the Organization of Eastern Caribbean States (OECS) to help it maintain regional security.

Two questions arise: By what ethical standards should the administration's arguments be judged? Were these ethical standards upheld in the administration's public communication? The purpose of this essay is to answer these questions and to determine whether Americans could have based sound judgments about the invasion on the arguments offered by the administration.

The administration's arguments were the primary—if not sole—source of information for the public's use in making judgments about the invasion. In order to appraise the ethicality of those arguments, proper criteria must first be defined. Because the invasion was a political act, the proper criteria are those relevant to a democratic political system.

A democratic perspective on communication ethics must be grounded in the values inherent to democratic government. Thomas Nilsen (1958) defines four fundamental values in a democracy. First, the human personality is believed to have intrinsic worth. Second, reason is regarded as the instrument of individual and social development. Third, self-determination is regarded as the means to individual fulfillment. Fourth, human fulfillment of potentialities is seen as desirable. Ethical communication in a democracy is communication that fosters and respects these values.

A democratic orientation must reflect concern for both means and ends. Ends are considered ethical to the degree they reflect the values of the system. But, Nilsen notes, there is also a high regard for means. "When being persuaded a man [or woman] is not only influenced directly or indirectly in his [or her] choice of a course of action, he [or she] is influenced by his [or her] method of making the choice. . . . In a democratic society—I do not think this can be denied—the method of decision is vital. Whether we vote for a particular candidate in a particular election may not be momentous for democracy, but how we make up our minds about candidates is indeed momentous" (1958, pp. 242–43).

How are democratic values upheld to maintain ethical quality? Dennis Day claims that democratic debate, or, "the confrontation of opposing ideas and beliefs for the purpose of decision," serves as the technology of decision making in a democracy (1966, p. 5). The commitment to open democratic debate and to the values inherent to democracy suggests ethical guidelines useful in preserving democratic institutions.

First, in order for debate to provide sound decisions, all evidence must be disclosed to listeners, whether or not it supports the arguer's viewpoint. If evidence is concealed or withheld, listeners' ability to make sound judgments is inhibited. Second, arguments must be presented clearly so as to be understood by the audience. Unclear arguments and faulty reasoning do not produce sound judgments.

There is a third consideration for ethical guidelines in democracy. Nilsen states that when we communicate in order to influence opinions or actions, the "ethical touchstone is the degree of informed, rational, and critical choice—significant choice—that is fostered by our speaking" (1966, p. 38). Significant choice depends upon the speaker's concern with truth, which includes "good intentions, the ability to appraise evidence objectively, knowledge of facts, knowledge of values, and most importantly, the exercise of goodwill" (p. 16–34).

Finally, because arguments invoke some degree of emotion, the proper goal of ethical arguers is "not to dissociate emotion from reason, but (p. 49). In stimulating appropriate emotion, arguers must be conscious of the truth, good reasons, intentions, and values (chap. 2).

PROTECTION OF AMERICANS ON GRENADA

The primary justification offered for the invasion was Reagan's concern that the Americans on Grenada would be "harmed or held as hostages" by the new government of Grenada. This threat justified action because "our government has a responsibility to go to the aid of its citizens if their right to life and liberty is threatened" (Transcript). Our contention is that President Reagan lied when he suggested the invasion was undertaken primarily to rescue imperiled American citizens (primarily medical students) on Grenada. Our case for this contention rests on the logical inconsistency of Reagan's arguments, the lack of evidence for claims of danger to American citizens, the existence of a motive to lie, and evidence that Reagan may have manufactured evidence.

Protection Was Only a Cover Story

If Reagan knew there was little or no danger to the Americans on Grenada, and if his decision to invade was not made with their safety as his primary concern, then his use of the threat to the Americans was merely a "cover story" designed to give the invasion a veneer of legitimacy. Irving Kristol has clearly stated the ethical questions raised by Reagan's use of such a cover story: "One of the most distressing aspects of American foreign policy today is the felt need of our government to lie to the American people when it takes an action, or adopts a policy, that it believes to be necessary for the integrity of our national interests. The invasion of Grenada was a most illuminating case in point" (1985, p. A26).

Why did the United States invade Grenada? According to the White House and State Department, the main reason was the danger to American medical students in Grenada because of the political turbulence there. A review of the evidence demonstrates that this was not, of course, the real reason. Further, "we simply could have airlifted those students out instead of sending the Marines in" (Kristol 1985, p. A26). Thus, the use of the marines is evidence that a rescue was not the real motive for invading Grenada.

Logically, rescuers might be expected to go directly to potential victims, whose location was known. But, as Joseph Treaster (1984, p. A10) reports, the "rescued" Americans later said over thirty hours passed before the "rescuers" reached some Americans. And, the invasion and delay actually provided both the motive and the opportunity for the "enemy" to harm the Americans. The vice-chancellor of the medical school attended by most of the Americans noted, "If in fact they had wanted to take revenge on the United States for launching the invasion, they could have come on campus and shot students" (Treaster 1984, p. A10). Or, as a member of President Carter's National Security Council argued:

> Common sense would suggest that the Grenadian government knew that the U.S. was eager to find a pretext for an invasion, and taking hostages would have provided the best one. The government would be more likely to take hostages if there were an imminent or probable invasion than if the U.S. government was in direct contact trying to gain assurances of safety for U.S. citizens. So, *in that sense, an invasion would have endangered the lives of U.S. citizens rather than protected them.* (U.S. House 1984, p. 82)

While no one can say for certain if the invasion actually increased the danger to the Americans, the administration advanced no arguments regarding why an invasion, rather than a simple evacuation, was necessary. Even if an invasion were necessary to evacuate the Americans, an "evacuation, in any case, does not require an occupation" (Which Threat 1983, p. A26).

Even if the invasion did not increase the danger, there is reason to doubt there was ever *any* danger to the Americans. Grenada's government had every reason to protect the school and students, which provided millions of dollars per year to the small, financially troubled island, and "everyone in Grenada regarded the medical school as a major asset" (U.S. House 1984, p. 3). Indeed, the Grenadian government went out of its way to satisfy both the U.S. citizens and the U.S. government. Grenada's ruler called the chancellor and offered to open a supermarket and to provide the students with transportation, despite a twenty-four-hour curfew. He also "sent one of his officers to check that everything was O.K. and gave [vice-chancellor] Bourne his home phone number if there were any problems" (U.S. House 1984, p. 82).

In Reagan's arguments, fears of a Cuban-Soviet subversion of the Caribbean "were conveyed to the American people only in an undertone, with the emphasis going to those presumably endangered students" (Kristol 1985, p. A26). We agree that "the real reasons" for the invasion were "the fear of other Caribbean governments before a new and potentially troublesome Soviet puppet-state in their area, and our own fear of still another Soviet military base in our 'backyard'" (Kristol 1985, p. A26). If we are correct, the incongruity between reality and Reagan's rhetoric is ethically troublesome. Day claims all arguments must be clearly expounded when decisions are being made, arguing that a "decision is meaningful only if there are alternatives from which to choose; it is intelligent only if the alternatives are understood" (1966, p. 6). Because the alternatives were not shared clearly with the American public and not clearly understood, meaningful judgments about the invasion could not have been made.

If these were the real reasons for the invasion, then the "rescue mission" was a cover story. Reagan's motive for using a cover story was that he wanted to portray the invasion as consistent with international law. Because international law does not allow a nation to invade another nation when the invader dislikes the other nation's foreign policy, Reagan's people "found themselves in a position where they could not explain their action without seeming to violate principles the U.S. government had been expounding for decades . . . the principles of international law" (Kristol 1985, p. A26).

Reagan wanted a legal basis to justify an illegal act, and he wanted to avoid making himself appear hypocritical. The transparent cover story Reagan selected apparently was not effective. Kristol reported one wit's suggestion that the United States should scatter medical students in nations it might want to invade someday, and found the wit's "contempt for our official hypocrisy" to be "perfectly justifiable" (p. 26A).

Some evidence suggests that the administration was deliberately deceitful. Pastor reported that the medical school's chancellor "received a phone call from U.S. Ambassador to Barbados Milan Bish as well as from others in the State Department designed to elicit a statement from him that the students were in danger." These calls may have been "aimed at obtaining a pretext for invasion." The chancellor refused to make the statement because "he knew this was not the case" (U.S. House 1984, p. 81).

This is a violation of basic ethical standards. The administration attempted to justify the end (i.e., the invasion) by unethical means (i.e., the arguments it offered the public). A democracy focuses upon both means and ends. This trait is the essence of democratic decision making. As Day put it, "a democratic society accepts certain ends, i.e. decisions, because they have been arrived at by democratic means" (1966, p. 4). Thus, even if the invasion was a good thing, justifying it with misleading arguments and evidence was wholly unethical.

There were troubling inconsistencies in Reagan's statements about the threat to the Americans. Reagan spokesman Speakes "had said the day before the invasion . . . that there was no indication of danger to Americans. After the invasion, he said that they had been in danger." Defense Secretary Weinberger said, three days after the invasion, that "there were 'indications' from 'intelligence reports' of plans to take American hostages. But intelligence sources later said there was no clear evidence of such a threat" (Taylor 1983b, p. 20A).

Thus far, we have argued that Reagan's arguments about the dangers of a hostage situation were exaggerated and grossly violated ethical standards. However, if he completely lied about the threat to Americans, ethical norms were more clearly violated. The American public was reminded of the horrors of the 444–day hostage incident in Iran, and told that everything had been done to prevent a similar crisis. If there was no such threat, Americans' emotions and thought processes were manipulated, decreasing their ability to make rational decisions.

Unethical Evidence Used to Support the Cover Story

Given Reagan's perception that he needed to justify the invasion and the transparency of the legal veneer discussed above, one might have expected Reagan to be anxious to supply rhetorically and ethically sound evidence for his case. Instead, Reagan failed to collect or produce rhetorically and ethically sound evidence, suppressed or ignored relevant evidence, and failed to use or rebut good evidence not consistent with his cover story.

After examining the evidence surrounding the invasion as well as the administration's attempts to justify the invasion, Pastor concluded that "the Reagan Administration did not want to receive any information about the students from their parents, or from the Grenadian government unless that information reinforced their own fear they were in danger" (U.S. House 1984, p. 83). This is hardly the diligent examination of evidence we would condone as ethically sound. "More importantly, the Reagan Administration did not *seek out* such information" (U.S. House 1984, p. 83). Democratic ethical standards demand that all evidence be examined, whether or not it supports the arguer's position. Day claims that when making a decision there is "an overriding ethical responsibility to promote full confrontation of opposing opinions" (1966, p. 6). All evidence and arguments need to be considered. If evidence or arguments are concealed or not sought out, inadequate decisions will be made.

The administration also claimed to have evidence that it either never had or refused to produce. For example, to bolster its claim that the threat to the students was genuine, the Reagan administration "suggested at one point that it had obtained secret documents purporting to show that the Grenadian government considered taking U.S. citizens as hostages." However, despite the fact that this was the evidence for "one of the most effective points made by Secretary [of State] Shultz in his first press conference," skeptics were still asking in 1984, "Where is that evidence, and how reliable do U.S. political analysts judge it?" (U.S. House 1984, p. 82). That question can still be fairly asked.

The administration "repeatedly said that its assertions were supported by . . . 'a treasure trove of documents' captured by the invaders." In truth, there was "no evidence that a terrorist training base existed or that Cubans had planned to take over Grenada either in the documents released Friday or in any other materials made public by the administration" (Taylor 1983b, p. A19). Lewis (1983, p. A19) demanded to know, "Where is the evidence for these terrifying assertions?" Reagan officials acknowledged their credibility was damaged by failure to provide "detailed evidence" to support their "sweeping charges about Soviet and Cuban influence" in Grenada (Taubman 1983, p. A22).

The value of evidence to the audience of arguments is that the audience can evaluate its reliability. Unless it is produced for examination, it cannot properly be called evidence. After questioning the missing evidence, Pastor built a strong case that no threat to the students existed that justified the invasion (U.S. House 1984, p. 82). These issues are related. The strong case for the absence of a threat necessitated reciprocally good evidence and reasoning from Reagan, but Reagan provided only unsupported assertions.

Reagan made some effort to demonstrate the existence of a threat to the students. For example, Reagan noted the expressed fear and gratitude of the "rescued" students. Yet as Representative Dymally testified, the "anxiety level of the students was only raised after two American consular officers visited the island and, of course, after the invasion" (U.S. House 1984, p. 3). The absence of fear before the officers' visit is suggested by the fact that "even as late as the Monday before the attack, the students could have left, and few did" (U.S. House 1984, p. 58).

There is further evidence that there was no threat to the students. A telex sent to a meeting of the students' parents informed the parents that the students had held a meeting at which "only 10% of the students expressed a desire to leave." When this telex reached the parents' meeting, the parents "sent a cable to President Reagan informing him that their children were safe and asking him 'not to move too quickly or to take any precipitous actions at this time'" (U.S. House 1984, p. 80). Reagan neither presented, rebutted, nor explained this evidence.

The students and parents were not the only involved parties to see no threat requiring a rescue. Ambassador Shelton compared the competing evidence in this way:

> President Reagan's justification for the . . . invasion of Grenada was based on the threat to Americans on the island and the threat to the Caribbean by the Cuban-Soviet buildup. In regard to the former justification, there is no supporting evidence as yet. Quite the contrary, the vice-chancellor of St. George's Medical School . . . who was on the ground and in close contact with the Government of Grenada, believed that what would jeopardize American lives would, in fact, be a U.S. invasion. (U.S. House 1984, p. 58)

Pastor quoted two medical school officials who "agreed at the time and in retrospect that the safety of the medical students . . . 'was never in danger.'" and that "'From the point of view of saving our students, the invasion was unnecessary'" (U.S. House

1984, p. 83). Chancellor Modica called the invasion "very unnecessary" (McQuiston 1983, p. A20).

Besides failing to offer the best available support for his decision to invade, Reagan also failed to explain why a military invasion, rather than a simple evacuation, was necessary. An explanation seemed in order because there seemed to have been "*no effort by the administration to . . . arrange an evacuation of U.S. citizens*" (U.S. House 1984, p. 82). As Modica noted, "those students could have been lifted out of there today and tomorrow with arrangements we had made" (McQuiston 1983, p. A20).

The need for an explanation was increased when the *New York Times* reported that the captain of a Cunard liner had offered to evacuate the Americans when he made his scheduled stop in Grenada on Tuesday—the morning of the invasion (Smith 1983). No satisfactory explanation was ever offered. The White House said only that it "came to distrust the offer" agreed to by the Grenadian government (p. A1). In an effort to show that an evacuation by air was not possible, Speakes "stressed that the airport on Grenada had been closed on Oct. 24, thwarting any possibility that the Americans . . . could have been evacuated peacefully." Confronted with the testimony of witnesses who saw at least four planes take off that day, Speakes admitted his assertion had "proved to be false" (Taylor 1983b, p. A20).

Thus, we have shown that Reagan ignored critical evidence and used faulty evidence to support the invasion. Lack of evidence not only potentially misguided the public in judging the situation, but may have misguided the administration's own policy decisions. Faulty evidence diminishes the ability of arguers and their listeners to decide rationally. We have seen that democracy adheres to such standards as truth, freedom of dissent, and justice (Wallace 1955). These were the very values violated and ignored by the leaders of America's democratic system.

SAVING GRENADA FOR DEMOCRACY

Reagan also justified the invasion by arguing that it was necessary to save the people of Grenada from the "self-proclaimed band of military men" who had overthrown the Bishop government and left Grenada "without a government" (Transcript 1983). Reagan said one purpose of the invasion was to "help in the restoration of democratic institutions in Grenada" (Taylor 1983a, p. A19).

A critic must first ask how, or if, democracy can be installed or restored by force. Senator Moynihan, in fact, called the invasion an "act of war" and asserted that the United States had no right to "bring in democracy at the point of a bayonet" (Taylor 1983a, p. A19). Forced democracy would seem to be an oxymoron.

Since the Revolutionary Military Council (RMC) had seized power in Grenada on October 12 and the decision to overthrow it was made no later than October 23, a critic must ask how the United States can determine the antidemocratic nature of a regime that has been in power less than twelve days. Reagan's only response to this obvious question was an assertion that the Soviets and Cubans "assisted and encouraged the violence" that led to the killing of Bishop. However, he "made public no evidence that supports its suggestions of a Soviet or Cuban role in the killings" (Taylor 1983b, p. A20).

Pastor suspected that this precipitous invasion was motivated by Reagan's desire to make sure the new government never got an opportunity to show its legitimacy and authority. Pastor asked, "Is it possible that the 'marines got there just in time' before the new Grenadian government could prove to the international community that it was a government, and that it could assure the safety of U.S. citizens?" (U.S. House 1984, p. 84). If so, Reagan was, in essence, destroying potential evidence that might disprove his assertions about the RMC.

RESTORING SECURITY IN THE EASTERN CARIBBEAN

Reagan's third justification for the invasion was that the coup in Grenada posed a direct threat to the security of the Eastern Caribbean and an indirect threat to the security of the United States. As evidence of these threats, Reagan reported that the invasion was requested by the Organization of Eastern Caribbean States because those nations feared for their security. The treaty under which the OECS was formed then was used to color the invasion as legal.

The veneer of legality lent by invoking the OECS treaty was thin indeed. The translucency of this legitimizing position results from Reagan's apparent failure to abide by the treaty itself, the absence of a regional threat, opposition by other states in the region, clear violations of other agreements the United States has signed, and evidence that the United States rather than the OECS actually initiated the request.

OECS Treaty Misrepresented to "Legalize" Invasion

The OECS treaty allows for making "arrangements for collective security against external aggression" provided that its members' decision to do so is unanimous (Taylor 1983a, p. A19). Reagan asserted that "six members of the Organization of Eastern Caribbean States joined by Jamaica and Barbados" had asked for help (Transcript 1983). In fact, the decision was not unanimous as required, because two of the seven members abstained and Grenada was not given the opportunity to vote (U.S. House 1984, p. 3; Taylor 1983a). Not satisfied with lying to the public himself, Reagan had a deputy secretary of state repeat the lie in testimony before the House Committee on Foreign Affairs. Only minutes after a member of the committee pointed out the actual OECS vote, Dam spoke of "the concerns of the OECS as unanimously expressed to us" as a reason for the invasion (U.S. House 1984, p. 22).

This clearly violates the standards for ethical communication in a democracy. As Dennis Gouran has noted, "deliberate falsification of information released to the public, especially under circumstances involving the general welfare, is inappropriate and irresponsible" (1976, pp. 20–31). The administration spokesperson's false testimony regarding the unanimity of OECS support for the invasion was irresponsible, and could only have served to impede public decisions about the use of troops in Grenada, the welfare of Americans in Grenada, the future of Grenada and its people, and U.S. foreign policy.

There were other violations of the OECS treaty that needed explanations that were never provided. For example, the treaty's arrangements for collective security are only to be invoked against "external aggression," and Secretary Shultz "did not cite any threat of external aggression in Grenada." Additionally, three participants in the invasion (United States, Jamaica, and Barbados) were not members of OECS (Taylor 1983a).

The need for this legal justification was that the invasion clearly violated the charters of both the United Nations and the Organization of American States—both of which the United States has signed. The secretary of state's "suggestion that the [OAS] charter's provisions were inapplicable" prompted legal experts to say they were "baffled" (Taylor 1983a, p. A19). Two key questions were unaddressed. How would compliance with the OECS treaty alter OAS and UN provisions forbidding invasions, occupations, and similar attempts to meddle in the internal affairs of other nations? How could Reagan claim compliance when the unanimity and external aggression requirements of the treaty were not met and three nonOECS members took part in the invasion?

There Was No Threat to the Region

Other questions were to arise. For example, was there really a threat to the region to justify Secretary Dam's assertion that the administration "took seriously the concerns of the OECS" (U.S. House 1984, p. 22)? Reagan had good reason to doubt Grenada was a threat to its neighbors after the prime minister of Barbados said, "in the presence of the President of the United States . . . that the Soviets and Cuba did not pose a threat to the islands from Grenada" (U.S. House 1982, p. 44). Further support for the claim that there was no threat necessitating a U.S. invasion is found in the neighboring countries' thoughts before and after the invasion. Prior to the invasion, "four important members of CARICOM, the other major regional grouping . . . opposed the invasion." These nations "subsequently condemned" the invasion (U.S. House 1984, p. 3).

Without attempting to refute Reagan's characterization of the Soviet Union as an omnipresent "evil empire" fomenting trouble wherever it could, we must assert that Reagan made no apparent effort to present the sound arguments and relevant evidence to support his claim that Grenada's new regime threatened its neighbors. There is still no proof for Reagan's assertion that Grenada was a "Soviet-Cuban colony being readied as a major military bastion to export terror and undermine democracy" (Transcript 1983).

Reagan should have explained why Cuba needed a base in the Caribbean, since Cuba is in the Caribbean. Reagan offered no explanation of how the new government constituted a threat and no evidence of the threat. Even in House hearings held well after the invasion, Secretary Dam had a difficult time explaining these matters in this exchange with Representative Stephen Solarz of the committee on Foreign Affairs:

> MR. SOLARZ: In what way could Cuba have promoted or fomented subversion in any of the countries of the eastern Caribbean that they could not have done even without using Grenada? . . . [I]f they were going to slip arms into the countries or . . . train cadres from those countries, could they not train them in Cuba or find other means of slipping the arms into those nations?
>
> MR. DAM: Well, perhaps. But it is all the more convenient to be just a few miles away. And also, we have seen a pattern of "deniability." Shipping things through Cuba to hide the Soviet hand and shipping through Grenada to hide the Cuban hand, et cetera, et cetera. There are many advantages to the Cubans in having as many bases of operation as possible.
>
> MR. SOLARZ: In other words, you are saying that it would make it easier for the Cubans, but they could have done it in other ways.
>
> MR. DAM: Whether they could have done it successfully or not is the question. They could have tried, and I think to a certain extent they are trying. (U.S. House 1984, p. 21)

What are the "many advantages"? Surely the United States did not invade Grenada just to create a public relations problem and some inconvenience for Cuba. The president had a duty to present some sound arguments and evidence to show that the regional subversion he feared would have occurred and would have been exacerbated by the Cubans' use of Grenada as a base.

As we have seen, Reagan continually denied, ignored, or was unaware of key information relevant to his and the public's judgment of the invasion. He repeatedly cited the Cuban presence as a motive for his action, yet offered no evidence to prove Cuba was a threat. One cannot accept as true an assertion that has no supporting evidence—yet that is exactly what Reagan would have us do. He continually violated ethical norms in presenting wholly inadequate evidence.

Lacking evidence before the fact, Reagan tried to rely on evidence of Cuban militarization found after the fact. We now know that President Reagan exaggerated when he spoke of the warehouses on Grenada that "contained weapons and ammunition stacked almost to the ceiling" and when he referred to the Cuban workers at the airport as a "military force" that was "much larger" than the "several hundred" the United States expected (Transcript 1983). The day after Reagan's national address on the invasion, an admiral announced that there were "at least 1,100" Cubans on the island, all "well-trained professional soldiers." Just a few days later, the State Department accepted Cuba's announced figure of 748 as accurate, and a few days later the military announced that "most of the Cuban prisoners had been classified after interrogation as workers, with only about 100 'combatants.'" These "up and down fluctuations" in Pentagon estimates of Cubans present on Grenada "have not been explained" (Taylor 1983b, p. A20; Halloran 1983, p. A1).

Ted Finan and Stewart Macauley (1966) have developed principles that can assure that statements made by public officials do not violate citizens' rights to disagree and will be, to that extent, ethical. One of Finan and Macauley's major concerns is that statements should be justified by reliable data. The continual fluctuation in numbers concerning the presence of Cuban military personnel violates this ethical standard. The constant changing of the figures inhibited dissent because statements essential to a judgment changed so often.

Administration reports that "several warehouses full of modern Soviet and Cuban weapons were discovered on Grenada" were also suspect. The warehouses, in fact, were "no more than half-full, and many weapons were antiquated." Reporters allowed to enter the warehouses found "Korean War-vintage British Bren guns" and some "Marlin 30-30 rifles made in 1870" (Taylor 1983b,p. A20; Taubman 1983a, p. A22).

On the day after Reagan's national address, Admiral McDonald reported the existence of a "terrorist training base" and accused the Cubans of "planning to put their Government into Grenada." As evidence, the admiral referred to then-unseen documents purported to show that Grenada had signed an agreement for "341 more officers and 4,000 more reservists" to be sent by Cuba to "take over the island." Before these documents could be examined, a "senior Pentagon official" admitted that the 4,341 military personnel were to be Grenadians, not Cubans (Taylor 1983b, p. A20). The promised evidence again did not live up to its advance billing.

Our conclusion, consistent with that of the Senate Select Committee on Intelligence, is "that the Reagan Administration had exaggerated Cuba's role in Grenada." The committee found that the "evidence of Cuban activity in Grenada does not support claims that Cuba was on the verge of occupying the island or turning it into a base for the export of terrorism and revolution" (Taubman 1983a, p. A19).

The OECS Did Not Originate the Request for Help

In his address on the invasion, Reagan told the nation that he had been "awakened in the early morning hours" of the previous weekend with an "urgent request" from the "small peaceful nations" of the OECS that "needed our help" in restoring "order and democracy to Grenada" (Transcript 1983). Clearly he wanted to portray the invasion decision as both originating with the OECS and as a last-minute response to a crisis begun by the ouster of the Bishop government. However, there is some concrete evidence that the United States had long planned and desired an invasion of Grenada, and may even have initiated the request from the OECS.

The first piece of evidence is that former Secretary of State Haig had long ago suggested "that a U.S. invasion might be the best solution to all of our problems" (U.S. House 1984, p. 3). Second, "an emissary from the State Department traveled to Barbados, prior to the meeting of the OECS ministers, with a memorandum suggesting that a U.S. invasion was a possibility" (U.S. House 1984, p. 3). The prime minister of Barbados said an American official approached one of his aides on October 15, and offered U.S. help in launching an operation to rescue Mr. Bishop. Although he later recanted by saying he had "misspoken," the U.S. ambassador to France on October 26 called the invasion "an action which had begun two weeks ago" (Taylor 1983b, p. A20). Perhaps, then, the "OECS request was drafted in Washington and conveyed to the Caribbean leaders by special American emissaries" (U.S. House 1984, p. 84).

Third, "U.S. ships were diverted to the region on October 20, even before the Caribbean leaders met" (U.S. House 1984, p. 84). Fourth, if the alleged threat to the Americans on Grenada was manufactured by Reagan, as we have previously argued, the case for deception is strengthened. Fifth, and finally, U.S. naval exercises held in 1981 indicate the possibility of a long-standing U.S. desire to invade. In the late summer of 1981, "U.S. military forces conducted exercises calling for the invasion of 'Amber and the Amberines,' a leftist country in the Caribbean that had seized American residents. The scenario unsettled the people of Grenada and the Grenadines" (U.S. House 1982, p. 92). These bits of evidence do not, of course, prove that the United States initiated the OECS request. They do, however, oblige the administration to provide a direct response. No such response has been provided to date.

Although, as Kristol (1985, p. A26) has noted, the threat to the region was expressed to the American people "only in an undertone," we are not surprised that the threat was portrayed as of communist origin. We have already discussed the direct threat to the region, but we have not yet dealt with Reagan's portrayal of the threat posed by the Point Salines airport under construction on Grenada.

Grenada Was No Threat to the United States

The Reagan administration had a long record of offering poor evidence and arguments regarding the threat posed to the United States by the airport. Grenada's airport seemed the most likely referent when Reagan spoke vaguely of "far away places" that can threaten "our national security." At least his description matched his ominous description of that facility given long before the invasion (Transcript 1983).

The administration had been asserting for some time that the airport was "being built by the Cubans for military rather than economic development purposes," when, in fact, an American company was the principal contractor for the project and "most of the money [came] from nonCuban sources" (U.S. House 1984, pp. 7, 16, 50). The administration's claim that there was no "economic justification" for the construction of the airport was used to suggest that it was a military project that threatened the United States although Reagan has never satisfactorily responded to Shelton's claim that the airport was being built by Grenada "to facilitate expansion of tourism," which was a "pillar of Grenada's economy." As Shelton noted, "every small island in the eastern Caribbean would give its eyeteeth to have Grenada's new international airport" (U.S. House 1982, pp. 38, 44–45, 58).

Grenada's tourism industry had long suffered from the absence of a large airport, without which tourists from America were forced to land in Barbados or Trinidad to take a small plane or boat to Grenada. Dellums saw the airport as having "the greatest development potential for Grenada" and noted that the European Economic Community, the World Bank, and "others of the international community" viewed the airport as "a priority undertaking for the survival of the country." Reagan's suggestion that the airport was larger than necessary for commercial purposes was answered by noting that the airport would be "the same length as the airport on the neighboring island of St. Vincent and on the island of Trinidad [and] smaller than that on Barbados" (U.S. House 1982, pp. 20, 49, 83).

Regardless of the airport's potential economic benefits, a case could be made that the airport was also a military threat. Following his own investigation, Representative Dellums thought it "absurd" and "totally unwarranted . . . to charge that this airport poses a military threat to the United States national security." Dellums visited the Atlantic fleet and left "with the absolute impression that nothing being done in Grenada constitutes a threat to the United States or her allies." The fleet commander "had no concern" over the airport. Dellums, "fully briefed by high level officials" of the Air Defense Command, was "assured that the airport . . . is of no consequence" to the United States and that it had "not now or ever presented a threat to the security of the United States" (U.S. House 1982, pp. 17–18, 20, 83).

There are two troubling inconsistencies in Reagan's portrayal of the threat posed by the airport. The first is in the nature of the threat. In 1982 the State Department and the Pentagon were arguing that the airport would be used by the Cubans as a staging area for their troops in South America and Africa (U.S. House 1982, pp. 16, 29). However, when Cuban military supplies suitable for transshipment to Cuban troops in those areas were found on Grenada, those supplies were used as evidence that a Cuban occupation of Grenada was planned.

The second inconsistency was over whether or not a strategic threat to the United States existed that could have justified the invasion. In 1982 Reagan appointees were expressing concern that the airport could be used as a servicing stop for Soviet bombers and as a base for the spread of communist (antiAmerican) influence in the region (U.S. House 1982, pp. 16, 29). Yet Reagan spoke of the communist threat in an undertone in 1983. In fact, Reagan's State Department told the Foreign Affairs Committee that the invasion had nothing "whatsoever to do with any strategic or geopolitical considerations" (U.S. House 1984, p. 22). Any hints of a threat to the United States must have been designed to mislead the public, since the president's official position was that such a threat was not relevant to the invasion.

THE BIG LIE?

Perhaps the worst lie told by the Reagan administration involved the attempt to make the American people and the world believe that the invasion had not been planned by the administration for quite some time when, in fact, it had been. The evidence for this being a deception is, admittedly, inconclusive. We have already seen that Secretary Haig had long said a U.S. invasion would solve the problems created by the Bishop regime on Grenada. We have seen that the administration was hostile to Grenada for quite some time. We have seen that the administration conducted provocative military exercises near Grenada. We have seen that an invasion and occupation were not needed to rescue stranded Americans on Grenada. We have seen that the administration may have been the source of the OECS request for U.S. assistance. We have seen that naval forces were directed to Grenada before the OECS requested U.S. assistance. We have seen that the administration worked to create evidence that would provide a plausible pretext for an invasion. And we now know the administration "understated the amount of planning that the administration had done before a formal request" from the OECS provided "one of the main stated legal justifications for [the invasion]" (Taylor 1983b, p. A20).

The question is whether the creation, suppression, and misrepresentation of evidence were done solely to provide a pretext to implement invasion plans made months or years before the RMC ousted Bishop. If so, the biggest lie of all was Reagan's denial of any such plan and elaborate attempts to portray the invasion as an unplanned response to an emergency.

Reagan's denial of a plan to invade was voiced in testimony before a House subcommittee in 1982. Grenada was taken to task because it had "charged on numerous occasions and without a shred of evidence that the United States is preparing an invasion of Grenada" (Bosworth 1982, p. 77). In retrospect, Reagan's report that his military planners had to work "around the clock to come up with a plan" for the invasion after the OECS request is not credible (Transcript 1983). The planning for the invasion apparently began long before the request was made.

CONCLUSION

"Ethical issues are inherent in ... communication ... to the degree that the communication can be judged on a right–wrong dimension, involves possible significant influence on other humans, and to the degree that the communicator consciously chooses specific ends sought and communicative means to achieve those ends" (Johannesen 1990, p. 2) Because the Reagan administration attempted to influence the American public by consciously choosing and communicating arguments and evidence, ethical issues are inherent in analyzing the rhetoric surrounding this invasion.

We have seen clearly that the four criteria for democratic ethical standards have been violated. The first criterion requires that all relevant evidence be disclosed. We have shown that "significant facts" were withheld from the American public (Taylor 1983b). The second criterion requires that all arguments be clearly presented and understood. We have concluded with Taylor (p. A20) that the administration "disseminated inaccurate information" as well as "many unproven assertions." Democratic ethics also require that individuals be allowed to make rational, well-informed choices. Since the American public was deliberately deceived, its ability to make significant choices was impeded. Finally, democratic standards require only appropriate emotion be used. Here, again, the Reagan administration failed by consistently appealing to fear for the safety of the Americans and the threat of communism as justifications for the invasion, when neither was justified. With the Iranian hostage crisis still fresh in American minds and world crises having prompted a national state of anticommunist fervor, a more calculated appeal to unchecked emotion would be difficult to imagine.

We have provided evidence for our inferences about the intentions and motives of the administration. We agree with Taylor that some factual errors can be attributed to "the confusion of a combat situation" while others "involved selective and incomplete reporting" or "deliberate distortions and knowingly false statements of fact" that were intentionally "designed to put Administration actions in a favorable light" (1983b, p. A20). We have not taken the government to task for the former, and many reported errors were omitted from this analysis for that reason.

The very nature of democracy depends upon the principle of representation. Representatives are elected to make decisions for the public good. Regardless of the validity of the decisions made, the American public has the right to know what actions were taken and why. Only then will the public be able to make judgments about actions taken and decide who its representatives will be. If the American public cannot trust its government, the very foundations of democracy are shaken. If democratic standards are to be upheld, leaders must set an example. If leaders withhold or distort information, they are responsible for manipulating the public and for violating the standards and values for which democracy stands. Wise expressed the threat to democracy as follows: "The American system is based not only upon formal checks and balances. . . . it depends also, perhaps most importantly on a delicate balance of confidence between the people and the government. . . . If the governed are misled, if they are not told the truth, or if through official secrecy and deception they lack information on which to base intelligent decisions, the system may go on—but not as a democracy" (Wise 1973. p. 18).

We believe that a number of important and fundamental ethical issues are involved in Reagan's exclusion of journalists from Grenada during the invasion and severe restrictions on their fact-gathering abilities for quite some time after the invasion (Lewis 1983; Burnham 1983; Weinraub 1983). These issues deserve a more comprehensive treatment than we can give them here, perhaps as part of an analysis of all of the "information-control actions" used by the Reagan administration "against the right of the public to obtain information" (Burnham 1983, p. A21).

The perennially dismal level of trust Americans have in their political leaders may be justified, particularly if this incident is typical of their leaders' communicative behavior. This study does not reveal how typical this incident is of the Reagan administration, of American presidents, of foreign policy rhetoric, or of any other general phenomena of which this incident is an example. A few related studies do shed some light on these questions (Hahn

1980; Johannesen 1985; Green and MacColl 1983). This study also does not speculate about what this episode says about the U.S. public, U.S. journalists, or other branches of the U.S. government and their respective performance of their roles in American democracy.

As we have examined in the previous pages, the standards and values of a democracy were violated in the postinvasion rhetoric. Arguments and evidence that were distorted and withheld inhibited the American public's ability to appraise the invasion fairly. Future administrations must recognize their responsibility to the American public. For it is only when that responsibility is recognized that democracy can function as it should.

REFERENCES

Bosworth, Stephen W. 1982, October. Grenada. *Department of State Bulletin*, 75–77.

Brandt, Richard B. 1959. *Ethical theory: The problems of normative and critical ethics*. Englewood Cliffs, N.J.: Prentice-Hall.

Burnham, David. 1983, November 3. Curbs on Grenada news coverage criticized in House hearing. *New York Times*, A21.

Day, Dennis G. 1966. The ethics of democratic debate. *Central States Speech Journal*, 17, 5–14.

Finan, Ted, and Stewart Macauley. 1966. Freedom of dissent: The Vietnam protests and the words of public officials. *Wisconsin Law Review*, 48, 632–723.

Gouran, Dennis. 1976. Guidelines for the analysis of responsibility in governmental communication. In *Teaching about Doublespeak*, ed. Daniel Dietrich. Urbana: National Council of Teachers of English.

Green, Mark, and Gail MacColl. 1983. *There he goes again: Ronald Reagan's reign of error*. New York: Pantheon.

Hahn, Dan F. 1980. Corrupt rhetoric: President Ford and the *Mayaguez* affair. *Communication Quarterly*, 28, 38-43.

Halloran, Richard. 1983, October 31. U.S. reduces force in Grenada by 700. *New York Times*, A1, 10.

Johannesen, Richard L. 1990. *Ethics in human communication*. 3d ed. Prospect Heights: Waveland.

———. 1985. An ethical assessment of the Reagan rhetoric. *Political communication yearbook 1984*, ed. Keith R. Sanders, Lynda Lee Kaid, and Dan Nimmo. Carbondale: Southern Illinois University Press.

Kristol, Irving. 1985, June 21. International law and international lies. *Wall Street Journal*, 26.

Lewis, Anthony. 1983, October 31. What was he hiding? Editorial. *New York Times*, A19.

McQuiston, John T. 1983, October 26. School's chancellor says invasion was not necessary to save lives. *New York Times*, A20.

Nilsen, Thomas R. 1966. *Ethics of speech communication.* New York: Bobbs Merrill.

———. 1958. Free speech, persuasion, and democratic press. *Quarterly Journal of Speech, 44,* 235–43.

Smith, Hedrick. 1983, October 27. Reagan aide says U.S. invasion forestalled Cuban arms buildup. *New York Times*, A1, 21.

Taubman, Philip. 1983a, October 30. Senators suggest administration exaggerated its Cuba assessment. *New York Times*, A22.

———. 1983b, November 1. The reason for invading. *New York Times*, 1, 17.

Taylor, Stuart. 1983a, October 26. Legality of Grenada attack disputed. *New York Times*, A19.

———. 1983b, November 6. In wake of invasion, much official misinformation by U.S. comes to light. *New York Times*, A20.

Transcript of Address by President Reagan on Lebanon and Grenada. 1983, October 28. *New York Times*, A10.

Treaster, Joseph B. 1984, October 28. Danger to Grenada students is still debated. *New York Times*, A10.

United States Congress, House Committee on Foreign Affairs. 1982. *United States policy toward Grenada.* Washington, D.C.: U.S. Government Printing Office.

———. 1984. *U.S. military actions in Grenada: Implications for U.S. policy in the Eastern Caribbean.* Washington, D.C.: U.S. Government Printing Office.

United States Department of State. 1983, December. Grenada: Collective action by the Caribbean peace force. *Department of State Bulletin,* 67–82.

Wallace, Karl. 1955. An ethical basis of communication. *The Speech Teacher, 4,* 1–9.

Weinraub, Bernard. 1983, October 29. U.S. press curbs: The unanswered questions. *New York Times*, 1, 7.

Which Threat in Grenada? 1983, October 26. Editorial. *New York Times*, A26.

Wise, David. 1973. *The politics of lying: Government deception, secrecy, and power.* New York: Random House.

CHAPTER 6

"I Respectfully Dissent": The Ethics of Dissent in Justice O'Connor's Metro Broadcasting, Inc. v. FCC Opinion

Jeffrey L. Courtright

> There never should be a dissenting opinion in a case decided by a court of last resort. No judge, lawyer or layman should be permitted to weaken the force of the court's decision, which all must accept as an unappealable finality. The decision should be that of the court, and not of the judges as individuals. The judges should get together and render a decision settling the points in controversy. The decision rendered should not reflect the opinion of this judge or that judge, but should be the opinion of the court. . . . Nothing of any benefit to the public can be gained by a dissenting opinion. (Wollman 1898, pp. 74, 75)

During the past century, the appearance of written dissent at the Supreme Court level has been both criticized and lauded by members of the legal community (e.g., Bennett 1991; Bergman 1991; Bowen 1905; Evans 1938; Rogers 1931; Stager 1925). Before that time, however, Chief Justice John Marshall made it a matter of policy to present a unified Court to the American public (Courtright 1991). Justices since have been divided on the appropriateness of public, written dissent (Brennan 1986; Douglas 1948; Hughes 1928; Kelman 1985; Powell 1918; Stone 1942).

Some members of the legal profession have expressed extreme viewpoints. Writes William Hirt, "Dissenting opinions do not contribute to the development of the law" (1960, p. 258) except in rare cases. In contrast, Matthew Bergman maintains that "[d]issenting opinions provide a talisman of where the Court is heading from which both the bench and bar can take their bearings in subsequent cases" (1991, p. 86). Some dissents actually become the basis for later reversal (indeed, many have noted the prophetic character of judicial dissent [e.g., Bartanen 1987]). Yet most remain footnotes to jurisprudence. Given the disparate reviews the publication of dissents has received, critics of legal argument well might contribute to the estimation of their value.

Although rhetorical critics and legal scholars have approached dissents as discourse in some small measure (Bartanen 1987; Campbell 1979; Corso 1981; Rodgers 1979; Vibbert 1987), none have recommended a standard to evaluate their worth. Legal scholars generally have limited evaluations of dissent to studies celebrating some "Great Dissenter" (e.g., Beth 1955; Ray 1988). Because the legal community is polarized as to the appropriateness of dissenting arguments being written at all, I suggest an *ethical* standard for the judgment of dissents, adapted from the writings of Henry Johnstone Jr. (1981). This standard defines four criteria: resoluteness, openness, gentleness, and compassion.

The selection of one or several dissents from Supreme Court case law poses great difficulties since so many have been filed in the past two centuries. The frequency of written dissent has increased dramatically since passage of the Judiciary Act of 1925 (Halpern and Vines 1977; Walker, Epstein, and Dixon 1988). Thus reasonable samples of multiple dissents yield far from generalizable results (e.g., Corso 1981; Courtright 1991; Levin-Epstein 1978; Rodgers 1979). Instead, a case study is more suitable for a demonstration of how ethical standards such as Johnstone's might be applied to argumentation. Sandra Day O'Connor's dissent in *Metro Broadcasting, Inc. v. FCC* (1990) exemplifies the kind of controversial opinion that draws both positive and negative commentary, thus meriting such critical analysis.

To illustrate Johnstone's "ethics of rhetoric" as an interpretive tool in the analysis of argumentation, several steps are in order. First, I review the rhetorical situation to which O'Connor brings her argumentative stance in *Metro*. Second, I discuss the problems the publication of Supreme Court dissent raises and introduce

Johnstone's four ethical criteria as they might be applied to the situation Supreme Court dissenters generally face. Third, I illustrate how O'Connor's opinion meets Johnstone's ethical criteria and his writings on rhetoric and argumentation quite generally. The chapter concludes by contrasting O'Connor's dissent with that of Justice Anthony Kennedy. O'Connor's *Metro* opinion thus serves as an exemplar of what constitutes good dissenting argument.

JUSTICE O'CONNOR AND THE QUESTION OF AFFIRMATIVE ACTION

Metro Broadcasting, Inc. v. FCC (1990) brought before the Supreme Court questions regarding the constitutionality of two affirmative action measures that the Federal Communications Commission had implemented to promote minority ownership of broadcast facilities. First, the commission chose to give preference to minority applicants in competitive applications for licenses of new radio or television stations. Second, broadcast licensees who face a license revocation hearing before the commission normally may not transfer the station prior to the hearing. Under a "distress sale" policy, the commission permitted licensees facing such a situation to sell the station to a minority for up to 75 percent of the station's value.

The two minority preference policies originally were challenged separately. Metro Broadcasting, Inc., had challenged the award of a new television license to Rainbow Broadcasting, since the minority ownership of Rainbow outweighed competitive factors favoring Metro as an owner. While the case was under review, the commission had terminated an inquiry into the validity of this practice due to lack of appropriations from Congress. The FCC's subsequent grant of the license to Rainbow then was reaffirmed by the Court of Appeals. In a second case, under a "distress sale" policy, Shurberg Broadcasting of Hartford, Inc., challenged the sale of Faith Center, Inc.'s television license to Astroline Communications Company Limited Partnership. Once the minority policy inquiry was closed, the commission reaffirmed its decision in favor of Astroline. The Court of Appeals reversed, ruling that Shurberg's right to equal protection under the Fifth Amendment had been violated.

The cases were united on appeal to the Supreme Court. The FCC argued that the policies served a compelling government interest, that is, to ensure broadcast diversity of viewpoints. Justice Brennan, writing for the majority, held that the policies bore the stamp of longstanding congressional approval, and therefore did not require an analysis of "strict scrutiny." Under a lower standard of analysis, the Court thus deferred to the FCC in the assessment of a nexus between minority ownership and the expression of diverse viewpoints. Brennan argued further that the link between ownership and diversity did not rest on impermissible stereotyping. The majority concluded that the minority ownership policies were substantially related to the goal of promoting broadcast diversity, and therefore were constitutional. Justice Stevens filed a brief concurring opinion, emphasizing that the specific elements required to establish the relationship between the minority classification and the goal of broadcast diversity were met without stigmatizing the minority owner in any way.

In an apparent about-face from his position in *City of Richmond v. J. A. Croson Co.* (1989), Justice Byron White joined the four minority justices in the latter case to form the majority in *Metro.* This placed O'Connor in the awkward position of disagreeing with a majority that relied, in part, on her plurality opinion in *Croson,* which rejected a municipal minority set-aside program under a heightened level of scrutiny. Briefly, O'Connor argued that racial classifications such as those in *Croson* and *Metro* were both subject to strict scrutiny. She found the *Metro* majority's arguments for an intermediate level of scrutiny to be counter to previous treatment of congressionally mandated affirmative action. Then, after illustrating how the FCC's policies would fail a strict scrutiny analysis, she proceeded to show how the policies failed to meet the lower level of analysis employed by the majority.

Justice Kennedy, also in dissent, was highly critical of the *Metro* majority, and compared its opinion to *Plessy v. Ferguson* (1896), the case in which the "separate but equal" doctrine was upheld, and to South African apartheid laws. Kennedy's dissent has been described as "trenchant" (Haggard 1990, p. 78) and "a scathing attack" (Sedler 1990, p. 1230) on the majority.

Assessments of O'Connor's performance in the *Metro Broadcasting* case have been somewhat mixed. Patricia Williams faults both the majority and minority for clouding the issues at stake: "There was a covert adjectival war taking place in *Metro Broadcasting*, in which words were inflated like balloons in order to make the issue of diversity large or trivial, compelling or merely important, natural or monetary, grandly futuristic or of the local past" (1990, p. 526). Thomas Haggard, in contrast, speaks of the consistency of O'Connor's views on affirmative action: "Her opinions *Croson* and *Metro Broadcasting*, rather, are now firmly based on fundamental principles of constitutional law, which she applies logically, rigorously, and without equivocation. When you cut through all the legal technicalities and details, her position is simple and clear" (1990, p. 87). Charles Fried acknowledges merit in both Brennan's and O'Connor's opinions, but these competing views leave the adjudication of affirmative action cases in flux: "But sooner or later the Court will have to choose between his [Justice Brennan's] collectivist perspective and Justice O'Connor's liberal, universalistic vision" (1990, p. 127).

Clearly, O'Connor's efforts in affirmative action are important. Yet legal scholars are divided as to the merit of her arguments. Perhaps an appreciation of her position might be found in a different field of argument (e.g., legislative hearings, public forums). Because of her role as the first woman justice on the Supreme Court, however, O'Connor's opinions on affirmative action have been obscured by seemingly greater concerns expressed in the popular press: the development of O'Connor's role on the Court, both as "freshman" justice (e.g., Justice O'Connor Carves Own Niche 1982; Scheb and Ailshie 1985) and "swing vote" (e.g., Ingwerson 1991; Skene 1989), and the impact of her vote on the abortion controversy (e.g., Gest 1991/1992).

Despite the media's preoccupation with these topics, Ingwerson maintains that O'Connor's "strongest stamp" on the Court is "developing in two areas of legal doctrine: establishment of religion and affirmative action" (1991, p. 12). Just as O'Connor's opinions on religion have articulated a narrow approach to a difficult area of adjudication (Courtright 1992), each opinion she has written regarding affirmative action has developed and refined a similarly narrow approach (Haggard 1990). In recent religion clause cases, O'Connor has written majority opinions or has concurred with them. However, the *Metro* opinion places her in the minority and presents the difficulties all Supreme Court dissenters face.

THE ETHICS OF DISSENT AND A JOHNSTONIAN APPROACH TO ARGUMENTATION

Jurisprudentially, a written dissent has little immediate impact on a given case. Dissenters have failed to convince their colleagues that their rationales are correct. The question may be asked, then, Why do justices file an opinion? Historically, some dissents have led to legislative correction, constitutional amendment, or an eventual reversal of the majority opinion by a future Supreme Court. But the majority of dissents seem to fall on deaf ears.

Dissents may seem ineffectual, in part, due to the fact that any majority opinion, provided that it is never overturned by a later case, enjoys the status of *stare decisis*, the "policy of courts to stand by precedent and not disturb settled point" (*Black Law Dictionary* 1979, p. 1261). When the facts in a subsequent case are essentially similar to those in an earlier one, the decision in the earlier one controls the decision in the later one. The establishment of the majority opinion as precedent is important to the credibility of the majority and of the Court itself, for "[t]hrough the use of *stare decisis* justices enhance their appearance of impartiality and strengthen perceptions of the continuity of the democratic system" (Bartanen 1987, p. 247). As a result, the dissent at best may weaken the majority opinion's claim as good law or obscure its meaning. Yet a positive reflection may obtain. Dissents can test the soundness of the majority's reasoning and can explain or clarify the meaning of the opinion. The presence of a dissent may draw greater attention to it (Wasby 1978).

The dissenter thus faces a dilemma: Can the publication of a dissent serve some purpose, present or future, without endangering the credibility of the current Court as a governmental body? If so, how can dissenters ethically approach present and future audiences to fulfill that purpose?

A Johnstonian View of the Dissenter's Purpose

Traditionally, legal scholars and commentators have suggested that dissenters have a limited function in the workings of the

Court. Having failed to convince their immediate colleagues, justices file a written dissent to persuade other audiences (e.g., state legislatures, Congress, future Supreme Court justices) that change is necessary. Such a contention ignores the service that a dissent performs for the immediate Court as an organization. Dissenters actually may justify their minority vote to themselves, and then file a written opinion in order to defend that vote before their colleagues and other interested parties. Johnstone's view of rhetoric and argumentation encompasses these concerns for self-persuasion and persuasion directed toward others.

Basic to Johnstone's approach to communication is a definition of *rhetoric* that presumes argumentation: rhetoric is "the evocation and maintenance of the consciousness required for communication. . . . Rhetoric, furthermore, studies the strategy of altering attitudes *in the service of propositions*. . . . Since it is communication that transmits propositions, rhetoric is thus the adjunct of communication" (Johnstone 1970, p. 121). Rhetoric, however, is distinct from communication in that

> it will focus not on propositions as such but upon the sentences that most effectively present them to others. Propositions need not be believed to be understood, and communication, in the weakest sense, solicits only the understanding of propositions; but rhetoric solicits belief first in the expectation that understanding will follow. Communication in the strongest sense essentially conveys information, but rhetoric essentially seeks to stimulate action, including the action of adopting a recommended belief. (Johnstone 1978, p. 64)

Communication, therefore, is the action that results from rhetoric. Rhetoric solicits action through gaining the attention of other minds: "[R]hetoric is fundamentally a *wedge* between a percipient and an object of perception" (Johnstone 1978, p. 139; see also Arnold 1987; Johnstone 1987, 1990; Yoos 1987).

Because of the breadth of this understanding of rhetoric, communication and the propositions developed in service to it may be the result of, in Johnstone's words, a "self-reflexive rhetoric" (1970, p. 127). Since rhetoric evokes and maintains the consciousness required for communication, according to Johnstone, rhetoric is as much intrapersonal as it is interpersonal. Thus rhetoric brings ideas to mind and reinforces personally held beliefs. The self is as much open to persuasion as are others to whom persuasion is directed.

Dissents indeed may perform both functions. The simplest purpose for a written dissent's existence may be to justify a justice's dissenting vote: "They [dissents] are the only means which a conscientious official has of recording his views in a case upon which he is required to render judgment. He, and he alone, must determine whether his differences are such as to justify a separate statement of his conclusions" (Evans 1938, p. 135). The dissent publicly discloses how the justice came to vote as she or he did. "[A] dissenting opinion . . . is some showing of how the author has fulfilled his [or her] judicial duty to consider and decide" (Stephens 1952, p. 396). Associate Justice Joseph Story provides an excellent expression of personal justification:

> It is a matter of regret that in this conclusion I have the misfortune to differ from a majority of the court, for whose superior learning and ability I entertain the most entire respect. But I hold it an indispensable duty not to surrender my own judgment, because a great weight of opinion is against me—a weight which no one can feel more sensibly than myself. Had this been an ordinary case I should have contented myself with silence; but believing that no more important or interesting question ever came before a prize tribunal, and that the national rights suspended on it are of infinite moment to the maritime world, I have thought it not unfit to pronounce my own opinion. (*The Nereide* 1815, p. 791)

Some suggest that this justificatory purpose of dissent is little more than self-expression. However, such a purpose is rhetorical from Johnstone's standpoint. Viewed as self-persuasion, this purpose is analogous to the persuasion of others. Don M. Burks explains:

> There is I suggest no intrinsic difference in the persuasion of another and the persuasion of self. The movement from dialectic to rhetoric, from investigation or the deriving of a position to promulgation or advocacy is best understood as a movement along a continuum, and, whether the advocacy is directed to self or to others, one of the highly characteristic features of the rhetorical end of the continuum is the presence of appeal or urging. In other words, once a position is arrived at through investigation and/or argument, there often needs to be an urging or appeal to take action in accord with or to accept a commitment to the finding. The urging or appealing may be to self or to oth-

ers or to both at once. So far as it is to self we are using rhetoric on ourselves. (1970, p. 112)

From this standpoint, the dissent may serve to maintain personal integrity and satisfaction (Evans 1938). Rathjen (1974) goes so far as to suggest that separate opinions serve to relieve cognitive dissonance in appellate justices.

Yet dissent as self-persuasion provides a forum for the dissenter to address many potential audiences in order to distinguish the majority position from the dissenter's, to indicate "that other members of the court have considered and rejected, not merely ignored" the dissenter's viewpoint (Barth 1975; Stephens 1952). The juxtaposition of the majority and dissenting positions within the dissent may serve to persuade others of the validity of the latter and induce a response.

A Johnstonian view of Supreme Court dissent, then, includes a strictly self-persuasive or reflexive understanding of rhetoric as well as a traditional, other-directed purpose for discourse. The dissenter may utilize the written opinion as a public record of the reasons for his or her disagreement; however, according to Van de Vate:

> This appeal to a new audience requires [the arguer] to "recast" the original audience, for their inability to grasp the truth of A unfits them for the audience function. The lapse from persuading to describing implied in uttering the constraining assertion signalizes this recasting. Now the original audience become "mere players," denied the double participation in the drama (as both player and audience) which the speaker attributes himself [or herself]. Now he [she] plays his [her] role for the new audience, and the original audience becomes "prop," a background feature necessary to the performance—but incapable of appreciating and applauding it. (1965, p. 255)

Not only do dissenters persuade themselves of the validity of their positions, but they direct their arguments to undesignated audiences, all the while presenting these arguments as a rebuttal directed to their colleagues on the Court. How dissenters simultaneously address three audiences (self, colleagues, and interested others) raises four difficult duties Johnstone suggests must be fulfilled in order for rhetoric and argumentation to be considered "ethical."

Johnstonian Ethics and the Dissenter's Audience(s)

Johnstone's ethics are based on the premise that human beings are *"persuading and persuaded* animals" (Johnstone 1966; 1981, p. 306). From this premise arises the axiom, a "basic imperative" (after Kant): "So act in each instance as to encourage, rather than suppress, the capacity to persuade and to be persuaded, whether the capacity in question is yours or another's" (Johnstone 1981, p. 310). Rhetoric thus serves to encourage further argumentation. Rhetoric is therefore not only self-reflexive, but *self-perpetuating* (Johnstone 1981), for "when an act of wedge-driving fails to be bilateral, the act exemplifies degenerate rhetoric" (Johnstone 1990, p. 336). To be ethical, and thus fulfill the basic imperative, arguers have four duties to fulfill, two duties toward themselves and two duties toward others. These duties encompass the three concerns of purpose in relation to Supreme Court dissent: the dissenting opinion as self-persuasive or reflexive; the opinion as addressed to other members of the immediate Court; and the dissent as an appeal to other interested parties, both immediate and future.

The situation in which a Supreme Court justice dissents limits the duties Johnstone directs toward the self to the case at hand and the immediate conflict between the justice and his or her colleagues. The first of these is *resoluteness*: "I am to act so as to perpetuate my own rhetorical faculties. Thus I have a duty to myself not to capitulate willy-nilly to the rhetorical demands of others. I must take a stand and bring my own persuasive powers into play with respect to propositions of which others are trying to persuade me" (Johnstone 1981, p. 310).

This duty falls clearly within the realm of self-persuasion as discussed earlier. The second duty, *openness*, refers to the need to listen to opposing viewpoints: "I ought not to turn a deaf ear to the attempts of others to persuade me. I ought to listen to them" (p. 310). Some dissents at least acknowledge and even agree with some lines of argument from majority and concurring opinions (Courtright 1991). Some dissents also refer to other parties to the case (e.g., oral arguments of counsel, lower court rulings), but how often such references appear in dissents is a matter of conjecture. The duties toward others include not only the immediate debate between dissenter and majority, but may reflect a concern for other audiences, in future as well as current public policy debates. These duties include *gentleness*, the obverse side of openness, and *compassion*, the obverse of resoluteness. Both, according to Johnstone, concern "our persuading others rather than being persuaded by them" (1981, p. 310).

Traditionally, how gentle a dissenter's arguments may be has been related to matters of style. A number of commentators contend that dissent is less constrained than the majority opinion in its modes of expression. Dissenting style has been characterized as "flamboyant . . . more vigorous and eloquent" (LeDuc 1976, p. 284). In Justice Benjamin Cardozo's words, the dissent places the justice in the role of "the gladiator making a last stand against the lions" (1931, p. 34). For example, some (but not all) of the stylistic choices in Justice Antonin Scalia's opinions have suggested the stance of a maverick rather than a consensus-builder (Barrett 1992; Kaplan and Cohn 1990; Ruhly 1991).

But the dissenter must balance the opportunity for self-expression with an image of collegial disagreement: "Although dissenting opinions are generally prompted by strong feelings and often connote a condemnation of the judgment of colleagues, there is a tradition in the Court that they ought to be stated in terms that indicate respect, and even deference, for the majority holding a different view" (Barth 1975, p. 6). Thus not every dissent can be deemed unethical due to a lack of gentleness toward the majority. How gently dissenters direct their arguments toward other audiences remains a question scholars have not addressed.

Johnstone's final ethical duty, *compassion*, is "a duty to listen to others not as much for our sake as for theirs" (Johnstone 1981, p. 310). Proponents in the legal profession attribute this altruistic quality to the ideal aims of dissent, exhortation, and, of course, correction. The most immediate audience for a dissenter is the group of colleagues on the bench at the time. In fact, appropriate appeals made during the course of circulation of opinions prior to their publication may obviate the need to publish the dissent at all. This occurs when the dissenter distinguishes his or her position from the majority to a moderate degree at most. Circulation of opinions allows for compromise and "massing a court." However, a potential dissent may have the opposite effect. Rather than unite the justices concerned, the opinion serves to divide them further, with two possible results: the dissenter's "opinion may force the Court or one of his [or her] colleagues to discuss matters that they would have preferred to leave unmentioned—indeed, the objective of the dissenter or concurrer may be to force the Court to take a *more* extreme rather than a less extreme position than would have been the case had he [or she] remained silent" (Schubert 1960, p. 130). The dissent thus may provoke the discussion of issues or produce adjustments in the majority's argument.

With regard to other audiences, J. Louis Campbell likens Supreme Court dissents to acts of civil disobedience: "The primary persuasive objective of disobedience is remedy—the remedy of perceived wrong" (1983, p. 309). Dissents propose policy change since the Court cannot enact law. The principal audiences called to action include the appropriate legislature (Carter 1953; Fuld 1962; Kelman 1985), and, via an appeal to the general public, the Court itself (Barth 1975). But the concept of audience may be more abstract, for the dissenter also addresses an "audience of a future day" (Campbell 1983, p. 308).

To apply Johnstone's four ethical duties to Supreme Court dissents as an example of argumentation, the relationship of audience to purpose is important. Dissenters may engage in self-persuasion, but the arguments they employ in defending their positions may serve to influence other audiences, perhaps even to persuade them that corrective measures are necessary. In either case, dissenting arguments function rhetorically to engage audiences in the consideration of propositions (Arnold 1987; Johnstone 1978) that the dissenter apparently deems worthy of public consideration.

AN ETHICAL APPRAISAL OF O'CONNOR'S OPINION

To analyze O'Connor's *Metro* opinion with Johnstone's ethical standards in mind, a central assumption to this study is that any discourse implies a speaker and an audience. As Edwin Black puts it, "the implied author of a discourse is a persona that figures importantly in rhetorical transactions. What equally well solicits our attention is that there is a second persona also implied by a discourse, and that persona is its implied auditor" (1970, p. 111). For the purposes of this study, O'Connor's "first persona" thus suggests indications of self-persuasion characterized by the duties of resoluteness and openness. The "second personae" revealed in her dissent are her colleagues on the Court, the FCC, and a "universal audience" (Perelman and Olbrechts-Tyteca 1969), abstract in character. O'Connor implies these audiences as she performs the duties of gentleness and compassion.

Ironically, the ways in which the four duties operate in O'Connor's dissent suggest relationships that Johnstone did not foresee. First, because resoluteness figures predominantly in her arguments, gentleness softens their character. Second, because a dissenter cannot be too open to counterargument, openness serves to introduce correctives through the duty of compassion. Thus, the duties Johnstone posits to be "obverse" function differently in O'Connor's argumentation. Resoluteness and its obverse, openness, pair respectively with gentleness and its obverse, compassion.

Resoluteness and Gentleness

O'Connor's *Metro* opinion betrays her resoluteness through arguments that are phrased in absolute terms. Such arguments could polarize in such a way that the dissent might appeal to few audiences; however, O'Connor tempers the dichotomy she creates between the majority and herself with the duty of gentleness. She softens the dissent with attention to three audiences: the Court, the FCC, and the broader public.

O'Connor remains resolute throughout the opinion, declaring her position on the Constitution, affirmative action adjudication, and its application to the FCC's minority preference policies. The majority's approach to the case unquestionably runs counter to her reading of the Constitution. She states early in her opinion: "Except in the narrowest of circumstances, the Constitution bars such racial classifications as a denial to particular individuals, of any race or ethnicity, of 'the equal protection of the laws.' The dangers of such classifications are clear. They endorse race-based reasoning and the conception of a Nation divided into racial blocs, thus contributing to the escalation of racial hostility and conflict" (*Metro Broadcasting* 1990, p. 487 [Hereafter, all references to the *Metro* opinion shall appear in parentheses with page number only]). The basis of affirmative action therefore lies in the Constitution: "The guarantee of equal protection extends to each citizen, regardless of race: the Federal Government, like the States, may not 'deny to any person within its jurisdiction the equal protection of the laws'" (p. 491).

O'Connor likewise is resolute in her defense of "strict scrutiny" as the appropriate adjudicatory standard in *Metro*. Such arguments include references to precedent and use of the "propositional" negative (Burke 1971, p. 20). Her defense of her majority opinion in *Croson* illustrates both:

> As we recognized last Term, the Constitution requires that the Court apply a strict standard of scrutiny to evaluate racial classifications such as those contained in the challenged FCC distress sale and comparative licensing policies. . . . Yet the Government's different treatment of citizens according to race is *no routine concern*. This Court's precedents *in no way justify* the Court's marked departure from our traditional treatment of race classifications and its conclusions that different equal protection principles apply to these federal actions. (p. 487, internal citation omitted, emphasis added)

Such polarization marks O'Connor's disagreement with the majority throughout the dissent (for similar appeals to precedent, see p. 494; for similar use of the propositional negative, see pp. 493, 503).

O'Connor's application of both standards of adjudication, demonstrating the failure of the FCC's policies to meet them, again displays the resoluteness of her position. She attacks the assumption that race and licensee programming behavior are somehow correlated (pp. 497–99), the incongruity of the law to its ostensible purpose (pp. 499–502), and the "less than substantial" (p. 502) nature of the asserted correlation (pp. 502–4). O'Connor again employs absolute terms to demonstrate the insufficiency of counterarguments: "First, the market shapes programming to a tremendous extent. . . . Second, station owners have only limited control over the content of programming. The distress sale presents a particularly acute difficulty of this sort. Third, the FCC had absolutely no factual basis for the nexus [between owners' race and programming] when it adopted the policies and has since established none to support its existence" (pp. 502–3). The policies themselves, like the majority's approach to affirmative action, do not pass muster in the face of O'Connor's arguments.

O'Connor moderates her resoluteness with statements directed at three ever-broadening audiences. Her principal target is the majority justices, but she later associates the FCC with them.

However, she addresses *any* interested parties (i.e., a "universal audience" [Perelman and Olbrechts-Tyteca 1969]) with gentleness in the opinion's introductory paragraph: "Social scientists may debate how peoples' thoughts and behavior reflect their background, but the Constitution provides that the Government may not allocate benefits and burdens among individuals based on the assumption that race or ethnicity determines how they act or think" (p. 487). The introduction thus calls into question the nexus between race and behavior posited by the majority and the FCC and invites audiences concerned with the social implications of such an argument. O'Connor gently reminds her audiences that the issue is far from resolved. To conclude the paragraph, like so many justices before her, she lets one and all know that she has disagreed with her colleagues with careful deliberation: "I respectfully dissent" (p. 487).

Apart from a paragraph in which the four ethical duties function together (p. 498), O'Connor confines her gentleness toward the Court and the FCC to arguments early in the dissent. Her comment to the majority reminds them that the precedent they cite, *Fullilove v. Klutznick*, contradicts their reasoning:

> Even Justice Marshall's opinion, joined by Justice Brennan and Justice Blackmun, undermines the Court's course today: that opinion drew its lower standard of review from the plurality opinion in *Regents of University of Calif. v. Bakke*, a case that did not involve congressional action, and stated that the appropriate standard of review for the congressional measure challenged in *Fullilove* "is the same as that under the Fourteenth Amendment." (p. 492, internal citation omitted)

O'Connor's choice to mention justices by name here seems to amplify the gentle chiding she gives her colleagues.

As O'Connor resolutely indicts the FCC's arguments, she exhorts the majority to reconsider its position. The asserted interest is the same one rejected in *Croson*, and thus lacks sufficient evidence: "The asserted interest in this case suffers from the same defects. The interest is certainly amorphous: the FCC and the majority of this Court understandably do not suggest how one would define or measure a particular viewpoint that might be associated with race, or even how one would assess the diversity of broadcast viewpoints" (pp. 494–95). In an appeal to the "universal audience," O'Connor further points out the majority's and

FCC's errors in reasoning concerning the potential effects of the majority opinion:

> [A] claim of insufficiently diverse broadcasting viewpoints might be used to justify equally unconstrained racial preferences, linked to nothing other than proportional representation of various races. . . . The FCC's claimed interest could similarly justify limitations on minority members' participation in broadcasting. It would be unwise to depend upon the Court's restriction of its holding to "benign" measures to forestall this result. (p. 495)

O'Connor also appeals to the "universal audience" through "depersonalization" (Courtright 1989) of the majority, thus maintaining a gentle, indirect attack on her fellow justices. With the exception of the aforementioned reference to Justice Marshall's opinion in *Fullilove*, she only mentions specific justices two other times, each time citing precedent (pp. 490–91). Reference to colleagues within the context of the *Metro* opinions remain anonymous as "the majority" or "the Court." This strategy simultaneously preserves a gentle public stance toward the majority and invites audiences outside the Court to "overhear" the disagreement.

O'Connor thus uses gentleness to gain a hearing with the Court, the FCC, and, failing these, a broader, "universal" audience. Throughout, however, she is resolute in her position. To demonstrate the validity of her position, however, she must balance these duties with a concern for the three audiences. She thus rounds out the opinion with the duties of openness and compassion.

Openness and Compassion

At several points in her arguments, O'Connor indicates to her audiences that she has listened to views differing from her own. O'Connor fulfills the duty of openness as a complement to the resoluteness of her own position but, more important, to the compassion she accords to her audiences. She remains open to the majority's arguments, but only as a means to listen for the sake of the majority of the Court and, by implication, the FCC. Her resoluteness toward these audiences translates into compassion for the "universal audience."

Early in the dissent, O'Connor acknowledges and even agrees with some lines of argument presented in the majority opinion. She proceeds, however, to counter each one. First, O'Connor agrees with the majority's constitutional premise but rejects the conclusion: "Congress has considerable latitude presenting special concerns for judicial review, when it exercises its 'unique remedial powers . . . under 5 of the Fourteenth Amendment,' but this case does not implicate those powers" (p. 489, internal citation omitted). In this manner, O'Connor remains open to the majority, but resolute in her own position.

O'Connor's openness to majority arguments also combines with her resoluteness with regard to the level of scrutiny required to adjudicate questions of affirmative action. For example, O'Connor demonstrates that her opinion and the majority's opinion operate from the same premise: "The Court evaluates the policies only as measures designed to increase programming diversity. I agree that the racial classifications cannot be upheld as remedial measures" (p. 493). This recognition summarizes O'Connor's concern over precedent and the standard of adjudication appropriate to the situation in *Metro*. These concerns, and their application to the FCC's policies transform the duty of openness to majority and FCC premises into a duty to correct the conclusions drawn from them with compassion.

O'Connor addresses each concern in turn, alternately addressing the majority and the FCC with a resolute statement of her own position. O'Connor appears to use the duty of compassion in the same way she did gentleness, softening the resoluteness of her opinion. The juxtaposition of the two duties presents a mixture of absolute terms with the use of qualifiers. For example, in her interpretation of *Fullilove*, O'Connor grants a majority premise with a compassionate qualifying phrase (a "refutational qualifier"; see Courtright 1991), but corrects it with a resolute refutation:

> [E]ven if Fullilove applied outside a remedial exercise outside of
> Congress' 5 power, it would not support today's adoption of the
> intermediate standard of review proffered by Justice Marshall
> but rejected in Fullilove. . . . *Although the Court correctly
> observes that a majority did not apply strict scrutiny*, six Members of the Court rejected intermediate scrutiny in favor of some
> more stringent form of review. (p. 490, emphasis added)

In contrast, O'Connor opens her attack on the majority's application of the intermediate scrutiny in absolute terms:

> The interest in increasing the diversity of broadcast viewpoints
> is clearly not a compelling interest. It is simply too amorphous,
> too insubstantial, and too unrelated to any legitimate basis for

employing racial classifications. *The Court does not claim otherwise.* Rather, it employs a novel standard and claims that this asserted interest need only be, and is, "important." This conclusion twice compounds the Court's initial error of reducing its level of a racial classification. (pp. 493–94, emphasis added)

O'Connor then utilizes refutational and traditional qualifiers to correct the majority's errors as she concludes the section: "*Even considered as other than a justification for using race classifications,* the asserted interest in viewpoint diversity falls short of being *weighty enough.* . . . *Even if an interest is determined to be legitimate in one context,* it does not suddenly become *important enough* to justify distinctions based on race" (p. 496, emphasis added).

As O'Connor moves to the application of strict and intermediate scrutiny to the *Metro* case's particulars, gentleness and openness give way to the pairing of compassion and resoluteness. Here she maintains the two types of compassionate argument, statement of the majority/FCC argument or a refutational qualifier accepting the argument temporarily. O'Connor's refutation of the majority assertion that race and behavior are somehow related illustrates both:

> The Court's lengthy discussion of this issue purports to establish only that some relation exists between owners' race and programming. . . . The Court understandably makes no stronger claims, because the evidence provides no support and because the requisite deference would so obviously abandon heightened scrutiny. For argument's sake, we can grant that the Court's review of congressional hearings and social science studies establishes the existence of some rational nexus. But even assuming that to be true, the Court's discussion does not begin to establish that the programs are directly and substantially related to the interest in diverse programming. (p. 502)

These two forms of compassionate argument also lead to compassion for the "universal audience." This audience, which may be divided into multiple publics for the Court (Makau 1984), appears as two "second personae" for O'Connor: members of the broadcast industry and jurists on future Courts. The former is of more pressing moment. O'Connor implies that those who make and follow broadcast policies should be wary of giving the majority opinion credence:

The FCC and the Court suggest that First Amendment interests in some manner should exempt the FCC from employing this direct race-neutral means [requiring licensees to provide programming that the FCC believes would add diversity] to achieve its asserted interest. . . . But the FCC cannot have it both ways: either the First Amendment bars the FCC from seeking to accomplish indirectly what it may not accomplish directly; or the FCC may pursue the goal, but must do so in a manner that comports with equal protection principles. And if the FCC can direct programming in any fashion, it must employ that direct means. (p. 500)

This and other indirect appeals to the FCC to reconsider its policies could be taken up by communication lawyers and members of the industry if the commission fails to act upon O'Connor's warnings.

Naturally, O'Connor's compassion toward future Courts appears in the earlier portions of the dissent devoted to interpretation of precedent and standards of review. Any number of such appeals could provide counsel to justices who cite *Metro*: "The Court's emphasis on 'benign racial classifications' suggests confidence in its ability to distinguish good from harmful governmental uses of racial criteria. History should teach greater humility" (p. 492). Likewise, O'Connor's dissent passes into history as a lesson to justices who follow her and attempt to build upon her efforts to refine affirmative action jurisprudence.

Justice O'Connor maintains an ethical stance in dissent, employing all four of Johnstone's duties: resoluteness, gentleness, openness, and compassion. She is resolute throughout the opinion, careful in her exposition of the Constitution, of the standards of adjudication required under the Fourteenth Amendment, and of their application to the FCC's minority preference policies. O'Connor moderates her resoluteness with gentleness, chiding the Court and the FCC for errors in reasoning, but refraining from personal attacks on her colleagues before a broader, "universal" audience. O'Connor displays openness to certain premises of the Court and the FCC, but often uses such opportunities to correct errors and to show compassion for the Court, the FCC, and a "universal" audience as well.

Although resoluteness and compassion tend to dominate O'Connor's *Metro* dissent, gentleness and openness temper her arguments to gain a hearing from several audiences: her colleagues, the FCC, the broadcast industry, and Courts of a future day. O'Connor moderates her firm stance on the Constitution and its standards and application with gentleness. She is willing to find common ground with her colleagues, but often uses those opportunities to correct those whose conclusions differ from her own. Her openness to the majority's and the FCC's arguments, while gently avoiding personal attacks, contributes to compassion toward them and members of a broader, "universal" audience.

O'Connor's Dissent in Context

Some might contend that O'Connor's efforts to force reconsideration of the constitutionality of the FCC's minority preference policies fail ethically because she does not balance the four duties Johnstone outlines. Given the problems dissenting justices face, however, O'Connor fulfills these ethical duties admirably. Certainly self-persuasion requires that a dissenter be resolute; but attention to credibility before a "universal" audience dictates that written, public dissent be open to counterargument, gentle in refutation, and compassionate in correction. In so doing, the dissenter sustains a forum in which other audiences may join the debate. When openness, gentleness, and compassion work in combination with the resoluteness a dissent requires, the practice of Supreme Court dissent is strengthened because the justice satisfies the expectations of multiple publics and enacts the very values these publics hold dear as Americans.

A comparison with Justice Kennedy's dissent in *Metro* illustrates the shortcomings that occur when a justice elects not to employ all four of Johnstone's duties. Sedler's (1990) and Haggard's (1990) critiques of his opinion as "scathing" and "trenchant" are justified because Kennedy exhibits only resoluteness and compassion. He is neither open to the majority's arguments nor gentle in his attack on them.

Unlike O'Connor, Kennedy finds no point on which to agree with the majority: "I cannot agree with the Court that the Constitution permits the Government to discriminate among its citizens on the basis of race in order to serve interests so trivial as 'broadcast diversity'" (p. 507). Kennedy's opinion is devoid of the refutational qualifiers O'Connor uses to soften her attack on the majority. His dissent, lacking openness, goes for the jugular, comparing the majority opinion with the laws of South African apartheid:

The Court is all too correct that the type of reasoning employed by the commission and Congress is not novel. Policies of racial separation and preference are almost always justified as benign, even when it is clear to any sensible observer that they are not. The following statement, for example, would fit well among those offered to uphold the commission's racial preference policy: "The policy is not based on any concept of superiority or inferiority, but merely on the fact that people differ, particularly in their group associations, loyalties, cultures, modes of life and standards of development." (p. 508, internal citation omitted)

O'Connor's use of openness balances resoluteness and compassion and extends some basis for future discussion; Kennedy's lack of openness creates a rift with little hope of reconciliation.

Kennedy's lack of gentleness deepens the rift. Instead of using case law to chide the majority as O'Connor does, Kennedy wages a historical indictment against it. He immediately opens the dissent with a comparison to the majority in *Plessy v. Ferguson*, which held that "race-conscious measures" were reasonable: "Plessy's standard of review and its explication have disturbing parallels to today's majority opinion that should warn us that something is amiss here" (p. 506). Toward the conclusion of his dissent, Kennedy's lack of gentleness turns to satire:

Whether or not such programs can be described as "remedial," the message conveyed is that it is acceptable to harm a member of the group excluded from the benefit or privilege. If this is to be considered acceptable under the Constitution, there are various possible explanations. One is that the group disadvantaged by the preference should feel no stigma at all, because racial preferences address not the evil of intentional discrimination but the continuing use of stereotypes that disadvantage minority groups. (p. 509)

This "explanation" and the one that follows maintain that the majority has little grasp of the facts of discrimination.

As in the passage just cited, Kennedy employs reservations ("if" or "until") rather than refutational qualifiers ("even if")in this indictment of the majority. He rejects a second explanation that suggests that racial stigma should be overlooked because "the disfavored class must bear collective blame, or because individual harms are simply irrelevant" (p. 509):

But these are not premises that the Court even appears willing to address in its analysis. Until the Court is candid about the existence of stigma imposed by racial preferences on both affected classes, candid about the "animosity and discontent" they create, and open about defending a theory that explains why the cost of this stigma is worth bearing and why it can consist with the Constitution, no basis can be shown for today's casual abandonment of strict scrutiny. (p. 509, internal citation omitted)

Kennedy earlier uses a reservation to demonstrate how the majority has misapplied case law since *Plessy*: "As to other exercises of congressional power, our cases following *Bolling v. Sharpe*, such as *Weinberger v. Wiesenfeld*, until they were in effect overruled today, had held that the Congress is constrained in its actions by the same standard applicable to the States: strict scrutiny of all racial classifications" (p. 507, internal citation omitted). Whereas O'Connor temporarily grants the majority's arguments a hearing with refutational qualification, Kennedy flatly contradicts their reasoning.

From a legal standpoint, Kennedy and O'Connor have similar concerns: a proper reading of precedent and maintenance of constitutional guarantees. From a Johnstonian standpoint, Kennedy accomplishes only in part what O'Connor performs *in toto*. The resoluteness found in both opinions achieves the dissenter's purpose in self-persuasion: justification. But resoluteness without gentleness and openness renders compassion hollow. As Burks puts it, "[P]ersuasion involves the risking of self for both speaker and listener" (1970, p. 111). Kennedy's dissent *evokes* the consciousness required for communication to occur, but O'Connor *maintains* it through a concern for her immediate audience, her colleagues on the Court. Indeed, Kennedy uses O'Connor's dissent as evidence for his position, but she in turn ethically cannot do the same.

O'Connor employs openness and gentleness to maintain the possibility of argumentative dialogue with each of her audiences. These duties achieve Johnstone's basic imperative through the use of what he calls *ad hominem* argument:

When the truth can be discovered through an act wholly distinct from that of communicating it, then the act of discovery can be formulated as an *argumentum ad rem*, an appeal to the truth in the form of a fact. . . . If *argumentum ad rem* is unavailable, then only *argumentum ad hominem* is available. . . . My present view is that a successful argument in philosophy is one that is intended to evoke, and does evoke, a response of a certain kind in the man [or woman] to whom it is addressed. (Johnstone 1978, p. 75)

Kennedy's reliance on resoluteness and compassion alone violates this ethical standard, for he neglects the relationship with his colleagues on the Court. In Johnstone's words, he uses rhetoric as a *terminating transaction* (Johnstone 1981). O'Connor forges an ethical, bilateral relationship through openness and compassion, and thus demonstrates compassion for other audiences as well, inviting them, as well as future Courts, to seek remedy for the majority's errors.

Engaging in what Johnstone calls *ad hominem* argument, O'Connor fulfills Johnstone's basic imperative, using argumentation to facilitate further communication. She moves beyond the mere need for public justification of her vote. Her use of openness and gentleness fosters a climate for ongoing discussion in three ways. Each contributes to the credibility of the Court itself. First, O'Connor shows respect and deference (Barth 1975) to the majority: "When expressed in moderation, with sincerity and conciseness, dissenting opinions will never detract from respect for courts nor will they develop unrest or dissatisfaction" (Evans 1938, p. 135).

Second, O'Connor's dissent considers many of the arguments raised by the majority. She applies both strict and intermediate scrutiny. She carefully discusses the assumptions and implications of the FCC's policies, and explains why her view differs. Kennedy attacks them in general. O'Connor's detailed consideration of the issues not only assures that the Court has not ignored the dissenter (Stephens 1952), but lets other audiences know that the case received the deliberation it deserves, and thus "reaffirm the credibility of the Court" (Bartanen 1987, p. 244):

Do [dissents] lessen public confidence in the court? Doubtless they do somewhat, particularly so far as the general, unthinking public is involved. To those who know that the law is not an exact science and cannot be made so, it is doubtful if a dissenting opinion ever weakens respect for the Court. In fact, such opinions must be, to the thoughtful reader, as well as to the litigants, proof conclusive that the questions presented were thoroughly and seriously considered and this conviction should go far to develop respect. (Evans 1938, pp. 128–29)

Finally, the exposition of counterarguments to the majority enacts core values held by the "universal audience" O'Connor addresses. Not only does she weigh constitutional doctrine against the social demands of affirmative action (Makau 1984), but O'Connor's written opinion is an act of responsible freedom of speech (Douglas 1948). Writes Stanley Fuld, "disagreement among judges is as true to the character of democracy, and as vital as freedom of speech itself. The affairs of government, no less than the work of the courts, could not be conducted by democratic standards without that right of dissent (1962, p. 926). Ethical dissent, then, embodies constitutional values in such a way that interested audiences may view the Court as a guardian of American culture (Vibbert 1987).

Although the four ethical duties are difficult to emphasize equally, O'Connor's dissent demonstrates that a well-argued dissent must employ all four in order to maintain an ethical stance toward interested parties to a Supreme Court case. Kennedy's dissent in *Metro* lacks the openness and gentleness requisite to temper an opinion so that it reflects well on the dissenter and the Court itself. O'Connor, in contrast, employs the duties in such a way that she listens to and respects the majority opinion, no matter how much she disagrees with it. In this fashion, O'Connor warrants a hearing from a broader audience, if not assent. She evokes and maintains the "consciousness required for communication" (Johnstone 1970, p. 121), thus preserving "the capacity to persuade and be persuaded" (Johnstone 1981, p. 310).

This analysis thus suggests that O'Connor maintains a stance that invites further contemplation and, perhaps, action. Ideally, such a conclusion would require ethical analysis of the majority and concurring opinions of *Metro Broadcasting* as well. Yet some brief implications can be drawn concerning the issues at stake in *Metro* and the value of Supreme Court dissent as well. Concerning affirmative action, O'Connor articulates her position well. Clearly she will be a force to be reckoned with, and this dissent may serve as a benchmark for correction. The FCC or Congress could act upon her concerns if future Courts do not. And her *Metro* dissent should echo in Court debates regarding the appropriate level of review under the Fourteenth Amendment. Such a prediction is open to debate, of course (Fried 1990; Haggard 1990; Sedler 1990; Williams 1990).

What may be instructive for those interested in written dissents as a visible artifact of the Court as an institution are the argumentative choices O'Connor makes in *Metro*. Resoluteness may be one of the few consistent characteristics of Supreme Court dissent (Courtright 1991), and thus could erode the Court's credibility among various publics. But "the reputation and prestige of a court—the influence and weight it commands—depend on something stronger" than "the illusion of absolute certainty and of judicial infallibility" (Fuld 1962, p. 928). I would maintain that they rest on the exercise of resoluteness in conjunction with openness, gentleness, and compassion. If O'Connor's *Metro* dissent is the exemplar I believe it to be, future studies will confirm these distinctions of good dissenting argument.

REFERENCES

Arnold, Carroll C. 1987. Johnstone's 'Wedge' and Theory of Rhetoric. *Philosophy and Rhetoric, 20,* 118–28.

Barett, Paul M. 1992, April 28. The loner: Despite expectations, Scalia fails to unify conservatives on the Court. *Wall Street Journal,* A1, A6.

Bartanen, Kristine M. 1987. The rhetoric of dissent in Justice O'Connor's *Akron* opinion. *Southern Speech Communication Journal, 52,* 240–62.

Barth, Alan. 1975. *Prophets with honor: Great dissents and great dissenters in the Supreme Court.* New York: Vintage Books.

Bennett, Robert W. 1991. A dissent on dissent. *Judicature, 74,* 255–60.

Bergman, Matthew P. 1991. Dissent in the judicial process: Discord in service of harmony. *Denver University Law Review, 68,* 79–90.

Beth, Loren P. 1955. Justice Harlan and the uses of dissent. *American Political Science Review, 49,* 1085–1104.

Black, Edwin. 1970. The second persona. *Quarterly Journal of Speech, 56,* 109–19.

Black Law Dictionary. 1979. 5th ed. St. Paul: West Law Publishing.

Bowen, William A. 1905. Dissenting opinions. *Green Bag, 17,* 690–97.

Brennan, William. 1986. In defense of dissents. *Hastings Law Journal, 37,* 427–38.

Burke, Kenneth. 1971. *A rhetoric of religion.* Berkeley: University of California Press.

Burks, Don M. 1970. Persuasion, self-persuasion, and rhetorical discourse. *Philosophy and Rhetoric, 3,* 109–19.

Campbell, J[eter] Louis, III. 1979. Justices Douglas and Black and the democratic ethos: Rhetorical criticism of concurring and dissenting opinions on obscenity, 1954–1975. Ph.D. diss., University of Minnesota.

————. 1983. The spirit of dissent. *Judicature, 66*, 304–12.

Cardozo, Benjamin. 1931. *Law and literature and other essays*. New York: Harcourt, Brace.

Carter, Jesse W. 1953. Dissenting opinions. *Hastings Law Journal, 4*, 118–23.

City of Richmond v. J. A. Croson and Co., 102 L.Ed.2d 854 (1989).

Corso, Diane Marie. 1981. The rhetoric of the United States Supreme Court: A generic approach. Ph.D. diss., University of Oregon.

Courtright, Jeffrey L[ee]. 1989, November. When experts disagree: A preliminary study of the generic aspects of Supreme Court dissents. Paper presented at the 75th annual convention of the Speech Communication Association, San Francisco.

————. 1991. 'Tactics' and 'trajectories': The argumentative resources of Supreme Court dissenting opinions. Ph.D. diss., Purdue University.

————. 1992. Justice O'Connor's messages to the American polity refining the boundaries of religious freedom. *Public Relations Review, 18*, 233–46.

Douglas, William O. 1948. The dissent: A safeguard of democracy. *Journal of the American Judicature Society, 32*, 104–7.

Evans, Evan A. 1938. The dissenting opinion—Its use and abuse. *Missouri Law Review, 3*, 120–42.

Fried, Charles. 1990. Comment: *Metro Broadcasting, Inc. v. FCC*: Two concepts of equality. *Harvard Law Review, 104*, 107–27.

Fuld, Stanley H. 1962. Voices of dissent. *Columbia Law Review, 62*, 923–29.

Gest, Ted. 1991/1992, December 30/January 6. Deciding on abortion's fate: O'Connor seeks to prevent 'undue burdens' on women. *U.S. News and World Report*, 70.

Haggard, Thomas R. 1990. Mugwump, mediator, Machiavellian, or majority? The role of Justice O'Connor in the affirmative action cases. *Akron Law Review, 24*, 47–87.

Halpern, Stephen C., and Kenneth N. Vines. 1977. Institutional disunity, the judges' bill, and the role of the supreme court. *Western Political Quarterly, 30*, 471–83.

Hirt, William E. 1960. In the matter of dissents inter judices de jure. *Pennsylvania Bar Association Quarterly, 31*, 256–60.

Hughes, Charles Evans. 1928. *The Supreme Court of the United States*. New York: Columbia University Press.

Ingwerson, Marshall. 1991, October 15. O'Connor marks decade on Court. *Christian Science Monitor*, 12.

Johnstone, Henry W., Jr. 1966. The relevance of rhetoric to philosophy and of philosophy to rhetoric. *Quarterly Journal of Speech, 52*, 41–46.

———. 1970. *The problem of the self.* University Park: Pennsylvania State University Press.

———. 1978. *Validity and rhetoric in philosophical argument: An outlook in transition.* University Park: Dialogue Press of Man and World.

———. 1981. Toward an ethics of rhetoric. *Communication, 6*, 305–14.

———. 1987. Response. *Philosophy and Rhetoric, 20*, 129–34.

———. 1990. Rhetoric as a wedge: A reformulation. *Rhetoric Society Quarterly, 20*, 33–38.

Justice O'Connor carves own niche. 1982, July 12. *U.S. News and World Report*, 46.

Kaplan, David A., and Bob Kohn. 1990, November 5. The Court's Mr. Right. *Newsweek*, 62–76.

Kelman, Maurice. 1985. The forked path of dissent. In *The Supreme Court review, 1985.* Chicago: University of Chicago Press.

LeDuc, Don R. 1976. 'Free speech' decisions and the legal process: The judicial opinion in context. *Quarterly Journal of Speech, 62*, 279–87.

Levin-Epstein, Eve. 1978. The rhetoric of the Supreme Court: A dramatistic analysis of First Amendment dissenting opinions. Ph.D. diss., Temple University.

Makau, Josina M. 1984. The Supreme Court and reasonableness. *Quarterly Journal of Speech, 70*, 379–96.

Metro Broadcasting, Inc. v. FCC, 111 L.Ed.2d 445 (1990).

The Nereide, 3 L.Ed. 769 (1815).

Perelman, Chaïm, and Lucie Olbrechts-Tyteca. 1969. *The new rhetoric: A treatise on argumentation.* Trans. John Wilkinson and Purcell Weaver. Notre Dame: University of Notre Dame Press.

Plessy v. Ferguson, 41 L.Ed. 256 (1896).

Powell, Thomas Reed. 1918. The logic and rhetoric of constitutional law. *Journal of Philosophy, Psychology, and Scientific Methods, 15*, 645–58.

Rathjen, Gregory. 1974. An analysis of separate opinion writing as dissonance reduction. *American Politics Quarterly, 2*, 393–411.

Ray, Laura Krugman. 1988. Justice Brennan and the jurisprudence of dissent. *Temple Law Review, 61*, 307–52.

Rodgers, Raymond Sinclair. 1979. Justice William O. Douglas on the First Amendment: Rhetorical genres in judicial opinions. Ph.D. diss., University of Oklahoma.

Rogers, Berto. 1931. Dissenting opinions. *Law Notes, 35*, 149–52.

Ruhly, Sharon. 1991, November. (Scalia, J., dissenting). Paper presented at the 77th annual convention of the Speech Communication Association, Atlanta.

Scheb, John M., II, and Lee W. Ailshie. 1985. Justice Sandra Day O'Connor and the "freshman effect." *Judicature, 69,* 9–12.

Schubert, Glendon A. 1960. *Constitutional Politics.* New York: Holt, Rinehart, and Winston.

Sedler, Robert A. 1990. The Constitution, racial preference, and the Supreme Court's institutional ambivalence: Reflections on *Metro Broadcasting. Wayne Law Review, 36,* 1187–1236.

Skene, Neil. 1989, September 30. O'Connor becoming the new Powell. *Congressional Quarterly Weekly Report,* 2598.

Stager, Walter. 1925. Dissenting opinions—Their purpose and results. *Illinois Law Review, 19,* 604–7.

Stephens, Richard B. 1952. The function of concurring and dissenting opinions in courts of last resort. *University of Florida Law Review, 5,* 394–410.

Stone, Harlan F. 1942. Dissenting opinions are not without value. *Journal of the American Judicature Society, 26,* 78–82.

Van de Vate, Dwight, Jr. 1965. Disagreement as a dramatic event. *The Monist, 49,* 248–61.

Vibbert, Candiss Baksa. 1987. The role of values in Supreme Court opinions as legal and cultural force. In *Culture and communication: Methodology, behavior, artifacts, and institutions,* Selected Proceedings from the Fifth International Conference on Culture and Communication, Temple University, 1983, ed. Sari Thomas. Norwood: Ablex.

Walker, Thomas G., Lee Epstein, and William J. Dixon. 1988. On the mysterious demise of consensual norms in the United States Supreme Court. *Journal of Politics, 50,* 362–89.

Wasby, Stephen L. 1978. *The Supreme Court in the federal judicial system.* New York: Holt, Rinehart and Winston.

Williams, Patricia J. 1990. Comment: *Metro Broadcasting, Inc. v. FCC:* Regrouping in singular times. *Harvard Law Review, 104,* 525–46.

Wollman, Henry. 1898. Evils of dissenting opinions. *Albany Law Journal, 57,* 74–75.

Yoos, George E. 1987. Rhetoric of appeal and rhetoric of response. *Philosophy and Rhetoric, 20,* 118–28.

PART 3

Ideological Approaches to Argument Evaluation

CHAPTER 7

Ideology and Argument Evaluation: Competing Axiologies in the Sanctuary Trial

Kathryn M. Olson and Clark D. Olson

"Ideology" is a problematic yet crucial concept for those interested in argument evaluation. It is problematic because people have assigned the term a plethora of different definitions, many of which are incompatible with each other (see Eagleton 1991, pp. 1–2). It is crucial because the concept, in its less pejorative formulations, enlivens internally consistent lines of argument and lies at the heart of many argumentative clashes. This essay examines the nature of ideology as a useful construct for argument evaluation, then uses the idea to develop a critique of arguments in the sanctuary trial *U.S. v. Aguilar* and of this critique itself.

DEFINING IDEOLOGY

While various definitions of ideology are useful for different purposes, our interest here is in a more social and power-centered than epistemological conception. A definition that Terry Eagleton (1991) locates midway between the most broad and most narrow conceptions of ideology is appropriate to a study of argument evaluation because it emphasizes discursive struggle while not making the overly broad claim that all political discourse is ideological. According to this conception, ideology attends to the promotion and legitimation of the interests of social groups in the face of opposing interests. Eagleton continues: "The interests in question must have some relevance to the sustaining or challenging of a whole political form of life. Ideology here can be seen as a discursive field in which self-promoting social powers conflict and collide over questions central to the reproduction of social power as a whole" (1991, p. 29). Ideology thus differs from the political in that political concerns are more narrow and linked to a specific goal, while ideology addresses the defense of or challenge to relative power distributions in the social scheme as a whole; so, while some political discourse is ideological, it need not all be.

This definition is especially useful for argument critics because it does not empty the term "ideology" of meaning by making it all-encompassing and because it sets aside, at least temporarily, the question of a particular ideology's truth or falsity. It allows for the fact that an ideology consists of a certain ratio of empirical propositions, many of which will be experientially verifiable, and a worldview, in which the latter has the edge over the former. More precisely, ideologies use empirical statements not for their own sakes, but as *supports* for the overall worldview advanced. Consequently, the ways in which empirical statements are selected and deployed are governed by the requirements of the worldview, and, if it seems necessary, a specific empirical truth may be bent to serve the purpose of supporting the worldview. For this same reason, proving a proposition of a particular ideology empirically false usually does not cause its proponents to reject the ideology, since the proposition is more likely a buttress for the ideology than the reason for adhering to it (Eagleton 1991, pp. 22–23). Further developing this conception of ideology for use in argument evaluation demands elaborating four aspects of the notion: ideologies' ubiquitous presence; their role as a matter of discourse; their concentration on discursive conflict; and the influence of ideologies on critics' arguments themselves.

First, in light of the foregoing definition, the ubiquitous presence of ideologies in a society should be obvious. While some ideologies command more popular support than others or are backed by people with the power to enforce them, ideologies are not limited to "false consciousness" nor to labels for the beliefs of only particular factions. Ideology as defined here cannot be used as a dismissive term that describes other people's interests rather than one's own (Eagleton 1983, p. 211). For example, ideology cannot be limited to a label for the justifications of belief and value patterns held by those currently in power, though incumbents have ideologies as well as some power to "normalize" their patterns as the most appropriate ones. Over the past several decades, Murray Edelman (1964, 1971, 1988), for one, devoted himself largely to demonstrating the ways in which language use expresses and perpetuates the ideologies of those wielding power. Conversely, ideology cannot be limited to a term labeling the belief and value patterns of those currently out of power, though these patterns are more regularly recognized as ideologies simply because they are based on priorities that challenge the patterns empowered subgroups have tried to make normative (see Eagleton 1983, p. 211). Finally, the concept of ideology cannot be confined to the provinces of activities examined by the humanities and social sciences. Recent work on the rhetoric of science, especially Thomas M. Lessl's (1989) discussion of science's "priestly voice," challenges Clifford Geertz's (1964) claim that science names situations in such a way that the attitude expressed toward them is one of "disinterestedness," while ideology names situations in such a way that the attitude contained toward them is one of "commitment" (p. 71). Recent analyses make clear that the vocabulary of disinterestedness obscures and protects, but does not eliminate, the ideological commitments to supportive power distributions of those involved in supposedly "objective" projects. So, if William R. Brown (1978) is correct, ideology is a function of symbolic process that is requisite to any worldview (p. 124).

Because an ideology actively privileges a particular perspective in the selection and organization of the propositions expressing one's worldview, one's ideology colors that worldview's three main components: ontology, epistemology, and axiology (see Pepper 1942). One's ontology is one's assumptions about the nature of reality, about how things and people *are*. One's epistemology is one's assumptions about how one *knows*, about how one gains an understanding of reality. And one's axiology is one's assumptions about how one should *judge*, about what is good or right. While they are interwoven and often are implicit rather than explicit, all three components are indispensable to a complete worldview. One's ideology is not synonymous with one's worldview, then, but plays a powerful role in coloring that worldview.

Second, ideology is a matter of discourse, not merely symbols. This claim has two implications. Initially, it indicates that no discourse (e.g., scientific discourse) is inherently nonideological and that, under particular circumstances, no discourse can be void of the ideological; the relationship between symbols and their context is the determining factor in deciding whether something is ideological. Because ideology concerns the actual uses of symbols between particular humans for producing specific effects, one must look at situated discourse to appropriately label and evaluate ideologies. While certain ideological "idioms" exist (e.g., the language of fascism), what is primarily ideological about them is the power interests served and the political effects they attempt to produce in context (Eagleton 1991, p. 9).

Additionally, claiming that ideology is a matter of discourse suggests that, even if one has never articulated his or her ideology, it is revealed in one's arguments. As Kenneth Burke explains, symbolic action is the "dancing of an attitude" (1973, p. 9). Like poetry, arguments involve strategies that "size up the situations, name their structure and outstanding ingredients, and name them in a way that contains an attitude toward them" (p. 1). By looking for the implied assumptions needed to make an arguer's statements compelling and internally consistent, the argument critic can uncover for analysis an advocate's ideology. The careful analyst examines the arguments themselves as clues to the motives embedded in an ideology. Burke notes that the critic will not need to "supply" these motives; the interrelationships revealed in the advocate's own work are those motives, disclosing how he or she defines and interprets the situation in which the arguments are made (1973, p. 20) and revealing preferred distributions of social power.

Third, ideology concerns discursive struggle. It does not focus merely on political discourse narrowly construed, but on discursive contests over something deemed worth controlling. Often, the focus of these contests is the terms that members of a society commonly value. Even if it supports an internal array of ideologies and subgroups, every group must have enough in common in order to remain a group. These commonalities are what Burke (1947) calls "myths," the prepolitical ground of ideologies. Different ideologies are each partial interpretations of the myths and their applications. So, a group may be united by a grounding in common myths, yet have subgroups whose ideologies clash fiercely in the struggle to own and interpret the symbols of these shared myths because to do so translates into power. The same myths thus sponsor a number of competing ideologies, each of which claims to promote the best interpretation of the shared myths. Consequently, this construction makes it clear that one's ideology is part of one's worldview, but is not the extent of it; one's worldview also includes allegiance to certain prepolitical myths.

Given this understanding of ideology, one can conclude with Lloyd A. Fallers that ideology is concerned actively with the establishment and defense of patterns of value and belief (1961, pp. 677–78). It involves the interpretation of shared prepolitical grounds according to particular patterns and the justification of those patterns; as V. William Balthrop (1984) notes, an ideology often is not articulated until the need arises to defend a particular understanding of a cultural myth from attack (pp. 343, 344). Consequently, there is a dynamic, rather than unidirectional, relationship between ideology and action. Edelman (1971) explains, "To a very significant degree ideologies are certainly the consequence, rather than the independent cause, of how the game is played. Men [and women] constantly create them to rationalize their behavior. They nonetheless become potent symbols once they are in existence, supplying gratifications, affect, and a justification for militancy on both sides" (p. 160). Ideologies can anticipate and direct action; conversely, actions can give rise to ideologies needed to justify them. This relationship is not static, as ideology and action may continue to modify each other over time. Furthermore, ideologies also must adapt in light of their clashes with other ideologies. It is important here to reiterate that "ideology" is not a synonym for "false consciousness" or merely a rationalization to act in one's own self-interest; as the following criticism will illustrate, the interests and power configurations one promotes need not be selfish ones.

Fourth and finally, given the ubiquitous presence of ideologies, their revelation in situated symbolic action, and the role of discursive conflict in understanding ideologies, they clearly are a subject of interest to the argument critic. However, the astute argument critic should recognize that these very qualities make his or her own criticism ideological as well. Each criticism is an act of situated symbolic action that defends a particular interpretation and evaluation of a text as better than conflicting critiques—and does so from the critic's particular ideologically tinted worldview. The ideologies engaged by critiques are disclosed by examining the qualities of the arguments deployed and the commitments they challenge or make to particular distributions of social power.

Eagleton (1983) succinctly argues the controversial point that academic criticism necessarily involves advancing particular political interests and/or advocating more general power distributions:

> For any body of theory concerned with human meaning, value, language, feeling and experience will inevitably engage with broader, deeper beliefs about the nature of human individuals and societies, problems of power and sexuality, interpretations of past history, versions of the present and hopes for the future. . . . [T]heories are not to be upbraided for being political, but for being on the whole covertly or unconsciously so—for the blindness with which they offer as a supposedly "technical," "self-evident," "scientific" or "universal" truth doctrines which with a little reflection can be seen to relate to and reinforce the particular interests of particular groups of people at particular times. (p. 195)

If critics, especially critics of contemporary arguments, refuse to acknowledge the unavoidably ideological nature of their own arguments, they are less likely to see the social relevance of their criticism. When critics so deny relevance to their criticism beyond the confines of the academy, the justification to write such criticism is reduced to the idea that, in the words of Jim Merod, "[c]riticism is necessary but useless, an urgent inadequacy" (1987, p. 1).

When we, as critics, acknowledge that our work inevitably takes sides and reinforces certain practical positions at the expense of others, we risk opening our views to scrutiny on the basis of their ideological content as well as their theoretical method (see, for example, Wander 1983, pp. 7–10). In the process, we take responsibility for the commitments our criticism makes that may be used—with or without our knowledge or consent—in sociopolitical controversies that reach beyond the confines of the academy. As Philip Wander (1983) suggests at the conclusion of his well-known article on "The Ideological Turn in Modern Criticism":

> An ideological turn in modern criticism reflects the existence of crisis, acknowledges the influence of established interests and the reality of alternative world-views, and commends rhetorical analyses not only of the actions implied but also of the interests represented. More than "informed talk about matters of importance," criticism carries us to the point of recognizing good rea-

sons and engaging in right action. What an ideological view does is to situate "good" and "right" in an historical context, the efforts of real people to create a better world. (p. 18)

Thus, to admit the inevitable partiality and advocacy of such symbolic acts involves not only rejecting the notion that academic critics' texts are "things-in-themselves" "assumed to be free of bias or distortion resulting from information that exists outside its boundaries," but also recognizing that critics are incapable of "innocent" or "pure" readings because they, too, always are situated in a historical context (Crowley 1992, p. 457).

In the remainder of this essay, we adopt a rather unique, two-pronged approach to evaluating historically situated arguments; the arguments are drawn from the discursive conflict in an admittedly political trial in which jurors had to affirm one ideology over a competing one. We analyze the struggle among ideological positions of four parties in a contemporary trial concerning the appropriateness of the U.S. government's policies with respect to certain Central American countries and to citizens protesting the government's actions on the issues involved, then briefly inspect how our own convictions are expressed by this analysis. Initially, we examine the competing ideologies couched in the arguments of the prosecution and the sanctuary movement defendants in *U.S. v. Aguilar*. Instead of merely explicating the arguments for a better understanding of the two ideologies, we juxtapose them and demonstrate how each side explicitly convicted the other's actions based on the axiology supported by its ideology. Then we survey how this ideological clash and, more concretely, the outcome of the trial were modified by the distinct ideologies of additional primary participants: the trial judge and the defense lawyers.[1] Lastly, the critique takes a reflexive turn as we examine what the analysis says about our own ideological commitments.

IDEOLOGICAL CONTESTS IN THE SANCTUARY TRIAL

The sanctuary movement began in 1980 as a loose coalition of individuals and churches seeking to help Central Americans fleeing their home countries for noneconomic reasons. Many Central Americans left their countries during the 1980s because they feared torture and death by political factions, factions that frequently received military and financial aid from the Reagan administration.[2] Sanctuary members aimed to help these Central Americans attain the legal protection of "refugee" status under domestic and international humanitarian laws, such as the 1980 Refugee Act and the 1967 U.N. Protocol Relating to the Status of Refugees, so that the foreigners could remain in the United States until it was safe to return home. Sanctuary workers soon realized that the legal channels for protecting refugees functionally were closed to Central Americans. Since the Reagan administration had to certify to Congress that human rights violations were not excessive in the countries it aided, the Immigration and Naturalization Service (INS) routinely denied even the most well-documented appeals for refugee status and deported countless Central Americans before they could file for protection. With the legal channels blocked, sanctuary workers turned to publicly shielding the Central Americans to call attention to the Reagan administration's foreign aid and asylum-granting policies and transported the foreigners to locations where they would have a better opportunity to file for refugee status (e.g., Canada or U.S. INS offices farther north of the Mexican border where immediate deportation was less likely). Because of the administration's role in Central America's unrest, the government wanted the sanctuary movement and its negative commentary on U.S. Central American policy stopped, particularly as sanctuary gained greater visibility and media attention over time. So, on January 14, 1985, after a ten-month investigation and infiltration of the religiously based movement, the government indicted sixteen sanctuary workers on charges of conspiracy and seventy counts of recruiting, smuggling, transporting, and harboring illegal aliens.[3]

A six-month trial, *U.S. v. Aguilar*, commenced in October 1985. The trial was characterized by a variety of motions designed to reduce the argumentative options of either side. These motions included a motion *in limine* or motion to exclude material considered "prejudicial" from a trial, including material deemed irrelevant, inadmissible, or inflammatory. In two separate moves, one at the time the original pretrial motion was filed and the second four months later on the eve of the trial, the judge granted special prosecutor Donald Reno a motion *in limine* that disallowed numerous entire lines of the accused's planned defense.[4] Fearing that the defendants' testimony only would subject them to conviction on more counts, since the *in limine* rulings prevented them from explaining either their motives or why they believed humanitarian laws protected their actions, the defense team instead concentrated on impugning the testimony of the prosecution witnesses. Ultimately, the defense lawyers rested without calling a single witness themselves. The defense team's lack of a cohesive and consistent strategy in light of the *in limine* rulings contributed to guilty verdicts against eight of the eleven defendants tried. At their sentencings, eighteen months after their initial indictment, the sanctuary workers who were found guilty had their first significant opportunity to address the court.

The Prosecutor's Ideology versus the Defendants' Ideology

Prosecutor Reno's arguments in *Aguilar* reveal a worldview colored by a consistent ideology. Reno urged the jury to espouse an ontology based on the idea that people are basically self-interested and act accordingly. The epistemology underlying his arguments assumes that one knows by relying on authorities and the testimony of those who represent authority. Finally, his axiology suggests that one should make judgments based primarily on whether laws or other authoritative directives are respected or violated.

Although the defendants did not testify at their trial, the expression of a worldview influenced by a consistent ideology emerges from their sentencing statements and stands in sharp contrast to the prosecution's position. Their ontology suggests that people are basically trustworthy and are not motivated predominantly by self-interest. Instead of looking to authorities to disseminate reliable knowledge, the defendants assume that one knows or confronts reality through personal experience or empathy with another's personal experience. Their axiology is consistent with these ontological and epistemological assumptions; they defended the idea that, based on personal experience, one should make judgments aimed at achieving affirmative justice (i.e., taking action to relieve human suffering and protect humans' dignity, instead of, for example, engaging in retribution), even if particular laws or legal interpretations must be violated in the process. Furthermore, their axiology explicitly calls for people to take constructive action to effect justice; simply avoiding breaking laws was not, for them, a defensible standard of human action. The contrast between the prosecutor's and the defendants' ideologies on each of these three dimensions illuminates a recurring discursive conflict over issues of social justice and power distribution; it also illustrates the approach and utility of argument critics focusing on the ideological structure that supports a particular set of arguments.

Contrasting Ontologies

Initially, the prosecutor and the defendants differed sharply on the ontological nature of reality as seen in human action. Reno's arguments imply that people are basically self-interested and usually act consistently with that self-interest. With any explanation of the defendants' humanitarian and religious motives explicitly excluded from the trial by the *in limine* rulings, Reno at one point suggested to the jury that the defendants may have helped the Central Americans for pecuniary gain, much like the professional coyotes who smuggle illegal aliens across the U.S.-Mexican border for profit. When he retreated from this position to acknowledge that the defendants may have acted from a desire to help others, the prosecutor's attack depended on two related ideas. First, he interpreted sanctuary members' violations of immigration laws as acts of self-interest designed to further a particular political or religious agenda at the expense of society as a whole. Second, the prosecutor intimated that the reason social welfare could be endangered even by violations of laws performed with good intentions and in the service of a hypothetically noble moral code is that such violations set a precedent for breaking laws. Even if the sanctuary defendants broke the law in the service of good, Reno implied, acquitting them would set a dangerous precedent. According to his ontological position, the people this example would encourage to break laws in the future would, more likely than not, do so to further selfish interests.

As we have argued in detail elsewhere (Olson and Olson 1994), the whole fabric of the prosecution's case reflects what Duncan Kennedy (1976) calls the "individualistic" mode of argument. Individualism sharply distinguishes one's interests from the interests of others and acknowledges that it is legitimate to prefer one's own interests. The caveat is that one must respect the rules that make it possible for everyone to pursue self-interest simultaneously and still coexist peacefully. Laws draw the boundaries that make coexistence possible for self-interested beings; consequently, one must not break or make exceptions to these laws, even in apparently exceptional cases, because excusing nonconforming action compromises the essence of the structure that makes society viable. In particular, Reno portrayed the sanctuary defendants as civil disobedients who deliberately defied immigration laws to serve their own political and religious agendas, however noble. For example, he argued:

> Personal advancement, financial gain, political reason, religious beliefs, moral convictions or some adherence to a higher law, even of nations, are well recognized motives of human conduct. These motives may prompt one person to voluntary acts of good, and another to voluntary acts of crime. Good motive is not a defense to intentional acts of crime. So if you find beyond a reasonable doubt that the acts constituting the crime charged were committed with the intent to commit the unlawful act and bring about the prohibited result, then the requirement that the act be done knowingly or willfully, as defined in these instructions, has been satisfied— . . . even though the defendant may have believed that his conduct was politically, religiously, or morally required, or that ultimate good would result from such conduct. (Trial, p. 12682)

The prosecutor insisted that the existence of legal channels for procuring refugee status, regardless of those channels' ineffectiveness for Central Americans, made sanctuary activities unjustified, dangerous acts of self-interest that compromised the integrity of the whole legal system. Thus, in his closing, Reno argued, "They may have had every single good purpose in the world for what they did, but, ladies and gentlemen, that doesn't change the fact they were violating the law" (Trial, p. 14201).

The defendants' ontological position is markedly different. They assume that people are basically good and frequently are motivated by altruistic concerns. For example, at her sentencing, defendant Wendy LeWin noted that she thought it was not remarkable, but routine for people to sacrifice for others without expecting personal gain:

> The Good Samaritan, who I don't think asked anything of the man that he helped, no green card or political opinion or anything else. But that that to me was just taken for granted as a human response to someone in need and not one that I had to be a hero or a heroine to do, but that I would be inhuman if I did not do, that was just taken for granted as the way I would respond in that kind of situation. . . . And I don't consider myself an exceptional person or someone who did something

exceptional either in the negative sense or the positive sense. I consider it just to be a human response to a situation that I found myself in living here. (Sentencings, p. 109)

The corpus of the defendants' sentencing comments is characterized by what Kennedy (1976) terms the "altruistic" mode of argument. In contrast to individualism, altruism does not endorse a sharp preference for one's self-interest over the interests of others. Sharing, mercy, and sacrifice are the positive human qualities underwritten by an altruistic ontology. At their sentencings, the defendants finally were allowed to raise the issues excluded from the trial by the *in limine* rulings: their perceptions that the Reagan administration disregarded both national and international humanitarian laws; their concern for the violence in Central America and the United States' role in perpetuating it; their belief that the INS illegitimately blocked channels for granting asylum to Central Americans in order to shield the administration's political interests; and their conviction that they were justified to follow what they saw as the natural human response to the persecuted Central Americans. Viewing the government's use of the immigration system as an illegitimate means to deny refugee status to deserving Central Americans for political reasons, sanctuary defendants supported the "taken-for-granted" human response of helping the Central Americans, even if that position necessitated violating certain immigration laws—or, more precisely, certain selective uses of immigration laws, laws that the defendants supported under usual circumstances—in order to fulfill the intent of the humanitarian laws ignored by the Reagan administration. Further illustrating their assumption that people usually can be trusted to do the right thing, defendant Darlene Nicgorski, a Roman Catholic nun, lamented the fact that the stringent *in limine* boundaries denied the jury the opportunity to decide the case based on a fuller disclosure of the issues: "I had always been willing to accept the judgment of a jury of our peers. What most discourages me is that we were never allowed to tell the jury why. I had always believed, perhaps naively, that under the American system of justice the courtroom is a place where citizens accused of crimes have a right to tell why they did what they did" (Sentencings, pp. 52–53). Thus, on the ontological dimension, the prosecutor defended the assumption that humans are basically self-interested and must be treated as such, while the defendants claimed that people are basically altruistic and often naturally sacrifice their own interests for the interests of others.[5]

Contrasting Epistemologies

According to the prosecution's position, the answer to the epistemological question "How do we know?" is "Authorities tell us." At the heart of Reno's arguments was the unquestioned assumption that one can and should believe the claims of those who hold positions of authority, such as members of the executive or judicial branches of government, as well as these authorities' agents, such as the informants who infiltrated the sanctuary movement. One trusts what authorities claim to know of reality simply because of their privileged status.

Several examples illustrate this epistemological commitment. For instance, although the *in limine* rulings precluded the defense team from openly challenging the government's execution of immigration procedures with respect to the Central Americans, Reno maintained in court that the government's conduct was justified. He claimed that both the use of immigration procedures to deny Central Americans asylum and the use of informants to infiltrate the sanctuary movement, whose members often met in churches and in conjunction with prayer or worship meetings, were justified because of the authorities' role in mediating issues of national concern for the American people. With respect to immigration laws, the prosecutor argued:

> Every nation has the absolute power to control [its] borders, to determine who comes in [its] country, when they come in, where they come in, how long they are going to be here, what they are going to do, how they are going to support themselves and when they are going to leave. No one in this courtroom questions the right of any government to pass a law to that effect. . . . Attempts to determine what aliens come in, where they come in, and attempt to monitor them, so that we as Americans know exactly who is coming into our country, what their business is and where they are going. (Trial, pp. 14191–92)

Since only the government authorities executing these entry procedures presumably "know" if a person is "truly" a refugee under the statute's definition, their judgment supersedes the judgment of nonauthorities, such as the foreigners themselves or the sanctuary workers. Reno told the jury:

The law that you will receive tomorrow will tell you that the
people of the United States have determined that regardless of
what a person may feel that he is before coming into this country, the citizens of the United States, through the law that they
have enacted through their elected representative[s] have said
every person coming into this country will present himself at the
Port of Entry to immigration. That is the law that you will
receive. It is not the law of Reverend Fife and as Mr. Hirsh
[Fife's lawyer] argued to you that so long as people are doing
good things, we have no border. (Trial, p. 14194)

The negative consequences of accepting sources of knowledge
other than authority appears in Reno's ensuing argument: "If that
were the law, all the refugees in this world that could find their
way to our border would become part of this nation. They would
be part of our entire socio-economic structure" (Trial, p. 14194).
Thus, no matter how compelling the evidence may appear to the
nonauthority, only the immigration officials, deputized by the
"elected representatives" of the people, can make a reliable determination of someone's rightful immigration and refugee status.
Only official determinations safeguard the established social hierarchy so that legitimate citizens can pursue their self-interest without such unsanctioned encumbrances as illegitimate intruders in
the socioeconomic structure.

Furthermore, in spite of the dubious nature of the government's practice of infiltrating a religiously based movement with
paid informants, Reno defended the credibility of the informant
witnesses because they were technically agents of the proper
authorities: "This was an alien smuggling conspiracy. Informants
are used in alien smuggling conspiracies as regularly as these cases
are prosecuted. They must be used, ladies and gentlemen. Informants are the only reasonable way of the Government protecting
the border and investigating alien smuggling conspiracies. And
that is why it is proper and lawful" (Trial, p. 12684). Again, self-
interest underwrites the authorities' method of gathering "knowledge" to disseminate to the jury. After the defense team had
impeached the credibility of the prosecution's star witness, Reno
argued that this informant, Jesús Cruz, still could be believed
because he acted on behalf and at the direction of government
authorities: "The motive may have been that he felt that he was
doing something that was right. That he was doing something that

was appropriate for the United States Government" (Trial, p. 14065).

In a similar vein, Reno urged the jury to accept and follow literally Judge Earl Carroll's interpretation of the law, an interpretation highly favorable to the prosecution's strategy (see Olson and Olson 1994; Davidson 1988, p. 146). The prosecutor specifically contrasted the defendants' lack of authority with the judge's position of governmental authority for imparting reliable knowledge in this case: "That may not be the law of Reverend Fife, that may not be the law of Mr. Conger, but ladies and gentlemen, it is the highest law of the land and you are going to receive it from His Honor tomorrow and it is the law that has come to you from all the people in this nation" (Trial, p. 14195). So, the prosecutor encouraged an epistemological stance heavily dependent on uncritical acceptance of statements by authorities and their agents.

Alternately, the defendants' trusted way of knowing was grounded firmly in personal experience or empathy for the personal experiences of others, instead of in the decrees of authority figures. Based on their own experiences with the displaced Central Americans, they claimed to know that these people "truly" fit the definition of "refugees" set forth in humanitarian laws. Defendant Peggy Hutchison defended her claim to know that the people she helped were indeed refugees based on her own observations in immigration detention centers and prisons:

> [I] went to the detention centers here in Southern Arizona. I went to the prison in Nogales, Sonora, Mexico, and I began to meet people from El Salvador and Guatemala. And so what was once an intellectual understanding, became an emotional, a physical understanding, because it was day after day after day that I saw torture marks, that I heard stories, that I cried with people. That was my experience. (Sentencings, p. 12)

She recounted how she and other sanctuary workers discouraged detainees from coming to the United States specifically for economic reasons; but with those who fled persecution, Hutchison shared her conviction that they had "a right to be here in the United States of America" under the Refugee Act of 1980 and the 1967 U.N. Protocol (Sentencings, pp. 12–13).

Sanctuary members were careful to offer their help only to those aliens whose stories persuaded the members that they faced persecution as defined by domestic and international humanitarian laws. For example, Hutchison's experience with certain Central Americans and their accounts of personal experiences in their home countries convinced her that she possessed reliable knowledge that the people she helped "have fled torture, they have fled imprisonment, civil war and death. . . . [T]hey have come here not because they want to, but because they have fled that torture and that death, because of fears of persecution, or actual persecution, because of their race, or their religion, or their nationality, or their participation in a social or political group" (Sentencings, pp. 10–11). The assumption that knowledge comes from sharing and personally evaluating experiences persists in LeWin's priorities. When we interviewed her some years after the trial, LeWin stressed that the Central Americans' problems are greater than her own legal ones and urged us to seek out the refugees' firsthand accounts of their experiences instead of concentrating on her account of her trial experience. She commented, "I think the most important thing to do is not to tell my story but the refugees' stories, and that's what most people need to hear" (LeWin, 1988). Thus, while personal and shared experiences all yield some knowledge, for LeWin the more important knowledge relates to genuinely life-threatening experiences of suffering.

Furthermore, the sanctuary defendants' experiences with U.S. immigration decisions convinced them that the government was misusing the system for political reasons and so prompted them to challenge the government as an authority that could not be trusted for reliable knowledge on the issues involved. Recounting her first experience at immigration court, Hutchison told the story of a young Central American who had fled to protect his life with only the clothes on his back; the immigration judge declared his petition for political asylum "a legally frivolous claim" because the man could not present documentation from an authority figure proving that he was a target of persecution (Sentencings, pp. 13–14). Another defendant, narrating the experience of her Salvadoran husband's struggle to gain asylum, tells Judge Carroll what she knows and how she knows it:

> I know about his telling about torture of family members, of his story of almost being killed, and I have every reason to believe that to be true after talking to his brother who also fled and applied for asylum in this country. I also sat in the courtroom when his case was denied. He doesn't have a piece of paper from

the person that did the torturing saying that they would do the same to him. He doesn't have any way of proving that they almost killed him. There was no reporter standing there with a camera and in most circumstances that is an impossibility. So perhaps the judge was in a very difficult situation with no proof either way. But because of that, my husband could be deported. His case is on appeal. (Sentencings, pp. 111–12)

Such negative experiences with those whose claim to know is based on their positions of authority prompted Hutchison to remark, "I am remorseful, Judge Carroll, but I am remorseful only for the plight of Central American refugees and the fact that our immigration laws are not administered fairly" (Sentencings, 18-19). Obviously, the defendants' assumption that knowledge comes from personal experiences or empathy with the personal experiences of others directly conflicts with the prosecution's epistemological assumption that reliable knowledge is disseminated by authorities and should not be challenged based on one's own assessments.

Contrasting Axiologies

Interwoven with the *Aguilar* prosecutor's and defendants' ontological and epistemological positions are their axiologies, or standards for judging what is good or right; each axiology indicts the ideologically motivated choices of the opposition. The prosecutor's axiology declares that actions are unequivocally wrong if they break laws. Uncritically abiding by the laws thus becomes an end in itself. In this axiology, there are no sins of omission nor negative judgments for good acts gone undone. One is only accountable for acts of commission that violate legal boundaries.

Reno's axiology is consistent with his ontological assumption that people are basically self-interested and with his epistemological assumption that one knows based on authority. The explanation behind his ontological position is that, even if everyone does not operate primarily from self-interest, enough people do to make legal boundaries necessary; one cannot make exceptions to these boundaries because making exceptions sets a dangerous precedent that the self-interested majority will use to justify their own violations of laws. Furthermore, according to the prosecutor, these legal boundaries should be obeyed because they are established by credible authorities who are responsible to protect the interests of society as a whole. On these grounds, Reno exhorted jurors, "[G]ive them the message that there is nothing higher, there is no higher law in this land than the law that has been passed by the people of the United States and by Congress" (Trial, p. 14206). Reno defended an axiology under which violating laws set forth by authorities is always "bad," while "good" consists of merely abstaining from breaking laws.

Consequently, the prosecutor was in a position to argue for abiding by laws as an end in itself. He contended, "They may have had every single good purpose in the world for what they did, but, ladies and gentlemen, that doesn't change the fact they were violating the law" (Trial, p. 14201). Under this axiology, it does not matter if the jury chooses to believe that the sanctuary defendants acted from self-interest or not. If they acted selfishly, they deserve to be punished for breaking the immigration laws to serve their own interests; if they acted from altruistic motives, they still deserve to be punished for setting a bad precedent and defying authority by transgressing legal boundaries. For instance, Reno's closing declared, "Their motive may be to help people, but His Honor, Judge Carroll, will instruct you that motive has nothing at all to do with whether or not these people knew and were willfully and knowingly involved in violating this law" (Trial, p. 14201). Here, the prosecutor reinforces his conclusion by referring to the trial's authority figure, Judge Carroll, and his instructions.

Obviously, winning the *in limine* rulings advanced Reno's ability to argue unambiguously that the defendants had violated laws. The *in limine* rulings precluded the defense team from referring to the humanitarian laws that the defendants perceived as supporting their behavior and as *only* conflicting with immigration laws in this specific case because of the administration's politically motivated use of these laws. The rulings also assisted the prosecution by excluding evidence of the defendants' motives or intentions; even so, Reno made explicit arguments to deter the jurors from acquitting the sanctuary workers should they come to a conclusion on their own that the defendants had acted from noble motives or necessity.

According to the axiology that Reno embraced, then, following the laws is an end in itself, and the role of the court system is simply to determine whether or not a law has been broken and to punish lawbreakers, not to realize justice in any larger sense. The prosecutor repeatedly argued that the evidence unequivocally showed the defendants indeed had breached the boundaries of the immigration laws. He declared:

> All the United States Government has to do is to prove beyond a reasonable doubt that they are violating the law. The Government is not at issue with them as to whether they are good or bad. We are here to prove to you, and under the evidence in this case have proved to you, that they have violated these acts beyond a reasonable doubt. . . . It is because they have very plainly and simply, and under the evidence of this case, violated the law. (Trial, p. 14202)

According to this axiological view, a jury is not to attempt to achieve justice nor to scrutinize the motives, needs, or intentions behind particular actions; it is only to decide if a defendant's actions technically violated particular legal boundaries. This position presumes that the laws established by the authorities are, in actuality, just and so warrants preempting complications that may arise in applying a particular law to a historically situated case.

The defendants' axiology is strikingly different from Reno's. At the sentencing, the sanctuary workers vigorously defended the ideas that law and justice are not identical and that achieving justice involves more than uncritically following laws for their own sake. According to the defendants' ideology, laws are only a means to achieve a more important end or social distribution of rights and power: affirmative justice. If laws—or, more precisely, the government's executions of laws—fail to serve justice (i.e., in the affirmative sense of reducing others' suffering and protecting their dignity, not in the sense of retribution for wrongs done to oneself), one must seek more effective means to achieve such justice and publicly expose the reasons and political motives that prevent laws from effectively serving justice. Furthermore, under this axiology, one can be held liable for failing to take constructive action to effect justice. Since justice is elevated as the ultimate goal, this axiology allows that, in special cases in which laws are interpreted to block justice, it is permissible to pursue justice at the expense of violating an interpretation of laws designed to serve the powerful's political agenda—at least as long as one first exhausts the legal avenues to such justice. Thus, the defendants did not justify outright civil disobedience. In this case, they argued that their actions fulfilled not only the "higher cause of justice," but also the specific domestic and international humanitarian laws excluded from the trial by the *in limine* rulings (i.e., the Refugee Act of 1980 and the 1967 UN Protocol). They further perceived that the immigration laws under which they were tried conflicted with these humanitarian laws and affirmative justice *only* because of the Reagan administration's self-serving practices of ignoring the latter two and pressing the former into the service of its political position on Central America. This complex axiological position demands a more detailed explication.

The central tenets of this axiology are that justice and law are not the same and that, when the two recommend different courses of action, justice is more important than law. Defendant Nicgorski's observation at the sentencing illustrates the first tenet: "I began to understand in 1983 what Justice Oliver Wendell Holmes, Jr. meant when he said and I quote, 'This is a Court of law, not a Court of justice.' . . . This trial has also caused me to think further about the crucial difference between justice and law, between what is just and what is legal. . . . The letter of the law will kill and quite literally kills" (Sentencings, pp. 49–50).

Laws are justified by their ability to effect justice, not because they are established or enforced by authority figures. Because achieving justice is the justification for having laws under this axiology, laws that inhibit the realization of justice or interpretations of laws that have this effect (e.g., the administration's use of immigration laws to deny Central Americans the asylum established by humanitarian laws) are illegitimate. Nicgorski continued:

> I accept this decision in the context of the current political climate in which dissent is being silenced at every level. I do still hope for justice and realize more clearly now than when we began, that I may need to look elsewhere for justice. . . . Laws for the most part are general directions which are subject to change as new circumstances develop. They are not to be absolutized as some have done. They are time dated guidelines. Law and Government are legitimized only by the fulfillment of certain duties for the maintenance of the general welfare of the body politic. Oftentimes the legal system lags behind the sense of right and justice as expressed by the community. I think we are now in one of those times. (Sentencings, p. 53)

She concludes that God, the ultimate embodiment of justice, expects nothing (e.g., human laws and legal interpretations) to take priority over this affirmative justice. However, Nicgorski recognized that it is difficult to separate law and justice in people's minds, saying, "The American people are taught to be obedient to the law. To get beyond the narrow concept of law and to respond to the issues of justice is very difficult" (Sentencings, p. 52). With this claim, Nicgorski acknowledged that many Americans are taught to accept uncritically a version of the prosecution's axiology.

According to the defendants' axiology, laws are warranted only if they work to achieve justice. Consequently, one needs to examine critically the legal code to determine which laws or legal interpretations are just. As in Reno's position, the defendants' ontological and epistemological assumptions point to their axiology by identifying how one recognizes justice. Initially, one cannot rely on impersonal legal codes, handed down by fallible authorities, to be applied blindly to every case without regard for the specific details. Nicgorski argued for this position, commenting, "There is no ethical handbook which we can consult for every situation" (Sentencings, p. 55). Instead, one follows one's altruistic nature in pursuit of affirmative justice. Based on one's personal experience and empathy for others' experiences, one follows "taken-for-granted" human altruistic tendencies; justice is realized when one responds with empathy to another's experience of suffering. For example, defendant Tony Clark, a Roman Catholic priest, stated, "I stand before this Court as a convicted felon, ready to be sentenced. And yet I know full well that if I ever failed to act in any other way than to respond to my fellow brothers and sisters in a less than genuine and authentic Christian manner, I would be guilty of a far greater crime" (Sentencings, pp. 181–82). So, when following the laws as directed by authorities conflicts with achieving justice, this axiology insists that one choose to advance justice over simply avoiding legal violations.

Consistent with this cardinal responsibility to justice, the defendants' axiology carries the requirement that one take constructive action to realize justice; merely avoiding technically violating laws is insufficient. Defendant Philip Willis-Conger summarized this affirmative responsibility: "[T]he most serious crime here is to see people in desperate need and to do nothing. . . . I cannot stand back and do nothing" (Sentencings, pp. 77–78). Similarly, defendant Reverend John Fife argued that all individuals, not only the authorities, are responsible for working to achieve justice: A passage from the Nuremberg trials "says clearly that each one of us, each one of us, carries a clear responsibility to the

law, to civilization, to human rights, the responsibility for observing and protecting refugees' rights to asylum rests on all of us[,]
not just on government officials, not just on immigration officials" (Sentencings, p. 165). While one should respect laws and
authorities, one's ultimate responsibility is to pursue justice.

Therefore, laws that perpetuate injustice or authorities that
use just laws for unjust purposes must be challenged. For example,
Father Clark stated that good laws can maintain justice only when
both the government and individuals are expected to obey them
(Sentencings, p. 184). If the government is allowed to ignore laws
that do not serve its immediate purposes (e.g., humanitarian
laws), then justice is thwarted. The defendants claimed that, in
this case, they fulfilled the just purpose of humanitarian laws,
while the government itself violated that purpose. Willis-Conger
explained the distinction, saying, "I believe that our Government
was breaking the law. And that by helping these refugees I was
upholding the law. . . . [W]e have not only a moral but a legal obligation to help political refugees" (Sentencings, pp. 86, 92). In the
defendants' eyes, only the government's self-serving interpretation
of immigration laws, laws that are not necessarily unjust in and of
themselves, brought them into conflict with the defendants'
attempts to fulfill the just aim of domestic and international
humanitarian laws. The defendants not only rendered a critical
judgment of their government's actions, but also committed themselves to the active pursuit of affirmative justice.

The defendants' first opportunity to defend and apply their
axiology in court came at the sentencing. Free from the *in limine*
restrictions that discouraged them from testifying in the trial
phase, the eight convicted defendants clearly explained their
beliefs that law and justice are distinct and that laws and their
interpretations or uses may or may not further the cause of justice.
In this case, they argued, sanctuary attempts to achieve justice by
fulfilling the intent of humanitarian laws conflicted with the
Reagan administration's abusive execution of immigration laws.
If the government itself abided by humanitarian laws, immigration and humanitarian laws would not be incompatible. They
argued that only the government's illegitimate use of immigration
laws, designed to conceal the fact that it was financing instead of
substantially curbing human rights violations by the factions
aided, necessitated the defendants' actions. Under the circumstances, the defendants claimed to feel morally compelled to take

action. Thus, their axiological standards vindicated their actions and condemned the government's position toward Central Americans and the sanctuary movement, just as the prosecution's axiology unequivocally condemned sanctuary activities.

The Modifying Influences of the Judge's and Defense Team's Ideologies

The legal showdown that the defendants had anticipated between their ideology and the government's, as represented by the prosecution, did not transpire during the trial phase. Since the defendants ultimately did not testify because of the *in limine* rulings, the clash between the argumentative position supported by their ideology and the one supported by the prosecution's was not apparent to the jury. However, as the previously cited quotations from the trial transcript illustrate, Prosecutor Reno was able to give a complete presentation revealing his ideology. This imbalance of access to the jury was aggravated further by the influences of the judge and the defense attorneys. The statements of these two parties reveal ideologies distinct from either the defendants' or the prosecution's. The axiological assumptions of these two additional ideologies are most relevant here. The judge saw "the law" as the sole avenue to justice; consequently, he did not allow for the possibility that conflicts may occur if one assumes the two are distinct and sometimes may be, or may be used in a way that makes them, incompatible. Most important, the judge was the party with the official power in this setting and, by virtue of this role, had the least conspicuous motives to insinuate his ideology into the jury's deliberations. Restricted by the *in limine* boundaries, the defense team reacted with a presentation that lacked a developed, internally consistent position on whether laws achieve justice or not (see Olson and Olson 1991, 1994). The axiologies of both the judge and the defense attorneys need elaboration.

By all accounts, Judge Carroll was a very influential force in the sanctuary trial. His statements and rulings suggest a consistent ideology inclined toward preserving existing power distributions. According to Carroll, there is a "universal sense of justice" (Pretrial, p. 1099). Justice is achieved only through the existing system of laws and government, not through individual action. When laws fulfill justice imperfectly, it is the fault of individuals, not the system. The only acceptable means for correcting such imperfections is to use the legal mechanisms for change built into the system. Because justice inheres in the system rather than in individuals' actions, all individuals are subject to the system. For Carroll, following the laws while working within the existing system is the only way to achieve justice. Under this ideology, instances in which laws conflict or otherwise fall short of achieving justice are rare, temporary aberrations that must be addressed from inside the system's own boundaries. For example, Carroll claimed at the sentencing that "a fuller use, a more determined use of the system" itself is not only possible but "has kept our legal justice system the best and fairest in the world for 200 years" (Sentencings, pp. 239, 236). Under this ideology, violating laws is never justified. Furthermore, there is no concept of justice other than that which the laws provide.

While Judge Carroll's conflation of laws and justice is different from Prosecutor Reno's position, which focuses on the importance of following the laws backed by authority regardless of whether or not justice results, in practice the prosecution's strategy benefited from the judge's position. The judge possessed the power to back his ideology with the jury, while simultaneously presenting himself as an "objective" representative of "the law"—choices that worked to the prosecution's advantage. For example, Carroll granted part of Reno's *in limine* motion in July; in a *sua sponte* (i.e., unprompted or voluntary) move just before the trial began in October, he greatly expanded the *in limine* boundaries, excluding at the last minute the defendants' most viable lines of defense on the grounds that the excluded material was incendiary or irrelevant to the case. The excluded defenses concerned the defendants' criticisms of the system and its inability to be revised within existing legal channels given the Reagan administration's politics, the defendants' justifications for the necessity of acting outside usual immigration channels in this instance, the humanitarian laws that might vindicate the defendants while casting doubt on the administration's conduct, and any discussion of the defendants' motives or intentions. The extensive exclusions not only discouraged the defendants from testifying (and so from making a forceful, consistent presentation of their ideology to the jury), but also circumscribed the defense attorneys' argumentative position in a way that blunted its effectiveness.

The judge's power to fashion the jury instructions further benefited the prosecution;[6] in fact the instructions so favored the prosecution that Reno spent large portions of his closing statement quoting them. And Reno's consistent refrain concerning the importance of obeying authority reinforced Carroll's tendency to present "the law" as univocal and himself as the embodiment of "objective law." Carroll charged the jury, "You must follow the law as I give it to you whether you agree with it or not and you must not be influenced by personal likes or dislikes, opinions, prejudices or sympathies. . . . You will recall that you took an oath promising to do so at the beginning of the case" (Trial, p. 14252). This presentation of the instructions arguably gave them added weight with the jury. According to defense attorney Robert Hirsh, Carroll gave each juror a copy of the instructions, but told the jurors not to write on the copies "as if the instructions were sacrosanct: 'This is my word, the word of the court'" (quoted in Davidson 1988, p. 148). Later interviews with the jurors clearly indicate the extensive impact that the judge's ideology had on the verdict and the ways in which it reinforced the prosecution's position with the jurors (see Pacelle 1986, 1989; Olson and Olson 1994).

The ideological underpinnings of the defense attorneys' arguments are the most murky of the four ideologies considered here, as they exhibit the lack of a single consistent, well-considered position. Part of the reason is undoubtedly the fact that the defense team included a dozen attorneys, since each defendant was represented by at least one lawyer; most of these attorneys had never worked together before, and they functioned without a clear leader. However, the last-minute *in limine* ruling, which perhaps they should have anticipated, also fragmented their prepared defense, sending them scrambling for whatever random "hooks" might persuade the jury. The result was that they offered the jury an underdeveloped, internally inconsistent justification for acquittal.

Deprived of their preferred, internally consistent defenses by the extensive *in limine* exclusions, members of the defense team by turns argued that law does lead to justice and that law does not lead to justice. For example, one defense tack was to argue that the prosecution had not met its burden of proof on many of the charges. For this reason, defense attorneys urged jurors to follow the legal standard on "reasonable doubt" and so to acquit the defendants. To illustrate, defense attorney A. Bates Butler told the jury, "The prosecution has the burden of proof beyond a reasonable doubt on each and every element of each and every crime. And that is a heavy, heavy burden. But that is our system of law and justice. And you have sworn to follow that" (Trial, p. 13595). Defense attorney James Brosnahan's argument urging the jurors to disregard the testimony of the prosecution's star witness reinforced the idea that law promotes justice in practice. He contended, "And [jury] instruction No. 10 says, 'If a witness is shown knowingly to have testified falsely in this case concerning any material matter, you have a right to distrust such witness's testimony in other particulars. And you may reject all the testimony of that witness or give it such credibility as you think it deserves.' The law is just, the law is right. The law is practical" (Trial, p. 13321). Additionally, despite the *in limine* prohibitions on such material, the defense cultivated the idea that certain laws do lead to justice by "oozing" information on the humanitarian laws that their clients believed sanctioned sanctuary activities into the trial. For instance, defense attorney Nancy Grey Postero took issue with Reno's analogy between the sanctuary movement and the nineteenth-century underground railroad for slaves:

> [The prosecutor] wants you to say just like the underground railroad people, these people are good humanitarian people with good motives, but they broke the law and you have to convict them. Don't fall into that trap. . . . [The defendants] did not break the law. . . . And if they put an informant, or a Mr. Nixon, in the underground railroad, they certainly wouldn't have had evidence like we have in this case that those people believed that they were acting lawfully. (Trial, pp. 13660–61)

On one hand, then, the defense lawyers endorsed the idea that following laws produces justice and encouraged jurors to apply certain laws in ways favorable to their clients.

On the other hand, the defense team suggested that laws do not yield justice. In such cases, it is permissible, perhaps even obligatory, to defy the laws in order to better serve justice, the defense attorneys sometimes implied. One defense argument that illustrates this second approach and apparently contradicts the Postero argument just cited is defense attorney Ellen Yaroshefsky's favorable reference to Rosa Parks, the woman whose admitted civil disobedience was instrumental in initiating the civil rights movement. The defense team further developed this apparently contradictory line of argument by suggesting jury nullification, which is a jury's right to set aside a law that they find unjust or that is used unjustly. As Brosnahan later acknowledged, arguing for jury nullification implies that the prosecution may have proven adequately that the defendants broke laws, thus compromising the contention that sanctuary functions within the laws (Brosnahan 1989). The defense's attempts to serve as role models for jury nullification by standing up to the judge led to repeated, one-sided power struggles with the courtroom's authority figure. It was a choice that not only further emphasized the apparent inconsistency in the defense lawyers' argumentative position, but also highlighted the nonauthorities' powerlessness and damaged the defense's credibility with the jury (see Olson and Olson 1991, 1994; Pacelle 1986). The defense's insufficient expression of when laws yield justice, when they do not, and how a juror regularly can recognize the two different situations exemplified the defense attorneys' failure to offer the jury a clear, internally consistent ideological position to compare to the prosecution's.

The important point here is that power differentials and the way they are handled can modify the outcome of a fundamentally ideological controversy presented as a legal contest. In this case, the prosecutor's ideological position benefited from the fact that the judge's commitments dovetailed with its objectives and allowed it to be presented to its fullest. This position's internal consistency thus was obvious, and the judge's exercise of his own ideology, through rulings, comments, and nonverbal behavior, further fortified the prosecution's position (see Olson and Olson 1994). The defendants' own internally consistent, well-reasoned ideological position was unavailable to the jury until after the verdict was submitted, largely because the *in limine* rulings convinced the defense team that it was too risky for the defendants to testify during the trial. The defense lawyers' efforts did not fill the resulting void adequately. While the judge's ability to exclude legally numerous lines of defense seriously limited the defense lawyers' options, the choices that they made further weakened their chances of prevailing (see also Olson and Olson 1991). Measured against the prosecution's complete, consistent ideology, the position that the sanctuary attorneys defended was underdeveloped and often appeared internally inconsistent. Furthermore, as the judge successfully squelched recurring defense challenges to his authority and rulings, the defense attorneys became unappealing models for the jurors. Now, certainly it is possible to develop a defensible, consistent argument concluding that laws sometimes serve justice and sometimes do not. The point is that the restrictions imposed on the defense attorneys by the prosecution and the judge, as well as their own failure to respond with one consistent, cogently argued ideological position, resulted in a situation in which the prosecution's case appeared more acceptable to the jury than it appears in a retrospective comparison of the primary trial participants' ideological stances. Thus, the courtroom does not offer a neutral forum for an open contest between two ideologies to be adjudicated by a disinterested jury; it offers a forum characterized by multiple competing and/or compatible ideologies, which may be fortified to differing degrees by prevailing distributions of power and authority.

ARGUMENT EVALUATION AND IDEOLOGICAL POSITIONS: WHAT THE ARGUMENTS REVEAL ABOUT THE TRIAL PARTICIPANTS AND THEIR CRITICS

This analysis of the fundamentally incompatible ideologies of the sanctuary trial's prosecutor and defendants demonstrates several important ideas for critics of argument. First, ideological positions tend not to be a random assembly of the arguments that one thinks will "win" in a controversy. A comprehensive analysis of the arguments revealing the various ideological positions evident in *Aguilar* shows the more profound, usually internally consistent political and ethical commitments of advocates that unite their arguments and make those arguments mutually reinforcing. If an advocate's auditors adopt his or her ideological interpretation of the society's shared myths, they are more likely to accept that advocate's arguments with little resistance. With respect to this case, sufficiently diverse and ambiguous strains exist in the mythology of our democratic, Judeo-Christian nation, with its legal system claiming ostensibly to operate by the "rule of law" instead of the "rule of individuals," to ground comfortably both the prosecutor's and the defendants' fundamentally conflicting ideologies. Whether the jurors came to the trial already embracing ideologies similar to the prosecutor's or whether Reno, with the judge's inadvertent or intentional assistance, convinced them of this interpretation is impossible to tell. Recent studies suggest that Americans without firsthand experience in the legal system tend toward Kennedy's "individualistic" view and accept the notions that laws are "objective" and that the "rule of law" largely describes legal practice in

America; at least they hold this view until they gain firsthand experience with the legal system (see Merry 1985, 1986; Sarat and Felstiner 1986). On the other hand, since the breadth of the *in limine* rulings encouraged the defendants to decline testifying on their own behalf for fear of being convicted on more counts with no compensatory opportunity to explain why they had acted and since the defense attorneys did not respond to the challenge by presenting a persuasive, consistent ideological position, the jurors may have been drawn to the prosecution's ideology simply because it was the only complete, internally consistent position presented by the trial's three groups of admitted partisans (i.e., prosecution, defense attorneys, defendants).

Second, this criticism underscores the importance of examining primary sources when evaluating arguments. While a critic's own ideology inevitably influences his or her impression of the primary materials, secondary sources already contain an additional layer of interpretation and evaluation colored by their authors' ideologies. In this case, our preliminary work with secondary sources led to an oversimplified view of the controversy and the trial participants' choices. Once we gained access to the actual trial transcripts, however, we modified this view. Analysis of the transcripts revealed that there were not merely two competing ideologies contending in the sanctuary trial (i.e., defendants'-defense attorneys' versus prosecution's or prosecution's-judge's), but at least four (i.e., defendants', defense attorneys', prosecution's, judge's, as well as the ideologies of the jurors and media representatives, which are not examined in this essay). The primary materials made it possible to reconstruct the different ideologies underlying these four parties' positions and so to gain a richer, more complex understanding of the trial and the ideological conflicts it engendered before rendering an evaluation.

Third, this examination of this trial shows that no ideology is "objectively" transcendent, in spite of claims to be grounded in something higher or more "objective" like "the law" or a moral code. (However, this claim does not mean that ideologies cannot be compared and judged as better or worse, as will become apparent later in this section.) Since *Aguilar* was an admittedly political trial with specific political goals at stake, one may wonder why this conclusion needs to be mentioned. The point, however, is that the ideological positions expressed by the prosecutor and the defendants make larger value commitments beyond the specific, more narrow political issue of determining refugee status for Central Americans. The ideology underwriting the prosecution's position commits to a fundamentally "conservative" set of values. This statement does not mean that the value set is "right-wing" but that it clearly favors perpetuating the status quo power distribution and policies of current executive and judicial authorities, whether that status quo leans left or right. The prosecutor's ideology ostensibly lays aside questions of whether the present system fosters right or wrong in particular cases in order to embrace a larger commitment to the inherent value of the prevailing governance system and its procedures. Under such an ideology, presumption is a powerful concept, especially in conflicts infused with doubt and/or in controversies pitting the powerful of the current system against those who challenge the legitimacy of their use of this power. The defendants' ideology shows its value priorities in its relentless privileging distributions that pursue an affirmative justice. The defendants would have been content to support the present system and authorities had they believed that this system enacted such affirmative justice toward the Central Americans; when they felt that the present system deliberately thwarted justice, however, they had no compunction about challenging it on both moral and legal grounds. Their value commitments were underwritten by their sense of altruism.

Fourth, our evaluation of the defendants' and prosecution's arguments based on analysis of their ideological groundings is mixed, but primarily favors the defendants' ideological stand for two reasons. First, the defendants' position allows for future evaluations based on relatively broader considerations of context. To us, the defendants' view that people are "naturally" motivated to sacrifice for the needs of others seems rather idealistic. Few people would be as altruistic as the sanctuary members, who were willing to risk their jobs, reputations, and freedom to defy a power configuration perpetuating unacceptable treatment of those less fortunate than themselves. While one may wish that more people were so dedicated to an affirmative commitment to relieve human suffering, their lawyers' characterizations of the defendants as exceptional people seem more accurate (see note 5). On the other hand, the prosecution's assumption that people are primarily self-interested, necessitating unbending enforcement of every law without respect to the circumstances, seems overly cynical. In practice, it seems that each person sometimes acts from self-interest and sometimes acts from altruism. And, of course, the prosecutor and defendants probably all would agree to this statement; their ideologies only emphasize one tendency over the other. If it is the case that people act variously for both self-interested and altruistic reasons, however, there is reason to accept the defendants' more flexible view of how laws should be used over the prosecutor's view. Only the defendants' position preserves the *possibility* of and consistent justification for legitimately considering the motives and intentions behind actions; the prosecutor's ideology sponsors blind application of legal codes without this flexibility. The more flexible approach does not justify wholesale violation of the legal codes nor does it necessitate letting motives and intentions consistently outweigh actions, but it allows consideration of boundary violations within a context.

The second reason we find the defendants' ideology more compelling than the prosecution's is that our reconstruction of their respective argumentative stands reveals a dangerous dimension of the prosecution's worldview: it encourages citizens to obey authorities uncritically. The prosecution's arguments assume that people should abide by directives given by authorities simply by virtue of those authorities' power positions and that one bears responsibility only for acts of commission against these directives. There is no sense that one is responsible to examine such directives critically for oneself; even the judge's position implies a greater degree of personal responsibility through its references to "changing the system from within" when one finds instances in which the system seems unjust or unacceptable. The prosecutor's arguments, however, imply that, as long as one obediently follows authorities' directives, one is not accountable for the type of society that following those directives creates. Reno himself seemed to adopt the attitude that prosecuting the sanctuary members was just part of his job. He had been directed to do so by his superiors and did not see it as his place to consider whether or how he prosecuted the defendants was just or unjust nor to weigh the consequences of his following those directives.[7] In his 1990 book *How Holocausts Happen*, Douglas V. Porpora launches an extensive critique of such an acquiescent position. Porpora traces the dangers of uncritically yielding to the directives of authorities from the Milgram experiments through the Kitty Genovese case and the Nazi Holocaust to contemporary citizens' acquiescence to genocidal U.S. government activities in Central America. As argument critics, it is especially important to reveal and resist ideologies that justify unreflective submission to authority and fail to promote any sense of personal responsibility or commitment beyond avoiding violations of legal boundaries. On this criterion, we again find the defendants' position more acceptable. While laws are not irrelevant to justice, they are imperfect means to realizing justice. When the two conflict, justice must take priority. Consequently, it is imperative to encourage the critical examination of the opinions and power distribution preferences of both authorities and nonauthorities. Grounded evaluations and commitments to action cannot result from uncritical capitulation to authorities' directives. As this particular case illustrates, it is dangerous to view laws as the sole path to justice; such an attitude nullifies individual responsibility in the name of "the system" and allows the legal system to extend its influence and guise of "objectivity" (see also Olson and Olson 1994).

This essay demonstrates the operation of ideological criticism on two dimensions. On one dimension, it shows how examining argumentative positions at the level of their ideological underpinnings offers insights unavailable when these underpinnings are ignored. The analysis also reveals how an ideology backed by power can silence or render impotent an ideology sponsoring superior moral and political arguments—even in a supposedly "disinterested" democratic legal system. Finally, the critique of the sanctuary defendants' ideology hopefully illustrates that claiming symbolic action is inherently value-laden is not the same as claiming it is inherently self-serving. These advocates held a vibrantly "interested," historically situated position centered on putting altruism into practice.

On a second dimension, the assumptions of this analysis demand that we, as argument critics, reflect on our own ideological commitments to the degree that one can engage in such self-reflexivity.[8] William G. Perry Jr.'s (1970, 1981) examination of progression in intellectual and ethical development gives structure to and underscores the importance of this critical move (see also Nelson 1989, 1993). Perry advances four progressive phases through which one must pass to become a mature critical thinker: dualism (or simple dualism), multiplicity (or complex dualism), relativism, and commitment (see especially Perry 1970, pp. 54–55; 1981, pp. 79–80). Each successive move through the subpositions of these four developmental phases includes and transcends the earlier ones in a way that the earlier ones cannot duplicate with the later ones (Perry 1970, p. 2; 1981, p. 78).

Initially people perceive the world dualistically. Truth appears to be simple and eternal. Conflicts are understood as having clear-cut right versus wrong, good versus bad answers that are available from proper authorities and/or from following the correct procedures. Knowledge is treated as a quantitative, collectible entity; not only outcomes, but also the amount of effort and hard work involved in reaching those outcomes count. Since a person in this stage has no way to understand or appreciate any position or set of value commitments other than the one that he or she accepts as "truth," he or she has no empathy with nor tolerance for different positions or value commitments embraced by others. In order to advance from dualism to multiplicity, a person must make the transition of recognizing that issues encompass "meaningful" uncertainty, uncertainty that is legitimate and unavoidable rather than the product of incompetent authorities or faulty procedures.

Once one accepts the existence of meaningful uncertainty on particular issues, he or she enters multiplicity in which one divides issues into two realms: the realm of issues on which proper authorities and procedures provide correct answers and the realm of issues on which uncertainty legitimately exists. On issues in the second realm, a person in this developmental stage believes that all opinions are equally acceptable or that each person's answer is appropriate for him or her. Choices among answers to uncertain issues are understood as arbitrary or intuitive choices instead of reasoned ones; an individual's opinions on uncertain matters need not even form a consistent pattern to be acceptable to one in this developmental phase. Since one in multiplicity need not understand another's position to grant him or her the right to embrace it, an individual in this stage has no need for empathy with, but has unlimited tolerance for, the choices of others on issues deemed uncertain. To escape such uncritical multiplicity, one must make the transition from treating all opinions as equally acceptable to learning to identify preferable ideas in spite of meaningful uncertainty.

Completing the transition to relativism positions one to recognize the inescapable pervasiveness of legitimate uncertainty and to use field-specific criteria and evidence to compare, evaluate, and select among competing opinions. In this phase, knowledge is treated as qualitative and contextual; one can analyze and evaluate a diversity of opinions, values, and judgments derived from a range of sources, ideologies, logics, patterns, and systems that are coherent and internally consistent, yet not certain. At this level of sophistication, an individual can justify why he or she sees one position as superior to another in a given context, but does not yet take personal responsibility for the use of these criteria nor for choosing when to apply which set of criteria. The ability to bring various sets of criteria to bear on a particular issue gives a person great empathy, for now he or she can appreciate why another who frames an issue in a certain way sees a particular position as most justified, and, by refusing to acknowledge one's responsibility in choosing among frames, he or she also displays almost unlimited tolerance for differing opinions. In relativism, one sees answers merely as contextually relative rather than individually relative. The person thus is capable of "playing" a wide range of context-specific games, but does not commit personally to any particular frameworks. Transition to the final level of sophistication in critical thinking involves linking values to critical analysis so that one can choose responsibly among and/or combine the various strengths of different approaches to face complex issues and accept the consequences of personal commitments to particular frameworks, commitments that cannot be grounded in certainty.

A person in the fourth and final phase, commitment, experiences agency as an individual responsibility and makes examined choices, affirmations, and decisions in the awareness of relative options. Such individuals can delineate the advantages and disadvantages of approaching an issue imbued with uncertainty from various potential frameworks, address trade-offs in the consequences of choice, and defend why he or she adopts a particular approach on an issue. Operating at this level of critical thinking involves self-reflexivity as well as acceptance of personal responsibility both for one's commitments and for making choices that make a difference in the world. At the commitment level, one has appropriately limited empathy with and significant, yet not unlimited, tolerance for other positions.[9]

Hopefully, our argument evaluation of the sanctuary trial reflects the qualities of this fourth phase of critical thinking. We have argued for the importance of embracing an ideological framework for this criticism. We have tried to explicate responsibly how and why the various parties in *Aguilar* justified their positions and the ways in which their ideologies influenced both their differing approaches to specific, complex political decisions and their varying interpretations of the broader myths undergirding their shared society. Furthermore, we have advanced, defended, and applied criteria (i.e., desirable flexibility to consider others' choices in a wider context that does not dismiss automatically— nor automatically privilege—motives, intentions, and interpretations for the sake of actions; the use of one's own critical skills and taking constructive action based on the outcome of such critical evaluation over passive acquiescence to authorities) for preferring one ideology expressed in the sanctuary trial over the others in the face of uncertainty. In this critique, we also have tried to model our commitment to values significant to our discipline, such as the importance of sophisticated critical thinking, the desirability of supporting claims with evidence, and the importance of examining assumptions. In the process, we commit to a distribution of power that promotes the critical examination of a range of positions, from nonauthorities as well as authorities, and action based on the resulting critical evaluations instead of on legalistic acquiescence to authorities. Finally, by publicly engaging contemporary conflicts and ideologies, analyzing and comparing them, taking sides and justifying our choices, then accepting responsibility for those choices by publishing our position, we hope to have enacted effectively our own commitments to create criticism that makes a difference in the world. Tackling contemporary arguments directly relevant to present social divisions of power and then disseminating the conclusions and reasoning behind them to these arguers involved (e.g., *Aguilar* trial participants), as well as to other members of the academic community, is one avenue by which critics of argument can demonstrate their own commitments, their acceptance of responsibility for those commitments, and the commitments' importance.

REFERENCES

Balthrop, V. William. 1984. Culture, myth, and ideology as public argument: An interpretation of the ascent and demise of "Southern culture." *Communication Monographs, 51,* 339–52.

Brosnahan, James. 1989, November 20. Interview with authors. San Francisco, Calif.

Brown, William R. 1978. Ideology as communication process. *Quarterly Journal of Speech, 64,* 123–40.

Browning, Daniel R. 1986, March 12. Don Reno: Sanctuary prosecution at ease despite his religious heritage. *Arizona Daily Star*, B1–2.

Burke, Kenneth. 1947. Ideology and myth. *Accent, 7,* 195–205.

———. 1973. *The philosophy of literary form: Studies in symbolic action.* 3d ed. Berkeley: University of California Press.

Colbert, Douglas L. 1987. The motion in limine in politically sensitive cases: Silencing the defendant at trial. *Stanford Law Review, 39,* 1271–1327.

Crowley, Sharon. 1992. Reflections on an argument that won't go away: Or, a turn of the ideological screw. *Quarterly Journal of Speech, 78,* 450–65.

Davidson, Miriam. 1988. *Convictions of the heart: Jim Corbett and the sanctuary movement.* Tucson: University of Arizona Press.

Eagleton, Terry. 1983. *Literary theory: An introduction.* Minneapolis: University of Minnesota Press.

———. 1991. *Ideology: An introduction.* New York: Verso.

Edelman, Murray. 1964. *The symbolic uses of politics.* Champaign-Urbana: University of Illinois Press.

———. 1971. *Politics as symbolic action: Mass arousal and quiescence.* New York: Academic Press.

———. 1988. *Constructing the political spectacle.* Chicago: University of Chicago Press.

Fallers, Lloyd A. 1961. Ideology and culture in Uganda nationalism. *American Anthropologist, 63,* 677–86.

Geertz, Clifford. 1964. Ideology as a cultural system. In *Ideology and discontent.*, ed. David E. Apter. New York: Free Press of Glencoe.

Kennedy, Duncan. 1976. Form and substance in private law adjudication. *Harvard Law Review, 89,* 1685-778.

Klumpp, James F., and Thomas A. Hollihan. 1989. Rhetorical criticism as moral action. *Quarterly Journal of Speech, 75,* 84–96.

Lessl, Thomas M. 1989. The priestly voice. *Quarterly Journal of Speech, 75,* 183–97.

LeWin, Wendy. 1988, January 31. Interview with authors. Phoenix, Ariz.

Merod, Jim. 1987. *The political responsibility of the critic.* Ithaca, N.Y.: Cornell University Press.

Merry, Sally Engle. 1985. Concepts of law and justice among working-class Americans: Ideology as culture. *Legal Studies Forum, 9,* 59–69.

———. 1986. Everyday understanding of the law in working-class America. *American Ethnologist, 13,* 253–70.

Nelson, Craig E. 1989. Skewered on the unicorn's horn: The illusion of tragic tradeoff between content and critical thinking in the teaching of science. In *Enhancing critical thinking in the sciences*, ed. Linda W. Crow. Washington, D.C.: Society for College Science Teachers.

————. 1993, June. Fostering critical thinking and mature valuing across the curriculum. Seminar presented at The University of Wisconsin System Faculty College 1993, Marinette, Wisc.

Olson, Kathryn M., and Clark D. Olson. 1991. Creating identification through the alignment of rhetorical enactment, purpose, and textually implied audience. In *Proceedings of the Second International Conference on Argumentation*, ed. Frans H. van Eemeren, Rob Grootendorst, J. Anthony Blair, and Charles A. Willard. Amsterdam: International Centre for the Study of Argumentation.

————. 1994. Judges' influence on trial outcomes and jurors' experiences of justice: Reinscribing existing hierarchies through the sanctuary trial. *Journal of Applied Communication Research, 22*, 16–35.

Pacelle, Mitchell. 1986, September. Law or justice? *The American Lawyer, 95*–103.

————. 1989. U.S. v. the Arizona sanctuary workers: Law or justice. In *Trial by jury*, ed. Steven Brill. New York: Simon and Schuster.

Pepper, Stephen C. 1942. *World hypotheses: A study in evidence.* Berkeley: University of California Press.

Perry, William G., Jr. 1970. *Forms of intellectual and ethical development in the college years: A scheme.* New York: Holt, Rinehart, and Winston.

————. 1981. Cognitive and ethical growth: The making of meaning. In *The modern American college: Responding to the new realities of diverse students and a changing society*, ed. Arthur W. Chickering. San Francisco: Jossey-Bass.

Piccarreta, Michael L. 1989, May 31. Interview with authors. Tucson, Ariz.

Porpora, Douglas V. 1990. *How holocausts happen: The United States in Central America.* Philadelphia: Temple University Press.

Sarat, Austin, and William L. F. Felstiner. 1986. Law and strategy in the divorce lawyer's office. *Law and Society Review, 20*, 93–134.

U.S. v. Aguilar. 1985–86. Pretrial, CR 85-008 PHX-EHC (Ariz. District Ct.).

————. 1985–86. Trial, CR 85-008 PHX-EHC (Ariz. District Ct.).

————. 1985–86. Sentencings, CR 85-008 PHX-EHC (Ariz. District Ct.).

Walker, William. 1989, June 2. Interview with authors. Tucson, Ariz.

Wander, Philip. 1983. The ideological turn in modern criticism. *Central States Speech Journal, 34,* 1–18.

————, ed. 1993. Special issue on ideology and communication. *Western Journal of Communication 57.*

CHAPTER 8

Arguing about
Fetal "versus" Women's Rights:
An Ideological Evaluation

Mary Keehner

In March 1990 the United States Supreme Court announced that it would hear oral argument on *United Auto Workers v. Johnson Controls, Inc.*, the case involving a company's legal right to exclude women from jobs it believes constitute a hazard to unborn and, indeed, unconceived fetuses. The Court, in March 1991, held that the company's "fetal protection" policy is illegal (Weyrich 1990). This case is only one instance of a growing controversy involving not only the employment of women in particular occupations, but also the prosecution of women who use drugs during pregnancy and the forced imposition of medical treatment on pregnant women (Caher 1990). Running through these controversies are arguments that frame "the issue" as a conflict between fetal and women's rights.

Most arguments concerning workplace protection, in addition to utilizing oppositional discursive strategies, tend to ignore the underlying economic and social issues involved. The controversy surrounding Johnson Control's fetal protection policy provides an excellent opportunity for argument evaluation that both examines

I wish to thank Dennis Mumby for his incisive comments on an earlier draft of this paper; Edward Schiappa for his assistance with revision; Kim Berg, Keith Hearit, and Angela Tretheway for their useful feedback, and particularly Anne C. Crenshaw, who is responsible for initially introducing me to the Johnson Controls case.

and critiques the ways in which the arguments are framed by institutions such as individual corporations or the legal system. This essay offers a critical examination of the argumentative discourse surrounding the Johnson Controls controversy. Such a critical stance presents a "normative reflection that is historically and socially contextualized" (Young 1990, p. 5). In particular, it is informed by feminist analysis that recognizes intersections of gender and class interests. Particular public arguments are discussed in light of their ideological suppositions and situated within the political and economic context of patriarchy in order to "create new frameworks which can reveal oppression which is concealed by traditional frameworks" (Oliver 1989, p. 11). Absent a critical stance toward public argument "many questions about what occurs in a society and why, who benefits and who is harmed, will not be asked, and social theory is liable to reaffirm and reify the given social reality" (Young 1990, p. 5).

My contention is that the intertwined ideologies of patriarchy, liberal legal philosophy, and capitalism all influence the arguments concerning hazards in the workplace for pregnant women. The texture of the debate is uniquely situated within the late twentieth-century American social epoch. The "fetal protection" policies single out women because women (unlike men) get pregnant. These policies are grounded within patriarchy: the "social, historical, and economic relations of power in society that create and reflect gendered inequality" (Eisenstein 1988, p. 21). The structural and institutional difference between males and females is articulated through "the male-oriented symbolization of *biological difference*" that is a dominant phallocratic discourse "construct[ed] and represent[ed] through a male viewing" (Eisenstein 1988, p. 21). Argument evaluation serves as an act of critical intervention; in this case, positioning a public controversy within dominant discourses that privilege the interests of men over women. The legal system and capitalist business interests undergird the "fetal protection" issue. Intimately connected to these strands, however, is a patriarchal view of women.

The dominant argumentative strategies in the Johnson Controls controversy function within a liberal legal framework to obscure significant class and gender interests. The issue of fetal protection can be productively viewed as occurring within a capitalist patriarchal framework—the dominant discourses of which use pregnancy to differentiate women and subordinate them to men. Argument within this controversy perpetuates a dangerous "conflict" between fetal and women's "rights." A more productive argumentative approach is nonoppositional in nature; that is, it is useful to cease viewing women and fetuses presumptively as separate enemies.

Accordingly, I first provide a brief historical background of the Johnson Controls case; second, I demonstrate how the discourse constituting the debate is premised on gendered capitalist and legal ideology; and finally, I propose an alternative argumentative-discursive framework within which to view the issue of hazardous workplace pregnancy.

BACKGROUND: ONE SKIRMISH
WITHIN A LARGER "BATTLE-GROUND"

In 1977 Johnson Controls, Inc., a car battery manufacturer based in Milwaukee, adopted a "fetal protection policy." This policy warned women working on the battery assembly line that exposure to lead in the workplace could endanger fetuses should they become pregnant.[1] The company compared the risk involved to that of smoking while pregnant and suggested that women who were planning to have children not work in the jobs that entail lead exposure.

The company concluded in 1982 that this voluntary policy was insufficient since during the five-year period six women in the high-exposure positions became pregnant and one of the children born showed elevated blood lead levels. Johnson Controls consequently adopted a new policy under which *no* woman capable of bearing children would be permitted to work in jobs exposing her to high lead levels. This policy applied to any woman under age seventy unless she could furnish medical documentation of her sterility and also excluded women from any job that could ultimately lead to a promotion into battery-making.

Some employees and the UAW challenged the policy as overt sex discrimination. Their challenge was based on Title VII of the 1964 Civil Rights Act that prohibits discrimination on the basis of sex unless there is a "bona fide occupational qualification reasonably necessary" to the performance of the job. Similarly, the 1982 Pregnancy Discrimination Act defined discrimination based on pregnancy or childbirth as sex discrimination for the purposes of

Title VII. The Seventh Circuit Court of Appeals, in a 7–4 decision, ruled in favor of Johnson Controls, arguing that "business necessity" justified the "fetal protection" policy. The court claimed that the policy was necessary for the company's "industrial safety" concern for protecting the unborn from exposure to lead. Upon appeal to the Supreme Court, Johnson Controls' policy was unanimously struck down in a plurality opinion.

Such "fetal protection" policies are not unique to Johnson Controls. General Motors, B. F. Goodrich, Allied Chemical, Monsanto, Gulf Oil, American Cyanamid, Olin Corp., Dow Chemical, Du Pont, and Union Carbide all have policies excluding women from certain positions on the basis of their potential to become pregnant. The disposition of these policies in the wake of the Court decision remains to be seen.[2] The issue of fetal protection is also not limited to the workplace. Anti-abortion groups argue for the unborn fetus's "right to life," child abuse statutes are being stretched to include the use of drugs during pregnancy, and doctors have sought court orders to force women to undergo transfusions, caesarean sections, and other medical treatments (Foster 1989).

Arguments over these policies characterize the situation as a forced choice between women's and fetal rights. For example, it is argued that "the rights of pregnant women and their fetuses are on a legal collision course as courts increasingly view the mother-to-be and unborn baby as separate individuals with competing interests" (Caher 1990). Decision making in these cases is described as the "balancing of fetal and maternal interests," and the attempt to resolve "the fundamental question of where maternal rights and fetal rights begin" (McNamara 1989). Some claim that a "woman's significant interest in her bodily integrity must be balanced against the state's interest in potential human life" (*In Re A.C.*). This is a "clash of rights," "maternal-fetal conflict," and a debate over "whether a fetus has rights—and whether those rights supersede that of the mother" (Protecting; Beck 1989; Foster 1989). Third parties become involved as a "balance" is needed between "the state's right to protect the unborn child against the mother's rights" (Folks and Caughron 1990). The "womb, increasingly, is a battleground" that "pits the rights of women against the interests of their unborn children" (Davidson 1989). It is interesting to note that many of these characterizations are not merely of *women's* rights versus fetal rights, but of *mothers* versus their *unborn children*. Joan Beck (1989), a columnist for the *Chicago Tribune*, goes so far as to characterize the conflict as between an unborn baby and *"his"* mother's rights. "Once *he* is born" *he* can be protected, but she regrets that until then, *"he* has no rights." One wonders if Beck is alone in seeing the conflict as between a woman and her unborn male child and if the debate would be seen differently if the unborn child were perceived as female.

These policies are debated as a conflict between women (mothers) and fetuses (children). Overlooked, often, are larger concerns that can provide an alternative framing of the issue. Specifically, within the current dominant oppositional discourse are unexpressed warrants about the nature of women, the law, and society that ought not go unnoticed.

THE LIMITS OF PROTECTION IN CAPITALISM

Johnson Controls characterizes its policy as altruistic: the protection of future generations' health and welfare. The company argues that it has a "moral responsibility" to protect fetuses, and that their "genuine desire" to protect the "health of unborn children" is their sole concern (Brink 1990; Crabtree 1990; Katz 1991; Rieger 1991). Granting, for the moment, the credibility of their concern, the substantial economic interests implicated in the adoption of their policy cannot go unnoted. Underlying it all is a tendency within capitalism to see procreation as a production process. Barbara Rothman, in *Recreating Motherhood*, argues: "We are facing the expansion of a way of thinking that treats people as objects, as commodities. It is a way of thinking that enables us to see not motherhood, not parenthood, but the creation of a commodity, a baby. . . . As babies and children become products, mothers become producers, pregnant women the unskilled workers on a reproductive assembly line" (1989, pp. 19–20). When women are seen as those who produce children, and (in patriarchy) those primarily responsible for rearing them, a fetal protection policy makes a sort of sense: if bearing children is women's most important role, if healthy children are important to capitalist institutions as future workers, and if a woman faces a choice between a job and a risk-free pregnancy, then the "logical" choice is to forego the employment in favor of "producing" a healthy child.

A second economic issue that deserves consideration in the debate over "fetal protection" is the felt-necessity of women to keep jobs in potentially hazardous environments. In capitalism, market forces produce economic concerns that often lead women to make choices they would not otherwise make (Oliver 1989, p. 97). These jobs do not constitute "pin money" for women; most women work because they must. For many unskilled women, these 20 million industrial jobs "may provide the only escape from poverty" (Bertin 1989). What Johnson Controls and other organizations do not consider in their justifications is that by foregoing these jobs, many women find themselves unable to support their families, losing valuable overtime hours, and often missing out on benefits and insurance that are essential to their efforts to provide for themselves and, often, their families (Kirp 1990, p. 203). Often it is the case that women are not just selfishly interested in a high-paying job (although their career interests ought be accorded the same respect as men's); they often choose to work in a given environment because "compared with the realistic alternatives for such women, filing forms in an office or collecting a welfare check, these jobs bring double and triple the income and deliver better health care" (Kirp 1990, p. 204). Unable to give up their jobs, many women choose sterilization. Betty Riggs, a twenty-six-year-old mother of one child, submitted to sterilization because "I thought there was no choice for me. That was my only way out, to keep my sanity, to keep my family afloat" (Kirp 1990, p. 204). Policies like Johnson Controls' require women to choose between their fertility and their job. While one of the appeals court judges defined the argument as "about the women who want to hurt their fetuses" (Kirp 1990, p. 203), it could just as reasonably be described as about a patriarchal system that allows women to work outside the home while it constrains their access to jobs and defines them, first and foremost, as mothers with a responsibility to society to produce undamaged goods.

A third consideration is the economic interest of these corporations to avoid liability suits—a motivation that encourages the exclusion of women from the workplace. Despite the fact that there were only six pregnancies in high-exposure areas at Johnson Controls in a five-year period, and despite the fact that, while one child showed high levels of lead, there has never been any evidence of birth defects or developmentally hindered children, the company persists in advocating this policy (Kirp 1990, p. 203). Why? Because they fear postnatal liability. Their concern is that a child will be born damaged, grow up, and sue the company. They could easily avoid lawsuits filed by parents by implementing informed consent waivers, but the problem is that the law does not allow parents to waive their *child's* right to a subsequent suit (Recent Cases 1990). In this case, the company finds this "ghost of company lawyers' imaginations" more of a risk than the exclusion of women from the workplace (Kirp 1990, p. 205). Given that, in general, "claims on behalf of the children of male workers outnumber those filed for" those of women workers, one must wonder why women are being singled out (Bertin 1989, p. B7). Perhaps it is because "potentially pregnant women look more vulnerable," and in patriarchy, they are more easily marginalized and excluded than men, given their history of exclusion from the public sphere of work and primary role as mother (Kirp 1989, p. 18).

Additionally, before accepting a description of these companies as "genuinely concerned about their future workers," it is important to note that such concern for women and fetuses only extends within the economic system to jobs where women are expendable. David Kirp argues that this is historically the case with protectionist measures: "The bottom line ultimately determined who was deemed worthy of protection. Because there was a ready supply of men to fill night-shift factory jobs, women became dispensable, but female nurses were too badly needed to be eased out" despite their equal exposure to hazards in the workplace (1990, p. 205). Women are not really necessary at Johnson Controls. However, in businesses that depend on women workers to clean computer circuit boards, operate video display terminals, or run day-care centers, for example, "no one proposes that no fertile women be hired in these places for no one else would fill these jobs" (1990, p. 205).

If liability were not a business concern, what would be the level of moral concern claimed by companies like Johnson Controls? The "bottom line" means that companies will continue to place women in hazardous workplaces so long as they need women working. However, when there are others (men) to fill the jobs, and when the specter of lawsuits is raised, women and their potential offspring will conveniently merit protection.

Additional evidence to support the conclusion that the moral interest in protecting the unborn is an argumentative strategy designed to conceal class/economic interests is corporate reaction to the Court's decision, epitomized by Johnson Controls itself. The company reports that it is considering eliminating workers by adopting robotic technology or by moving their production off-shore to avoid the legal issues altogether (Under a civil rights cloud 1991). If they really care about the health of children, not only would their risk assessment include the risks incurred by women taking lower-paying jobs elsewhere, but they would not suggest moving overseas to avoid legal problems. By taking production offshore, the company can endanger fetuses without incurring any liability. Given the economic issues involved and the company's rather cynical consideration of moving overseas, their claims for the moral high-ground seem disingenuous.

The argumentative context in which the "fetal protection" debate is taking place, then, is one in which women are seen as mothers—the producers of babies-as-commodities. Our particular capitalist system conveniently excludes women from jobs that it can afford to and is likely making an economic calculation rather than a humanitarian gesture to protect individuals as individuals. Organizations like Johnson Controls can afford to exclude women from jobs in order to avoid the potential of future lawsuits because they can continue to produce their goods by substituting male labor for female labor. The women, however, cannot in most cases afford to lose their jobs. For some, the choice of sterilization is the only alternative. For most, the risk to future unconceived potential fetuses that might be damaged by exposure to hazardous substances is more than outweighed by the needs of their concrete, present, nonpotential (actual) selves and families.

THE LIMITS OF EQUALITY
IN THE LIBERAL LEGAL TRADITION

The "fetal protection" debate is situated not only within a particular economic system, but also within a liberal legal tradition that frames the issue in gendered and oppositional terms. Law is the authorized discourse of the state. Zillah Eisenstein argues that while power is not centered in *a* state, it is "concentrated in a state defined by the relations of power that are dispersed" (1988, p. 18). She continues: "The relations of the state reflect and construct the relations of power in society and yet the state does not fully uncover the entirety of power relations themselves. The state, rather, condenses the relations of power in society" and does so through discourse. She argues that the discourse of the law is based on the patriarchal privileging of man over woman. "The sexual discourses in law constitute and construct the problem of 'difference' for a theory of sex equality because the phallus is privileged along with the patriarchal structure of meaning itself" (1988, pp. 19–20).

Within the liberal legal tradition, males define and constitute the norm and are privileged over females. Consequently, when equality is discussed, it is an equality that is premised on *sameness*—the sameness of women to men. This means that for women to be equal to men, they must be *like* men. Since maleness defines the norm, and femaleness is considered "other," the discourse of equality uses the male as the measure of equality. With the acceptance of women as independent persons with rights to equality, issues of sex discrimination have been framed along male-centered lines. To be equal, men and women need to be "the same." To the extent that women can be seen as like men, then the absence of "difference" between men and women means that men and women should be treated the same (Eisenstein 1988, pp. 53–60). The problem is that once a "real difference" between men and women can be articulated to the satisfaction of the law, then discrimination against women is justified because "real differences" require different treatment (Eisenstein 1988, pp. 64–66). So, for example, the Supreme Court has argued that not registering women for the draft is acceptable since women are disallowed by legislation from serving in combat roles. Here we have a "difference" between women and men articulated in such a way as to justify differential treatment.

The area in which this notion of equality as "sameness" becomes problematic is pregnancy. Women get pregnant, men do not. Eisenstein argues: "Man is never viewed as '*not* pregnant,' so pregnancy must be constructed as woman's 'difference' and not man's lacking. Part of the misrepresentation of the female body, as one and the same as the mother's body, is to define it as 'different'" (1988, p. 77). Thus, because the potentially pregnant woman is *unlike* man, she cannot be his "equal" in the hazardous workplace.

The Supreme Court based its decision in the Johnson Controls case on the Pregnancy Discrimination Act's interpretation of Title VII of the Civil Rights Act (*Autoworkers* 1991, p. 173). The PDA is premised on a "sameness" notion of equality, however, so the Court's decision only perpetuates the gendered legal tradition on which it is based. As a sex-specific law (only women become pregnant) it is gendered because is "assumes woman's engendered inequality at the same time that it is supposed to challenge it" (Eisenstein 1988, p. 206). Additionally, the PDA only protects pregnant women from being treated less favorably than men; pregnant women only have the right "not to be treated *worse* than male, or nonpregnant female employees" (Eisenstein 1988, p. 212). The Court ruled that pregnancy cannot be used to exclude women from the workplace unless it "interferes with the employee's ability to perform the job" (*Autoworkers* 1991, p. 177). Of course adequate performance of the job remains defined by male performance; if pregnancy means that a woman cannot perform the job the same as a man, then her exclusion is fair game. The standard for equality in the PDA, on which the Court relies, is still the less inclusive standard of sameness premised on the "norm" of the male body.

A related concern within the liberal legal framework is that the tendency to see the fetus as "other" perpetuates the opposition of woman and fetus. The Court decision does nothing to mitigate such an opposition. NOW's Molly Yard happily read the decision as a vote for women and against the fetus; the opinion upholds the rights of women over fetal rights, and "the rights of women come first" (Katz 1991). Interestingly, those in favor of fetal protection policies viewed the Court decision as not only a defeat for fetal rights but also as a victory for *women* at the expense of *mothers*. The Concerned Women for America says the decision "really minimizes the value of motherhood" (Ceol 1991), the American Life League says the ruling "makes motherhood a second-class profession" and denigrates woman's "natural role as a wife and mother" (Terrell 1991).

By claiming their individuality and autonomy, women have made significant strides toward remedying the ill-effects of patriarchy. Often feminists have downplayed or ignored pregnancy in an effort to avoid being "different" from men (Eisenstein 1988, pp. 85–87). Particularly in the area of procreative rights, women have claimed rights to bodily integrity and privacy, and have differentiated themselves from their fetuses in order to claim their autonomy (Rethinking Motherhood 1990). The problem is that this separation has turned into an argument for why women will not act in their fetuses' interests and, in part, has justified the oppositional discourse in the fetal rights conflict. A federal appeals court judge's comments illustrate that this opposition is perceived as significant. He asserts that being a "'force in the workplace' may warp a working woman's judgment, leading her to 'discount this clear risk' to the physical and mental development of her own child" (Kirp 1991, p. 73). Women may have won a battle for equality by distancing themselves argumentatively from their childbearing capacity and by asserting their rights to autonomy and privacy. These arguments risk a larger war, however—one in which their interests will be increasingly characterized as mutually exclusive with those of their unborn children.

Furthermore, the liberal legal tradition that recognizes equality of rights for "persons" is increasingly coming to see the fetus as a person or at least as a potential person (Brown el al. 1986). Such an argumentative move complicates matters even more. If women were merely separate from the interests of a fetus and not separate from the interests of a potential person, then the perceived conflict could be solved easily. However, the issue is increasingly framed as two individuals with competing claims rights. As abortion rights become increasingly endangered, and as medical technology continues to advance, the automatic presumption in favor of women's rights becomes more and more suspect.

The liberal legal tradition, then, privileges the male as "norm" and marginalizes the pregnant woman as "different" and thus not deserving of equality. Equality, though, is being defined in male terms. The Johnson Controls case is being argued along "rights" and "discrimination" lines. To the extent that this legal notion of equality is gendered, the pregnant/potentially pregnant woman is devalued and the individuality of the fetus privileged.

ENVISIONING AN ALTERNATIVE:
DECENTERING THE PHALLUS

When the preferred norm in patriarchy and liberal law is the male, women are defined as "different" or as similar, but always *the male is the measure* (Eisenstein 1988, p. 54). The "fetal protection" debate, viewed within this context, is resolved along lines defining equality in *male* terms—hence treating women and men "equally" means treating women "like men." In the current context, the female body does not "displace the silent privileging of the male body" (Eisenstein 1988, p. 1). Therefore, rather than privilege the male in the male/female opposition, it is productive to imagine the hazardous workplace situation from the viewpoint of *the pregnant body* as "norm."

Eisenstein argues that our theories of sex equality need to introduce the pregnant body "in order to decenter the privileged position of the male body" (Eisenstein 1988, p. 1). Her position is not that pregnancy thus would be a "model" to apply to everyone (since obviously no male could meet it), but that the pregnant body makes the current standard of "sameness" problematic for a theory of equality. Such a turn would be productive, Eisenstein suggests, because it would require a redefinition of "difference" in unengendered, plural terms. For example, argumentation that did not define the pregnant woman as the "different other" would open up the possibility to argue for workplace safety defined with the pregnant body as the standard.

At the very least, making the workplace safe for potentially pregnant women is preferable to excluding women from the jobs. The UAW has argued that "improved ventilation or other engineering controls" are available that would allow Johnson Controls to lower lead levels in the workplace without eliminating all workers of one sex (Swoboda 1990). Industry spokespersons have claimed that they are *unable* to make the workplace any safer, but critics suggest that the industry is more likely *unwilling* since it is much less costly for business to exclude fertile women from certain jobs than to tackle a problem of lead or other dangerous substances. Given that these jobs can be filled by men, there is no economic motive for the companies *not* to bar women from the jobs and plenty of motivation to exclude women.

Companies often have been less reluctant to take action to clean up the workplace while protecting men's jobs. When the toxic chemical DBCP was found to cause male sterility "the chemical was banned, not the worker" (Bertin 1989). A related issue is the interpretation of studies regarding the risks to *male* workers from exposure to lead. More studies have been done on women because the dominant assumption is that women (because they can get pregnant) are the focus of fetal lead exposure. However, the studies that examine male lead exposure also suggest that there are similar reproductive hazards for men. When research on the male reproductive system has shown a threat, "safety policies change: The toxins are banned or new safeguards rushed into place. Meanwhile, rather than lowering lead levels on the line, companies give women" the ax (Kirp 1989). Thus far, however, the risks of men's exposure to lead is ignored while women's is made the focal point. The high amounts of lead exposure to children from paint, soil, water, and air—often higher than exposure found in sites like Johnson Controls—are not treated seriously (Kirp 1990, p. 203).

If institutions were really as concerned about the health and welfare of women and their potential future children as they claim to be, then the standard for workplace safety would be what is considered safe for the *pregnant* worker. Now, however, the standard by which safety is measured is the male worker; the pregnant woman's "difference" is justification for companies to exclude her from the work environment. The Supreme Court decision does not alter this calculus—the safety standard is still the male worker. The difference is that now women bear the burden of risk assessment rather than employers.

There is value in not defining "fetal protection" as an inevitable conflict between women's and fetal rights. Instead, a perspective of cooperation and connection is equally valid and less prone to the further subordination of women as persons. Here the goal is to affirm the mother-child relationship without accepting the reduction of all women to mothers and without using the potential for women to become pregnant as a pretext for privileging male interests. Rothman argues that phallocratic discourse makes it difficult to view pregnancy as a relationship: A "blindness to the presence of the baby for the woman" is encouraged by this discourse through which "the fetus is increasingly seen and valued, while the relationship with the woman in whom it resides is disvalued. And so the fetus becomes a patient, a captive, an 'unborn child,' needing protection—including protection from its mother" (1989, pp. 85–86).

The spokespersons for "fetal protection" reveal in their arguments a devaluing of the pregnancy relationship and a suspicion of women's ability to make choices within that relationship. Jean Beaudoin, manager of health, safety, and environmental control at Johnson Controls, justified the company's shift from a voluntary to a mandatory policy in these terms: "It's like dealing with human nature in general, making them make a choice between an immediate economic issue and something that is hard to understand and is not of immediate concern. You can do it by locking them up, but you can't expect to accomplish it until they decide to do it themselves" (State Probes 1989, pp. D9–10). The inference is that we have women who opt for short-term economic benefits, in part, because they are incapable of understanding the long-term risks. Charles Fishburn, a physician who works for Johnson Controls, claims that "Somebody has to be responsible and you have to ask: Is the policy responsible for protecting the people it is designed to protect?" (State Probes 1989). The inference is that the company is being forced to be "mature" and responsible because women are not.

Pablo Rodriguez, the medical director of Planned Parenthood for Rhode Island, views with suspicion the growing impetus toward favoring the rights of the fetus: "This is a dangerous trend, because it continues to view women as mere vessels, ignoring the true realities of pregnancy and motherhood" (Making Cocaine 1989). At issue is a woman's ability to make reasoned, informed decisions, to use contraception if she wishes to avoid pregnancy, and to make a choice about abortion should she become pregnant. Mostly implicit, but expressed explicitly by Dr. W. Nat Richardson, medical director for certain divisions of General Motors Corporation, is the assumption that "we never know when a woman may become pregnant" and "once she is it's too late to do anything about it" (State Probes 1989). Not only is it naive to suggest that we cannot know when a woman may become pregnant, but it is most presumptuous to assume that her pregnancy is a "done deed." Perhaps the woman will weigh the risks of remaining on the job and decide to have regular pregnancy tests to learn early if she should become pregnant. Perhaps she will decide that the risk of a damaged fetus is not worth the money and opt to leave her job early in the pregnancy or before becoming pregnant. Perhaps she will decide that the risk of a damaged fetus is less important than her children or her career. What is never made clear by industry spokespersons is the rationale for having a company (which has its own interests quite distant from those of the child) make decisions for women workers (whose interests are clearly more closely related to those of the fetus).

Shirlee Holder, an employee of Johnson Controls, believes that "women have the tendency to want to protect their children" (Ambrose 1990). The ACLU's Joan Bertin argues that, at the very least, women should be trusted in these decisions more than employers: "Women usually worry about reproductive risks at work a lot more than the boss does. And they certainly are better equipped to decide whether they should stay or go" (quoted in Kirp 1990, p. 204). Such an argumentative stance does not rely on an essentialist view of women as *inherently* nurturing (which underlies the arguments made by advocates of fetal protection). Rather, it recognizes a dominant, socially constituted set of discourses that position women in a particular relationship with their children. Women have a "strong interest in the health and safety of their unborn children. It is unlikely that women adequately informed of fetal workplace hazards will intentionally become pregnant or carry unplanned pregnancies to term. Moreover, even if an employee chooses to carry a pregnancy to term, she is better able than her employer to evaluate the relative risks to the unborn child of toxic exposure in the workplace, on the one hand, and the harms that will result from the termination of her employment and health insurance, on the other" (Recent Cases 1990, pp. 981–82).

In the case of forced medical treatment, Hutton Brown et al. argue: "A mother rarely will refuse medical treatment that is necessary to protect the health of her fetus." A decision that fetal rights must prevail "will lead to a society that will require monitoring of all pregnant and potentially fertile women to assure effective enforcement of those fetal rights" (1986, p. 849). Pregnancy can be viewed as a "condition of continuous connection and dependence" (Rethinking Motherhood 1990, p. 1337). Within patriarchy women are socialized into cultural roles of selflessness and nurturance. "Fetal protection" policies further compel women into this duty of care. The alternative discourse of women's experience of "connectedness, both physically, in pregnancy and intercourse, and psychologically, as caretakers" allows a view of pregnancy as both the source of positive values and the source of women's vulnerability in patriarchy. If we were to construct the fetal-maternal relationship from this perspective of vulnerability, responsibility, and interdependence, we can identify the way in which fetal protection policies disempower women as moral decision makers (Rethinking Motherhood 1990, pp. 1337–39).

Such a construction of pregnancy would argue for women making the decision about workplace hazards on two accounts: first, the intimate connection between woman and fetus implies that "there is no norm of noninterference, of disconnection" available to the mother. Second, connectedness in motherhood suggests that a pregnant woman's physical and psychological position "makes her a uniquely appropriate decision maker"

(Rethinking Motherhood 1990, p. 1338). While not all women experience pregnancy—nor do they all experience pregnancy in the same way—a discourse of need and responsibility and connection reflects women's experience more adequately than does describing pregnancy as a conflicting, adversarial relationship (Rethinking Motherhood 1990, pp. 1342–43).

CONCLUSION

This essay has adopted a feminist critical stance for the analysis and evaluation of the arguments surrounding the Johnson Controls "fetal protection" controversy. The current debate surrounding "fetal protection" issues provides an opportunity to examine critically particular policies as they interact with the gendered institutions of capitalism and a liberal legal system. The current argument tends to be framed within the opposition of women's and fetal rights. A decentering of the privileged male body would require a perspective that views the pregnant body as "normal," not as "different" or "same" as judged by phallocratic standards. Such a perspective is useful because it opens up the possibility of a discourse of equality that, in the case of workplace pregnancy, would advance the goals of worker (and fetal) safety. Further, such a perspective would encourage a recognition of pluralism and diversity as preferred standards by which to determine sex equality.

REFERENCES

Ambrose, Eileen. 1990, May 20. Court to review pregnancy policy. *Aurora Beacon News*. [Newsbank 1990 SUP: 257, C7].
Autoworkers v. Johnson Controls. 1991. 113 L Ed 158-177.
Beck, Joan. 1989, November 27. In maternal-fetal conflicts, guess who has no rights. *Chicago Tribune*, 1:11.
Bertin, Joan. 1989, November 27. Fix the job, not the worker. *Los Angeles Times*, B7.
Brink, Susan. 1990, October 15. Workplace hazards. *Boston Herald*. [Newsbank 1990 EMP: 73, A8].
Brown, Hutton et al. 1986. Maternal rights v. fetal rights. *Vanderbilt Law Review*, 39, 819-50.

Caher, John. 1990, April 1. Mothers held liable for behavior while pregnant. *Albany Times Union*. [Newsbank 1990 LAW: 46, E3].

Ceol, Dawn Weyrich. 1991, March 21. Court says safety rule is sex bias. *Washington Times*. [Newsbank 1991 EMP: 21, G12-13].

Crabtree, Peter. 1990, September 11. Company policy barring women faces challenge. *Rutland Daily Herald*. [Newsbank 1990 EMP: 73, B1].

Davidson, Jean. 1989, April 25. Drug babies push issue of fetal rights. *Los Angeles Times*. [Newsbank 1989 HEA: 46, B14].

Eisenstein, Zillah. 1988. *The female body and the law*. Berkeley: University of California Press.

Elsasser, Glen. 1990, March 27. Court to get fertile women's job case. *Chicago Tribune*, 1:1.

Folks, Mike, and Chele Caughron. 1990, April 27. Court favors women's rights over unborn child's. *Washington Times*. [Newsbank 1990 LAW: 46, E6].

Foster, Catherine. 1989, October 10. Fetal endangerment cases increasing. *Christian Science Monitor*, 8.

In Re A.C. 1987. 533 A. 2d 613 (D.C. 1987).

Katz, Diane. 1991, March 21. Ruling opens more jobs to women. *Detroit News*. [Newsbank 1991 EMP: 14, A10-11].

Kirp, David L. 1989, December 13. The next right to life battle-ground. *Christian Science Monitor*, 18.

―――. 1990, May. Health. *Vogue*, 203–5.

―――. 1991, March–April. The pitfalls of "fetal protection." *Society* 28, 70–76.

Kleiman, Carol. 1990, August 27. 20 million industrial jobs hinge on "fetal protection" court case. *Chicago Tribune*, 4:2.

McNamara, Eileen. 1989, October 3. Fetal endangerment cases on the rise. *Boston Globe*. [Newsbank 1989 LAW: 127, F7].

Making Cocaine Mothers Criminal. 1989, September 3. *Providence Journal*. [Newsbank 1989 HEA: 114, F7].

Oliver, Kelly. 1989. Marxism and surrogacy. *Hypatia, 4*, 95–115.

Protecting Unborn Babies from Lead. 1990, April 1. *Chicago Tribune*, 4:2.

Recent Cases. 1990. *Harvard Law Review, 103*, 977–82.

Rethinking Motherhood: Feminist Theory and State Regulation of Pregnancy. 1990. *Harvard Law Review, 103*, 1325–43.

Rieger, Susan. 1991, March 3. Fertile women need not apply. *Berkshire Eagle* (Pittsfield, Mass.). [Newsbank 1991 EMP: 13, G2].

Rothmann, Barbara. 1989. *Recreating motherhood: Ideology and technology in a patriarchal society*. New York: Norton.

Savage, David. 1990, March 27. Court to rule on ban on women in perilous jobs. *Los Angeles Times*, A20.

Significant Decisions in Labor Cases. 1990, March. *Monthly Labor Review*, 59–61.

State Probes Fairness of Johnson Controls Rule. 1989, January 16. *Milwaukee Business Journal*. [Newsbank 1989 MAN: 1, D9-10].

Swoboda, Frank. 1990, January 7. High Court will be asked to review company's "fetal protection" policy. *Washington Post*, A4.

Terrell, Gaynell. 1991, March 21. Rights groups hail landmark job bias ruling. *Houston Post*. [Newsbank 1991 EMP: 13, G14].

Under a civil rights cloud, fetal protection looks dismal. 1991, April 15. *Washington Times*. [Newsbank 1991 EMP: 21, G3].

Weyrich, Dawn. 1990, March 27. High Court to rule on keeping women from perilous jobs. *Washington Times*. [Newsbank 1990 EMP: 20, A5].

Young, Iris Marion. 1990. *Justice and the politics of difference*. Princeton: Princeton University Press.

CHAPTER 9

Public Policy Argumentation and Colonialist Ideology in the Post–Cold War Era

Rebecca S. Bjork

Dramatic changes in the international scene, marked primarily by the end of the cold war and its replacement with what George Bush referred to as the "new world order," created a sense of relief and hope among many observers of international relations. The dangerous and delicate game of nuclear power politics that governed U.S.-Soviet relations for so many years abated as the Soviet empire collapsed and a new era of detente and cooperation between former adversaries emerged. As the superpower nuclear stalemate appeared to lessen its deadly hold on the planet, many came to believe in the promise of a new world order, one unfettered by the polarizing and costly legacy of a bipolar international structure. As is becoming all too clear, however, this sense of relief and hope for a peaceful future has been replaced with heightened concern about regional conflicts. The tragedies in Somalia and the former republics of Yugoslavia are grim reminders of just how fragile, or perhaps illusory, a new world order of peace and prosperity for all can be. But perhaps this revelation of the intractability of war is not so surprising, for it is important to remember that the public pronouncements concerning this new world order reached a zenith during the largest deployment of U.S. military

The author wishes to thank Reginald Twigg for his helpful comments and suggestions in the preparation of this manuscript.

might since the Vietnam War: the 1991 war in the Persian Gulf, dubbed by the military establishment as Operation Desert Storm.

The prosecution of this war raised fears that the new world order would not necessarily usher in an era of peace. Fears about the proliferation of weapons of mass destruction and advanced delivery systems have reached the forefront of concern, not only because of the use of Scud missiles in the Gulf War, but also due to fears about nuclear terrorism and the security of the nuclear arsenal in the Commonwealth of Independent States (Payne 1991). Although the threat of a superpower nuclear exchange seems to have diminished substantially, fears about the spread of nuclear technology to "emerging" nations led both the Bush and Clinton administrations to order a redirection of the Strategic Defense Initiative program to counter such "limited" threats. According to Assistant Secretary of Defense for International Security Policy Stephen J. Hadley (1991), the objectives of Bush's plan, dubbed Global Protection Against Limited Strikes (GPALS), were to provide protection for the United States, its forces deployed overseas, its friends, and its allies against accidental or unauthorized launches of ballistic missiles, and limited attacks from terrorists or third world nations. The system would consist of both ground-based and space-based interceptors (the controversial Brilliant Pebbles system), along with space-based sensors (Brilliant Eyes), in order to attempt to intercept ballistic missiles virtually anywhere around the globe before they reach their targets (Cooper 1991; Broad 1991). In the autumn of 1991, when many in the United States were still celebrating Operation Desert Storm, Congress passed legislation mandating deployment of the Phase I of GPALS, a ground-based antiballistic missile system, designed to be the first part of a comprehensive system to protect the U.S. territory against limited attacks (Lumpe, Gronlund, and Wright 1992).

Clinton's plans for the program, now called the Ballistic Missile Defense Organization, were described by Secretary of Defense Les Aspin on May 13, 1993, as the "end of the Star Wars era" (Second Coming 1993). Its objectives, however, are surprisingly similar to those of Clinton's predecessor. Requesting $3.8 billion for the program in the 1994 budget, Clinton hopes to develop a defensive system designed to deal with ballistic missile threats by third world and terrorist sources. Research into space-based systems will continue, as will a focus on development and deployment of ground-based antimissile systems (Second Coming 1993; Reagan's Missile Shield 1993). Although only time will tell whether Clinton's plan differs substantially from Bush's GPALS, some of Aspin's aides acknowledged that the name change codified by his announcement amounted to a recognition of the changes in direction in the Strategic Defense Initiative that had been taking place for several years (Reagan's Missile Shield 1993).

A close evaluation of recent public policy arguments justifying these ballistic missile defense programs reveals how they function ideologically to solidify the dominant role of the United States in the post–cold war world. Undertaking an ideological evaluation of argumentative strategies, rather than simply explaining whether an argument is inferentially sound or achieves the effects sought, involves making an ethical and political judgment about the arguments employed. One of my guiding assumptions is that it is important for argument scholars to be aware of how power, as constituted discursively in all argumentation, is manifested ideologically in and through language. Specifically in the case of nuclear proliferation and ballistic missile defense, I contend that public policy arguments in these arenas represent emerging nuclear nations through language that reproduces and perpetuates colonialist ideologies, along with the racist and sexist representations they employ. Calling upon Edward W. Said's (1979, 1981, 1983, 1989) and Abdul R. Jan Mohamed's (1985) discussions of a postcolonial critical stance, I claim that arguments advocating GPALS construct a linguistic transformation of the dualistic argumentative structures of the East-West conflict into the post–cold war world. As such, these argumentative strategies not only serve to perpetuate colonialist ideologies (and their attendant material and cultural exploitation), but also strengthen U.S. geopolitical, military, and economic hegemony in the post–cold war world. I conclude that argument theories that fail to take into account, or even acknowledge, the various ideological undercurrents in public policy argumentation participate in the perpetuation of injustice at a critical time in world history.

Importantly, my argument is not that there is some conspiratorial imperialist and patriarchal "plot" that is responsible for the dangers and problems of the post–cold war world. Rather, I am concerned with the ways in which public policy arguments (and academic arguments) participate in "word politics" (Said 1981) that over time come to be taken for granted as somehow real or natural manifestations of understanding about the world around us. As linguistic interpretations of reality circulate throughout a culture, they acquire legitimacy and authority through their articulation in conjunction with changing relations of power. As Said (1979, p. 12) argues, a postcolonialist critique of language does not seek to trace the outlines of "some nefarious 'Western' imperialist plot," but rather, to explore the ways that ideological constructions of colonialism are expressed in various texts, including aesthetic, economic, political, historical, and even scholarly texts. The purpose of exposing how such interests are manifested in arguments is to illustrate the particular ways that they participate in constructing relationships of power. Specifically, the purpose of a postcolonial critique of argumentation is to reveal how geopolitical concerns are shaped by and exist symbiotically with arguments—scholarly and otherwise. Ideological criticism, then, seeks to understand and expose how "obvious" or "commonsense" assumptions about society and the individual's role in it operate to obscure realities of power and solidify social order (Kavanagh 1990).

This type of approach to the evaluation of public policy arguments attempts to trace the ideological functions of language as it appears in a variety of sites. Following James Der Derian and Michael J. Shapiro's strategy of reading "intertextually" (1989), I examine the ways that a variety of "texts," or "textual fragments" in Michael Calvin McGee's (1990) terms, form together in the minds of readers and critics as apparently whole, finished, and closed "texts." Hence, as McGee claims, traditional understandings of texts as somehow separate and conceptually distinct from contexts obscure the degree to which all discourse is inextricably embedded in context, which I argue is constituted discursively as well. Although I do not wish to deny the importance of material (nondiscursive) conditions in any understanding of the function of language, my concern is with articulating the ways that taken-for-granted meanings interpenetrate and circulate throughout public policy arguments justifying a need for ballistic missile defense in the post–cold war period. As such, I do not examine any one particular text, but rather explore how various textual sites converge in their representations of third world nations.

The first task of such criticism is the recognition that texts are "acts of will and interpretation that take place in history, and can only be dealt with in history as acts of will and interpretation" (Said 1981, p. 41). Interpretations of events are *made*, not natural, and they are made by individuals who are situated in specific historical, social, cultural, and political circumstances. To assume that we, as argument critics, can somehow behave as if our work goes on in a sterile, clinical laboratory, objective and removed from the circumstances of our discourse, is to ignore the fact that we are situated social actors, whose views of reality are shaped by our places in history. Similarly, to assume that public policy arguers are free from the constraints of their historical circumstances is to ignore the powerful influence of culture in all of its ever-changing, contested manifestations. Once these assumptions are granted, it is the task of the critic to trace the relationships between uneven distributions of power and textual practices, and to explore the ways particular arguments construct and "naturalize" social relations, which are not "natural" and given, but created through discourse. In other words, a critic concerned with the role of ideology in argumentation looks for the ways that argumentative strategies serve to consolidate the authority of the powerful, and similarly, how the less powerful attempt to find a stronger voice in the dialogue. As Said points out in a recent interview, "every cultural document contains within it a history of a contest of rulers and ruled, of leader and led" (Marranca, Robinson, and Chaudhuri 1991, p. 59). With these thoughts in mind, I hope to illustrate the ways in which public policy arguments about nuclear proliferation and ballistic missile defense represent so-called third world nations in terms that reinforce the domination and hegemony of the United States in historically coded and ideologically powerful ways.

FINDING A VOICE IN THE INTERNATIONAL DIALOGUE

The existence of a Soviet superpower made centralized state control a legitimate form of government elsewhere, and provided a handy complementarity for those Third World states eager to take up anti-Western, post-colonialist postures. With the conceding by the leading communist power of the virtues of pluralism and markets, this political space has narrowed sharply. Anti-Westernism now has no great-power supporter and no convincing alternative political model. (Buzan 1991, p. 439)

With the end of the cold war and the collapse of the Soviet Union as a "superpower" (a term that reveals the global relations of power in stark terms), nations that sought refuge from colonial rule in Soviet-style communism find themselves, as Buzan indicates, with no "great-power" supporter. The phrase "third world nations" originated as a way to speak about formerly colonized nations, those who were somehow not "first" or "second world" nations in the global balance of power. In attempting to understand how such nations conceive their role in today's international community, and why they might be tempted to seek security in nuclear weapons, it is important to keep their colonial experiences in mind. Up until the seventeenth century, for example, the Ottoman Empire and the rise of Islam represented the strongest political, military, and religious challenge to European Christianity (Said 1979). In conjunction with the "Age of Discovery," however, the consolidation of European global power in the eighteenth century resulted in the collapse of the Ottoman Empire and the colonial occupation of nations throughout Asia, Africa, and the Americas. The slave trade, the extraction and export of valuable natural resources, and the destruction of indigenous cultures and political systems, not to mention the imposition of direct colonial rule, created a historical relationship between the colonizers and the colonized with effects that linger today. Although formally and institutionally "decolonized," these nations still suffer from the experience of colonization, resulting in social conditions marked by poverty, dependency, underdevelopment, and political corruption (Said 1989).

At the close of World War II, the United States, with its atomic monopoly, occupied center stage as the dominant power in the world. Although the imperial expansion of the United States has been traced back to the earliest moments of American history (Gardner, LaFeber, and McCormick 1973), during the twentieth century its role as the dominant global power became much more explicit. In the Middle East in particular, U.S. geopolitical interests (countering the Soviet threat during the cold war) and its need for oil, combined to create a situation whereby one imperial system—European—was replaced with another—American (Said 1981). Although the newly-independent states began to emerge from direct colonial rule at the close of World War II, the experience of colonization continued in subtle and not-so-subtle ways.

One way in which the experience of colonization continues, and the ideology that justifies it is perpetuated, is through public policy argumentation that represents third world nations in ways that are dehumanizing and debasing. As Abdul R. Jan Mohamed (1985, p. 64) explains, "the discursive practices do to the symbolic, linguistic presence of the native what the material practices do to his physical presence; the writer commodifies him so that he can be exploited more efficiently by the administrator, who, of course, obliges by returning the favor in kind." If one conceptualizes international relations as "text," looking for the ways in which critics can "read" global geopolitical events as dialogues between interlocutors (Der Derian and Shapiro 1989), it is important to acknowledge that some voices in the international arena are louder and stronger than others. If it is the case that power relations are imbued in and through language, then it is clear that so-called third world nations, those at the "periphery" of international relations (Buzan 1991), have a more difficult time being heard in the global dialogue than the superpowers. One way these emerging nations attempt to empower their voices in the international arena is, unfortunately, through the acquisition of arms. As an ultimate expression of technological progress, in that what distinguishes a modern nation from a backward one is high technology, nuclear weapons represent power in many forms; power over nature, power over nations, and, of course, destructive power. If one of the defining characteristics of being a superpower is the possession of weapons of mass destruction, those in less powerful positions can attempt to make their voices heard by playing this dangerous game of nuclear politics. Said (1989) describes these attempts to participate in the global dialogue of power as desperate attempts by the colonized to find ways to be taken seriously as interlocutors. From this perspective, the arms trade can be read either as an attempt to be taken seriously in the global conversation, or as a radically antagonistic stance, which is perceived by the colonized to be the only appropriate position from which to address colonial authority.

Read in the context of the new world order, given that the United States claims to have "won" the cold war, U.S. military strategy is being reformulated to address such emerging threats, while at the same time guaranteeing that it protects the dominant military and political position enjoyed by the nation at present. A secret internal Pentagon document, leaked to the *New York Times* by an official who believed the debate over post–cold war military strategy should be held in public, proclaims that "America's political and military mission in the post–cold war era will be to ensure that no rival superpower is allowed to emerge in Western Europe, Asia, or the territory of the former Soviet Union" (Pentagon Policy 1992, p. A1). One result of such a stance is to guarantee U.S. hegemony in a dangerous time of transition, by ensuring that those in less powerful positions in international relations stay in their place at the bottom rung of the hierarchy. Buzan (1991, p. 451) argues that one result of the collapse of the bipolar power structure and its replacement by the "capitalist security community" in world politics is to weaken the position of "periphery" states relative to "the centre," making "the periphery more subordinate, than at any time since decolonization began."

The use of terms like "center" and "periphery" to describe international relations between nations of the industrial north and the former colonies of the south serves to reinforce the domination of one by the other. A person who is on the periphery is one who is barely present, one whose voice holds no authority or power, one who is irrelevant to what goes on in the center. I am also troubled by Buzan's (1991, p. 440) claim that the twenty-first century will be the era of "post-decolonization," where periphery countries can no longer blame their "many failings in their political and economic performance" on colonization, and that they cannot use "colonial rationalizations" anymore. Arguments like these attempt to erase and obscure the history of suffering and exploitation imposed by colonial rule, as if those experiences are irrelevant to the present problems faced by these nations. Scholars interested in the evaluation of foreign policy argumentation must not forget Saddam Hussein's explanation for the invasion of Kuwait: colonial boundaries between the two nations that were drawn by Great Britain were perceived as illegitimate. Geoffrey Kemp (1991, p. 58) alludes to the importance of this point in his testimony before Congress, saying, "I think one of the *most dangerous* things Saddam Hussein did was to raise the issue of colonial boundaries" (emphasis mine). Regardless of what American audiences may think about this argument, Muslims from many countries who protested the war were influenced by their shared colonial experience and their perception that artificially drawn postcolonial boundaries have weakened Islamic unity (Azzam 1991). Buzan does have a point when he claims that the collapse of the Soviet Union means that states wishing to articulate an anti-Western, postcolonialist voice have no place to turn for support in the new world order. Although I certainly do not condone the massive human rights violations carried out by Saddam Hussein's regime throughout the past decade, perhaps his drive to acquire weapons of mass destruction represents an attempt to find such a voice, given that his invasion of Kuwait was explicitly grounded in claims to postcolonial self-determination. If scholars and public policy arguers refuse to consider this explanation, the opportunity to understand the motivations for nuclear proliferation will be lost, and the stakes are much too high to ignore any possibility.

THE PERSIAN GULF WAR
AND THE DISCOURSE OF UNDERDEVELOPMENT

> Countries with embryonic ballistic missile forces are likely to lack the technical safeguards and practical experience necessary to ensure that missiles cannot be launched without proper authorization, or as a result of mechanical malfunctions or human error. (Payne 1991, p. 97)

"Third world" countries, "lesser developed" countries, "underdeveloped" countries, "developing" countries: these terms signify an implicit belief that indigenous cultures are somehow backward, and are in need of modernization by benevolent nations of the first world. Social Darwinist thought, along with the drive to convert "savages" to Christianity, provided philosophical, scientific, and moral justifications for American and European imperial expansion (Gardner, LaFeber and McCormick 1973). Social Darwinism, with its implication of evolutionary progress as grounded in biological superiority, functioned to solidify this perceived difference between modern and savage cultures. Historically, native people all around the world, from tribal cultures in Africa to Native American cultures in the Americas, were designated by great power occupiers as uncivilized, in need of high Anglo-European culture. This designation, perpetuated and naturalized through argumentative practices in public policy and academia, circulates throughout various discursive sites and becomes a kind of self-fulfilling prophecy. As Said (1989, p. 207) argues, "Thus the status of colonized people has been fixed in zones of dependency and peripherality, stigmatized in the designation of underdeveloped, less-developed, developing states, ruled by a superior, developed, or metropolitan colonizer." The danger seen by many in the post–cold war world, however, is that such backward nations will somehow acquire modern military technology, in the form of nuclear, chemical, and biological weapons.

Arguments attributing images of savagery, barbarity, and irrationality to the enemy in times of war did not suddenly appear during the 1991 war in the Persian Gulf. Robert Ivie (1980, 1982, 1984), among others (Bjork 1992; Wander 1984), illustrates the historical functions that such arguments serve in wartime. Dualistic argument structures, such as those so prevalent during the cold war (remember Ronald Reagan's description of the Soviet Union as an "evil empire") describe the world in stark, oppositional terms that make any attempt to locate similarities or compromises difficult. But when read in the context of wars prosecuted against non-European people of color, such arguments take on more dangerous and nefarious implications of racism and sexism, especially given that these arguments have historically been used to demonstrate the supposed racial superiority of whites, and the sexual "threats" posed by people of color (Gilman 1986). Hence, it is important to consider carefully the functions of dualistic arguments articulated during the Persian Gulf War.

When the rationale for war is cast in Manichean terms, as an ultimate epic battle between the forces of good and the forces of evil, the only acceptable course of action is ultimate defeat, unconditional surrender. In a speech before the United Nations, George Bush (1990a, p. 151) characterized Operation Desert Storm in such terms: "Forty-five years ago, while the fires of an epic war still raged across two oceans and two continents, a small group of men and women began a search for hope amid the ruins. They gathered in San Francisco, stepping back from the haze and horror, to try to shape a new structure that might support an ancient dream. . . . Two days from now, the world will be watching when the cold war is formally buried in Berlin. And in this time of testing, a fundamental question must be asked. . . . Can the collective strength of the world community, expressed by the United Nations, unite to deter and defeat aggression? Because the cold war's battle of ideas is not the last epic battle of this century." An epic battle of ideas is quite different than one between human adversaries; the ultimate forces of good and evil compete for dominance, implying an apocalyptic struggle of near-Biblical proportions. In such a war, it is assumed, more is at stake than geopolitical or economic interests. In a speech before U.S. troops, Bush (1990b, p. 260) underscored the stakes in the Persian Gulf War, and he did so in starkly dualistic terms: "Today in the Persian Gulf, the world is once again faced with the challenge of *perfect clarity*. Saddam Hussein has given us a whole plateful of clarity, because today, in the Persian Gulf, what we are looking at is *good and evil, right and wrong*" (emphasis mine). Bush's claim about "perfect clarity" rendered voiceless and invisible those who would speak out against the war; the implication was that anyone who has eyes and ears would obviously support military action, since it was so clearly the right course of action. More important, however, such an argumentative strategy erases historical particularity from the situation, and creates an abstract, essentialized understanding of a complicated, historically grounded conflict, and it does so in ways that are important to the ideology of colonialism.

Jan Mohamed (1985) claims that the central feature of the colonialist cognitive framework as revealed in literature is the Manichean allegory, which divides the world into opposing binary terms that imply power relations. Dualisms like white-black, good-evil, superior-inferior, civilization-savagery, intelligence-emotion, rationality-sensuality, self-other, and subject-object are products of Western Enlightenment thought that posit abstract essences devoid of historical particularities as the basis for human relations and subsequent actions. One implication of dualistic structures of thought, in other words, is to obscure the concrete, lived realities of individuals, and submerge them in grand covering terms. Feminist theories of discourse, particularly those that articulate concerns about representations of women of color, similarly point to the ways in which dualistic, binary modes of thought serve to erase and render invisible the experiences of people who are culturally coded by gender *and* by race (Caraway 1991). When theories posit universal characteristics of human experiences, they ignore the lives of those who exist either on the boundaries of categories, or who exist in multiple categories. Importantly, as Gilman (1986) argues, the intersection of race and gender as culturally and socially constructed categories of meaning, served to perpetuate the colonialist project, in that "backward" nations were described in gendered terms, and images of "primitive" sexuality served to justify oppressive racial practices. It is not difficult to find examples of the same kind of dualistic argumentative strategies being employed not only in the 1991 Persian Gulf War, but also in nuclear nonproliferation discourse.

Repeatedly, Saddam Hussein is described in public argument as uncivilized and backward. Secretary of State James Baker (1990, p. 235) claimed that "If we reverse [Saddam's] aggression, we'll help define the world that lies beyond the cold war as a place where civilized rules of conduct apply." Bush (1990a, p. 152) echoed this sentiment, arguing, "Today, the regime stands isolated and out of step with the times, separated from the civilized world, not by space but by centuries. Iraq's unprovoked aggression is a throwback to another era, a dark relic from a dark time." Calling forth images of time, and coupling them with the metaphor of darkness, Bush's argument implies that Saddam Hussein's regime and its outrageous actions are primitive and evil. Later in the speech, Bush (p. 153) explicitly called upon such colonialist metaphors, when he argued that Saddam's aggression "threatens to turn the dream of a new international order into a grim nightmare of anarchy in which *the law of the jungle* supplants the law of nations" (emphasis mine). Social Darwinist notions of evolution (humans literally emerging from the jungle), represented most clearly in the cultural celebration of science and technology, are relevant here as primitive, savage beasts are contrasted with modern, industrial nations. Specific images of beast-like savagery were prevalent in public arguments during the Persian Gulf War. Bush (1990c, 1990d) described Saddam Hussein in subhuman, animalistic terms, claiming that he "devoured" and "swallowed whole" a peaceful neighbor, like a fierce beast in need of taming and subjugation. He claimed that the invasion was characterized by "raping," "brutalizing," "kidnapping," "intimidating," "coercing," and "ruthless aggression."

Similarly, arguments in favor of ballistic missile defense, grounded in fears about the proliferation of weapons of mass destruction, center on the irrationality and instability of third world leaders, whose quest for even a "primitive" weapon is dangerous. For example, Keith B. Payne (1991, p. 32) argues that by the year 2000, twenty-four or more emerging nations could have ballistic missile technology, and that the list of these countries includes "bellicose countries hostile to the United States, its allies, and friends," and "autocratic regimes capable of reckless and possibly irrational acts of aggression." Speaking specifically about the threat that nuclear proliferation would pose to U.S. interests, retired Marine Corps Lt. Gen. Bernard Trainor (1991, p. 50) claims that "The message to the world is, 'Look, if I can get or build some sort of primitive missile, it doesn't have to be particularly effective, but if I can get a nuclear weapon to go with it, I am the master in this region. Even the United States with all its high tech weapons might be reluctant to engage us because of the fear that this nuclear weapon might be used.'" Images of the jungle, darkness, rape, savage beasts, and eerie, primitive irrationality certainly call on historical experiences of colonization, when "savage" primitive tribes (like those found on "The Dark Continent") fought for survival against their European conquerors. Such imagery brings to mind colonialist literature, such as Joseph Conrad's *Heart of Darkness,* which depicts European forays into the wilderness as dangerous and eerie adventures, barely understandable to "rational" minds (Jan Mohamed 1985).

Images of primitive savagery and irrationality, when read in the context of a war against an Arab nation, take on particularly troubling consequences, given the ways in which historically, representations of Arab peoples have been constructed in racist and sexist terms. The colonialist dualism is represented in Orientalist literature, which variously described people of "the Orient" as irrational, depraved, fallen, childlike, sexually titillating and different, in dialectic opposition to people of Europe, who were rational, virtuous, mature, sexually pure, and normal (Said 1979). Writings in the early twentieth century, for instance, characterize Europeans as "naturally" logical and rational, and Arabs as "singularly deficient in the logical faculty. They are often incapable of drawing the most obvious conclusions from any simple premises of which they may admit the truth" (quoted in Said 1979, p. 38). Similarly, Harold W. Glidden (1972, pp. 984–88) claims that Arab culture "naturally" is "characterized by anxiety expressed in generalized suspicion and distrust, which has been labeled free-floating hostility," and that "strife, not peace, was the normal state of affairs because raiding was one of the two main supports of the economy." In other words, people of Arabic descent are "naturally" hostile and warlike, childlike, irrational, and unpredictable, simply by virtue of their culture and race.

Merging these images of savagery and backwardness with the prospect that such people could acquire modern, high-technology weapons produces a frightening argumentative synthesis for proponents of nonproliferation policies. Combining traits of irrationality, recklessness, and primitive ways of life with the most powerful and destructive force known to humanity, strikes fear in the hearts of many. Baker (1990, p. 235) articulated this position shortly before the onset of the Persian Gulf War, arguing that "While the international community tries to build on the successful ending of the cold war, Saddam Hussein seems hell-bent on a revival of hot war. He marries his old-style contempt for civilized rules with modern destructive methods; chemical and biological weapons, ballistic missiles, and—if he could—nuclear weapons." Vice President Dan Quayle (1990) gave voice to the usually unspoken assumption underlying such arguments; the fear that nuclear proliferation will challenge the global hegemony of the United States by creating new superpowers. He argued that "Saddam's ambitions are not confined to Kuwait. Rather, his goal is to dominate the Persian Gulf region and use its vast wealth to become the greatest Arab hero of modern times, the leader of a new Arab superpower. . . . And, of course, the prospect of Saddam Hussein strutting across the globe at the head of a malevolent global power, armed to the teeth with weapons of mass destruction, and controlling a large portion of the world's energy supplies, is something no sane person would welcome. That is why we are working to contain Saddam Hussein's bid for hegemony today—just as we worked to contain other bids for hegemony yesterday." In other words, Saddam Hussein is in a quest for power in the international arena; a power that, according to Quayle, is dangerous because it is "malevolent" and "Arab," it constrains U.S. access to "our" oil in the Middle East, and anyone who disagrees with this interpretation of the threat is almost certainly insane. It is also important to keep in mind the phallocentric tendencies of such arguments, in that the possession of nuclear weapons, and ballistic missiles in particular, connote images of aggressive male sexuality (Cohn 1987). Read in this way, Saddam Hussein's quest for nuclear weapons represents a sexual threat to the West: Quayle does not want to see a "malevolent Arab superpower" "strutting" his stuff across the world stage, competing against the United States for attention.

Thinly veiled sexism and racism, however, are not the only assumptions operating in arguments such as these. A discourse of underdevelopment, which contrasts the "modern" nations of the industrial north with the "backward" nations of the south, although certainly related to racist assumptions, functions to keep high technology in the hands of the privileged few. Payne's (1991) claim that countries with "embryonic" nuclear forces lack the practical experience, technical skill, and know-how to safely handle high-technology weapons seems curious, since in this view, the United States in 1945 apparently *did* have such experience to justify its own nuclear arsenal development. Many commentators have noted the ethnocentric tendencies in the nuclear nonproliferation regime, arguing that claims of irresponsibility, irrationality, and backwardness represent a war of words between the technical haves and the technical have-nots (Kapur 1990; Dhanapala 1990; Subrahmanyam 1991). Resentment grows as the 1995 extension conference for the Nuclear Non-Proliferation Treaty approaches, given that many emerging nations feel that the United States and the Soviet Union failed to live up to Article VI of the treaty, requiring them to dismantle their own nuclear arsenals, in conjunction with efforts to control the spread of these heinous weapons. They argue that even with the completion of the Intermediate Nuclear Forces and Strategic Arms Reduction Treaties, the superpowers will have 20 percent more nuclear warheads than when SALT I was signed— hardly progress toward disarmament (Dhanapala 1990). Some argue that the superpowers never intended to disarm, using Article VI as a smokescreen to continue their own weapons development at the exclusion of other members of the international community (Kapur 1990). Tragically, given the realities of international power politics, it seems that former colonial states are being driven to more and more desperate means, in an attempt to overcome the stigma of "underdevelopment," and to participate as equal voices in the international dialogue. Given the scope of global problems facing humanity in the years ahead, such an outcome can only serve to endanger the lives of all on this fragile planet.

MAINTAINING U.S. HEGEMONY THROUGH BALLISTIC MISSILE DEFENSE

"Did not the Americans almost hit you . . . when you were asleep in your homes? If they knew that you had a deterrent force capable of hitting the United States, they would not be able to hit you. If we had possessed a deterrent—missiles that could reach New York—we would have hit it at the same moment. Consequently, we should build this force so that they and others will no longer think about an attack." This statement [by Col. Qadhafi] reflects an appreciation of the deterrent value that ballistic missiles may provide to Third World leaders vis-a-vis the United States. In other words, the weak may paralyze the strong if there is no protection against this threat. (Cooper 1991, p. 68)

Nuclear deterrence has been the staple of U.S. defense policy throughout the past forty-five years. The theory of deterrence postulates that if the U.S. nuclear arsenal is strong and credible, no nuclear-armed state would risk attacking, for fear of retaliation. The nuclear standoff that characterized the cold war was grounded in the logic of deterrence, at least until March 23, 1983, when Ronald Reagan proposed the Strategic Defense Initiative, a program he claimed would "render nuclear weapons impotent and obsolete" (Bjork 1992). As the raucous public debate over SDI developed during the 1980s, proponents articulated a less drastic mission for the program, claiming that it would actually serve to strengthen nuclear deterrence by creating uncertainties in the minds of Soviet attack planners who, unable to predict how many ICBMs would actually reach their targets, would not attempt a first strike (Bjork 1992). With the apparent disappearance of the Soviet nuclear threat at the end of the cold war, however, some proclaim that SDI is "a program in search of a rationale" (Auster 1990).

Given the experience, however, of the first major military confrontation in the post–cold war era, the 1991 war in the Persian Gulf, some argue that the rationale for proceeding with SDI is self-evident. Bush's Secretary of Defense Dick Cheney argued, for example, that "If there was ever evidence that supported the notion for aggressively going forward with the program, it would seem to me it was watching those Scuds fly at Tel Aviv and Riyadh" (quoted in Thompson 1991). The dramatic live television coverage of apparent Patriot missile interceptions seemed to verify Cheney's claim that now, more than ever, the time is right to proceed aggressively with SDI. In his 1991 State of the Union address, Bush officially announced that the SDI program had been redirected to counter limited ballistic missile threats, whatever their source (Hadley 1991), and GPALS was born.

Despite controversies concerning the actual effectiveness of the Patriot missile's performance in the Gulf War (Safire 1991; Patriots May Have Missed 1992), the redirection of SDI to a focus on limited attacks proceeds apace. Given fears about nuclear, chemical, and biological weapons proliferation, along with high-technology ballistic missile delivery systems, the program has acquired momentum, and seems destined for deployment in some form. But given that these fears about proliferation, as I argued earlier, are cast in terms that reinforce the ideology of colonialism, it is important to examine carefully the arguments justifying the objectives of ballistic missile defense, with an eye toward revealing their relationships with changing distributions of power in the new world order.

At the end of the cold war, the United States found itself to be the only remaining nuclear superpower in the world. Put squarely at the top of the global hierarchy of power, the United States did not hesitate to communicate to other nations that it alone was in a position of power and leadership sufficient to assemble a coalition to disengage Saddam Hussein from Kuwait. As Bush (1991, p. 67) put it, "Among the nations of the world, only the United States of America has had both the moral standing and the means to back it up. We are the only nation on this Earth that could assemble the forces of peace. This is the burden of leadership and the strength that has made America the beacon of freedom in a searching world." Calling on the historical image of America as a nation with a moral mission to free the world from war, poverty, and oppression, Bush echoed a vision of the United States' role in the world that has deep roots reaching back to the earliest moments in the nation's history (Bjork 1992). This destiny of the United States, backed up by the strongest military force in the world, allows it to lead the way toward a new world order in which peace and freedom will reign, unfettered by tyrants who wish to challenge the authority of the powerful. The outcome of the stunning victory in the Gulf War, according to Trainor (1991, pp. 47–48), was to underscore this authority and power vested in the United States by virtue of its military might. He argued, "in the end we will win this war and the United States will be dominant in the region. We will have shown that we not only have the capability to reach half way around the world in the interest of world security but we have credibility, by virtue of having done it at considerable cost but with a great deal of efficiency."

One result of this demonstration of the United States' "efficient" military capability in distant places around the world is to consolidate the power that was granted by default with the collapse of the Soviet Union. Echoing the racist undertones I pointed to earlier, Trainor (1991, p. 48) claimed, "If nothing else, the nations of the world, particularly in the Arab world, respect power. They may not like us but they will respect us. The United States is in the position of winning that war down there and is in a position to set the agenda for the Middle East in interests of not only the United States but more importantly for the Middle East." According to this line of argument, Arabs, somehow more so than other races, only understand the language of power, and the United States is certainly in a position of power at the end of the war, one that gives it the authority to "set the agenda" for the nations of the Middle East for their own good, if not to preserve the geopolitical interests of the United States. The primary danger associated with such a stance, however, is that this articulation of unilateral American power in a region half way around the world will stir up resentment among the Arab "masses," who will respond in ways unbecoming to the new world order. Although fears that Islamic uprisings would spread throughout the Middle East during the prosecution of the war were not ultimately realized, arguments articulating the continued threat of "Arab" resentment, and proposing ways to avoid it, are evident in public policy arguments at the end of the war.

Leonard S. Spector, a respected advocate for nuclear nonproliferation policies, testified before Congress about his concerns about maintaining a long-term U.S. troop presence in the Middle East. In response to a question from Rep. Lee Hamilton about whether troops should be withdrawn as quickly as possible, Spector (1991, p. 52) stated, "I would tend to favor that because I think in peacetime their presence may be a provocation. U.S. troops will remain a symbol of American intervention in the region, which could stimulate the backlash that we are all fearing." As a symbol of U.S. military intervention, troop presence, therefore, comes to represent the history of colonization experienced by nations in the Middle East, along with the resentment feared by American policymakers. Reducing the force levels actually deployed on Middle Eastern soil, however, does not mean reducing the authority, power, and prestige won by the United States in the war. In fact, some argue that the best course of action would be to maintain a "low profile," which would avoid sending an *explicit* symbol of intervention, without actually scaling back U.S. forces. As Trainor (1991, p. 48) argued, "it is clearly in our interest to withdraw, insofar as we can, and maintain a low profile."

One way suggested to accomplish the symbolic purpose of withdrawal without actually reducing the United States' presence in the region is to maintain the appearance of multilateralism, which was highlighted during the actual prosecution of the war. Martin Indyk (1991, p. 86) executive director of the Washington Institute for Near East Policy, explicitly suggested such a course of action: "We must avoid the impression that the U.S. is out to impose a *Pax Americana* on the region. We will be the dominant power in the region after the war. . . . However, just as we prosecuted the campaign against Saddam as a multinational effort, so too must we maintain the image of a joint enterprise to deal with the region's post-war problems. Drawing down our ground presence in the Gulf will help to bolster this image and undermine the perception of 'neo-imperialism.' However, we should remember that we have maintained a force presence in the Persian Gulf for forty years and will need to continue this presence to protect our interest in the free flow of oil at reasonable prices. What we need is a 'low profile' not 'no profile.'" Avoiding the *appearance* of imperialism, according to this line of argument, is of primary importance in the post–Gulf war period; whether or not the *actual* practice of imperialism is a wise course of action is not addressed. Indyk explicitly revealed the extent of U.S. involvement in the Middle East during the past forty years, arguing that geopolitical and economic concerns have always guided policy decisions. As we have learned recently, moreover, the United States has even subverted its concern for human rights in Iraq under its desire to protect geopolitical interests in the region. Evidence mounts that the Reagan and Bush administrations knowingly strengthened Saddam Hussein's regime and fed his military machine, both during the Iran-Iraq war and up until two months before the invasion of Kuwait, in an attempt to counter Iran's quest for regional hegemony after its revolution (Frantz 1992; Memos Prove U.S. Knew 1992).

Evidence of a desire to maintain U.S. military hegemony, especially in regional "hot spots," can be found in statements describing how the Pentagon sees its role in the post–cold war era. Deployment of ballistic missile defense is emerging as a centerpiece of U.S. military strategy in responding to regional threats to American hegemony. In describing the new U.S. defense strategy, which consists of three parts (forward presence, crisis response, and force reconstitution), Hadley (1991, pp. 5–6) argued that the concept of forward presence "emphasizes the importance of U.S. presence abroad, albeit at reduced levels. Presence can take many forms. The stationing of forces in selected forward bases is perhaps the most tangible demonstration of U.S. commitment in key areas. Our missile defenses, in combination with those our allies and coalition partners might deploy, will protect us and them in maintaining a forward military presence in those areas threatened by ballistic missiles, and *will support our aim of continuing to play a leadership role in international events*" (emphasis mine). Deployment of an antiballistic missile system that can deny new nuclear nations the ability to strike against U.S. forces or our allies and friends will in this way strengthen the ability of the United States to "project its power" all around the globe, and thereby ensure a continued "leadership" role for the nation. Articulating one of the greatest security risks involved in nuclear proliferation, Payne (1991, p. 50) argued that "proliferation would impose significant constraints on future U.S. military and foreign policy options. In considering power projection alternatives, U.S. leaders would have to calculate the possibility of Third Party ballistic missile strikes." He clearly spelled out the implications that such a situation would have for the maintenance of U.S. hegemony in the post–cold war era: "In short, merely by acquiring long-range ballistic missiles, Third Parties could gain international prestige, constrain U.S. diplomacy, undermine U.S. security guarantees, and deter U.S. and allied power projection into local conflicts" (Payne 1991, p. 54). In this view, it is inconceivable that the leader of a third world nation would want to "gain international prestige" and deter military intervention by outside powers—ironically the same objectives sought explicitly by the United States and justified by arguments appealing to "national security."

Finally, it is important to acknowledge a deeper symbolic role that ballistic missile defense would play in the maintenance of U.S. political, military, and economic hegemony. As I noted earlier, one of the objectives of GPALS was to provide *global* protection against ballistic missile attacks, to protect U.S. forces deployed overseas as well as those of our allies. In order to achieve this objective, however, a significant portion of the technology would need to be deployed in outer space, to provide early warning, surveillance, and boost-phase protection against the launch of missiles anywhere in the world (Cooper 1991). A space-based ballistic missile defense system seems to be the perfect, transcendent solution to the problem outlined earlier; that is, how to maintain a "low profile" U.S. military presence without risking anti-Western resentment in former colonial states. "Brilliant Eyes" orbiting far above the globe would provide constant surveillance of troubled areas, while avoiding the risks associated with the deployment of intelligence personnel, seen recently in Iraqi protests over inspections of military facilities carried out by United Nations teams. In this way, ballistic missile defense would allow the United States to maintain a "distant presence" that is more politically acceptable than troop deployment on the ground (Payne 1991, p. 48). Striving to maintain a distant, almost invisible presence brings to mind one of the primary characteristics of ideology as performed in culture; always present, but rarely articulated codes of conduct that serve to obscure relations of power and maintain social (and in this case, international) order.

It is risky to take a position that might appear, on the surface, to justify attempts by nations to acquire weapons of mass destruction; for even giving voice to deeply submerged issues such as these leaves one open to charges of radical fanaticism, anti-Americanism, or worse. But when I read statements like Qadhafi's that I quoted earlier, I am struck by the ways in which what I perceive to be a double standard emerges so clearly. The avowed purpose of the U.S. nuclear arsenal is to deter attack by other nations; yet when others articulate a similar position, they are labeled fanatical dictators, irrational and unstable leaders who threaten the very security of the world. I am left wondering why it is that so many observers of international politics apparently believe that the leadership of the United States has a monopoly on rationality and self-control, when in the past two decades it has engaged in acts of military intervention against sovereign states all around the world.

IMPLICATIONS

The facts are that we have vast global interests, and we prosecute them accordingly. There are armies, and armies of scholars at work politically, militarily, ideologically. (Said 1989, p. 214)

Perhaps the most compelling feature of Said's (1979) *Orientalism* is the careful, detailed account he constructs of the historical relationships between academic scholarship and colonial expansion in the eighteenth and nineteenth centuries. The assumption, all too often taken for granted in academic circles, that scholarship takes place in an "ivory tower" that has no relationship to the real world, is problematic in light of Said's thorough critique of the discursive practice of Orientalism and his advocacy of "worldly" criticism (Said 1983). As I have attempted to demonstrate in this essay, all scholars and public policy arguers, myself included, cannot escape the cultural embeddedness of their positions, authority, and work. If it is the case that human beings are constantly shaped by their surroundings, and form attitudes, beliefs, and values in response to their circumstances, then it seems clear that attempts to "objectively" discover and communicate knowledge are doomed to fail. It is my belief that formalist argumentation theory, with its goals of accurately describing arguments and applying "rational" tests to determine whether they warrant assent, clings to this goal of objectivity. Furthermore, presuming that "rational" argument takes place between equally empowered voices in an "ideal" civic and democratic society, obscures the role of power relations as they are culturally and historically coded in society (Fish 1990). Once it is granted that academic discourse circulates throughout culture and becomes part of the taken-for-granted assumptions that drive society, then it is imperative that scholars who produce such discourse are vigilant and aware of the power and implications of their work.

In this essay, I have attempted to illustrate the ways in which public policy argumentation (scholarly and otherwise) concerning the threats posed by nuclear proliferation, and the potential deployment of ballistic missile defense as a way of alleviating those threats, depict "other" nations in ways that are racist and sexist, and which serve to perpetuate global inequalities. Some might argue that it is easy to point fingers, lay blame, and complain about the current state of international relations without offering any concrete solutions to the dangers that face our world each day. Adopting a critical stance to the evaluation of arguments, however, represents a first step toward constructive change, in that awareness of the ideological power of argumentation opens up possibilities for reconceptualizing the role of scholarship. Listening to the voices of "others," with sensitivity to the particular situations from which such voices emerge, seems to be logically prior to suggesting alternatives. One difficulty with adopting a postcolonialist critical stance toward argumentation, for instance, involves grappling with the question, "when does my speaking *about* the struggles of the 'other' become an attempt to speak *for*?" After all, I am privileged, as a middle-class, white, professional American, and I must acknowledge my privileged status. Listening carefully to the voices of the colonized, however, and attempting to open up a critical space for their arguments, moves the study of argumentation in new directions. Exposing the colonialist functions of dualistic argumentative structures, and striving to allow subjugated voices to emerge, allows critics to cultivate a sense of "respect for the concrete detail of human experience, understanding that arises from viewing the Other compassionately, honestly" (Said 1981, p. xxxi). Guarding against the temptation to abstract and essentialize whole cultures, societies, and peoples, and replacing it with scholarship sensitive to the concrete historical factors shaping human action, serves to "humanize" academic practice and, perhaps, makes inroads against the dehumanizing practices so characteristic of argumentation in the formulation and justification of American foreign policy. I can only hope that my efforts will encourage others to engage in the debate over ideological criticism, and that the result will be a humane, vigilant dialogue that is sensitive to the power and influence of scholarship.

REFERENCES

Auster, Bruce. 1990, June 11. Remember Star Wars? Now it's a program in search of a rationale. *U.S. News and World Report*, 32.

Azzam, Maha. 1991. The Gulf crisis: Perceptions in the Muslim world. *International Affairs, 67,* 473–85.

Baker, James. 1990, November 5. Why America is in the Gulf. *U.S. Department of State Dispatch*, 235–36.

Bjork, Rebecca S. 1992. *The Strategic Defense Initiative: Symbolic containment of the nuclear threat*. Albany, N.Y.: State University of New York Press.

Broad, William J. 1991, January 31. New course for "Star Wars," from full to a limited defense. *The New York Times*, A18.

Bush, George. 1990a, October 8. The UN: World parliament of peace. *U.S. Department of State Dispatch,* 151–53.

———. 1990b, November 12. Remarks to U.S. troops. *U.S. Department of State Dispatch*, 260.

————. 1990c, November 26. Thanksgiving Day address to U.S. Forces in Saudi Arabia. *U.S. Department of State Dispatch*, 279–80.

————. 1990d, September 17. Toward a new world order. *U.S. Department of State Dispatch*, 91–94.

————. 1991, February 4. State of the Union address. *U.S. Department of State Dispatch*, 65–67.

Buzan, Barry. 1991. New patterns of global security in the twenty-first century. *International Affairs, 67*, 431–51.

Caraway, Nancie. 1991. *Segregated sisterhood: Racism and the politics of American feminism*. Knoxville: University of Tennessee Press.

Cohn, Carol. 1987. Sex and death in the rational world of defense intellectuals. *Signs: Journal of Women in Culture and Society, 12*, 687–718.

Cooper, Henry F. 1991. The SDI as it relates to the ABM Treaty. In *Hearings: Committee on Foreign Relations, U.S. Senate*. Washington D.C.: U.S. Government Printing Office.

Der Derian, James, and Michael J. Shapiro, eds. 1989. *International/intertextual relations: postmodern readings of world politics*. Lexington, Mass.: Lexington Books.

Dhanapala, Jayantha. 1990, July–August. Disappointment in the third world. *Bulletin of the Atomic Scientists*, 30–31.

Fish, Stanley. 1990. Rhetoric. In *Critical terms for literary study*, ed. Frank Lentricchia and Thomas McLaughlin. Chicago: University of Chicago Press.

Frantz, Douglas. 1992, April 26. Bush imprint all over support to Saddam. *Salt Lake Tribune*, A16.

Gardner, Lloyd C., Walter F. LaFeber, and Thomas J. McCormick. 1973. *Creation of the American empire*. Chicago: Rand McNally.

Gilman, Sander L. 1986. Black bodies, white bodies: Toward an iconography of female sexuality in late nineteenth-century art, medicine, and literature. In *Race, writing and difference*, ed. H. L. Gates Jr. Chicago: University of Chicago Press.

Glidden, Harold W. 1972. The Arab world. *American Journal of Psychiatry, 128*, 984–88.

Hadley, Stephen J. 1991. The SDI as it relates to the ABM Treaty. In *Hearings: Committee on Foreign Relations, U.S. Senate*. Washington D.C.: U.S. Government Printing Office.

Indyk, Martin. 1991. Post-war policy issues in the Persian Gulf. In *Hearings: Committee on Foreign Affairs, U.S. House of Representatives.*. Washington D.C.: U.S. Government Printing Office.

Ivie, Robert L. 1980. Images of savagery in American justifications for war. *Communication Monographs, 47*, 279–94.

————. 1982. The metaphor of force in pro-war discourse: The case of 1812. *Quarterly Journal of Speech, 68*, 240–53.

————. 1984. Speaking "common sense" about the Soviet threat: Reagan's rhetorical stance. *Western Journal of Speech Communication, 48,* 39–50.

Jan Mohamed, Abdul R. 1985. The economy of Manichean allegory: The function of racial difference in colonialist literature. *Critical Inquiry, 12,* 59–87.

Kapur, Ashok. 1990, July-August. Dump the treaty. *Bulletin of the Atomic Scientists,* 21–22.

Kavanagh, James H. 1990. Ideology. In *Critical terms for literary study,* ed. Frank Lentricchia and Thomas McLaughlin. Chicago: University of Chicago Press.

Kemp, Geoffrey. 1991. Post-war policy issues in the Persian Gulf. In *Hearings: Committee on Foreign Affairs, U.S. House of Representatives.* Washington, D.C.: U.S. Government Printing Office.

Lumpe, Lora, Lisbeth Gronlund, and David C. Wright. 1992, March. Third world missiles fall short. *Bulletin of the Atomic Scientists,* 30–37.

McGee, Michael Calvin. 1990. Text, context, and the fragmentation of contemporary culture. *Western Journal of Speech Communication, 54,* 274–89.

Marranca, Bonnie, Marc Robinson, and Una Chaudhuri. 1991. Criticism, culture, and performance: An interview with Edward Said. In *Interculturalism and performance: Writings from PAJ,* ed. Bonnie Marranca and Guatam Dasgupta. New York: PAJ Publications.

Memos Prove U.S. Knew Iraq Was Pursuing Nukes. 1992, July 5. *Salt Lake Tribune,* A3.

Patriots May Have Missed Every Scud. 1992, March 19. *Salt Lake Tribune,* A10.

Payne, Keith B. 1991. *Missile defense in the 21st century: Protection against limited threats.* Boulder, Colo.: Westview Press.

Pentagon Policy Casts U.S. as Singular Power. 1992, March 9. *Salt Lake Tribune,* A1.

Quayle, Dan. 1990, December 10. America's objectives in the Persian Gulf. *U.S. Department of State Dispatch,* 310–11.

Reagan's Missile Shield in Space, "Star Wars," Is Pronounced Dead. 1993, May 14. *New York Times,* A20.

Safire, William. 1991, March 7. The great Scud-Patriot mystery. *New York Times,* A19.

Said, Edward W. 1979. *Orientalism.* New York: Vintage Books.

————. 1981. *Covering Islam.* New York: Pantheon Books.

————. 1983. *The world, the text, and the critic.* Cambridge: Harvard University Press.

————. 1989. Representing the colonized: Anthropology's interlocutors. *Critical Inquiry, 15,* 205–25.

Second Coming. 1993, May 22. *The Economist*, 31–32.

Spector, Leonard S. 1991. Post-war policy issues in the Persian Gulf. In *Hearings: Committee on Foreign Affairs, U.S. House of Representatives.* Washington D.C.: U.S. Government Printing Office.

Subrahmanyam, K. 1991, June. Some nations are more equal than others. *Bulletin of the Atomic Scientists*, 21.

Thompson, Mark. 1991, March 10. Command system, high-tech weapons win high marks. *Salt Lake Tribune*, 4A.

Trainor, Lt. Gen. Bernard. 1991. Post-war policy issues in the Persian Gulf. In *Hearings: Committee on Foreign Affairs,U.S. House of Representative.* Washington D.C.: U.S. Government Printing Office.

Wander, Philip. 1984. The rhetoric of American foreign policy. *Quarterly Journal of Speech*, 70, 339–61.

PART 4

Alternative Evaluations of The Final Report of the Attorney General's Commission on Pornography

CHAPTER 10

Examining an Argument by Cause: The Weak Link Between Pornography and Violence in the Attorney General's Commission on Pornography Final Report

Ian Fielding

In July 1986 the Attorney General's Commission on Pornography (hereafter referred to as the commission) issued its final report to the American public, the first extensive governmental study on the subject since the President's Commission on Obscenity and Pornography published its multivolume report in 1970. According to its charter, the objectives of the commission were "to determine the nature, extent, and impact on society of pornography in the United States, and to make specific recommendations to the Attorney General concerning more effective ways in which the spread of pornography could be constrained, consistent with constitutional guarantees" (U.S. Department of Justice 1986, p. 1957).

Although the commission's report was unveiled with great hue and cry, the attention has long since dissipated and the little in the way of implementing the report's nearly ninety recommendations on how to curb the "spread of pornography" has been accomplished. While it is possible to question the extent to which the commission's report has functioned as a progenitor to the formation of public policy in the area of pornography, this by no means diminishes the importance of the report. If nothing else, the report is a watershed for those interested in the field of argument criticism.

This essay examines the commission's use of causal argument in its final report. A major part of the scope of the commission's study, a scope that the commission admits was very broad, included, "a review of the available empirical evidence on the relationship between exposure to pornographic materials and antisocial behavior" (U.S. Department of Justice 1986, p. 1957). The commission concluded that causal relationships exist between exposure to pornography and various types of harm, including acts of sexual violence. In fact, of all the points raised in the commission's report, it is the causal argument linking pornography and violence that has received the greatest amount of public attention and it has been disputed by various groups including, not surprisingly, the American Civil Liberties Union. This argument is also the commission's most obvious causal claim in that it is made, from the commission's viewpoint, with the greatest possible degree of certainty. The commission's discussion of the causal connections between pornography and harm is found in Chapter Five of Part Two of the report entitled, "The Question of Harm" (U.S. Department of Justice 1986, 1: 299–352).

A careful examination of the commission's causal reasoning is important since causal arguments are employed for a number of reasons (Zarefsky 1977, pp. 177–90). For example, causal argument permits control over events through understanding them. If we have knowledge of the causes of events then we are able to bring about those events again or prevent them from occurring in the future. Also, the effective use of causal argument improves the rigor of the advocate's analysis and the fairness of argumentation as a decision-making process because causal reasoning demands that we ask the question, "How?" An acceptable answer to this question compels the advocate to prepare and present a well-documented argument to which decision makers are likely to adhere. Finally, causal arguments provide a basis for one's commitment to public policy choices or to systems of belief depending on the strength of the causal warrant. By applying Zarefsky's points to the commission's report it is clear that if a causal link can indeed be established between exposure to pornography and violent behavior then such behavior may be controlled. In addition, the report, which relies heavily on causality, can be expected to offer strong arguments as to how this link is manifested. If a cause-effect relationship is demonstrated, then the document may be considered credible. Finally, if pornography and violence are shown to be directly connected, then policy-makers and the public are likely to be committed to a program of control or prevention. Unfortunately, as the analysis that follows makes clear, the commission's report fails in each of these areas largely because of the weaknesses of the commission's causal reasoning in the areas of definitions, standards of proof, use of evidence, and flaws in the commission's causal warrant linking exposure to pornography and violence.

THE COMMISSION'S PORNOGRAPHY-VIOLENCE CAUSAL ARGUMENT

Although the chapter on harm in the commission's report is relatively brief in relation to the entire work (152 out of 1,960 pages), it is the pivotal part of the study. In this chapter the commission sets forth its causal arguments identifying a connection between exposure to pornography and antisocial behavior by dividing its conclusions about harms into four categories of pornography: (1) sexually violent materials; (2) nonviolent but degrading materials; (3) nonviolent and nondegrading materials; and (4) nudity. The concern here is with the first category because it is in this category that the commission asserts its clearest causal argument that exposure to sexually violent materials leads to acts of sexual violence.

The category of sexually violent materials consists of "material featuring actual or unmistakably simulated or unmistakably threatened violence presented in a sexually explicit fashion with a predominant focus on the sexually explicit violence" (U.S. Department of Justice 1986, p. 323). The commission contends that the most prevalent forms of pornography, as well as an increasing prevalent body of less sexually explicit material, fit this description (p. 323). According to the commission, this is the category upon which most of the evidence has focused (p. 323). In describing the causal significance of this body of material the report states: "In both clinical and experimental settings, exposure to sexually violent materials has indicated an increase in the likelihood of aggression. More specifically, the research, which is described in much detail later in the Report, shows a causal relationship between exposure to material of this type and aggressive behavior toward women" (p. 324).

It is important to bear in mind that, for the commission, making this causal connection between aggressive behavior and sexual violence required making "assumptions not found exclusively in the experimental evidence" (p. 325). According to the commission, the assumption of a causal relationship is supported by a variety of types of evidence, including experimental evidence, clinical evidence, "less scientific evidence," and common sense (p. 325). The commission states its causal argument in this way:

> Thus we make our conclusions by combining the results of research with highly justifiable assumptions about the generalizability of more limited research results. Since the clinical and experimental evidence supports the conclusion that there is a causal relationship between exposure to sexually violent materials and an increase in aggressive behavior toward women, and since we believe that an increase in aggressive behavior toward women will in a population increase the incidence of sexual violence in that population, we have reached the conclusion, unanimously and confidently, that the available evidence strongly supports the hypothesis that substantial exposure to sexually violent materials as described here bears a causal relationship to antisocial acts of sexual violence and, for some subgroups, possibly to unlawful acts of sexual violence. (pp. 325–26)

In short, the commission argues that exposure to pornography leads to aggression which, in turn, creates sexual violence.

The Commission's Definitions

One of the principal shortcomings of the commission's report concerns the defining of pivotal terms. While defining "pornography" is a difficult task at best ("I can't tell you what it is but I know it when I see it), the commission should have reached some level of agreement as to the meaning of the term. Such agreement is especially important when trying to determine the impact of pornography. Without agreed-upon terms it is uncertain whether all of the members of the commission had in mind the same materials when trying to ascertain the harms resulting from pornography. The members of the commission, however, could not reach consensus on the meaning of this centric term. The commission states that references to material as pornographic "means only that the material is predominately sexually explicit and intended primarily for arousal" (pp. 228–29). According to commissioners Judith

Becker and Ellen Levine, who dissented from the report's conclusion that pornography and violence are causally linked,

> One critical concern of this Commission was to measure and assess pornography's role in causing antisocial behavior; but although the commission struggled mightily to agree on definitions of such basic terms as "pornography" and "erotica," it never did so. This failure to establish definitions acceptable to all members severely limited our ability to come to grips with the question of impact. Only the term "obscenity," which as a legal meaning, became a category we all understood. In fact, the commission failed to carve out a mutually satisfactory definition of "antisocial behavior." (p. 200)

Moreover, although the commission claims to have tried to minimize the use of the word "pornography" because of its perceived connotations (p. 228), the word appears repeatedly throughout the text, even in the title of the final report. The failure to arrive at agreed-upon definitions, as well as the extensive use of a word with admitted negative meanings, casts doubt on the commission's conclusions particularly as they relate to harm.

"Antisocial behavior," the harm allegedly resulting from pornography exposure, is likewise never defined by the commission. In their personal statements contained in the report, however, Becker and Levine use the phrase to describe forced sexual acts, that is, "acts involving coercion of any kind of lack of consent" (p. 200). The report, however, does not limit itself to such behavior. According to the report, a number of commissioners

> reject the idea that the only noticeable harm is one that causes physical or financial harm to identifiable individuals. An environment, physical, cultural, moral, or aesthetic can be harmed, and so can a community, organization, or group be harmed independent of identifiable harms to members of that community.
>
> Most importantly, although we have emphasized in our discussion of harms the kinds of harm that can most easily be observed and measured, the idea of harm is broader than that. To a number of us, the most important harms must be seen in moral terms, and the act of moral condemnation of that which is immoral is not merely important but essential. From this perspective there are acts that need be seen not only as causes of immorality but as manifestations of it. Issues of human dignity and human decency, no less real for their lack of scientific mea-

surability, are for many of us central to thinking about the question of harm. And when we think about harm in this way, there are acts that must be condemned not because the evils of the world will thereby be eliminated, but because conscience demands it. (p. 303)

In discussing harms, the commission draws a distinction between primary and secondary harms. Primary harms are those in which the alleged harm is commonly taken to be intrinsically harmful. Acts such as murder and rape are examples of primary harms not because of where they will lead, but because of what they are (p. 304). Secondary harms are those that result from some other act. The concern here is not with what the act is, but where it will lead (p. 304). The commission contends that the harms from pornography, such as loss of human dignity, are secondary harms because "the allegation of harm presupposes a causal link between the act and the harm, a causal link that is superfluous if, as in the case of primary harms, the act is quite simply the harm" (p. 305).

There is, as well, a problem with the commission's definition of "harm" itself. As the American Civil Liberties Union points out:, "Our legal system normally defines and compensates 'harms' which represent serious, concrete injury to individuals. The sweeping compendium of 'harms' included here, including even 'harm' to moral and aesthetic considerations, sets up this Commission as a roving arbiter of tastes and values, a wholly inappropriate venture for an official body of this kind" (1986, p. 60). It is open to discussion whether moral and aesthetic issues should be part of the discussion on the potential harmful effects of pornography, but if the commission is going to identify such issues as areas of legitimate concern then the commission should offer some way to assess harm in those areas. It is not surprising that the commission cannot do this, since it cannot even determine what is said to be causing the harm—whatever that may be—in the first place.

The Commission's Standard of Proof

In addition to lacking agreement on the meaning of pivotal terms, the commission's final report also lacks a clearly defined standard of proof (American Civil Liberties Union 1986, p. 61). The standard of proof is used to judge the credibility of the witnesses who testified at the various public meetings of the commission and to assess the accuracy of the evidence submitted to the commission. The commission states: "It would be ideal if we could put our evidentiary standards into simple formulas, but that has not been possible. The standards of proof applicable to the legal process— preponderance of evidence, clear and convincing evidence, and proof beyond a reasonable doubt—are not easily transferred into a nonjudicial context" (pp. 308–9).

It is true, of course, that judicial standards are not easily transferred to a commission of the type the attorney general assembled for examining the potential harms of pornography, yet the development of guidelines for weighing the veracity of claims is important from both argumentative and public policy perspectives. The success of an argument is not measured only by the extent to which it achieves its end, but also by the extent to which it adheres to identifiable standards. The closest the commission comes to identifying standards is the rejection of suggestions that a causal link must be proved conclusively before a harm can be identified and that assertion of a fact is not necessarily proof of that fact (p. 307). In between these two extremes, the commission argues, the issues are much more difficult. That the issues are difficult, however, does not excuse the commission from making clear its standard of proof. The commission's extremes do not help in judging the accuracy of the evidence as it relates to the discussion of harms alleged to result from exposure to pornography.

The Commission's Use of Evidence

The lack of clearly defined standards of proof highlights two things that are especially disturbing about the evidence on which the commission relies in supporting its causal reasoning. First, throughout all of the chapter on harm in the final report, the commission never identifies the specific studies relied on in drawing its conclusions about harms. The chapter is replete with references such as "the research indicates," or "significant scientific empirical evidence," or "some researchers have found"; however, these undocumented references are so vague as to be meaningless. As a result, it is difficult, even impossible, to assess the credibility of the commission's claims. The report notes that the research is described in detail later in the report (p. 324), and there is an entire chapter in Part Four devoted to this subject (pp. 901–1033), but even in that chapter the commission does not specify which studies were given weight in drawing conclusions or why counter-vailing studies were ignored or dismissed altogether (American Civil Liberties Union 1986, p. 61).

The second problem is the lack of any effort by the commission to judge or independently verify the credibility of the witnesses who were relied on in drawing the final conclusions about harm. A considerable amount of attention was paid to those identified in the report as "victims of pornography." The report states, "Most of the people who have testified about personal experiences . . . have been women reporting on what men in their lives have done to them or their children as a result of exposure to sexually explicit materials" (p. 313). The witnesses, then, are being asked to provide the causal link between exposure to pornography and violence by stating that the "use" of pornographic materials by men led the men to commit certain violent acts on their families. Nowhere, however, does the commission explain how the credibility of the witnesses was determined, how the witnesses were selected to testify, or what factors, such as competency or trustworthiness, played a role in assessing their credibility. As the American Civil Liberties Union argues, "There is no question that many of the life-histories of these individuals are sad tales of sexual abuse. There is serious doubt, however, as to how significant a role 'pornography' played in their worlds—which were blighted by a plethora of abusive practices, including drug problems, alcoholism, severe psychopathologies, and broken homes" (1986, p. 65). The commission justifies its reliance on the witnesses by not drawing statistical conclusions from their testimony and by offering their testimony as simply one more perspective from which to view the harm phenomenon. According to the commission, a more complete understanding emerges when a phenomenon is viewed from multiple perspectives (p. 314). However, such anecdotal evidence is of little use in identifying possible negative effects precisely because no statistical conclusions can be drawn. Lacking such conclusions, the commission's report can reasonably be accused of committing a hasty generalization in relying on anecdotal evidence to draw conclusions about harm.

The other forms of evidence used by the commission have similar problems with respect to credibility verification. Correlative data play a significant role in the commission's attempt to establish a causal link between pornography and violence. An example of correlative data in the final report is seen in this passage:

For example, we heard much evidence from law enforcement personnel that a disproportionate number of sex offenders were found to have large quantities of pornographic material in their residences. Pornographic material was found on the premises more, in the opinion of witnesses, than one would expect to find in the residences of random samples of the population as a whole, in the residences of a random sample of nonoffenders of the same sex, age, and socioeconomic status, or in the residences of a random sample of offenders whose offenses were not sex offenses. To the extent that we believe these witnesses, then there is a correlation between pornographic material and sex offenses. (p. 316)

Evidence like this is labeled as "less scientific" in the commission's report (p. 316), but the commission refused to discount it simply because the "researcher did not have some set of academic qualifications" (p. 316). Perhaps, then, the commission should have discounted it because law enforcement officers do not conduct random samplings of the homes of nonoffenders. What is most interesting about this passage is that the commission is arguing not from cause, but rather by sign. This weakens the commission's argument because sign reasoning can only connect an event with the existence of some other phenomenon; it cannot establish a causal link between the two events. That such material was present in an offender's home is not proof that the material caused or even contributed to the offense. At best, the only connection that can be drawn in this case is that sex offenders also look at pornography (as do teachers, corporate employees, doctors, engineers, homemakers, and assembly line workers).

The more scientific correlations studies deal with circulation of sexually explicit materials and sex offense rates. The commission is correct in stating that the correlational evidence suffers from an inability to establish a causal connection between the correlated phenomena and in stating that frequently two phenomena are positively correlated because they are both caused by a third phenomenon (p. 317). While the commission states it is important to assess the plausibility of any third variable, it fails to do so. Unless this is done, the commission can be reasonably accused of committing the fallacy of ignoring a common cause. That is, rather than identifying a possible third variable, or common cause, the commission assumes that there is a causal relationship between the two positively correlated phenomena. The report demonstrates this when it states, "But the fact that correlational evidence cannot definitively establish causality does not mean that it may not be some evidence of causality, and we have treated it as such" (p. 317).

The Commission's Causal Warrant

The analysis thus far has demonstrated the problematic nature of definitions, the lack of a clearly articulated standard of proof, and the commission's overreliance on correlational data as a substitute for evidence of causation in the commission's final report. At this point it would be useful to examine the commission's causal reasoning in terms of commonly recognized standards for evaluating causal argument. Such standards seek to evaluate the warrant/backing complex in a causal argument. According to Toulmin (1958), the warrant is the part of an argument that links data (evidence) to the claim (conclusion) while the backing serves as support for the warrant. An application of the Toulmin model of argument to the commission's causal argument under discussion yields the following:

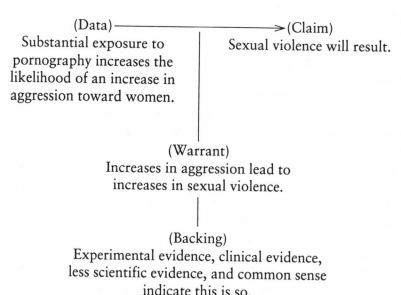

(Data) ————————————→(Claim)
Substantial exposure to pornography increases the likelihood of an increase in aggression toward women.

Sexual violence will result.

(Warrant)
Increases in aggression lead to increases in sexual violence.

(Backing)
Experimental evidence, clinical evidence, less scientific evidence, and common sense indicate this is so.

With this model of the commission's argument in mind, standard tests of causal reasoning can be applied to the argument in an effort to assess its strength. One of those standards considers whether the argument demonstrates that the cause is capable of producing the effect. If a causal connection exists between exposure to pornography and acts of violence, then the commission's report would carry considerable weight in forming public policy. The commission, however, overstates its causal claim when it argues that the "available evidence strongly supports the hypothesis that substantial exposure to sexually violent materials . . . bears a causal relationship to antisocial acts of violence" (p. 326; one cannot help but wonder what constitutes a "social" act of violence). The commission admits that its asserted causal link "requires assumptions not found exclusively in the experimental evidence" (p. 325) because the experimental and clinical evidence indicates only a possible increase in the likelihood of aggression. The commission goes on to assert that such aggression will lead to sexual violence, but this assertion is never substantiated in the report. The only support the commission can muster is the statement that "the evidence says simply that the images that people are exposed to bears a causal relationship to their behavior" (p. 326). No mention is made of where this evidence comes from or to what specific images the relied-upon evidence refers.

In making the leap from exposure to pornography to the likelihood of an increase in aggression to sexual violence, the commission places great stock in "common sense." Although commonsense reasoning is not inherently flawed, the common sense used by the commission's members provides little in the way of justifying the commission's leaps in its chain of causal reasoning. The commission, however, also offers "clinical evidence and less scientific evidence" to support its warrant. The commission includes as "less scientific evidence" the testimony of sex offenders to support the conclusion that the causal connection the report identifies relates to actual sexual offenses rather than aggressive behavior. The report, however, casts doubt on the credibility of such testimony when it states: "Much research supports the tendency of people to externalize their own problems by looking too easily for some external source beyond their own control. As with more extensive studies based on self-reports of sex offenders, evidence relying on what an offender thought caused his problem is likely to so overstate the external and so understate the internal as to be of less value than other evidence" (p. 325). Thus, although this "less scientific evidence" is of dubious value, the commission relies on it to support its argument that exposure to pornography results in sexual violence.

The clinical evidence that purports to establish a causal connection between pornography and violence is difficult to evaluate because, as mentioned above, the commission does not indicate in its report which studies were viewed as most conclusive. While this does not entirely invalidate the commission's connection between pornography exposure and various harms (i.e., aggression), such omissions cast doubt on the credibility of the report as a whole and, in turn, on the commission's assertion that a causal link exists between exposure and sexual violence. Some have argued that the studies on which the commission may have relied were flawed. In its review of all the conceptual models from which the commission may have drawn conclusions, the American Civil Liberties Union concluded that the scientific data from test results in the laboratory and from clinical results of working with sex offenders are contradictory and ambiguous. The results produced only moderate correlations from which causation can be only tentatively extrapolated (American Civil Liberties Union 1986, pp. 70, 75–88). Even some commissioners were not convinced that exposure to pornography and violence are causally linked. In a joint statement, Levine and Becker argued: "To state that exposure to pornography in and of itself causes an individual to commit a sexual crime is simplistic, not supported by social-science data, and overlooks many of the other variables that may be contributing causes" (p. 206).

That the commission was unwilling or unable to clearly articulate which studies were given weight in drawing its conclusions points to a failure of the commission's causal argument to meet two other important standards for judging causal reasoning: that the warrant should demonstrate that the effect is produced by the cause and does not occur coincidentally with the cause, and that the warrant should demonstrate that the effect has consistently followed from the cause. Because the report does not identify the relevant studies, it is not possible to know if the research on which the commission relied actually meets these standards.

Another reason why these standards are difficult to assess in the commission's reasoning has to do with multiple causality. The standard of multiple causality states that the warrant should point to other potential causes of the effect and demonstrate their secondary importance to the cause under examination. Depending on the number and strength of other causes of a phenomenon, determining coincidence and consistency becomes more difficult because of the number of causes it is necessary to consider. The commission does point out that other causes of violence exist:

> But when we identify something as a cause, we do not deny that there are other causes, and we do not deny that some of these causes might bear an even greater causal connection than does some form of pornography. That is, it may be, for example, and there is some evidence that points in this direction, that certain magazines focusing on guns, martial arts, and related topics bear a closer causal relationship to sexual violence than do some magazines that are . . . "degrading." If this is true, then the amount of sexual violence would be reduced more by eliminating the weaponry magazines and keeping the degrading magazines than it would be reduced by eliminating the degrading magazines and keeping the weaponry magazines. (p. 310)

While the commission points to other potential causes of violence, it does not indicate the secondary importance of those causes. On the contrary, the commission demonstrates that other potential causes of violence, like weaponry magazines, are more significant causes of the identified harm than are pornographic materials.

The commission provides a sweeping definition of causation when it contends that a causal relationship exists if "the evidence supports the conclusion that if there were none of the material being tested, then the incidence of the consequences would be less" (p. 310). This interpretation of causation is too broad because no judgment can be made about the significance of any potential element of causation. Thus, it is impossible to know the extent to which exposure to pornography is responsible for acts of sexual violence because there is no distinction drawn in the commission's definition between a cause that is .01 percent responsible for the effect and one that is 99 percent responsible (American Civil Liberties Union 1986, p. 62).

The most important critique of the commission's report with respect to multiple causes comes from the commission itself. In Chapter Six of Part Two of the report, "Laws and Their Enforcement," the commission states, "[M]ost of the harms that we have identified in Chapter Five of this part are not caused exclusively or even predominantly by pornography" (p. 358). By its own admission the commission invalidates much of its causal reasoning linking pornography with sexual violence.

CONCLUSION

Although one of the principal goals of the Attorney General's Commission on Pornography was to ascertain the harms resulting from pornography in the United States, the analysis presented here demonstrates that the commission was unable to establish a valid causal connection between exposure to pornography and violence. There are several flaws in the commission's reasoning. First, the members of the commission failed to agree on the meaning of pivotal terms including "pornography" and "antisocial behavior," which severely limited the commission's ability to delineate potential negative effects arising from the material the commission was established to study. As well, the commission's interpretation of "harm," which included moral and aesthetic considerations, sets up the commission for the charge that it functioned as "a roving arbiter of tastes and values." Second, the commission never articulated a standard of proof by which it judged the credibility of witnesses who testified or by which it assessed the accuracy and reliability of the evidence on which the commission relied. Third, the evidence the commission made use of was weak. The commission's "common sense" is not subject to evaluation by common tests of evidence; the "less scientific evidence" offered by the testimonies of both "victims" of pornography and sex offenders suffers because the witnesses are relied on to establish the missing causal link even though the commission presents no way to verify the witnesses' credibility; and the clinical evidence, at best, supports only a correlation between pornography and aggression, not a causal relationship between pornography and sexual violence. Finally, the commission's causal reasoning falls short of meeting common standards for a causal warrant. Neither common sense, less scientific evidence, nor clinical evidence could establish that the cause is capable of producing the effect the commission identified; the commission's failure to identify its sources makes it difficult to determine if the effect was mere coincidence or if the effect consistently followed the cause; and the commission, while identifying other possible causes, admits that those other causes play a greater role in the harms it specified than does pornography.

So why did the commission's causal analysis fail on so many levels? Some have speculated that one reason for the commission's spurious argumentation concerns the motives of the commission and the underlying political reasons surrounding its formation. The confirmation or denial of such speculation is beyond the scope of this essay; however, the commission identified at least two reasons why the final report is rife with shortcomings: lack of money and lack of time. With respect to the former, the commission states:

> The budgetary constraints have limited the size of our staff, and have prevented us from commissioning independent research. We especially regret the inability to commission independent research, because in many cases our deliberations have enabled us to formulate issues, questions, and hypotheses in ways that are either novel or more precise than those reflected in existing thinking about this subject, yet our budgetary constraints have kept us from testing these hypotheses or answering these questions. (p. 218)

The time factor, according to the commission, also hindered its work:

> The time constraints have also been significant. We all wish we could have had much more time for continued discussion among ourselves, as the process of deliberation among people of different backgrounds, different points of view, and different areas of expertise had been perhaps the most fruitful part of our task. Yet we have been required to produce a report within a year of our creation as a Commission, and our ability to meet together has been limited. (p. 219)

Limited resources such as time and money, however, do not excuse the commission for presenting an argument that is largely unsatisfactory in demonstrating a causal link between exposure to pornography and harms to society. The implications of the commission's reasoning process can best be seen in light of Zarefsky's uses for causal argument outlined at the beginning of this essay. The first use of causal argument is that it permits control over events through understanding them. The idea is that if we have knowledge regarding the causes of events, then we can bring about those events again or prevent them from recurring in the future. The commission gives no real insight into the causes of the event it identifies (that event being harm generally and sexual vio-

lence specifically). At best, the commission can only assert a correlation between pornography and harm. The result is that if the
commission's report is used in an attempt to control sexual violence in our country then no true understanding of the event will
occur. That is, because the commission's causal analysis fails, it
cannot help in controlling violence because the report does little
to generate an understanding of violence as it relates (if, in fact, it
does relate) to pornography.

The second use of causal argument is that it improves the rigor
of the advocate's analysis and the fairness of argumentation as a
decision-making process by demanding that we ask the questions
"How?" and "Why?" It might appear that this use of causal argument is restricted to the collegiate debate round; however, this use
has a much wider application. Future commissions like the Attorney General's Commission on Pornography, as well as future
research into the potential effects of pornography on society,
might look to the commission's final report to see how the commission fell short of its mandate because of its ineffective causal
analysis. Perhaps the mistakes of the commission will aid the work
of others involved in explaining how or why there might exist a
connection between pornography and harm.

The final use of causal argument is that it provides a basis for
commitment to policy choices or to systems of belief depending on
the strength of the causal warrant. It is in this regard that adherence to the commission's final report has the greatest potential for
danger. Because the causal reasoning in the report is flawed, it
cannot serve as a basis for commitment to policy. Such policy
might entail legislation curtailing so-called pornography or the
means by which such materials are made available to the public.
A commitment to solving the "pornography problem" must begin
from the standpoint that pornography is in some important ways
harmful. The commission's causal argument does not support this
basic assumption. In addition, the causal argument analyzed here
does not provide the basis necessary for a commitment to the
belief that pornography is harmful in the ways the commission
contends.

Although the purpose of this essay has been to examine the
pivotal causal argument in the final report of the Attorney General's Commission on Pornography, I hope that a greater awareness of the difficulties involved in arguing from cause to effect will
result. My intention has not been to demonstrate that there exists

no causal link between exposure to pornography and various harms, but rather to show that the commission does not demonstrate such a link. It is important to realize that answering questions of cause and effect is rarely a simple task. Often, usually, cause and effect issues are highly complex, and searching out the cause of a particular phenomenon requires careful study. The causal reasoning of the commission is a prime example of what can happen when the necessary effort is not put forth in ascertaining the cause of something. The implications of such fallacious reasoning are that the understanding process is thwarted, the advocate's analysis is hindered, and a firm basis for commitment to policy or belief is prevented.

If nothing else, the commission's report illustrates how not to argue from cause. As a case study in fallacious causal argument, the report is most insightful. As an aid in the formation of public policy, it leaves a great deal to be desired.

REFERENCES

American Civil Liberties Union. 1986. *Polluting the censorship debate: A summary and critique of the final report of the Attorney General's Commission on Pornography*. Washington, D.C.: American Civil Liberties Union.

Toulmin, Stephen. 1958. *The uses of argument*. Cambridge: Cambridge University Press.

U.S. Department of Justice. 1986. *Attorney General's Commission on Pornography final report*. Washington, D.C.: U.S. Government Printing Office.

Zarefsky, David. 1977. The role of causal argument in policy controversies. *The Journal of the American Forensic Association, 13*, 179–90.

CHAPTER 11

Survivor Testimony in the Pornography Controversy: Assessing Credibility in the Minneapolis Hearings and the Attorney General's Report

Catherine Helen Palczewski

The use of consciousness-raising and personal testimony in women's discourse is not new. Karlyn Kohrs Campbell (1989) identifies a feminine style that inhered in early feminist discourse. She argues that women's gender presented unique rhetorical problems for women rhetors and, hence, generated a distinctive rhetorical style. This style is typified by a personal tone; reliance on experience, anecdotes, and examples; inductive structure; invitation for audience participation; treatment of the audience as peers; and goal of empowerment (Campbell 1989, p. 13). Women were confined to a particular sphere and used the resources available in that sphere to persuade.

The personal process of consciousness-raising that arose during the "second wave" of feminism paralleled the feminine style of the turn of the century. During the 1970s the politicization of the personal was effected through consciousness-raising groups. These groups' exploration of women's experience, and their process of self-validation, enabled women to identify themselves as a group and to understand the systematic nature of their subordination; women, through consciousness-raising, named their oppression. Feminism thus became defined by the politicization of the personal as it attempted to uncover the political power hidden in the private sphere (MacKinnon 1987, 1989; Koedt et al. 1973).

Moving beyond the small-group recognition of the power that inheres in the private sphere, women are now speaking publicly about the harm done to them in private. Women are taking the private process of consciousness-raising and introducing it to the public sphere in the form of personal testimony about the sexual violence women experience as a result of their gender. This use of personal testimony has played a central role in the contemporary pornography controversy.

According to Catharine MacKinnon, women long spoke of their experiences, but their words were given no credibility, and hence no power, in the public sphere (MacKinnon 1987, p. 188). Eventually, social science data began to corroborate women's experience and the voice of the survivor gained volume. However, the criticism of personal testimony is still problematic for argument scholars because we have no vocabulary to describe the dual role a victimized woman fills when she testifies in pornography hearings. She is both a victim, in that force was used on her, and she is a survivor, in that she is publicly proclaiming that she was forced and that it should never happen again.[1] Argument scholars also lack a model that can describe the liminal location of testimony in relation to the objective, subjective, and intersubjective worlds. Finally, survivors' rhetorical problems are further compounded because they not only face the possibility that they will not be believed, but also the possibility that their words will be coopted.

Survivor testimony has been used in two instances as evidence justifying restrictions on pornography: the 1983 Minneapolis city council hearings concerning an amendment to its civil rights ordinance and in the 1986 Attorney General's Commission on Pornography. While the two instances tend to overlap because of the commission's use of the Minneapolis hearings as a source of evidence, formal and ideological distinctions exist. While the Minneapolis hearings' structure encouraged empowerment, the Meese Commission had witnesses testify behind screens, imparting a sense of guilt or shame (Vance 1990, p. 55). While the Minneapolis city council was persuaded to treat pornography as a violation of women's civil rights, the commission saw pornography as a moral scourge. Accordingly, interesting contrasts arise between the commission's framing of survivor testimony and the Minneapolis hearings' framing of it.

For argument critics, the status of personal testimony is an important practical and theoretical issue. Consistent with Aristotle's early dismissal of testimony as a weak form of evidence because it is not from "detached persons" (*Basic Works* 1376a, p. 15), contemporary scholars treat testimony as a means of confounding argument, not as a part of argument. How one assesses the credibility of personal testimony and how one distinguishes a personal statement from a generalizable knowledge claim have not been addressed. Scholars have found it easier to dismiss testimony as a subjective and nongeneralizable form of evidence (e.g., Fielding 1987; Hauser 1987).

Instead of explaining how personal testimony problematizes validity tests used in public argument, critiques of testimony simply assume that the credibility of the witnesses, and hence the validity of the testimony, is fixed. Credibility is defined in relation to traditional Aristotelian notions of objectivity. Hauser argues that "credibility requires more than deference to authority or compassion; it requires detachment and objectivity to entertain the possibility of alternative accounts" (1987, p. 258). He writes that the witnesses who testified to the commission about pornography's linkage to their victimization "were not in a position to form an objective or competent opinion" (1987, p. 260). Experience of an event did not qualify one to speak of it. For Hauser, objectivity was necessary for a speaker to be persuasive, yet the objective voice is precisely what the marginalized, most notably women, have always been denied.

Fielding also critiques the use of survivor testimony, arguing that "guidelines for weighing the veracity of claims is still important" (1987, p. 265) in determining the power of an argument. Unlike Hauser, Fielding recognizes that witnesses may be credible, and their statements valid, even if the witness is not detached. However, even after Fielding establishes that a potential for testimony validity exists, he discredits any generalizing potential, arguing that to reason from the testimony of survivors would be to engage in "hasty generalization" (1987, p. 266). Hauser also indicates that the witnesses are not able to establish a causal connection between pornography and their abuse (1987, p. 266). Accordingly, one is left wondering what role, if any, is left for testimony in the discussion of public policy concerning pornography.

Fielding and Hauser's conclusions are limited further by their failure to distinguish between the Minneapolis and the commission use of testimony. Even though the commission extensively relied on the Minneapolis hearings' use of survivor testimony, they accept the vocabulary of the commission, referring to those who testified as "'victims'" (Fielding 1987, p. 266) and as "those who . . . saw themselves as victims" (Hauser 1987, p. 256). Given that this essay argues that ideological framing is an important aspect of determining the validity of testimony, recognition of our *own*, as well as others', vocabulary becomes important to our assessments of validity. By ignoring the distinctions between the two instances of testimony, Fielding and Hauser create a theoretical apparatus that tends to discount all testimony, not just testimony that has been recuperated by the dominant discourse.[2]

At the heart of the dismissal of survivor testimony is the traditional, and apparently immutable, distinction between the objective and the subjective. Such a distinction not only appears in the assessment of survivor testimony in the commission report, but also in other public controversies. Lorraine Code (1988), in a study of Toronto's investigation of infant deaths, discovered that when doctors (who were primarily male) were questioned, they were asked about what they *knew*, while nurses (who were primarily female) were asked about what they had *experienced*. This distinction between knowledge and experience that confers authority to doctors is representative of the larger distinction between men's public knowledge and women's "narrowly circumscribed private spheres of knowledge and expertise" (Code 1988, p. 64).

A similar stratification seems to be in operation with the criticism of personal testimony in the pornography controversy. Critics tend to assume that personal testimony is attached and subjective, as opposed to detached and objective, and, hence, is incapable of speaking to broader, generalizable understandings. Instead, argument critics should view survivor testimony as an important source of claims about "reality" and one that ought not to be dismissed, out of hand, as an illegitimate source of evidence. Personal testimony is more than the mere retelling of some isolated person's subjective experience of an incident, and hence problematizes traditional validity tests. As scholars continue to explore the ideological biases in our conceptions of objectivity (i.e., Code 1988, 1991; Jaggar and Bordo 1989; Harding and Hintikka 1983), argument scholars should integrate those explorations into their assessments of argument validity.

As argument critics, we need to recognize that personal testimony, when placed within a framework of assessing argument validity that recognizes the problematic relationships among the objective, subjective, and intersubjective worlds, can be understood as a legitimate and powerful form of evidence within public policy controversy. If marginal and silent groups are to gain a voice in public discourse, an understanding of the processes of gaining a voice, and the dangers that inhere in taking "personal" experience public, must be analyzed. Survivor testimony in the pornography controversy provides an excellent case with which to examine the interplay of the objective, subjective, and intersubjective and how the terms and their understanding may be bound by a masculinist bias.

FEMINIST THEORY AND TESTIMONY

While argumentation has not yet investigated the implications of testimony on the relations among the objective, subjective, and intersubjective worlds, feminist theoretical debate proceeds. The questions within feminism concerning the survivor regard what it means to speak as a survivor: Is it a reaffirmation and embrace of women's powerless position, or is it the means of deconstructing that position?[3] The determination of what a survivor's voice means is not a simple one, for the ability to name, and hence to impart credibility and power, extends beyond women who consider themselves feminist. When women, as survivors, enter into the political sphere of public argument to speak in their own voice, the potential for their voice to be taken from them emerges. Other actors in a public argument may frame and redefine the meaning and implications of women's personal testimony.

Jean Bethke Elshtain argues that feminists must be critical of the discourse that they use and, thus, "the nature and meaning of feminist discourse itself must be a subject of critical inquiry" (1982, p. 607). As a result of this critical inquiry, key questions arise concerning language, identity, how to "redescribe social reality and experience in order to reflect on what makes this reality and experience what it currently is, whether what is must be, or whether dramatic alterations are either possible or desirable?

And what models for emancipatory speech are available?" (p. 607). The form of discourse that Elshtain fears is that which appears to embrace the victim role. She questions the use of survivor testimony that presents the victim as speaking in a "pure voice" and hence tends to enshrine, through repeated evocation, "images of female helplessness and victimization" (p. 612). She questions the notion that, because someone has suffered, she speaks with moral purity. Elshtain fears that through reliance on victim testimony feminism will lose its critical edge (p. 612).

In contrast, Catharine MacKinnon argues that survivor testimony is powerful due to its consciousness-raising potential. For MacKinnon, consciousness-raising is feminist method (MacKinnon 1982, pp. 519–20). In turn, the method of consciousness-raising determines what counts as evidence for drawing particular conclusions: "Method shapes each theory's vision of social reality. . . . Method in this sense organizes the apprehension of truth; it determines what counts as evidence and defines what is taken as verification" (p. 527). According to MacKinnon, the only valid way to discover the status of women, or to understand women's condition, is to listen to women's voices (p. 535). For MacKinnon, women's status as survivors defines their experience as women (p. 536).

However, dangers inhere in the use of the survivor as a source of evidence in public argument. Because survivors are powerless in many ways, their discourse is easily appropriated; those who control the discourse in the public sphere can frame the meaning of testimony to meet their own ends. The dilemma facing survivors is that if they do not speak, they assure themselves of anonymity; yet if they do speak, the potential exists for the dominant discourse to coopt their statements and use them to reinforce the existing structure.

THE MINNEAPOLIS HEARINGS

In the fall of 1983, the city of Minneapolis was considering alterations to its zoning law in an attempt to control pornographic materials. The city council requested that feminist scholars and activists Catharine A. MacKinnon and Andrea Dworkin testify to them about the zoning approach. In their testimony, they argued that this approach was ineffective because it did not lessen the amount of pornography, but rather concentrated it in the socio-economic areas least equipped to counter its effects. As an alternative, they wrote an amendment to the city's civil rights ordinance. As part of the policy discussion of that amendment, public hearings were organized in an attempt to gather information and to establish a legislative history for the amendment. The hearings were distinctive because they created a forum in which survivors of abuse, who attributed their abuse to pornography, could exercise their voice (MacKinnon 1987, p. 188).

The amendment to the civil rights code, which came to be known as the MacKinnonDworkin Civil Rights Ordinance, found that "*Pornography is central in creating and maintaining the civil inequality of the sexes. Pornography is a systematic practice of exploitation and subordination based on sex which differentially harms women.*" The ordinance defined pornography as "the sexually explicit subordination of women, graphically depicted, whether in pictures or in words" that also includes women presented as sexual objects who enjoy pain or humiliation, experience sexual pleasure in being raped, are tied up or cut up, are presented in postures of sexual submission, are reduced to body parts, are presented as whores by nature, are presented being penetrated by objects or animals, and/or are presented in scenarios of degradation (*Amendment*).

At the outset of the hearings concerning the Ordinance, MacKinnon saw no need to justify the survivor testimony as legitimate evidence. Instead, she explained: "The understanding and the evidence which we will present to you today to support defining pornography as a practice of discrimination on the basis of sex is a new idea" (*Public Hearings* 1983, p. 1). MacKinnon also established the validity standard against which the testimony should be judged: Were those testifying relaying facts? She explained: "The purpose of this hearing is principally factual. We think that we have found a large part of the way that women have been kept silent for a very long time and that is that pornography silences women. . . . we will provide a factual basis for a legally sufficient sex discrimination statute" (*Public Hearings* 1983, p. 2). The statements of the women were to be taken as factual, not subjective. If a woman claimed to have been sexually assaulted, she was; if a woman claimed to know the cause of that assault, she did. This privileging of women's experience placed opponents to the ordinance in a difficult position. In order to refute the survivors' claims, as those claims had been framed by MacKinnon, opponents either had to deny that an incident of sexual abuse occurred or had to respond to MacKinnon's framing of the issue.

The ordering of the witnesses also is informative. Social scientist Edward Donnerstein followed the short introductions offered by MacKinnon and Dworkin. After Donnerstein came Linda Marchiano, formerly known as Linda Lovelace, who was then followed by social scientists Pauline Bart and Kathleen Barry. In other words, a survivor was given the same placement as institutionally recognized experts on the subject of violence against women.

Marchiano began her testimony by justifying her right to speak at the hearings (*Public Hearings* 1983, p. 13) and then described the problems faced by survivors when telling their stories. Accordingly, the testimony the committee was about to hear represented acts of courage:

> I tried to tell my story several times. Once to a reporter, Vernon Scott, who works for the UPI. He said he couldn't print it. Again on the Regis Philbin Show and when I started to explain what happened to me, that I was beaten and forced into it, he laughed. Also at a grand jury hearing in California after they had watched a porno film, they asked me why I did it. I said, "Because a gun was being pointed at me" and they just said "Oh, but no charges were ever filed." (*Public Hearings* 1983, p. 14)

Marchiano, with this short history, created her audience. Either they could be like the callous reporters and courts in her past, or they could accept the statements of the witnesses as truth.

After Marchiano's testimony, Dworkin read a part of a letter from sociologist Kathleen Barry (*Public Hearings* 1983, p. 17). Testimony by Pauline Bart, also a sociologist, followed. Bart used various quotations from women describing "the things that they have been asked to do because of pornographic pictures, and this was by their husbands and boyfriends" (*Public Hearings* 1983, pp. 18–19). The words of women were presented as equally valuable and informative as social science research. However, Bart did place some constraints on the evidence offered by survivors because of "insufficient probing by the interviewers to determine the exact nature of the unwanted sexual experience" (*Public Hearings* 1983, p. 20).

After Bart concluded her testimony, Dworkin quickly introduced the survivors and requested that they be able to speak from the same location as did the experts (*Public Hearings* 1983, p. 37). Dworkin's request located the survivors in a place of authority and differentiated them from the generic audience. Witnesses "L" through "Z" then testified.[4]

Each of the survivors, in her or his own way,[5] defined what they were doing with their discourse. The witnesses believed they empowered themselves by claiming a place and a voice in public discourse. For example, Ms. M defined her activities as a means of self-preservation and as a way to reclaim self-worth (*Public Hearings* 1983, p. 39). Ms. N voiced a similar reason for testifying, explaining, "This for me is also a way of purging my own shame about this" (*Public Hearings* 1983, p. 41). For these witnesses, their testimony functioned as more than evidence for the ordinance; it functioned as evidence that their lives were worth something. Through testimony, the speakers transformed themselves from acted-upon victims to acting survivors and challenged the social order by speaking the unspeakable.

Another witness, Ms. X, told the council that she testified as a means of helping her children (*Public Hearings* 1983, p. 66). Through her testimony, she could protect others. Ms. X, an American Indian woman, was raped by two white men acting out the pornographic video game *Custer's Last Stand* (actually entitled *Custer's Revenge*). Explaining the linkage among pornography, racism, and rape, Ms. X argued that the linkage did not surprise her because the three are "perfect partners. They all rely on hate. They all reduce a living person to an object." By allowing the distribution of video games like *Custer's Revenge*, society "gives white men permission to do what they did to me." In order to protect others, "I bring my screams of that night here to you today, hoping that they will help you decide to stand against the dehumanization and violence of pornography" (*Public Hearings* 1983, p. 67). Ms. X sought to recreate the emotions experienced during sexual abuse, giving concrete meaning to the abstract numbers presented by the social scientists.

The totality of the testimony provided a chronicle of the various ways survivors' lives had been impacted by pornography, ranging from mental humiliation to rape and battery. Attempting to contextualize the statements of the witnesses, so that they could not be dismissed as unrepresentative anecdotes, Dworkin remarked, "All of the stories that you have heard are representative of a thousand more stories" (*Public Hearings* 1983, p. 50). In like manner, MacKinnon tied the statements of the individual witnesses to the reports of the "experts," explaining: "Also, the men are not doing what they are doing to the women because of alcohol and drugs. The data that we had earlier on today [from Donnerstein, Bart, and Barry] showed a direct causal relationship between pornography and aggression toward women" (*Public Hearings* 1983, p. 50). MacKinnon and Dworkin were careful to tie the reports of sexual abuse to pornography, and one of the means by which they did this was to use social science data as the warrant for generalization. The incidents proved not only that sexual abuse occurred, but that the sexual abuse was tied to pornography.

The hearings concluded with the testimony of people who work at battered women's shelters, rape counseling centers, and sexual assault centers, as well as people who work with sex offenders, all of whom linked pornography to sexual abuse. MacKinnon also submitted the court reports of ongoing cases of sexual assault.

The effect of the Minneapolis hearings was not confined to the city council. MacKinnon and Dworkin used much of the testimony in later speeches. Two themes run through MacKinnon and Dworkin's use of the hearings in their arguments against pornography. First, echoing the words of the survivors, the act of testifying is an act of empowerment (MacKinnon 1987, p. 188) that is intimately linked to the ordinance, which "unlike pornography and its defenses, was written in the speech of what has been their silence" (Dworkin and MacKinnon 1988, p. 35). Second, testimony about women's actual experience is as good as, or better than, speculative social science research for establishing the linkage of pornography to violence against women (MacKinnon 1987, pp. 163, 188; Dworkin 1988, pp. 247–48; 1984, pp. 3, 6). Even though MacKinnon and Dworkin combined social science evidence with women's testimony in the hearings, they believe the testimony can stand on its own as proof of pornography's harm.

As a result of the Minneapolis hearings, and MacKinnon and Dworkin's advocacy, the ordinance was twice adopted by the Minneapolis city council, in 1983 and 1984, but twice vetoed by Mayor Fraser. In 1984 Indianapolis, relying on the Minneapolis hearings, adopted a narrower version of the ordinance that covered only explicitly violent pornography. Minneapolis delayed further action, awaiting the judicial outcome of the Indianapolis Ordinance. The Seventh Circuit Court in *American Booksellers Association, Inc. et al. v. William H. Hudnut III et al.* (771 F.2d 323), decided that the Indianapolis ordinance was unconstitutional because it did not employ the standards the Court had established to judge a document "obscene" and hence did not pass First Amendment scrutiny.

RESPONSES TO MINNEAPOLIS SURVIVOR TESTIMONY

While people generally are willing to accept women's claims that abuse occurred, they are not yet willing to accept the survivor's explanation of the cause. As part of the debate over the Minneapolis ordinance and the judicial scrutiny of the Indianapolis ordinance, various people and groups critiqued survivor testimony, most notably the Feminist Anti-Censorship Taskforce (FACT) and the American Civil Liberties Union (ACLU), primarily represented by Barry Lynn.

While members of FACT never directly attacked the witness statements, they did attack MacKinnon and Dworkin for using survivor testimony. Ann Snitow argued that the statements of "victims" created a setting in which rational policy discourse was impossible and hence it diverted attention away from "real" feminist issues.[6] In a 1983 talk, Snitow argued that "today's antipornography campaigns achieve their energy by mobilizing a complex amalgam of female rage, fear and humiliation in strategic directions that are not in the long term interests of our movement." Seeing antipornography action as "a politics of outrage," she predicted it will "fail women in our efforts to change the basic dynamics of the sex-gender system" (1985, p. 108).

Snitow attributed the failure of the pornography critique to its division of the world into two absolute categories, "victims and oppressors," and, similar to "the nineteenth-century debates on sex, lust is male, outrage female" (1985, p. 113). By highlighting distinctions between women and men, the only role offered to women is that of victim, and it becomes the primary focal point of action:

> The antipornography movement . . . requires that we oversimplify, that we hypothesize a monolithic enemy, a timeless, uni-

versal, male sexual brutality. . . . All are collapsed into a false unity, the brotherhood of the oppressors, the sisterhood of the victims. In this sisterhood, we can seem far closer than we are likely to feel when we discuss those more basic and problematic sources of sexual mores: ethnicity, church, school and family. (1985, p. 113)

The fear that such distinctions would be reinforced by the ordinance and the testimony surrounding it were voiced in FACT's *amici curiae* brief (1985, p. 18). For FACT, once a person claims to have been a victim of sexual abuse, or once a law operates from the assumption that women, *as a class*, disproportionately suffer sexual abuse, women are locked into the victim role. Where MacKinnon and Dworkin saw empowerment, FACT saw protection (FACT 1985, p. 8).

In response to the claim that pornography is or causes violence, FACT relied on traditional liberal defenses of obscene material. FACT employed the distinction between speech and act and argued that no evidence proves that pornography causes violence against women. However, the only evidence FACT challenged is social science research (FACT 1985, pp. 18–27). Apparently, MacKinnon and Dworkin's argument that the testimony of women is sufficient to establish harm was either forgotten, ignored, or dismissed out-of-hand by FACT.

Barry Lynn, the ACLU's primary spokesperson against the ordinance, while avoiding directly attacking those who testified, did attempt to diminish the power of the testimony by framing it as inauthentic and narrow. Lynn dissociated the process of testifying from those who testified. For example, in Lynn's description of the Minneapolis hearings, one finds hints that the hearings were artificially created by MacKinnon and Dworkin. In other words, the "victims'" voices were not pure, but rather had been filtered by MacKinnon and Dworkin: "The hearings in Minneapolis were orchestrated to pay particular—if not exclusive—attention to those who had something quite devastating to say about the role which pornography had played in their lives" (1986a, pp. 74–75). While the statements of the "victims" may be true, their intersubjective importance is called into question because of the setting in which the statements were uttered. The "self-selected" voices were not random and hence their claims were not generalizable (1986a, p. 75).

Generalizability was further diminished because the speaking of the "harmed" silenced the voices of those who benefit from pornography. Lynn described speech as, in some cases, a zero sum game, much like MacKinnon and Dworkin argued that pornographer's speech is a zero sum game for women. He argued that the "victim impact" approach served as a disincentive to testify for those who benefit from pornography, whom Lynn identified as "equally voiceless" (1986a, p. 75). By creating a scenario in which advocates of pornography were "silenced," Lynn cast the survivors' claims as isolated and unique. In a sense, he drowned out the survivors' voices by calling forth alternative voices.

However, Lynn went to great lengths not to question the legitimacy of the survivors' statements, at times making explicit that he was not "attack[ing] the credibility of anyone who has spoken." However, he also went to great lengths to contest the intersubjective attribution of pornography's link to violence. He warned the Meese Commission, on the basis of his reading of the Minneapolis hearings:

> There will be considerable testimony before the commission from persons characterized as victims of pornography. The claim here is not some generalized interference with the good life, but specific personal injury. There is no doubt about the truth of these personal tragedies. . . . When you look at specific claims of victimization, however, it is crucial to determine the real cause of the abuse so that symptom control does not become the substitute for genuine remedies. (1985, p. 165)

Lynn appears not to attack the truthfulness of the "victim" nor the truth of abuse. Instead, he frames the claim that pornography is abuse as an objective claim that is verifiable only through social science research or as an intersubjective claim that is not "right" because the judgment of the survivors is not universalizable. The survivors only are able to report credibly that abuse occurred; they are not able to report credibly on the cause or the meaning of that abuse.

FACT and Lynn isolate survivors by locating their claims in the purely subjective world. The survivors merely are given the power (at best) to report that abuse happened to them or (at worst) merely to report that something happened. Survivors were not allowed to attach intersubjective meaning to their experiences. Survivors were powerless to name their abuse. The reactions of

FACT and Lynn demonstrate how rigid distinctions among objective, subjective, and intersubjective may operate to exclude women's voices from the sphere of public argument.

The fact that these absolute distinctions have influenced theories of public argument and controversy is demonstrated by Donald Alexander Downs' (1989) analysis of the Minneapolis hearings. He, like Elshtain, rejects the notion that the experience of sexual violence, and hence victimization, defines women's lives, arguing that "disempowered women . . . are likely a minority among women" and that to "reduce the plurality of women's experience to the most extreme cases of powerlessness and silence is to deny both the complexity of social life and the full reality of women's lives" (p. 70). To Downs, the claims of the survivors were not generalizable, but instead only represented the singular, subjective experience of the (minority) victimized woman.

In addition to isolating the testimony as atypical, Downs also argued that survivor testimony undermined rational policy-making. Downs contrasted the testimony of survivors to objectivity, explaining that the testimony, and the attention it brought to "women's special sensitivities to [pornography's] degrading aspects . . . seems to have . . . unleashed a psychology of victimization that jeopardized objectivity and perspective" (pp. 71–72). Even though the statements of the women were true, or perhaps because they were true, the testimony of the survivor undermined objectivity and polluted the environment of policy-making. Downs did not claim the statements were invalid, even though he did discredit them by attributing them to women's "special sensitivities"; they simply were inappropriate to the "objective" public forum. Downs believed that the testimony harmed the political process because it "bred an emotionalism that was ultimately anti-political, since politics is a process of legitimate compromise, the acknowledgement of conflicting viewpoints and understanding, and an overcoming of the purely personal in favor of a communal understanding" (p. 74).

Not only did Downs reinvigorate the tired notion of women's special sensitivities, but he also reinvigorated the old distinction between public and private by quoting Minneapolis Councilmember Barbara Carlson calling pornography a "personal issue." While Downs was not arguing that public policy should avoid addressing harms that occur in private, he was arguing that personal harms are highly emotional, and hence discussing them in public undermines decision making.

Downs' primary criticism of the hearing process was *not* that the survivor testimony did not prove that pornography was a form of sex discrimination, nor was his position that the survivors lied. Rather, his argument was that the emotional nature of the evidence rendered it inappropriate for the public policy realm. His criticism was not of the validity claims inherent to the evidence, but rather was an argument about the appropriateness of such evidence in an "objective" public policy-making arena. Ultimately, Downs' approach to public argument requires that issues about which people care deeply, and of which they have personal experience, should not be discussed in the hallowed halls of government.

THE ATTORNEY GENERAL'S COMMISSION ON PORNOGRAPHY

Kaminer
1992

Just as controversy arose surrounding the Minneapolis hearings, so, too, did advocates react to the 1986 Attorney General's Commission on Pornography. While the commission conducted hearings of its own, it also relied heavily on the Minneapolis hearings. However, instead of treating the activities of the witnesses as empowering, the commission grouped the testimony of witnesses with the rest of the evidence. The commission recognized nothing unique about the personal statements of survivors that privileged the information. The testimony was merely a means toward reaching the end of morally condemning pornography.

The casual grouping is evident in the commission's *Final Report*, which used evidence from "personal experience of witnesses, some from professionals whose orientation is primarily clinical, some from experimental social scientists, and some from other forms of empirical science" (1986, p. 35). However, the commission did note that not all of the "victim" evidence was the same and isolated two types of "victims": (1) the "user," whose testimony the commission discounted as "less valuable than other victim evidence" because of the "tendency of people to externalize their own problems by looking too easily for some external source beyond their own control" (p. 35), and 2) abuse "victims," whose testimony was useful insofar as subjective interpretations of the world were necessary to describe and inform about the harms of pornography. While the commission rejected the usefulness of this evidence in terms of drawing a causal connection, the commission's description of this evidence as identifying harms assumed that a causal connection existed. The commission wrote:

> [W]e do not deceive ourselves into thinking that the sample before us is an accurate statistical reflection of the state of the world. . . . Nevertheless, as long as one does not draw statistical or percentage conclusions from this evidence, and we have not, it can still be important with respect to identification and description of a phenomenon. . . . [M]any of the stories these witnesses told were highly believable and extremely informative, leading us to think about possible harms of which some of us had previously been unaware. (1986, p. 36)

Elsewhere in the report the commission argued that subjective experiences could not be tested against standards applied to objective or statistical methods of inquiry. However, the commission found subjective interpretations of the world to be useful as "part of the basis for our conclusions" because "the most complete understanding emerges when a phenomenon is viewed from multiple perspectives" such as "the subjective meaning that individuals attribute to their own experiences" (p. 36).

The commission framed the survivor evidence much like FACT, Downs, and Lynn did; the statements of the survivors may accurately reflect what they experienced, but generalizations made in the claims were dismissed. However, unlike FACT, Lynn, and Downs, the commission did not dismiss the utility of "victim" testimony. Instead, the commission recognized varying degrees of credibility among witnesses, and, even though standards to determine the credibility of a witness were not discussed, the commission acted as an expert mediator of the testimony's meaning.

In its description of the subjective interpretations of the survivors, one finds the ambiguity with which the commission played. The commission donned the guise of traditional objectivity, in which it rejected the "conclusions" drawn from "anecdotal evidence"; yet the commission was willing to accept as valid and informative the subjective interpretations of survivors that linked pornography to violence.

The commission devoted a section of the report to "Victim Testimony" that relied heavily on the Minneapolis hearings. However, the commission, while wanting to capture all of the persuasive appeal of survivor testimony, failed to frame the testimony in a theoretically consistent manner. While MacKinnon and Dworkin placed the testimony of women within a framework that explained women's subordination and silence, the commission could not locate a place for survivor testimony in its theory of pornography, a theory that focused on pornography's impact on men and the social fabric (as defined by men). The commission qualified the survivors' claims and was unable to justify the hair-splitting done with the qualifications. The commission admitted that survivors could identify and describe phenomena (presumably phenomena associated with pornography), but it was unwilling to accept other generalizations the survivors made. Additionally, the commission was unable to identify the precise role subjective interpretations of situations played in policy formation; it was unclear whether the statements of survivors were more or less valid than social science research.

RESPONSES TO COMMISSION TESTIMONY

One of the primary criticisms of the commission's methodology focused on its use of survivor testimony. The criticisms ranged from claiming that the "victims"—while real—are not representative of the majority experience, to arguing that subjective attributions of harm cannot serve as the basis for public policy, to questioning the authenticity of the "victims."

Many indicted the report for manufacturing a false controversy by using the emotional appeal of witnesses. The hearings were not public policy discussions, but were high political drama in which the commission artificially created a controversy through the use of survivor testimony. In a move similar to Lynn's dissociation of the Minneapolis testimony from the process of testifying, Larry Baron, lecturer in sociology at Yale University, dissociated the testimony to the commission from the commission's motive for the format. Baron argued that the format of public hearings on local levels was created "In an attempt to garner public support for a crackdown on pornography" and described the format as an orchestrated "scare campaign designed to stir up antipornography activism" (1987, p. 10). Again, while the testimony may be authentic, the results are orchestrated by the commission. The testimony itself is one thing; its meaning is another.

Critics attempted to recontextualize the survivor testimony in order to limit its suasory power. Instead of discrediting the claims of the witnesses, respondents argued that the evidence did not prove what the commission wanted it to prove; in fact, the evidence was misused (Baron 1987, p. 7). According to Brannigan, the intent of the commission was not to find facts, but to find ways of stopping pornography: "[T]he Meese commission, with its parade of anonymous and unexamined pornography victims, who appeared behind screens, and with its containment mandate, appears to have been little more than a sounding board for anti-pornography crusaders of every kind—religious, feminist, and academic. Judging from the makeup of the panel, and its timing and budget, this was probably inevitable" (p. 13).

A broad Commission definition of evidence allowed it to inflate the impact of pornography. Baron believed that "the uncorroborated testimony of self-proclaimed victims of pornography" undeservedly constituted evidence (p. 8). Here one sees not only an attack on the credibility of the survivors as "victims," but also an attack on the meaning of survivor testimony. For Baron, the statements of survivors appear to have no place in public policy formation but were merely a ploy of the commission to "prove" its preordained conclusions.

As many of the above quotations indicate, the actual meaning of "victim" is called into question. Barry Lynn, who had been so careful not to question the authenticity of the "victims" in his response to the Minneapolis hearings, was more than willing to question the right of the "victim" to that label in response to the commission's *Final Report*. Lynn, in a mock commission created by Philip Nobile and Eric Nadler in their book *United States of America vs. SEX: How the Meese Commission Lied about Pornography* (1986), wrote: "[The commission] simply filled in the gaps of science with the legion of their own preoccupations and intuitions buttressed with some Gestalt derived from the sometimes plaintive, sometimes pathetic, voices of alleged 'victims' of pornography" (1986b, p. 330). The "alleged 'victims'" who testified to the commission were not survivors who reported their abuse, but instead were pathetic (deserving pity, not credibility) and plaintive (expressing suffering, not truth). Lynn's placement of quotation marks around the word "victim" also called into question whether the person claiming to be a victim actually is one. The ambiguity created by this description casts doubt not only on the commission's claims concerning survivors but also on the survivors' claims as "victims." It is as though the respondents argued that the survivors are incorrect in perceiving themselves as having been victimized. The survivors' subjective interpretations of incidents were questioned.

The credibility of the testimony was attacked indirectly as well. Because the commission established no standards for the evaluation of such evidence, all of it needed to be dismissed. Baron wrote, "Despite the seriousness of some of these allegations, there was little or no attempt on the part of the commissioners to assess the credibility of the witnesses or the truthfulness of their testimony" (1987, p. 10). This approach is an interesting one for it calls into question the truth of witnesses' statements, as well as the truthfulness of the witnesses, while not placing the blame on the witnesses for deception; instead, it was the commission's responsibility to test the validity of the statements.

The credibility of the witnesses was further undermined by the way in which commentators described them. For example, Hendrick Hertzberg categorized the "victims" as follows: "The 'victims' who testified before the commission included former prostitutes, former abused wives and children, former junkies, and people who complained that a relative had spent the family savings on dirty books. All blamed their troubles on pornography, though the causal connections were never clear" (1986, p. 22). Hertzberg then detailed one of the more atypical "victims," a man who started using pornography and claimed that he became a drug addict because of his pornography addiction. Hertzberg then concluded: "Even the most ardently antiporn commissioners were embarrassed by this sort of testimony—much of which, Chairman Hudson admitted during one of the working sessions, was written and structured by the commission staff" (1986, p. 22). Hertzberg offers the man as the synecdochic witness, making all of the witnesses appear ludicrous and deranged. P. J. O'Rourke offered similar descriptions of those who testified, writing, "In addition to weird filth, the commission examined weird witnesses" (1986, p. 60).

Ultimately, one finds respondents to the *Final Report* attacking the survivors indirectly through attacks on the commission and directly through attacks on the "victims." Opponents of the commission frame the survivors as mere dupes and pawns of the commission. Insofar as the commission's integrity was questionable, so too was the survivors'. No notion of empowerment appeared in public critiques of the commission. No credence was given to the claims that pornography causes and is violence against women. The survivors' voices were heard only as mediated through the commission.

CONCLUSIONS

Argument critics' assumption that the objective is the only acceptable type of evidence has relegated the subjective, the realm to which the powerless (in particular women) have access, to meaninglessness in public policy discourse. Regardless of the world to which the survivor speaks, her claims, and her location of those claims in relation to a world, are contested. Argument critics minimize the survivors' claims by arguing that their statements speak only of the subjective world, and have no relevance to the other worlds. Advocates also refute survivors' claims either by arguing that they are atypical (the survivor cannot identify a universal, objective truth), that the survivors' perceptions of events are incorrect (the survivor is not adhering to intersubjective interpretations of right and wrong), or that survivors lie (the survivor is not being truthful).

Traditionally, objectivity in argument is held as a good and has meant nonattachment or disengagement; if one has immediate and direct experience of the subject of controversy, one is assumed to be merely the provider of evidence. Framing is reserved for the unattached and disengaged. In contrast, this essay seeks to expand the range of what is considered acceptable evidence by making explicit the ideological framing of personal testimony. Depending on the format and ideological frame, personal testimony can be more or less valuable.

The powers of framing have been contested in the pornography controversy; survivors speak not only of their own experiences, but also of what they think their experiences mean. Thus, survivor testimony has advanced the controversy surrounding pornography by introducing the civil rights perspective into the stalled debate between moralists and free speech advocates, while, at the same time, problematizing the process of argument because the standard validity tests of evidence were declared irrelevant. Testimony, such as that provided in the Minneapolis hearings, where survivors are empowered to speak in their own voices, unmediated by "experts," can open a closed system of discourse and foster a recognition of previously unnamed relationships and harms.

From this study of the use of survivor testimony in the pornography controversy, argument scholars may begin to understand that personal testimony is theoretically more problematic than first thought. Those people who advocate legal change based on the experiences of the survivor cast the testimony of the survivor as empowering and as sufficient to prove harm. The recognition that one has been harmed, through no fault of one's self, was viewed as self-affirming. But in order for the testimony to work as a means of empowerment, the audience must assume that the survivor is being truthful. In turn, the process of empowerment fostered an approach in which women named pornography a violation of their civil rights, and eschewed the traditional morality approach condemning pornography (see MacKinnon's "Not a Moral Issue" in *Feminism Unmodified* [1987]). Advocates of the ordinance, by reconfiguring world relations and locating survivor testimony as simultaneously subjective, objective, and intersubjective, provided an innovative form of proof for an innovative approach to pornography.

The ACLU and anti-ordinance feminists, recognizing that a personal attack would be counterproductive because it would be seen as an attack on women as opposed to an attack on arguments, sought alternative ways to refute survivor testimony, and in so doing, redefined the meaning of being a survivor. Others, who are not known for advocacy of feminist issues, were not as careful in their response and were willing to attack the truthfulness of the survivors' statements, returning us to a time when women were not believed when they reported instances of sexual abuse. However, the response was moderated depending on which hearing was being discussed, evidencing that we implicitly recognize the effect of framing on credibility.

Feminists who oppose the ordinance, yet recognize that violence against women is pervasive, saw survivor testimony as locking the witness, and all women, into the role of victim. The dialectical balance between claiming that one has been victimized, and proclaiming that persona as a form of empowerment, was not recognized. Anti-ordinance feminists also feared that if women speak as "victims" that other social forces will use this to disempower them.

Confirming the fears of anti-ordinance feminists, the commission sought to recuperate the voices of survivors into the dominant discourse's approach to pornography that sees it as a moral scourge from which women need to be protected. The commission's discussion of survivor testimony provided a unique mixture of utilitarianism and protection. While the commission discounted the user-victim's testimony, it accepted the survivors' testimony as proof of the evil of pornography. As much of the critique of the commission indicated, the commission went into its research project with a conclusion in hand, and the words of the survivors merely served to reinforce that conclusion. Hence, the commission was not compelled to recognize as empowering the public statements of the survivors, but instead masked the survivors behind screens and treated the testimony as the revelation of something shameful and guilt-ridden. The commission's move to protect "victims" speaks to the danger of losing control of one's voice, a danger survivors must face when they consider speaking publicly.

The media response to the testimony further undermined the process of empowerment. Respondents argued that the survivors were unique; in other words, something about the individual brought on the abuse. The general response to survivor testimony indicates the continuing problems women, and other marginalized groups, face when making personal experience political in an attempt to invigorate public policy argument.

The varied responses to survivor testimony evidence that, in public argument, even the process of giving evidence is not a politically neutral one. When issues of truthfulness, truth, and rightness intersect, the potential for both empowerment and disempowerment exists. Additionally, that intersection confounds the traditional process of argumentation, a process that assumes that validity tests are not arguable in and of themselves.

As critics of argument, we need to understand that the presuppositions we carry with us in the analysis of argument and evidence tend to discredit personal experiences as evidence. Such an approach is not only dangerous to those who are disempowered and who rely on personal experience as one of the sole areas of knowledge to which they have access, but it also functions as a blinder to much of the evidence presented in contemporary controversies. The power of AIDS-infected Kimberly Bergalis's final testimony to Congress stemmed from its linkage to personal experience. The conundrum presented by the Clarence Thomas–Anita Hill hearings was the inability of the media and scholars to critically assess the validity and meaning of their conflicting testimony. The plight of the homeless, those ill with AIDS, the racial minority, and the political prisoner is not understood through statistics or an awakening of social conscience; it is understood through the testimony of those who have personal experience. In like manner, a complete understanding of the controversy surrounding pornography will not occur until argument critics recognize the validity of personal testimony as a source of evidence.

REFERENCES

Alcoff, Linda, and Laura Gray. 1993. Survivor discourse: Transgression or recuperation? *Signs, 18,* 260–90.
Amendment to the Civil Rights Ordinance. 1983. City of Minneapolis.
Aristotle. 1941. *The basic works of Aristotle,* ed. Richard McKeon. New York: Random House.
Baron, Larry. 1987, July–August. Immoral, inviolate or inconclusive. *Society, 24,* 6–12.
Brannigan, Augustine. 1987, July–August. Is obscenity criminogenic? *Society, 24,* 12–19.
Campbell, Karlyn Kohrs. 1989. *Man cannot speak for her.* Vol. 1. New York: Greenwood Press.
Code, Lorraine. 1988. Credibility: A double standard. In *Feminist perspectives,* ed. Lorraine Code, Sheila Mullett, and Christine Overall. Toronto: University of Toronto Press.
———. 1991. *What can she know? Feminist theory and the construction of knowledge.* Ithaca: Cornell University Press.
Downs, Donald Alexander. 1989. *The new politics of pornography.* Chicago: University of Chicago Press.
Dworkin, Andrea. 1984. Letter to Mayor Fraser, unpublished, dated July 5. Available from Minneapolis city council.
———. 1988. *Letters from a war zone.* London: Secker and Warburg.
Dworkin, Andrea, and Catharine A. MacKinnon, 1988. *Pornography and civil rights.* Minneapolis: Organizing Against Pornography.
Elshtain, Jean Bethke. 1982. Feminist discourse and its discontents: Language, power, and meaning. *Signs, 7,* 603–21.
Feminist Anti-Censorship Taskforce et al. 1985, April 8. *Brief Amici Curiae.* American Booksellers Association, Inc. et al., Plaintiffs-Appellees v. William H. Hudnut et al., Defendants-Appellants. In the United

States Court of Appeals for the Seventh Circuit on appeal from the United States District Court for the Southern District of Indiana.

Fielding, Ian. 1987. Causal argument in the final report of the Attorney General's Commission on Pornography. In *Argument and critical practices: Proceedings of the Fifth SCA/AFA Conference on Argumentation*, ed. Joseph W. Wenzel. Annandale, Va.: Speech Communication Association.

Final Report of the Attorney General's Commission on Pornography. 1986. Introduction by Michael J. McManus. Nashville: Rutledge Hill Press.

Harding, Sandra, and Merrill B. Hintikka, eds. 1983. *Discovering reality*. Boston: D. Reidel.

Hauser, Gerard A. 1987. Defining publics and reconstructing public spheres: The final report of the Attorney General's Commission on Pornography. In *Argument and Critical Practices: Proceedings of the Fifth SCA/AFA Conference on Argumentation*, ed. Joseph W. Wenzel. Annandale, Va.: Speech Communication Association.

Hertzberg, Hendrik. 1986, July 14 and 21. Big boobs. *The New Republic, 195*, 21–24.

Jaggar, Alison M., and Susan R. Bordo, eds. 1989. *Gender/body/knowledge*. London: Rutgers University Press.

Koedt, Anne; Ellen Levine, and Anita Rapone, eds. 1973. *Radical feminism*. New York: Quadrangle.

Lynn, Barry W. 1985. Testimony to the Attorney General's Commission on Pornography. *Transcripts of Proceedings*, 144–94.

———. 1986a. 'Civil rights' ordinances and the Attorney General's Commission: New developments in pornography regulation. *Harvard Civil Liberties-Civil Rights Law Review, 21,* 27–122.

———. 1986b. Fathers who know best. In *United States of America vs. SEX: How the Meese Commission lied about pornography*, ed. Philip Nobile and Eric Nadler. New York: Minotaur Press (A Penthouse International Company).

MacKinnon, Catharine A. 1982, Spring. Feminism, Marxism, method and the state: An agenda for theory. *Signs, 7, 515*–44.

———. 1987. *Feminism unmodified*. Cambridge: Harvard University Press.

———. 1989. *Toward a feminist theory of state*. Cambridge: Harvard University Press.

O'Rourke, P. J. 1986, September 25. Dirty Words. *Rolling Stone, 59*–61.

Public Hearings on Ordinances to Add Pornography as Discrimination Against Women. 1983, December 12 and 13. Minneapolis city council. Government Operations Committee. Available from Organizing Against Pornography, Minneapolis.

Snitow, Ann. 1985. Retrenchment versus transformation: The politics of the anti-pornography movement. In *Women against censorship*, ed. Varda Burstyn. Vancouver: Douglas and McIntyre.

Vance, Carole S. 1990. The pleasures of looking: The Attorney General's Commission on Pornography versus visual images. In *The critical image: Essays on contemporary photography*, ed. Carol Squiers. Seattle: Bay Press.

CHAPTER 12

Constituting Publics and Reconstructing Public Spheres: The Meese Commission's Report on Pornography

Gerard A. Hauser

The ebb and flow of society's ongoing self-production is influenced significantly by the arguments of social actors and the availability of a public sphere. The relationship between argument and the public sphere is not incidental. The rational and critical validity of the public opinion that legitimates state policies is contingent on the quality of public argument: of what is said, of how it is interrogated, of the persons and groups included in or excluded from the process of deliberation. Assessing why a society acts as it does involves evaluating the reasons its members advance as rational and ethical justification for its measures and the methods for their advancement. Moreover, such an assessment requires considerations beyond what is uttered. The discursive conditions under which public deliberations proceed also require scrutiny since they inevitably are conducive to certain argumentative possibilities while inhospitable to others, encouraging selective voices

I wish to acknowledge the assistance of Robin Reese, who aided in the collection of materials used in this study and provided useful criticisms of my thinking. I alone am responsible for any defects in this research project and its argument. Earlier versions of this project were presented at the joint AFA/SCA Conference in Alta, Utah, July 30–August 1, 1987, and at the Speech Communication Association meeting in Boston, November 5–8, 1987.

while silencing others. I refer to the defining conditions of the public sphere.

The public sphere is a discursive space in which ideas appear to be heard and evaluated by social actors forming their common sense of reality (Hauser 1985). In a significant sense the shape of the public sphere serves as a barometer of a society's freedoms. Its defining characteristics of accessibility, availability of information, means of dissemination, and audiences qualified to form as publics (Habermas 1974; Hauser and Blair 1983), are necessities for social actors to achieve autonomy; their absence promotes domination. Consequently, the unique character of a given public sphere sets parameters for the discourse that a society can accommodate. Alterations to its character introduce corresponding effects on society's meaning. Possessing or losing one's franchise to participate in the public sphere alters power, shifts freedoms, and redefines the normative structures on which social relations hinge (Giddens 1984). As Touraine (1981) teaches, one cannot escape domination without first appropriating historicity—one's capacity to define one's own meaning and the legitimacy of one's place and aspirations as a social actor. Such a shift was proposed in the *Final Report of the Attorney General's Commission on Pornography* (1986).

"Pornography" comes from the Greek *pornē* , meaning prostitute, and *graphein*, meaning to write, or literally "writings of prostitutes." It is a form of communication that has existed since antiquity as a natural expression of humankind's sexuality. As such, it is value-neutral. At the same time, it has been a source of controversy historically, reflecting both social attitudes toward the explicit portrayal of sexual subject matter and the judgments of society on the manner in which sexual subject matter is portrayed, often depicting women and children as sexual partners lacking equal power and therefore to be subjected to degradation and humiliation. As a source of complex social issues, therefore, pornography is of interest to communication scholars. Considered as a natural extension of human sexuality, it may be regarded as inherently neutral. Censoring it is an infringement on rights of free expression. On the other hand, considered as a mode of expression that degrades women and children as inferior or powerless, it is a source of political imbalance with dangerous social implications.

The final report of the Meese Commission, issued in 1986, became an instant source of controversy due to the way it chose to address these complexities. It called for radical initiatives with profound implications for what could appear in the public sphere and, ultimately, for the shape and character of that sphere itself.[1] In this essay, I wish to examine the report as a source of controversy in relation to the public sphere. I am interested in how the report served as an argumentative instrument of legitimation and as a contest over the right to speak and be heard.

A CALL TO RESHAPE THE PUBLIC SPHERE

In 1970 the President's Commission on Obscenity and Pornography reported that it could find no public harm caused by pornography and obscenity. That commission's report did not receive a warm reception from the Nixon administration or Congress. But its finding seemed in keeping with a Supreme Court that thirteen years earlier had afforded First Amendment protection to all materials except those that could be considered as "utterly without redeeming social importance" (*Roth v. U.S.*). Nor was it removed from the mood and tenor of a nation emerging from the Sturm und Drang of national protests over the war in Vietnam, civil rights, and university policies, not to mention the so-called sexual revolution.

The years following the commission's report saw a proliferation of sexually explicit books and magazines, music, film, videos, and photographs available for public consumption. Moreover, the market for these materials seemed strong and growing throughout the 1970s. For example, the monthly circulation for the thirteen most widely distributed male entertainment magazines peaked at approximately 16.5 million in 1980 (*Report*, p. 1410). In the 1980s this volume subsided, most likely with a shift of consumption patterns to sexually explicit fare accessible on cable TV and videocassettes. The expanded availability of pornography also increased its variety, ranging from nudity to the disturbing extremes of sadomasochism and pedophilia.

The Supreme Court's refinement of *Roth* in *Miller v. California* (1973) left each community with the responsibility of determining its standards of obscenity. Although some might say that the period following the 1970 report witnessed America's taste for erotic and pornographic materials go from the risque to the raunchy, the fact remains that few obscenity cases were successfully tried. The reluctance of most communities to introduce a more conservative censorship of the public sphere served as a tacit endorsement of the 1970 commission's views. The report did not endorse pornography, only its right to appear, suggesting that without proof of social harm caused by pornography, there was wisdom in tolerance.

Sixteen years later, with *Playboy* and *Penthouse* having become common items on convenience store shelves, and with *Deep Throat, The Devil in Miss Jones*, and *Debbie Does Dallas* having entered the arena of middle-class experience, the Reagan administration determined to have the harmful effects of pornography on society reexamined. Thus, on February 22, 1985, William French established the Attorney General's Commission on Pornography. The rationale behind the commission's formation remains a point of controversy, though the ostensible reason was the enormous technological change that had transpired during the intervening years since 1970. Basically there was more porn more readily accessible to more people, which gave moral conservatives, religious fundamentalists, and selected feminists reason for sounding an alarm.

One year later, on July 9, 1986, at a Justice Department news conference held under the gaze of the "Spirit of Justice," French's successor, Attorney General Edwin Meese III, accepted the commission's report. The irony of the scene—America's chief law enforcement official accepting a commissioned study on the ill-effects of public depictions involving sex while the Reubenesque statue symbolizing his office looked over his shoulder, arms uplifted and right breast exposed—escaped few, least of all that element of the press aching for a fight over a perceived attack on an area of First Amendment rights (Kurtz 1986; McDaniel 1986; *Time* 1986, pp. 13–14; Wines and Sharbutt 1986). The report triggered an immediate controversy that sustained itself in the popular press for the balance of the summer.

The expressed hope of the commission report was to encourage public discussion of the issue of pornography's effects on its consumers and on the community. Commissioners Becker and Levine and Commissioner Schauer, in fact, explicitly emphasized this hope in their personal statements (*Report*, pp. 179, 195). Surely this was an important objective in light of the growing concern of many over the effects that explicitly sexual depictions have on public and private perceptions and behaviors. Dismay over the characterization of women as sex objects had long been voiced by feminist critics of male-oriented magazines. While one may quibble over whether the contents of *Playboy* display liberated sophistication or adolescent fixation, serious concern had been raised about literatures that depict women as objects to be attacked, humiliated, mutilated, and raped, as enjoying physical abuse, or as consumed with desire for bestiality. Moral objections had also been raised against the depiction of pedophilia and the uses to which such portrayals were sometimes put as lures for children to cooperate as subjects of pornography or as sexual partners.

For many groups, these matters appeared to support the formation of the commission and to invest it with the hopes of those who either saw themselves as victims of exploitation and violence or who questioned the redeeming social value of such portrayals. Yet these hopes were denied because, from the moment of its inception, these normative concerns never became the focus of the debate. Rather the focus was the commission itself. Why was this so, especially when the commission offered a report seemingly understanding of and sympathetic to these very concerns? I believe that the answer lies in the way in which the commission itself and its final report were perceived as a threat to the public sphere.

The commission's charter charged it "to determine the nature, extent, and impact on society of pornography in the United States, and to make specific recommendations to the Attorney General concerning more effective ways in which the spread of pornography could be contained, consistent with constitutional guarantees" (*Report*, p. 215). The charter continued to outline a mandate of broad scope, including such items as studying "the dimensions of the problem of pornography," reviewing "the available empirical evidence on the relationship between exposure to pornographic materials and antisocial behavior," and exploring "possible roles and initiatives that the Department of Justice and agencies of local, state and federal government could pursue in controlling, consistent with constitutional guarantees, the production and distribution of pornography" (*Report,* p. 1957).

Thus charged with the task of finding a remedy for a situation assumed to be evil, the commission had its subject and its publics identified. Unfortunately, it found great difficulty in constructing an operational definition of the subject matter that caused this evil (*Report*, pp. 227–32), a problem that eventually bedeviled its findings. After reviewing the difficulties encountered in providing a generally acceptable definition of hard core pornography, the commission reported that it sided with Justice Stewart who, when confronted with the same difficulty, admitted that although unable to define hard core pornography, "I know it when I see it" (*Report*, p. 229).

The commission's publics were easier to identify. The examination of pornography as a problem of social significance had potential publics of wide scope: women, parents, and practicing members of an organized religion come immediately to mind. At the same time, that segment of society already actively opposed to pornography and committed to curbing its spread was much more narrow. Here is a list of those who, in keeping with what the *Washington Post* reported as the Moral Majority's call[2] for 1985 to be the year to clean up "filth," organized against pornography at the time the report appeared: The National Federation for Decency, Women Against Pornography, Citizens for Decency Through Law, Inc., Parents Music Resource Center, Concerned Women for America, Eagle Forum, Liberty Federation, Morality in Media, Citizens for Legislation Against Decadence, and Feminists Against Pornography. The leadership and agenda for many on this list embraced assumptions with a narrow band for accommodating diversity: moral conservatives, religious fundamentalists, and law enforcement officials were commonly in this constituency. Added to this list were selected feminists who defined the issue in simple causal terms. These were not the assumptions of liberals, the publishing industry, or a substantial number of feminists who defined the issue in complex terms of power and health. Such groups included: The National Coalition Against Censorship, The Media Coalition (drawn from publishers' associations), and the Feminist Anti-Censorship Task Force. Nor were the commission's initial assumptions shared by a sizable portion of Americans who consumed pornography for enhancement of their sex lives. For example, a few weeks before the report was issued, the citizens of Maine rejected a referendum much in the spirit of the report in its proposed curbs on pornography. The margin of defeat was 2:1.

This division of perspectives, present from the commission's formation, had serious consequences for public response. To endorse the report became tantamount to endorsing a morally conservative and Christian fundamentalist interpretation of not only an issue of personal and ethical concern, but of what may appear in the public sphere. The report was perceived and presented by its opponents as a threat to open and honest dialogue and debate on the issue. At the same time, the moral stigma associated with pornography had consequences of equal magnitude for the public dialogue. To oppose the report required an escape from the appearance of favoring the sexual abuse of women and children and the subordination of community norms of morality to unqualified First Amendment protections for vile and degrading portrayals of sexual relations. The public debate may have centered on the commission and the validity and balance of its report; however, the transcendent issue of the public controversy spawned by the report was whether or not the public sphere was properly limited in portrayals of human sexuality.

THE FINAL REPORT: VERSION I

Were one to read the commission report without prior knowledge of the venomous attacks to which it was subjected, one might conclude that it was at least struggling to present balanced and responsible analysis and recommendations, especially if one focused on the first quarter of the two-volume document, or its initial 458 pages (Vance 1986, p. 78). These contain the specific statements of the commissioners, occupying nearly two hundred pages. Each expresses his or her views on selected issues addressed in the report, their reasons for the positions they took, their general endorsement of the report itself, and their disclaimers about time, money, and the recognition that not every recommendation was unanimously endorsed. This section also contains a dissenting opinion authored by two members, Judith Becker, associate professor of clinical psychology in psychiatry at Columbia University, and Ellen Levine, editor-in-chief of *Women's Day* magazine and a vice-president of CBS magazine. This is followed by a 218-page statement written by Frederick Schauer, a commission member and professor of law at Michigan, and endorsed by the other members. The Schauer statement offers the commission's analysis and argument. This is followed by a section specifying ninety-two recommendations to curb the spread of pornography. The remainder of the 1,960-page document consists of selected testimony and evidence, excerpts from pornography, summaries of pornographic books and movies, a rather extensive bibliography of pornographic literature and videos, and photos of the commission in action. These materials composed by the commission staff, more strident in tone and less thoughtful in analysis, led Becker, among others, to encourage the reader to stop after Schauer's report had been completed.

The Schauer report is a smoothly written document that is scholarly in tone. It recognizes the complexity of its subject matter and is peppered with qualifying statements suggesting the need for caution in drawing conclusions. In this sense, it does not read as the conservative broadside the liberal community had anticipated and feared. Consequently, it can be interpreted to argue a most reasonable position. It recognizes that the term "pornography" is problematic because it conveys a conclusion (pp. 227–32). It elects to favor "obscenity" instead because it has a legal meaning and, therefore will enhance objectivity and fair treatment. It recognizes that recommendations to limit pornography are warranted only if harm is shown, but is candid in admitting its inability to provide scientific demonstration of the causal link between pornography and harm (pp. 299, 306–12). At the same time, in matters of social behavior causation is always complex; it would be simplistic to maintain that one variable brought about a social consequence in a definitive manner. While admitting the limitations, therefore, of a strictly positivistic approach to drawing inferences about pornography and public harm, it offers as a substitute criterion "common sense" (pp. 360, 381). For example, it is not in the best interests of a child to be sodomized or raped for purposes of making a pornographic video, nor is it in the child's interest to have his or her introduction to human sexual relations through exposure to such materials. Although it is impossible to show that adult antisocial behavior was caused by childhood experiences such as the foregoing, "common sense" suggests that these would not likely act as a deterrent.

To illustrate the commission's argumentation, consider this example of one of the milder depictions of the problems associated with pornography, the typical peep show:

> The peep show is often separated by a doorway or screen from the rest of the establishment, and consists of a number of booths in which a film, or, more likely now, a video tape, can be viewed. The patron inserts tokens into a slot for a certain amount of viewing time, and the patron is usually alone or with another person within the particular booth. The peep show serves the purpose of allowing patrons to masturbate or to engage in sexual activity with others with some degree of privacy, at least compared to an adult theatre, while watching the pornographic

material. In a later portion of our report describing these establishments we note in detail the generally unsanitary conditions in such establishments. The booths seem rarely to be cleaned, and the evidence of frequent sexual activity is apparent. Peep shows are a particularly common location for male homosexual activity within and between the booths, and the material available for viewing in some of the booths is frequently oriented toward the male homosexual. (p. 290)

Even if this does not establish a causal link to social harm, the repulsiveness of the scene encourages a "commonsense" conclusion that such establishments are a blight on the community. "Common sense" suggests that eliminating certain kinds of pornography and restricting others would eradicate this social cancer.

The committee continues to recognize that not all pornographic materials are of this nature and that all legitimate First Amendment protections must be honored (p. 250). Hence it divides pornography into three classes: sexually violent, nonviolent but degrading, and nonviolent and nondegrading materials (pp. 323–49). The first two require government and citizen action while the third is beyond the realm of official redress since it clearly has First Amendment protections. Finally, the Schauer report leaves the reader with a series of recommendations that place emphasis on citizen action (pp. 433–58). It recognizes that the courts will not prohibit the distribution and sale of lurid materials, and accordingly instructs the public on the stance to take on this issue. The public is encouraged to exercise its options of dissent through pickets and economic boycotts as effective local means to discourage the accessibility of pornography in the community (pp. 300, 361, 419–29).

These may be conservative claims but they are neither unreasonable nor necessarily oppressive. Why, then, did they represent a threat to the public sphere? For this we must examine the commission and its report in terms other than its apparent presentation on pornography. We must examine how the final report was portrayed in the public press.

THE FINAL REPORT: VERSION II

The Meese Commission report may have experienced brisk sales, but the report that the public responded to was the one that appeared on the pages of America's newspapers and magazines. Although sparsely covered by television, the report became a source of national debate at the newsstand. Its notoriety was principally attributable to Barry Lynn, ACLU attorney, who became a self-appointed commission watchdog—following the panel to each location, securing a court order for the release of information, and providing the working press with a steady stream of information and quotable interviews. From the moment of its inception through the time the final report was received and debated in the popular press, Lynn succeeded in galvanizing a press portrayal that depicted the attorney general's commission as an object of suspicion to the liberal community, as anathema to the publishing industry, and as a palpable threat to the civil liberties of the average American.

The generally negative reporting and commentary on the commission's activities and findings insinuated that the validity of the report was questionable along several lines. In part, the commission itself was an obvious target for attack as a legitimate body capable of dispatching its charge, especially since its charter fore-ordained it to collide with its 1970 predecessor. But the contrast between it and the President's Commission on Obscenity strongly suggested that the current panel was a stacked deck appointed as a payoff to religious fundamentalists and the radical right who had staunchly supported President Reagan. As bodies impanelled to address similar questions, the contrast could not have been more stark, a fact on which the press embellished in a manner suggesting that this commission's findings should be regarded with caution (Hertzberg 1986, p. 21; Lipton 1986; Scheer 1986b, p. 160; Vance 1986, pp. 78–79). The 1970 commission was given a budget of $2,000,000 and two years to complete its task. It was chaired by the dean of the University of Minnesota Law School, a renowned scholar of constitutional law. Its executive director was a social scientist, its staff consisted primarily of trained social scientists. Its membership included representatives from law, medicine, the publishing and film industries, education, the social and behavioral sciences, and the clergy. Of its eighteen members, only the three clergy and one other had expressed a prior view about pornography. It saw its work as getting scientifically valid findings on which to make recommendations. Hence, it held only two public meetings but commissioned eighty studies to gain information relevant to its charge. Critics of the Meese Commission suggested that such factors lent credibility to the 1970 panel's conclusion that one could not demonstrate a causal relation between pornography and social harms.

By contrast, the Meese Commission was portrayed as a partisan effort intended to gloss over analysis while advancing a politically expedient recommendation. It was given a budget of $500,000, or 16 times less than its predecessor in real dollars, and one year for its work. The chair and executive director of the 1986 panel were local prosecuting attorneys who had earned a reputation for successful records prosecuting pornography. Its professional staff included three attorneys and three of its full-time investigators were police officers. Eight of its eleven members had expressed opposition to pornography prior to joining the panel. It saw its work as curbing pornography. Hence, it commissioned no studies to determine the effects of pornography. Its charge to curb pornography assumed that pornography had harmful effects. So the panel relied on extrapolations from the existing literature to form "scientific" support for its recommendations while documenting the effects of pornography on social behavior through the aforementioned personal testimony recorded in meetings of several days each held in six different cities. Even panel members were critical of this final difference, since it denied the commission an opportunity to explore testimony in private without subjecting witnesses to press coverage of their private consumption of sexually explicit materials (*Report*, pp. 196–98).

Since this was a government commission, it spoke with an official voice. It was a body charged to study a problem of national concern and to make recommendations. The trappings of authority graced its findings, whatever they might be, giving them the weight of legitimation. Critics saw the combination of official charge to a panel with this one's predispositions as legitimating conservative and religious fundamentalist views that, in another form, would have been subject to challenge (Vance 1986, p. 78). Hence, the qualifications of the Meese Commission, as an official body, were questionable from the outset and critics responded to it as such by making the commission itself the issue (Clark 1986; Kurtz 1986; Shenon 1986b; Smith 1986; Wald 1986).

Further concern was aroused by the commission's methodology. If the press harbored reservations about the panel's composition, it was derisive in its portrayal of how the commissioners collected data and drew inferences. Commissioners Becker and

Levine's dissenting statement had already commented on the one-sided testimony received in the public hearings and on the difficulty of drawing valid inferences when such partiality could distort the panel members' judgment "about the proportion of such violent material in relation to the total pornographic material in distribution" (*Report*, p. 199). Their view was extended in the coverage available at the newsstand. Highlighted were examples such as the above-mentioned visit to a Houston peep show (*People* 1986, pp. 28–29), the scarcity of witnesses from the book industry (Bob 1986, p. 39), the selectivity with which witnesses were chosen (Hefner 1986, p. 58), and the extreme nature of the testimony received (*Time* 1986, pp. 14–15). Reports and commentaries such as these strongly implied, and sometimes asserted, that the commission received, reported, and based recommendations on seriously skewed data.

The briefest consideration of consumption data indicates that depictions of the panel as prudish, at best, spoke to a broad-based predisposition concerning sexually explicit materials. The fact of the matter is that since 1970, the pornographic movie and publication industries have thrived. More important, in 1970 the home video business did not exist. Its explosion since 1980 has made the consumption of X-rated movies common. As many as 40 percent of VCR owners reportedly bought or rented X-rated cassettes during 1985 and adult tapes were estimated to account for 20 percent of the total video market (Duggan 1985, p. C1). The growth in public distribution of X-rated videos coupled with continued substantial sales of male-oriented magazines are meaningful data. A significant number of adult Americans consume pornography without apparent ill effects. Such liberality toward private consumption of sexually explicit materials may explain why few public prosecutors have been willing to bring suit against a producer or distributor of erotica. In addition to First Amendment guarantees, community standards exhibiting tolerance make a successful action extremely unlikely. Such data also suggest a widely shared but not commonly disclosed attitude predisposed toward debunking the *Final Report* while simultaneously jeopardizing the likelihood of balanced commission findings.

Typically adults watch and read pornography for sexual stimulation, a reason that is extremely private and not commonly made a theme of public discussion. Consequently, although large numbers of Americans may consume and approve of certain types of pornographic literature, magazines, films, and videos, few were willing to appear before the commission to testify that they consumed erotica for personal sexual fulfillment without suffering harmful side effects. The lack of such witnesses deprived the commission of testimony that could have confirmed or denied whether the extreme forms on which they had focused were representative of the "mainstream," or were giving sex a bad name. In light of the apparent widespread consumption of sexually explicit materials without corresponding social harms in the vast majority of cases, the press portrayal of the Meese Commission's findings made them appear one-sided and a fait accompli.

Beyond its implicit assumption of harm, the methodology was indicted for the types of witnesses to appear and the manner of their selection. The press focused on the types of witnesses that appeared and the special view of pornography they held. Most witnesses who testified against pornography had opinions colored by the negative and extreme circumstances in which they experienced sex accompanied by violence. Such witnesses, accounting for 77 percent of those who testified, called for greater control or elimination of sexually explicit materials. The force of such numbers was undermined, however, by allegations that only those with a supportive view were invited to appear. As one critic wrote, "The vice cops on the staff energetically recruited the alleged victims to testify, assisted by antipornography groups and prosecutors. The same zeal was not applied to the search for people who had positive experiences" (Vance 1986, p. 77).

Law enforcement officers were present in significant numbers (68 of 208 witnesses). They were opposed to pornography because they associated it with crimes they had investigated—vice, rape, and child abuse, to name a few. Victims of incest, child abuse, pedophilia, mutilation, and rape, plus former porn queens and hookers opposed pornography because they associated it with the degradation to which they were subjected in contexts of sexual contact or the production of lurid materials. As presented in the popular press, their accounts seemed extreme and were depicted in a manner that questioned the conclusions these witnesses advanced. For example, *Time* cited the testimony of Larry Madigan, age thrity-eight, with this air of incredulity: "[Madigan] told the commission he had been 'a typically normal, healthy boy,' whose subsequent life of solitary masturbation, bestiality, and drug addiction could all be traced to finding a deck of pornographic playing cards when he was twelve" (1986, p. 15). *Time* reported this to illustrate its claim that "there were times when the commission seemed to be on a kind of surrealist mystery tour of sexual perversity, peeping at the most recondite forms of sexual behavior known—though mostly unknown—to society" (14).

If this were a mystery tour, the commissioners were not unaware of the terrain they were covering. One commissioner described the experience of gathering data and taking testimony on the degradation reported as akin to sailing through a sewer in a glass-bottomed boat. Doubtless such a depiction was in part due to the commission's strange fascination for the scatological. Even the most casual perusal of the descriptions of pornographic materials examined by the commission reveals a striking preoccupation with degrading acts involving fecal matter. Similarly, though to a lesser extent, sexual depictions involving animals occur frequently. Press accounts used such details to suggest that the commission's concerns were with materials far beyond the mainstream (e.g., Grove 1986, pp. D1, 8–9). At the same time, with a limited range of witnesses, the panel was basing its conclusions on a biased sample that encouraged identifying the most extreme cases as the norm, with depictions of rape, incest, bestiality, and sexual violence as typical pornographic fare. Undoubtedly the police officers to testify were competent investigators of criminal offenses. Equally, there is no reason to doubt the devastation of sexually abusive behavior on the witnesses who testified. But press portrayals suggested that credibility required more than deference to authority or compassion; it required detachment and objectivity to entertain the possibility of alternative accounts.

Although Meese made much ado over the commissioners' qualifications to deal with the subject, press focus on the commissioners' qualifications suggested that their religious biases and experiences as proactive agents opposed to pornography or as dealing with victims of sex-related offenses were signs that they would have a difficult time being objective in their reception of testimony. This problem surfaced at the very first meeting of the commission in Washington. One of the witnesses, Bill, recounted his molestation of two fourteen-year-old girls who were visiting his home. Bill was prepared to tell the commissioners what he had done and the role pornography played in it. His account was so pat, in fact, as to raise doubts in Commissioner Levine's mind. She cross-questioned him as follows:

LEVINE: Can you tell me whether drinking was also a problem of yours and whether or not it continues to be?

BILL: Drinking was a problem in my life. I was drinking approximately two to three six-packs of beer daily.

LEVINE: Was drinking in any way one of the triggers that allowed you to do things that otherwise you wouldn't have done?

BILL: Yes, it certainly was.

In an analysis of the commission's work published by *Playboy*, *LA Times* writer Robert Scheer points out that when Levine suggested to commission chair Hudson in private that the witness appeared to be coached, her concern was evaded. Concludes Scheer, "The commission's questioning of Bill was typical of what would happen for the rest of the year—pandering to the antiporn witnesses to buttress the case and attempting to discredit those with a different position" (p. 160).

At issue, then were the witnesses' qualifications to determine the role of pornography in the behaviors they reported. And as a corollary, at issue was the level of understanding the commissioners were able to form of the problem from such a sample. These concerns, which were common in the opinion pieces that appeared in major newspapers and magazines, portrayed a version of the *Final Report* that went beyond the commissioners' own statements and Frederick Schauer's report. They drew rather from the materials that appeared elsewhere in the document, the data base on which the commission's findings rested. To place the matter in context, one must turn to that datato determine how it was presented in the report itself and in the press.

In the graphic excerpts of testimony cited to support the claim that pornography causes adverse effects (pp. 767–835) the reader of the report encounters brief depictions that can only be described in terms of distress, shock, and rage. These excerpts are used to support the report's claim that pornography is socially devastating.

Here is a summation based on the report's characterizations of the ghastly consequences that the witnesses attribute to pornography:

A. Physical harms of rape, forced sexual performance, battery, torture, murder, imprisonment, sexually transmitted diseases, masochistic self-harm, and prostitution.

B. Psychological harms of suicidal thoughts and behaviors, fear and anxiety caused by seeing pornography, feelings of shame and guilt, fear of exposure through publication or display of pornographic materials, amnesia and denial and repression of abuses, nightmares, compulsive reenactment of sexual abuse and inability to feel sexual pleasure outside of a context of dominance and submission, inability to experience sexual pleasure and feelings of sexual inadequacy, feelings of inferiority and degradation, feelings of frustration with the legal system, abuses of alcohol and other drugs.

C. Social harms of loss of job or promotion, sexual harassment, financial losses, defamation and loss of status in the community, promotion of racial hatred, loss of trust within a family, prostitution, and sexual harassment in the workplace.

The pathos of the testimony narrating this scene is unspeakable. And one cannot avoid noticing throughout this section that common reference is made to such magazines as *Playboy* and *Penthouse* as sources of sexual stimulation for their attackers. The obvious implication of this joining is that male-oriented entertainment magazines caused these horror shows. Although the Schauer report is explicit in qualifying its stance so as not to call for action against this genre, the suggestion later presented is that this genre is indeed among the culprits. For example, a woman alleged that her father used *Playboy* as an enticement to his molestation of her as a small child. The text reads as follows: "This father took a *Playboy* magazine and wrote her name across the centerfold. Then he placed it under the covers so she would find it when she went to bed. He joined her in bed that night and taught her about sex" (p. 775).

Obviously this is a staff report of witness testimony, not a direct quote. Further, this report, as with those throughout this section, contains no indication of witness interrogation. Similar traits characterize this account by a mother whose son committed autoerotic suicide:

My son, Troy Daniel Dunaway, was murdered on August 6, 1981, by the greed and avarice of *Hustler* Magazine. My son read the article 'Orgasm of Death', set up the sexual experiment depicted therein, followed the explicit instructions of the article, and ended up dead. He would still be alive today were he not enticed and incited into this action by *Hustler* Magazine's 'How To Do' August 1981 article; an article which was found at his feet and which directly caused his death. (p. 797)

A reader must take or leave these accounts at face value, including the featured roles of *Playboy* and *Hustler* clearly implicated in the crimes reported.

Such presentations created complications for the report's recommendations. The violence depicted was so serious as to require attention and remedy. At the same time, because they raised issues of human degradation and civil liberties that cut so deeply to the core of what it means to live in a civilized society, these episodes required more careful analysis than the witnesses themselves could provide of events so traumatic. Here is a typical instance of victim testimony that illustrates the analysis witnesses often provided (pp. 774–75):

> When I first met my husband, it was in early 1975, and he was all the time talking about Ms. Marchiano's film *Deep Throat*. After we married, he on several occasions referred to her performance and suggested I try to imitate her actions. . . . Last January . . . my husband raped me. . . . He made me strip and lie on our bed. He cut our clothesline up . . . and tied my hands and feet to the corners of the bedframe. (All this was done while our nine month old son watched.) While he held a butcher knife on me threatening to kill me he fed me three strong tranquilizers. I started crying and because the baby got scared and also began crying, he beat my face and my body. I later had welts and bruises. He attempted to smother me with a pillow. . . . Then, he had sex with me vaginally, and then forced me to give oral sex to him.

What one may conclude from this account is taken as self-evident by the report, since it explicitly eschewed any commentary or findings. Instead, in its own words, "we have tried in this chapter to allow victims to speak in their own words, without interpretation or commentary" (p. 769). Thus a reader is left with witnesses' analyses, often based on the emotional distress that accompanies the degrading violence of sexual assault to which they were subjected. The reader is not asked to make a rational inference of causation, but to deal with the victim's hurt. The rhetorical dynamics of inflammatory testimony of this sort enrages and cries for action. It preempts the ethical foundations of the issue, making it difficult to question the implied causes or to advance remedies without appearing to lack moral sensitivity.

For example, one might suggest that the general indictment of magazines of *Hustler's* ilk as a cause of sexual violence is an over-simplification at best. Were it true, the several million monthly readers of these publications would constitute a public menace of massive proportions, not to mention the corrosive effects on the commissioners who were steeped in far worse for a full year. Without the antidote of wider, perhaps more analytical testimony, however, the commission may have denied itself a repertoire of alternative accounts to critically test their evidence.

Moreover, one might wonder at the types of conclusions permissible from the savage assault allegedly sparked by *Deep Throat*. Is it evident that this would not have occurred had the perpetrator not seen *Deep Throat*? That pornography or certain types of pornography or too much pornography causes crime? That sexual relations or certain types of sexual relations are dangerous? That the husband required psychological treatment? And what of the lurking hints that there may have been drug or alcohol abuse? That the husband may have had a problem accepting his role as father? That the marriage was generally troubled? Nor do we know the events prior to the episode that may have acted as a trigger. In the context of a report charged to suggest legal remedies for the spread of pornography, these questions went unasked.

The provocative nature of this testimony, coupled with the absence of analytical assessments of witness accounts, only added fuel to the depiction of the commission as engaging in an ideological witch hunt. Doubtless because the pathos of such vicious attacks is so overwhelming, though equally because there was little rhetorical advantage to be gained by challenging the victims' own analyses, these accounts seldom reached the public. When they did, it was usually to illustrate how the wacky reasoning of witnesses skewed the data. A favorite example reported was the testimony of Larry Madigan, cited above. More commonly the press focused on problems of methodology that undermined the report's claims.

Lacking an operational definition of what constituted pornography, the commission could not specify with precision what caused the misery being paraded before it. Without the methodological requirements of cross-examination nor the presentation of expert interpretation and analysis of testimony, the commission's thinking appeared to be reductionistic. The report discussed the testimony only in terms of the presumed problem of pornography and the presumed solution of legal changes. On the other hand, the debunking version suggested that pornography wasn't the real problem, from which it followed that the report's recommendations were no cure (Goleman 1986, p. A35; C. Hefner 1987, pp. 28–29; Scheer 1986b, p. 167; Shenon 1986a). The report was challenged for the unrepresentative sample of pornography examined and for being prudish in its shock at what millions of middle-class Americans take as commonplace (Nelson 1986). Rather than a problem of sexual portrayal requiring legal remedy, it was equally plausible to ask whether the victimage examined was not more basically a problem of health and welfare requiring a completely different analysis and remedy.

In light of the profound implications for a democratic society that accompany any restrictions on its access to the public sphere, the aforementioned concerns made the Meese Commission and its report seem threatening to a significant range of citizens—journalists, publishers, physicians, lawyers, and educators, among others (e.g., Wines and Sharbutt 1986). Consequently, the findings themselves were challenged on the grounds that the commission had failed to establish a causal relation between pornography and sexual violence, that it was using an emotionally loaded topic to abridge civil liberties. Thus it was that in the public controversy surrounding the report, the commission's major burden of proof became the demonstration of a causal link between pornography and physical, psychological, and social harm.

The attacks demanding a causal link were widespread in press coverage of the report. No less than thirteen articles and editorials appeared between May 11 and July 20 in the *Los Angeles Times*, *New York Times* and *Washington Post* objecting to the failure of the commission to demonstrate causality. Specifically, the commission was pilloried for its failure to base its recommendations on a scientifically established causal relation between pornography and harm.

Certainly this objection was not a distortion of the commission's position, since, as previously indicated, the commission had not advanced a scientifically based argument for causation. Instead it had argued that social behavior had multiple causes that could not be accounted for in social scientific research. The "commonsense" criterion was advanced in its place, buttressed with extrapolations from social science research on pornography. It concluded, for example, that extended exposure to increased aggressive behavior directed at women will increase one's level of sexual violence and that substantial exposure to violent sexually explicit material will cause an increase in the rape myth (pp. 325, 327).

This admitted absence of the strongest possible causal claim became problematic in press accounts, since the press made little of the commission's rationale of complexity and made much of the absence as an indication that the commission was raising a smoke screen on the causal issue because no causal relationships existed. News coverage pointed to the fact that social scientists who appeared before the commission did not believe their studies supported the causal claim the panel had advanced, especially in its reportage of sexual violence. Speaking in the *New York Times*, University of New Hampshire sociologist Murray Strauss observed, "The panel seems to have deliberately released its findings before we [the social scientists who testified or were cited by the commission] could meet [at the Surgeon General's request], because they were afraid that the social scientists' conclusions would contradict theirs. . . . I dispute their conclusions because they are not in accordance with my understanding of the scientific data" (Goleman 1986, p. A35). The article continues to cite Professor Strauss' report that social scientists have found eleven factors that correlate with rape, but none that relate causally. Second, the report encouraged the inference that pornography was the cause of sexual assault. But the scientific community contended that sexual assault was not a problem of pornography but of violence. As already noted, the research cited to support the point did not specifically investigate the relationship between violent pornography and sexual behaviors. It was more concerned with violence than with sexuality. The assumed relationship between pornography and antisocial behavior became self-confirming as the panel interpreted aggressive behavior toward women as a portent of a *sexual* offense rather than one of violence, as the researchers had maintained (e.g., Donnerstein 1986). The irony of this shift in focus was underscored by Michael Kinsley, who remarked in the *Washington Post* that one could not conclude that viewing sexual violence induced violent behavior with any significance beyond that encouraged by, say, slasher films or a steady diet of Sylvester Stallone (1986, p. A25).

Again, one responding to the aspects of the report emphasized by the press could hardly avoid the strong impression that the commission's contention of a link between pornography and violence was reinforced by the skewed body of testimony it received. Many of the witnesses who averred that pornography caused irreparable tragedy were not in a position to form an objective or competent opinion: law enforcement officers, who formed judgments based on their encounters with a highly selective sample of society and always in the context of crime, religious fundamentalists (Hiaasen 1986, p. 53), and victims, whose own tragic circumstances tended to confuse the fact that they were victimized by another's sexual behavior with pornography.

Finally, the dissenting members of the commission, Barker and Levine, were commonly cited in front-page coverage of the report upon its release. They also were invoked by the report's antagonists as specifically arguing that the conclusion of causality could not be teased from the data at the commission's disposal. Their demurrer suggested that in the presence of substantial methodological flaws, one reached the claimed causal link only by smuggling in an ideological bias (Fields 1986, p. 14).

Collectively, these difficulties with the commission's methods and assumptions made the Schauer report, seemingly even-handed and well-reasoned, appear a threat to the public sphere and to selected publics of some significance. The Schauer section discusses pornography in terms that are more general than the examples I have been considering. But when one turns to the latter portions of the report, the exclusively extreme nature of examples such as these suggest that they are the norm. Consequently, despite the commission's disclaimers to the contrary, when focus is trained on what appears after the Schauer section, the impression is created that all of pornography is a social scourge.

By contrast, the press version strongly intimated that freedom of speech was the central issue, albeit one given relatively little consideration, consistent with the commission's determination to focus its attention on materials that would satisfy a legal test of obscenity. It is discussed by Schauer as a "constraint" on what the committee might recommend and it also receives consideration near the end of the report when social scientific and legal evidence bearing on the harms and regulation of pornography are under consideration. Indeed, out of a total report of nearly two thousand pages, slightly less than eighty are devoted to this topic—a disturbing balance in light of the panel's charge to honor First Amendment protections. By contrast, press accounts were ashimmer with reminders of First Amendment rights (e.g., Kurtz 1986, p. A8; *LA Times* 1986, p. 114; Shenon 1986b; Smith 1986; Wald 1986).

RECONSTRUCTING THE PUBLIC SPHERE

Had Version I remained uncontested regarding the commission's composition and methodology, a national debate on pornography conceivably might have ensued. But Version II so challenged the credibility of the *Final Report* as to make the commission itself the focus of controversy (e.g., Scheer 1986a). On the one hand, it portrayed itself as a champion of the public's right to know, to discuss, and to decide. Conversely, by virtue of seeking legal restraints on what may appear in public, it acted as an antagonist toward the public sphere. The commissioners could protest in the public press as loudly as they chose about the balance and responsibility of the report, but the nature of its rhetoric shouted a completely different message. Inflammatory testimony coupled with specific recommendations for public action gave the document incendiary potential, especially for local mentalities distrustful of a complex world and fearful that it meant them harm.

For the vast majority of Americans whose knowledge of the commission's findings were informed by the press, the document seemed to argue for an interpretation of all explicit treatments of sexual relations as deleterious to the public welfare. It seemed to address particular audiences vulnerable to appeals that confirmed a predisposition against sexually explicit depictions. To readers of Version II, the report seemed addressed, in part, to those who lacked experience with pornography. For that audience, pornography appeared as the clear cause of child abuse, incest, rape, physically violent sex, pederasty, homosexuality, and as contributing to the welfare of the underworld and to urban blight. Version II portrayed a second audience segment as moral conservatives and religious fundamentalists, for whose views the report provided legitimation, with the now added authority of governmental voice. A third audience seemed to include feminist concerns about the relation between pornographic portrayals and the specific issue of sexual crimes as well as the larger issue of stereotyped and degrading depictions of females as sex objects.

For those who may have been consumers of erotic literature and films, the press accounts of the report depicted an environment of hostile judgment about their private lives. Rather than encouraging dialogue, Version II introduced the terror of moral predispositions that could only discourage them from speaking out. More than anything, Version II encouraged a spiral of silence, a condition of public expression in which the individual's sense of what everyone believes provides an indication of what one must or must not say in public to be acceptable, a judgment made irrespective of personal beliefs or commitments (Noelle-Neumann 1984). Freighted with the above associations, there was too much ground to defend. Prudence dictated safety in silence. For those who chose to address the issues being contested in the national debate, its focus on the commission itself was counterproductive for enlightened discussion of the serious problems associated with hard core pornography. By underspecifying the cause of the harms it reported, the final report served more as an invitation to polemics than to discussion, since Version II left no ground for one to disagree without appearing to support the morally reprehensible practices depicted in the cited testimony or callousness toward the cruelty to which many of the witnesses were subjected.

Since pornography itself was thus suppressed as a viable issue of debate, dissenting voices gravitated toward the quality of the report's reasoning. The problematic character of the causality claim made the specific recommendations of the commission necessarily appear as a form of censorship (Baker 1986; C. Hefner 1987, pp. 27–28; Hertzberg 1986, p. 24; Vance 1986, p. 81). Especially troubling was the invitation to form citizen watch groups for surveillance of merchants trafficking in pornography. There was the explicit recommendation that they picket and boycott to exert economic and moral pressure. For many this appeared an open invitation to vigilante action as a form of censorship. The potential to intimidate patrons from doing business with a merchant extended clearly beyond "adult only" establishments to those who were not primarily trafficking in pornography but carried such items as Penthouse or X-rated films in their inventory.

This fear was not without foundation. The call apparently was heeded, if increased mobilization by antipornography groups shortly after the report appeared were an indicator (Kurtz 1986; Quinn 1986; Rangel 1986; Sharbutt 1986; *Washington Post* 1986, p. C7), and the fear was only intensified by the infamous Sears letter. Alan E. Sears, who served as executive director of the commission, sent a letter to convenience stores following the testimony of the Rev. Donald Wildmon, a notoriously outspoken opponent of all sexually explicit matter. Included in his crusade were magazines of the *Playboy* variety and their common outlet, America's convenience stores. Mr. Sears' letter outlined Rev. Wildmon's charges and offered the accused an opportunity to reply. Unfortunately, in an act of questionable judgment, he further specified that failure to respond within ten days would be taken as an indication that they did not contest the claim. The furor created was substantial, leading to a court order that the letter be withdrawn. But it is significant to note that the 7-Eleven chain took *Playboy*, *Penthouse*, and the like off its shelves. The public reason for their action was their own polling data that showed their customers wished these magazines withdrawn from display. Whether this was so, or a response to the perception of a new moral militancy with which the commission was in tune, the fact remains that a form of censorship was being exercised. From the point of view of the parent Southland corporation, it was no longer safe to display that merchandise. In effect Southland became accomplices to a spiral of silence, intensifying the perception that it was dangerous to be identified publicly as a consumer of sexually explicit magazines.

The aura of moral militancy encouraged by the commission's urging of citizen action and the Sears letter were not out of keeping with the Rev. Jerry Falwell's much publicized crusade against *Playboy*. Two weeks after the report's release, *Newsweek* (McDaniel 1986) suggested this mood was spreading when the Wal-Mart chain ordered its 890 outlets to remove thirty-two rock magazines from the racks. The *Washington Post* suggested that the Rev. Jimmy Swaggart's criticisms of rock magazines as a form of pornography had done its part in encouraging the wisdom of such a decision (1986, p. B3). In light of the massive television audiences commanded by fundamentalist evangelists, the threat of citizen action leading to mass censorship seemed more likely now that the commission had given a form of legitimation to the idea.

For the concerned citizen reading of such events in the daily paper, the message was clear: it was not safe to say you read erotica, it was not safe to say that pornography does not commonly turn its consumers into antisocial maniacs. The very terms in which the issue was presented made such an admission of belief equivalent to relinquishing one's claim to being a moral person.

Thus, the argument of the report, especially the portion written by Frederick Schauer, was perceived as encouraging legislative and citizen initiative for a conservative and fundamentalist interpretation of sexually explicit matter. Moreover, because the Schauer portion was written in language that seemed to have taken a sober and moderate view, the *Final Report* seemed to legitimate this interpretation with its own voice. Ironically, the report's force was enhanced by Schauer's version which put in moderate tones the more extreme views presented in the later sections. He wrote with an audience in mind, having been prompted by the blatant overstatement of the commission's work, which he professed would not be acceptable for any responsible person to sign. His massaging of the data put them into more temperate language that saved the report and the commission from being publicly laughable. It was now a document to be taken seriously, one with the potential to bring about action with serious implications for freedom of expression in the United States on sexually related matters.

CONCLUSION

The Meese Commission did not have a profound effect on the spread of pornography. The antipornography initiatives that did surface during the Reagan administration issued primarily out of the attorney general's office. One reason for the absence of legislative taste to pursue the commission's recommendations is found in the Maine referendum noted earlier. Given the chance to endorse measures in the spirit of the *Final Report*, two out of three Maine voters said "no." The message was clear to politicians looking for votes.

But there is another reason for the report's apparent lack of impact. The intent of the commission was to provoke an informed dialogue on pornography. But it was impossible to have a dialogue when the methodology of the report seemed to satisfy voyeur interests with sensational testimony accompanied by summaries and bibliographies of the most degrading pornography available. How was it possible to have a dialogue when the report made it impossible to take the other side without indicting oneself as morally corrupt? Consequently, those whose issues were other than legal found themselves lacking an informed context for discussion, although it was one well suited for polemics or for ridicule. The *Final Report* did not promote discussion on pornography because it did not provide insight into pornography.

This failure reflects, in part, the public envisioned by the commissioners and the public sphere that would accommodate them. The innuendoes of immorality through resistance had profound implications for reconstructing the public sphere along conservative and religious lines. It distorted the public realm as an open discursive space for those looking beyond the legal restraints on pornography. In its open instruction on citizen action tactics, the report became an invitation to vigilante disruption of discursive spaces. While citizen dissent has been a strength of the American political process, heretofore it had not been exercised to contravene private rights. In its silence on the public welfare and health issues and its insistence on treating social and cultural questions of gender power as legal problems, the panel subordinated an alternative analysis of pornography to a conservative legislative agenda. In its presentation of data in a sensationalistic fashion, and in its method for selecting witnesses and deriving conclusions, it projected a public more attuned to respond to titillation and power than analysis. Ironically, it replicated in its communication the terms of relationship whose extreme it was attempting to eradicate.

The critics of the report may have won the public debate about its value on a censorship issue; however, that does not remove the intimidating effect of the report on open discussion of sexually explicit materials. The commission's failure was not in its inability to reconstruct the public sphere, but in its failure to explore its possibilities for open discussion of a complex mode of communication with enormous implications for intimate and public life.

REFERENCES

Baker, John F. 1986, July 11. An American dilemma. *Publishers Weekly*, 230, 31.

Bob, Murray. 1986, October 15. The right questions about obscenity. *Library Journal, 111,* 39–41.

Clark, Henry. 1986, June 9. Don't turn back the clock on reality by fighting *Playboy. Los Angeles Times,* 115.

Donnerstein, Edward. 1986, August. Research misused. *Playboy, 33,* 42.

Duggan, Lisa. 1985, September 1. The dubious porn war alliance. *Washington Post,* C14.

Fields, Howard. 1986, May 30. Two on Meese Ppanel dissent from report's conclusion. *Publishers Weekly, 229,* 14.

Giddens, Anthony. 1984. *The constitution of society.* Berkeley: University of California Press.

Goleman, Daniel. 1986, May 17. Researchers dispute pornography report on its use of data. *New York Times,* A1, 35.

Grove, Lloyd. 1986, June 7. Descent into the world of porn. *Washington Post,* D1, 8–9.

Habermas, Jürgen. 1974. The public sphere: An encyclopedia article. *New German Critique, 3,* 49–55.

Hauser, Gerard A. 1985. Common sense in the public sphere: A rhetorical grounding for publics. *Informatologia Yugoslavica, 17,* 67–75.

———. 1987. Features of the public sphere. *Critical Studies in Mass Communication, 4,* 437–41.

Hauser, Gerard A., and Carole Blair. 1983. Rhetorical antecedents to the public. *Pre/Text, 3,* 139–67.

Hefner, Christie. 1987, January–February. Meese Commission: Sex, violence, and censorship. *The Humanist, 47,* 25–29, 46.

Hefner, Hugh. 1986, January. Sexual McCarthyism. *Playboy, 33,* 58–59.

Hertzberg, Hendrik. 1986, July 14–21. Big boobs. *New Republic, 195,* 21–24.

Hiaasen, Carl. 1986, December. Commentary. *Playboy, 33,* 53.

Kinsley, Michael. 1986, June 12. Apostle of violence. *Washington Post,* A25.

Kurtz, Howard. 1986, July 10. Attorney General's panel says some porn causes sexual violence. *Washington Post,* A1, 8.

Lipton, Morris. S. 1986, July 18. No, the evidence against porn is shoddy. *Los Angeles Times,* 115.

Los Angeles Times. 1986, June 9. 114.

McDaniel, Ann. 1986, July 21. A salvo in the porn war. *Newsweek,* 18.

Miller v. California. 1973. 413 U.S. 15.

Nelson, Milo. 1986, September. Meese's peep show. *Wilson Library Bulletin, 61,* 4.

Noelle-Neumann, Elisabeth. 1984. *The spiral of silence: Public opinion—our social skin.* Chicago: University of Chicago Press.

People. 1986, June 30. 28–33.

Quinn, Krystal. 1986, August 7. Ex-Bunny leads antipornography rally. *Washington Post*, C4.

Rangle, Jesus. 1986, July 26. Church leaders make a target of pornography. *New York Times*, A31.

Roth v. United States. 1957. 354 U.S. 476.

Scheer, Robert. 1986, May 1. Commission founders on limits to sex. *Los Angeles Times*, A1, 24.

———. 1986a, August. Inside the Meese Commission. *Playboy, 33,* 60–61, 157–67.

Sharbutt, Jay. 1986, May 30. Mahoney's porn attack zero's in on cable TV. *Los Angeles Times*, V1, 14.

Shenon, Philip. 1986, May 18. A second opinion on pornography's impact. *New York Times*, E8.

———. 1986a, May 20. Playboy and booksellers suing *Playboy* panel. *New York Times*, A24.

Smith, Jack. 1986, May 29. *Los Angeles Times*, V1.

Time. 1986, July 21. 12–22.

Tourain, Alain. 1981. *The voice and the eye: An analysis of social movements,* trans. Alan Duff. London: Cambridge University Press.

U.S. Department of Justice. 1986. *Final report of the Attorney General's Commission on Pornography*. Washington, D.C.

Vance, Carole S. 1986, August 2 and 9. The Meese Commission on the road. *The Nation, 243,* 65, 76–82.

Wald, Matthew. 1986, June 16. "Adult" magazines lose sales as 8,000 stores forbid them. *New York Times*, A1, 14.

Washington Post. 1986, July 23. B3.

Wines, Michael, and Jay Sharbutt. 1986, July 10. Critics see report as a reflection of rising intolerance. *Los Angeles Times*, 15.

ABOUT THE CONTRIBUTORS

Rebecca S. Bjork is Associate Professor of Communication at the University of Utah. She was a recipient of the Speech Communication Association Dissertation Award in 1990. She is author of *The Strategic Defense Initiative: Symbolic Containment of the Nuclear Threat* and has written extensively on the discursive construction of U.S. foreign policy and nuclear weapons strategy.

Jeffrey L. Courtright is Assistant Professor of Communication at Miami University in Oxford, Ohio. A student of issues surrounding church and state, Courtright has published (with Mark P. Gibney) "Arguments for the Elimination of Religious Broadcasting from the Public Airwaves" in *Notre Dame Journal of Law, Ethics, and Public Policy* and "Justice O'Connor's Messages to the Polity Refining the Boundaries of Religious Freedom" in *Public Relations Review.*

Ralph E. Dowling (J.D., Indiana University, 1993; Ph.D., University of Denver, 1984), formerly director of Graduate Studies in Speech Communication at Ball State University, is employed by Wilson, Kehoe and Winingham in Indianapolis. Dowling has published in such journals as *Indiana Law Review, Journal of the American Forensic Association, Journal of Communication, Central States Speech Journal, Communication Education, Political Communication and Persuasion, Terrorism: An International Journal,* and *Conflict Quarterly.*

Ian Fielding is Assistant Professor and Director of Forensics in the Department of Communication at Loyola University of Chicago. His research interests include developing methods of evaluating value arguments, the criticism of argumentation concerning social issues, and the application of rhetorical criticism to legal discourse. He has published in the *Proceedings of the Seventh Biennial SCA/AFA Conference on Argumentation* and the *Proceedings*

311

of the Second International Conference on Argumentation on argument in children's television and the influence of children's television on the development of children's argument patterns. He is currently working on a book critiquing the arguments advanced by the U.S. military in support of its policy of discriminating on the basis of sexual orientation.

Gabrielle A. Ginder is now the Education Director at the Huntertown United Methodist Church in Huntertown, Indiana. Her work with Ralph Dowling has been published in *Western Speech Communication Journal*.

Dennis S. Gouran is Professor and Head in the Department of Speech Communication at The Pennsylvania State University. Professor Gouran has been president of both the Central States Communication Association and the Speech Communication Association as well as editor of *Central States Speech Journal*. He is author of numerous books, articles, and reviews dealing with communication in decision-making groups. In 1992 Professor Gouran was named first recipient of the Howard B. Palmer Faculty Mentoring Award at Penn State and was one of the first ten recipients of the Speech Communication Association Distinguished Scholar Award. In 1993 he received the Penn State University Faculty Scholar Medal in the Social and Behavioral Sciences.

Gerard A. Hauser is Professor of Communication and Department Chair at the University of Colorado at Boulder. He has also held an appointment on the faculty of the Pennsylvania State University, where he was Professor of Speech Communication and Director of the University Scholars Program. There he was recipient of the College of the Liberal Arts' Distinguished Teaching Award. He has been named a Visiting Scholar by the Eastern Communication Association, and received an Excellence Visiting Professor appointment at Temple University. In addition to articles and reviews on the subject of rhetorical theory and criticism, he is author of *Introduction to Rhetorical Theory* and consulting editor of the international journal *Philosophy and Rhetoric*.

Mary Keehner is Assistant Professor of Rhetorical Studies in the Communication Department at Purdue University. Her research emphasizes a feminist approach to rhetorical theory and argumentation, and her work has been published in *Communication Studies*, *Argumentation and Advocacy*, and *Argument and Controversy: Proceedings of the Seventh SCA/AFA Conference on Argumentation*.

Michael K. Launer is Professor of Russian at The Florida State University. After fifteen years of research in applied semantics, syntax, methodology, and translation studies, he began analyzing Soviet crisis rhetoric. Co-author of *Flights of Fancy, Flight of Doom: KAL 007 and Soviet-American Rhetoric*, Professor Launer's research has been published in *Russian Language Journal*, *Quarterly Journal of Speech*, *Argumentation and Advocacy*, *Journal of Communication*, *FORUM for Applied Research and Public Policy*, *Bulletin of Concerned Asian Scholars*, and *Current World Leaders*. Professor Launer is also a State Department certified interpreter specializing in civilian nuclear power safety initiatives.

Clark D. Olson is Director of Forensics and Associate Professor of communication at Arizona State University. He has published over a dozen articles and his work appears in the *Journal of Applied Communication Research*, *The Forensic*, *Proceedings of the Second International Conference on Argumentation*, and in the proceedings of the Biennial SCA/AFA Conferences on Argumentation.

Kathryn M. Olson is Assistant Professor of Communication at the University of Wisconsin, Milwaukee. She is a critic primarily of contemporary political and religious discourse, and her work appears in such journals as *Quarterly Journal of Speech*, *Philosophy and Rhetoric*, *Journal of Applied Communication Research*, *Argumentation and Advocacy*, and *Communication Quarterly*. Olson is the 1992 winner of SCA's Karl R. Wallace Award.

Catherine Helen Palczewski is Assistant Professor of Communication at the University of Northern Iowa. Her prior publications include a feminist critique of Ronald Reagan's abortion discourse, an analysis of George Bush's Michigan Commencement Address that attacks PC, and critical rhetorical biographies of anarchist Voltairine de Cleyre and feminist lawyer Catharine A. MacKinnon. Her research interests include women's rhetoric and feminist criticism, rhetorical theory and criticism, argumentation, social movements, and political communication.

Edward Schiappa is Associate Professor and Director of Graduate Studies in Communication at Purdue University. His work on classical and contemporary rhetorical theory has appeared in such journals as *Quarterly Journal of Speech, Philosophy and Rhetoric, Rhetoric Society Quarterly, American Journal of Philology,* and *Communication Monographs.* He is author of *Protagoras and Logos: A Study in Greek Philosophy and Rhetoric* and editor of *Landmark Essays on Classical Greek Rhetoric.*

Carol Winkler is Associate Professor and chair of Communication at Georgia State University. Her essays on presidential rhetoric and terrorism appear in *Political Communication and Persuasion* and *Terrorism.* With David Birdsell and William Newnam, she recently co-authored a multivolume series on argumentation and debate, entitled *Lines of Argument: An Approach to Policy and Value Debate.*

Marilyn J. Young is Professor of Communication and Director of the International Center for the Study of Political Communication and Argumentation at The Florida State University. A former Director of Forensics at FSU, Professor Young is co-author of *Flights of Fancy, Flight of Doom: KAL 007 and Soviet-American Rhetoric* and author of "When the Shoe Is on the Other Foot: Comparative Treatments of the KAL 007 and Iran Air Shootdowns" in *Studies of the Reagan Presidency and Public Discourse,* Michael Weiler and Barnett Pearce, eds. Her research has also been published in *Quarterly Journal of Speech, Argumentation and Advocacy, Journal of Communication, Bulletin of Concerned Asian Scholars,* and *Current World Leaders.* Professor Young's current research interest entails an analysis of the rhetorical aftermath of the Chernobyl nuclear accident.

NOTES

CHAPTER 1. EVALUATIVE CRITERIA FOR CONSPIRACY ARGUMENTS

1. © 1984 by The Nation Company, Inc. Portions reprinted by permission.

2. Anonymous (1984); Johnson (1983); Sampson and Bittorf (1984). In addition, the Soviet Union published "Prestuplenie prezidenta" *(The President's Crime)*, a translation of a Japanese study by Akio Takahashi, the pseudonym for an unknown author. For an extensive listing of publications devoted to explanations of the incident, see Young and Launer (1988b, pp. xxiv–xxv).

3. Examples include two call-in talk shows: "Larry King Live," CNN, September 2, 1986, and "Donahue," September 16, 1986. See also Cutler (1986) and Parenti (1986).

4. The survey was conducted by the G. Lawrence Company of Santa Ana, California, for the National Strategy Information Center (NSIC). This information was provided by Ronald H. Hinckley, formerly a Senior Fellow at NSIC (see NSIC 1986).

5. All official administration statements can be found in this document.

6. Oberg (1988) catalogs numerous instances of Soviet forces attacking border violators without warning (chap. 3). In one case, the Soviet Union actually admitted culpability eight years after the fact in direct response to Oberg's published charges. See Illesh and Shal'nev (1989) and Andrjushkov (1986).

7. The typical mission orbit of an RC-135 is a figure eight paralleling the coastline of the Soviet Union. The Soviet government contends that as the RC-135 was returning to its base in the Aleutians, it made an unexpected turn in order to position itself near the flight-path of KAL 007 and effect a rendezvous; in a diagram presented by Marshal Ogarkov at a September 9, 1983 press conference, this alleged "second loop" enabled the RC-135 to fly parallel to the route of KAL 007 (Foreign Broadcast Information Service 1983). The U.S. government, of course, denied the existence of this anomaly in the route of the RC-135.

8. Much of this information appears to be faulty. In the words of James E. Oberg (1985), a spaceflight operations engineer and noted science writer, Pearson delivers "an avalanche of technical and military terminology which gives a good appearance of true expertise." But the material is "replete with the most elementary technical errors." In Oberg's opinion, Pearson "counts on—and cultivates—the ignorance of his readers" (pp. 36–37).

9. Aside from fervent U.S. denials of the authenticity of Ogarkov's map, there exists one independent fact that argues for fabrication: on the map the time of the shooting was placed at 1824 GMT, two minutes earlier than that indicated in all American and Japanese materials, including the voice-activated tape of Soviet fighter pilots. No one in the West ever challenged the authenticity of 1826 GMT as the time at which the airplane was destroyed or that it was still in Soviet airspace when fired on. However, in an updated report issued in June 1993, based on information recently released by the government of the Russian Federation, ICAO revealed that the airliner had actually left Soviet airspace when it was shot down. Additionally, it was not the Soviets who introduced the variable of the RC-135; the presence of the reconnaissance aircraft was first revealed by then House Majority Leader Jim Wright.

10. One may infer that the Soviets did not record their own radar, and hence could not know for certain where KAL 007 was at the moment it was hit and did not know what U.S. intelligence might be able to prove.

11. "No evidence was available to either support or refute the contradictory information from the USSR and the United States concerning the proximity of KE007 and the reconnaissance air-craft" (UNO 1983, p. 40). Newly released information demonstrates that the two aircraft were never less than 150 kilometers apart.

12. For further discussion of the question of surveillance, see Young and Launer (1988b), chap. 8.

13. For a complete discussion of the errors in this passage, see Launer et al. (1986).

14. Between February and May 1991, then again in October 1991, *Izvestija* journalists Andrei Illesh and Aleksandr Shal'nev published approximately thirty articles revealing that nearly all of the official Soviet version was fallacious. In particular, the pilot who shot down KAL 007 denied that established international procedures were followed during the interception. The new ICAO report confirmed that only an IFF inquiry was attempted by the Soviet pilot.

15. Maertens (1985), p. 29. This view was confirmed in a private communication from Harold Ewing, a 747 pilot cited extensively by Hersh (1986).

CHAPTER 3. THE FAILURE OF ARGUMENT IN DECISIONS LEADING TO THE "CHALLENGER DISASTER"

1. Launch decisions involve four levels of review. Representing Level IV are contractors responsible for various system components. Level III personnel are employees of NASA's three centers (Marshall, Kennedy, and Johnson) who conduct flight readiness reviews of the system components for which they are responsible. These individuals report to other personnel at Levels II and I, who, in turn, feed relevant data to the Mission Management Team. Those at Level II conduct the review of preflight readiness of all systems, and those at Level I certify overall flight readiness (*Report* 1986, pp. 82–84).

2. Elsewhere, I (Gouran 1984) have discussed the concept of "counteractive influence," which, in general, refers to efforts designed to restore movement to a group's goal path when disruptive influences have diverted it from the goal path and inertial forces are sustaining movement away from the goal. Opponents of the *Challenger* launch seemed to face precisely this sort of situation; however, their efforts were largely reactive rather than proactive. They allowed themselves to be put on the defensive when, in fact, it was unnecessary for them to take such a posture. If anyone needed to justify a position on the question of whether to launch, it was those in favor. Unfortunately, the opponents permitted proponents to turn the tables early on, and they never broke loose from this defensive position.

CHAPTER 4. ALIGNING ETHICALITY AND EFFECTIVENESS IN ARGUMENTS

1. Usually, however, such standards automatically force argument scholars to look outside their own discipline for evaluative criteria by which to appraise an argument's end.

2. Herrick (1992) criticizes the basic imperative as "prescriptive or maximal" and so "freighted with the same problems as other ethical systems that impose external guidelines on the practitioners of rhetoric" (p. 137). As this is the extent of his comments specific to Johnstone's ethic, Herrick's objection is somewhat unclear. If the problem with a prescriptive or maximal ethic is that Herrick sees such ethics as "universalist" and so "anchor[ing] truth in some idea external to people and social contexts" (p. 136), then the criticism does not seem to apply to the basic imperative for a number of reasons. First, though Herrick does not develop the problems with external guidelines imposed on rhetoric, the argument in the main body of this text raises such issues and demonstrates why the basic imperative is not an "external guideline" pressed

on practitioners of rhetoric; it emerges from rhetoric itself in a way that seems consistent with Herrick's preferences for generating ethics for rhetoric. Second, the basic imperative prescribes a process of persuading that preserves indefinitely the human tendency to persuade rather than a particular telos; since Johnstone's ethic prescribes "how" rather than "what," it hardly seems anchored in a "truth" external to people and social contexts. Third, because the basic imperative combines elements of both what Herrick calls human nature perspectives and dialogical perspectives, it is not external to people and social contexts; Johnstone's ethic emerges from particular assumptions about human nature and, as a result, suggests guidelines for rhetorical interactions in a way that presumes a social context. If Herrick's objection is simply that the basic imperative provides a prescription for rhetorical action, it raises the question of what ethic would not violate this standard; ethics of rhetoric are inherently prescriptive, whatever their origins. If the problem is that a prescriptive ethic is unattainable, the upcoming case analysis will demonstrate that the basic imperative can be approximated closely in actual rhetoric, rhetoric that is also effective. For these reasons, Herrick's puzzling objection seems to fall short of satisfactorily discrediting the power of the basic imperative.

3.   The record of CNLC debates and membership responses shows that the opponents' association between law, in this undesirable sense, and the proposed inclusiveness percentages was a site of contestation. For example, proponents argued that the Lutheran Church still embraces and uses laws as guidelines for human behavior (e.g., the Ten Commandments), though it does not view them as directions for an alternative means of salvation (i.e., one's own works) to grace. The author thanks Pastor George A. Olson for reviewing the theological ideas presented in this section.

4.   Booth's rhetorical stance assumes that an arguer addresses an actual, practically identifiable intended audience(s) (e.g., other CNLC commissioners; the members of the three merging churches). Others (e.g., Black 1970; Charland 1987; White 1984) have demonstrated how a text may constitute its own audience, but, for the sake of evaluating effectiveness using the rhetorical stance, Booth's understanding of "audience" is most useful here.

CHAPTER 7. IDEOLOGY AND ARGUMENT EVALUATION

1.   We are concentrating in this essay on the relationship between the prosecution's and the defendants' arguments because we have analyzed the positions of and interactions among the judge, jurors, defense lawyers, and prosecution in other essays (e.g., Olson and Olson 1991,

1994). These analyses did not involve the defendants' ideology because they focused more closely on the trial's legal dimensions; since the sanctuary defendants did not testify during the trial phase, their position and its relationship to the prosecutor's position remain to be examined.

2. The Carter administration began aid programs to some of these Central American factions, but the Reagan administration greatly expanded them.

3. Only eleven of the sixteen, mostly clergy or lay church workers, ultimately stood trial: María del Socorro Pardo de Aguilar, Father Tony Clark, Philip Willis-Conger, Mary K. Espinosa, Reverend John Fife, Peggy Hutchison, Wendy LeWin, Sister Darlene Nicgorski, Father Ramón Quiñones, and Quakers Jim Corbett and Nena MacDonald. The eleven defendants were tried as a group, partly due to the conspiracy charge accompanying the specific indictments on such charges as alien-smuggling, and each was represented by at least one lawyer. Twelve lawyers participated in the trial.

4. Prosecutorial motions to exclude entire lines of defense, rather than individual items of evidence, appear with increasing frequency in the politically sensitive trials of defendants charged with conduct that challenges government policies (Colbert 1987, p. 1272).

5. It is interesting to note that these defendants, whose ontology assumes that people are basically good, were cited as examples of good people by both the defense attorneys and the prosecutor. Both at the sentencings and in interviews conducted some time after the trial, defense attorneys characterized their sanctuary clients as "some of the best among us"; "a person of moral character that I would long to have the same morals . . . and fiber that she has"; "never had a better client"; "just very, very good people"; "the best people I've ever met. . . . I was overpaid a thousand times. I'd do anything for them—they're truly good people"; and the kind of people who, instead of going out for a $50 meal, would take that $50, eat for $5, and give $45 to others who had nothing (Sentencings, pp. 188, 21, 92; Brosnahan 1989; Piccarreta 1989). While the defense attorneys' comments may not be particularly remarkable, the fact that the prosecutor also allowed for the possibility that the defendants fit the image of humanity found in their ontology is; Reno said, "[L]adies and gentlemen, they are not indicted in this case for being bad people. We don't have to prove in this case that they are bad people. . . . The government is not in issue with them as to whether they are good or bad" (Trial, pp. 14201–2).

6. In cases such as *Aguilar* in which pattern instructions are not required, both the prosecution and the defense can suggest jury instructions, but the judge makes the final determination.

7. While it is arguable that the prosecutor merely espoused this particular ideology as a useful strategy for the sanctuary trial, other evidence

suggests that this is the ideology he regularly embraces. Carole Reno, the prosecutor's wife, notes, "Don looks at [a trial] from the point that it's the constitutional aspect that fascinates him. What these people [i.e., sanctuary workers] are doing and what their cause is really is of no concern to Don. What fascinates him is the law" (Browning 1986, p. B2). Additional support for this claim is provided by Reno's behavior toward the sanctuary defense team outside the courtroom and after the trial (Walker 1989). His practice of trying to be friendly with the defense lawyers in these contexts suggests that in practice he is able to separate "his job" from whatever moral commitments he makes in the other areas of his life. Such evidence suggests that Reno consistently sees what occurs in the courtroom as unconnected to social consequences or to one's relationships outside the boundaries of the legal "game."

8. Another intriguing, self-reflexive, and often relatively personal set of approaches to ideology and communication appears in a special issue of the *Western Journal of Communication* edited by Wander (1993).

9. For more on the special role of criticism as moral action, see Klumpp and Hollihan (1989).

CHAPTER 8. ARGUING ABOUT
FETAL "VERSUS" WOMEN'S RIGHTS

1. The following narrative is based on Ambrose (1990); Elsasser (1990); Kirp, (1990); Kleiman (1990); Savage (1990); Recent Cases (1990); and Significant Decisions (1990).

2. General Motors, for example, will "review" its fetal protection policy, which is similar to Johnson Controls, but may continue the policy despite the court's decision. "It'll take a while to digest this," a company spokesperson says. "We've always felt, and I guess we still do, that the policy was aimed at protecting the fetus which has no vote in a decision whether to stay in a job or leave a job" (Ceol 1991).

CHAPTER 11. SURVIVOR TESTIMONY IN THE
PORNOGRAPHY CONTROVERSY

1. I will use the term "survivor" instead of "victim" because I seek to recognize one of the primary reasons women cite as a justification for testifying: empowerment. Women's testimony is a means of transforming themselves into survivors. "Victim" tends to connote powerlessness in that a victim is someone who is acted on, not someone who acts. The

victim, through testimony, claims control over her experiences and becomes an actor as opposed to someone who is acted on.

2. See Alcoff and Gray (1993) for a discussion of this process.

3. For example, Alcoff and Gray (1993) analyze rape survivors' appearances on talk shows. In their essay, they explore the tensions that exist between survivors' transgressive discourse and the dominant discourse's attempts at recuperation.

4. Although the witnesses did not testify anonymously or in disguise, the names and addresses of those who testified have been deleted from the transcript of the hearings available to the public. Additionally, I am using the Organizing Against Pornography (the group started by MacKinnon and Dworkin in support of the Ordinance) version of the hearing transcript, which refers to the witnesses by letter.

5. Of those who testified, thirteen were women and survivors, and two were gay men, one of whom was also a survivor.

6. Snitow's speech was originally written in response to the broader antipornography movement. While this talk predates the MacKinnon–Dworkin ordinance, Snitow writes that much of it applies to their activities (1985, 107).

CHAPTER 12. CONSTITUTING PUBLICS AND RECONSTRUCTING PUBLIC SPHERES

1. By public sphere I refer to a discursive realm in which the disinterested but actively attending members of society may exchange views on the issue before them, discover their common interests, and form their shared opinions on what they take to be reality (Hauser 1987).

2. The Moral Majority was a fundamentalist Christian movement in the early to mid-1980s, spearheaded by the Rev. Jerry Falwell. It sought to advance a political agenda that centered around traditional values of the family and the church, and was opposed to the liberal legislative and social accomplishments of the two preceding decades. Its most visible advocates were the fundamentalist Christian preachers whose televised services were quite popular during this period.

NAME INDEX

SUBJECT INDEX